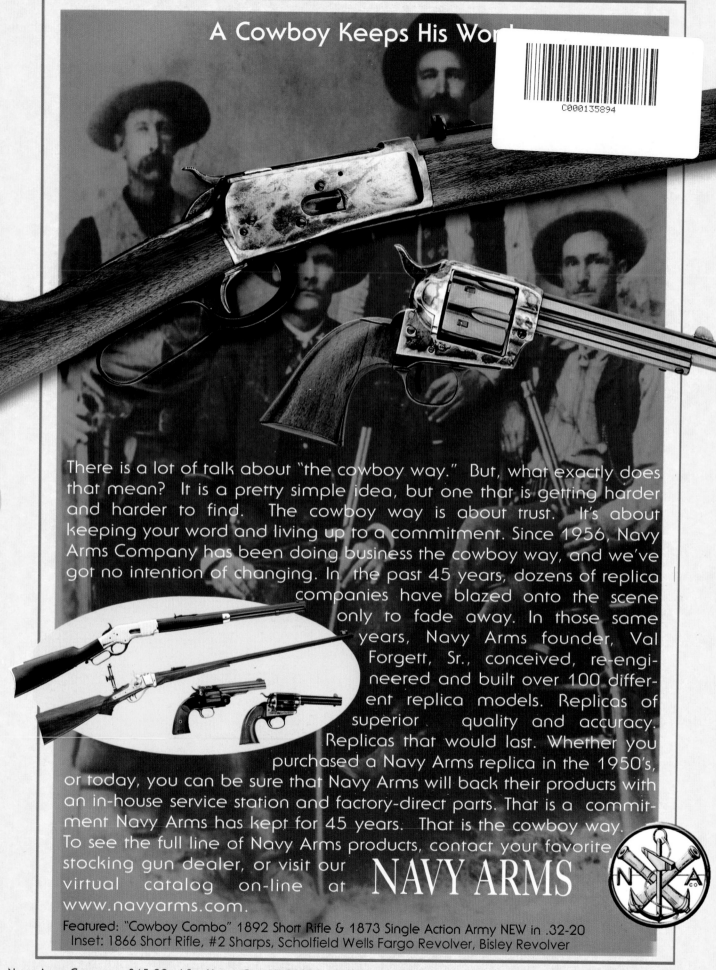

SHOOT! MAGAZINE'S
Black Powder and the Old West

Editorial Comments and Suggestions:

We're always looking for feedback on our books and magazines. Please let us know what you like about this publication. If you have suggestions for articles you'd like to see in future editions, please contact:

Andy Fink, Editor-in-Chief
1770 W. State Street #340
Boise, ID 83702
email: editor@shootmagazine.com

Published by:
Shoot Magazine Corporation
1170 W. State Street #340, Boise, ID 83702
Telephone: 208-368-9920, Fax: 208-338-8428
Website: www.ShootMagazine.com

Contact **SHOOT! MAGAZINE** at 1-800-342-0904 or 208-368-9920 (outside the US) to obtain a free **SHOOT! MERCANTILE** catalog, to place an order, or to submit editorial comments.

ISBN: 0-9726383-0-X

SHOOT MAGAZINE'S

Black Powder and the Old West *Featured Writers*

JOHN TAFFIN, AKA SIXGUNNER

John, a consultant and technical editor, has been a professional gun writer and shootist for over 19 years. In addition to **SHOOT! MAGAZINE**, he is a staff writer for *Guns* and *American Handgunner* and is the author of *Big Bore Sixguns* and *Action Shooting Cowboy Style.*

RAY WALTERS, AKA SMITH N' JONES

Writer, editor, and Events Manager for **SHOOT! MAGAZINE**, Ray has been shooting antique firearms since he was a youngster and participating in CAS since 1996. He is the co-founder of the Oregon Trail Rough Riders in Boise, Idaho and also teaches firearms safety courses.

KENNY DURHAM, AKA KID DURHAM

SHOOT! MAGAZINE staff writer Kenny Durham has over 30 years of experience with black powder firearms, and has become known as an expert in this field. He has won the Idaho State Muzzle Loading Championship three times and numerous awards at the National level in BPCRS and target shooting.

MIKE BELIVEAU, AKA BOTTOM DEALIN' MIKE

Mike Beliveau has been a freelance magazine writer and photographer specializing in 18th and 19th century firearms since 1988. He writes the black powder column for *Guns of The Old West* magazine and he is a regular contributor to *Gun World* magazine.

MIKE CUBER, AKA KID QUICK

Staff writer for **SHOOT! MAGAZINE**, Mike has over 10 years of experience in handling Old West firearms, excellent attention to detail, and is involved in reloading, firearms testing, and western gear articles. He has been shooting cowboy for a number of years.

OTHER CONTRIBUTING WRITERS:

Andy Fink, aka Chucky; Dave McDonald; Katha Higginbotham; Lee Anderson, aka Bull Chip; G. Scott Jamieson; Bob Benbough, aka Not So Bad Bob; Steve Matlock, aka Maddog; Captain George Baylor; Jocko Jackson; Jim Henley, aka Red Desperado; Terry Nibarger, aka Red River Drifter; Daniel Alley, aka Big Pete; and Corby Christensen, aka Rex O'Hurlihan.

KEEPING THE PAST IN OUR FUTURE.

FROM THE FOOTSOLDIER AT GETTYSBURG
TO THE BUFFALO HUNTER ON THE PLAINS.
OUR FINELY DETAILED REPRODUCTIONS
WILL PUT YOU THERE. OUR QUALITY AND
CUSTOMER SERVICE WILL KEEP YOU THERE.
TAYLOR'S EMBODIES HISTORY.

SEND $5.00 FOR A COMPLETE FULL-COLOR CATALOG

TAYLOR'S & CO., INC.

304 LENOIR DRIVE • WINCHESTER, VIRGINIA 22603
TEL: 540-722-2017 • FAX: 540-722-2018

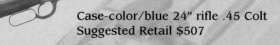
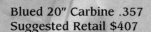

Foreward

By: Andy Fink, aka Chucky

When we hear the term "The Old West" it brings back nostalgic thoughts of days gone by; of sitting in front of the television and watching shows like *Bonanza, Wyatt Earp, The Rebel, Wanted Dead or Alive, High Chaparral, Hopalong Cassidy, Roy Rogers, Gunsmoke, Cheyenne,* and *Have Gun Will Travel.* In more recent times, movies such as *Quigley Down Under, Crossfire Trail, The Shadow Riders, Tombstone, The Outlaw Josey Wales,* and TV shows such as *The Young Guns* and *The Magnificent Seven* have brought life in the Old West back to us. These shows also remind us of the days when we used to play Cowboys and Indians, when the good guys wore white (except for Hoppy), when there was always a moral to the story, and when the violence was not nearly as bloody nor as violent as the vast majority of cop shows shown today on television and in the movies. There was usually a clear message that made the viewer, whether child or adult, sympathize with the "good guys" and want to be like them. Western novels have also been a popular genre for years, and now even appear to be making a comeback. Most of these also provide good moral examples of people doing the right thing, surviving against close-to-impossible odds, and end with the heroes or heroines winning. There is, and will always be, a love for the adventure of The American Old West.

Chucky, Editor-in-Chief of **SHOOT! MAGAZINE** *shooting a pair of AFF 1860 Army conversions in .44 Colt.*

Most of the movies and TV shows depicted appropriate firearms, though not always period-correct with the time frame that was trying to be portrayed. In the Old West, black powder was used exclusively until smokeless powder and the Winchester 1894 came about in the late 19th century. Even early in the 20th century, you were more likely to find black powder being used over smokeless powder in Arizona, New Mexico, Texas, Wyoming, Colorado, Idaho, the Dakotas, and the other western states, as well as in Mexico.

This book is about firearms of The Old West and is for anyone interested in original and replica firearms of the 1800's, especially when loaded with black powder ammunition just as they originally were. The trappers, miners, pioneers, settlers, Indians, cowboys, and outlaws all used black powder, be it cap-n-ball or brass cartridges. Some firearms and their ammunition made the transition to smokeless powder, others, because of their design, never did. This book is about shooting these firearms with the gunpowder of their era, black powder. There is something for everyone with in these pages, whether they are an experienced shooter wanting to start shooting black powder in their current battery of firearms, a new shooter with little or no experience, or someone who has had quite a bit of experience shooting black powder.

If you are an experienced black powder shooter, you might want to delve right into the *Firearms* chapter. If you already shoot in Western-action or cowboy action events, but shoot in one of the smokeless powder categories and are interested in possibly getting into black powder, you might want to read the *Shoots & Tips* chapter first. The *Ammunition & Reloading* chapter is pretty extensive if you wish to pick up some new ideas for loading, however the *Firearms* chapter does have pertinent loads associated with the firearm covered in many of the articles. The new shooter, or someone thinking about getting involved in Western-action shooting and black powder, may want to read the *Introduction to Black Powder* chapter first. Regardless of where you fit, this book covers the majority of the firearms used in all categories of shooting with both original and replica Old West firearms, such as Cowboy Action, Black Powder Cartridge Rifle Silhouette (BPCRS), Buffalo Matches, and Hunting. The detailed section on *Ammunition & Reloading* is informative and extremely useful for both the new and experienced shooter. I do recommend reading other books covering black powder as well, such as Lyman's *Black Powder Handbook and Loading Manual* and Mike Venturino's series of books, including *Shooting Sixguns of The Old West, Shooting Lever Guns of The Old West,* and *Shooting Buffalo Guns of The Old West.* **SHOOT! MAGAZINE**, the authors, and staff all hope that this book provides you many hours of enjoyment and helps bring The Old West into your life.

Andrew J. Fink, aka Chucky
Editor-in-Chief, **SHOOT! MAGAZINE**

PS: A special thanks to all of the authors that have contributed to this book, as well as my staff. This book would not have been possible without their hard work, excellent skills, and dedication.

SHOOT! MAGAZINE'S

Introduction

Old West Firearms and Replicas

Old West Firearms and Replicas Continued

Black Powder and the Old West
TABLE OF CONTENTS

Table of Contents Continued on Next Page.

SHOOT! MAGAZINE'S

Ammunition, Reloading and Cleaning

Ammunition, Reloading and Cleaning Continued

History, Hunting and Tall Tales

Black Powder and the Old West
Table Of Contents

Editor-In-Chief: Andy Fink "Chucky"
Graphic Designer: Carrie Uhlorn "Carrie Concealed"
Marketing and Sales Director: Juliette Dean "Penelope Jane"
Technical Directors: Bob Benbough "Not So Bad Bob," Ray Walters "Smith n' Jones," Kenny Durham "KID Durham."
Copy Editors: Juliette Dean "Penelope Jane," Tonya Uhlorn, Carrie Uhlorn "Carrie Concealed."

Front Cover: Photo by Andy Fink, guns provided courtesy of Andy Fink, all originals: Colt 1883 Shotgun, Rabone Smoothbore, Winchester 1873 .44 WCF, Marlin 1889 38 WCF.

Back Cover: Photos by Carrie Uhlorn and Andy Fink. Gun engraved by Dale Miller of Miller Enterprises.

Black Powder and the Old West
Chapter 1
Introduction

Introduction to Black Powder

By: Andy Fink, aka Chucky

What is that wonderful smelly stuff that makes billowing clouds of smoke as your sixgun bucks in your hand and the sound of a big "BOOM" that crashes into your ears? Black powder not only produces more smoke than smokeless powder, it has a distinctive booming sound as the cartridge is fired and the acrid smell of sulfur hangs in the air. It seems that everyone at a cowboy action shoot can easily tell who is shooting black powder.

Black powder is the original gunpowder propellant and consists of a mixture of charcoal, sulfur, and saltpeter (potassium nitrate). Early gunpowder was a simple mixture

the same rate, whether confined or unconfined, and thus requires special safety precautions.

WARNING: Do not attempt to make your own powder! This is extremely dangerous and will probably end up with someone getting seriously hurt. Black powder mill explosions, even today, occur too often, and most black powder manufactured today is done by remote control. Regardless of whether you load your own or buy factory-loaded black powder cartridges, always be sure that you obtain your supplies of powder or cartridges from qualified

of these ingredients finely-ground, and eventually became known as "green powder" as the powder making process was refined. The stuff worked, but was inconsistent. The addition of water to the mixture, thus making the ingredients wet, then compressing it into cakes and breaking or "corning" the dried cakes into granules of various sizes, and finally screening, glazing, and polishing the granules, became the standard method of making black powder. This is referred to as corned powder and is much more powerful than the earlier green powder. Black powder was merely referred to as "gunpowder" until the introduction of smokeless powder, and was so named due to its color. Unlike smokeless powder, black powder is considered a "low explosive" by the government definition. Black powder, unlike smokeless powder, burns at

and authorized manufacturers. Shooting guns loaded with black powder not only brings us back to the Old West, but to the Eastern frontier as well, for this was the propellant used by our forefathers when Europeans first arrived in America. The puffs of smoke from Kentucky rifles and the Minutemen fighting off the British remind us of our fight to make this land free. I sometimes wonder what it was really like inside a saloon when multiple shots were fired. I imagine that after the first couple of shots, the antagonists couldn't even see each other and were just guessing where their opponents were. When I hunker down over cross-sticks and aim at the steel buffalo 600 yards away, I can imagine what it was like in the 1870's when the buffalo herds, numbering in the thousands, lumbered over the plains. It is sometimes hard to explain the thrill of the big "BOOM" of my 1874 Sharps as the rifle butt pushes hard against my shoulder and the white cloud of smoke goes wafting slowly off, moved by the wind. Then it is quiet. But if my shot was true, I hear the loud "CLANG" a couple of seconds later as the target is hit.

Shooting black powder is really fun, and if all precautions are adhered to, as safe as when shooting or loading smokeless powder. When shooting muzzleloaders, standard powder charges that are recommended by the manufacturer should be used.

There are several granulations of black powder: the larger the number, the finer the powder:

FFFFg (4F) is the smallest granulation available and is recommended for priming the pan of flintlocks and as the main charge in some small caliber pistols.

FFFg (3F) is used in revolvers, including cartridge revolvers, most muzzleloading pistols, smallbore rifles, and for target loads in big-bore rifles.

FFg (2F) is a coarser grain powder that is used in big-bore rifles and shotguns, though it may also be used in larger bore pistols and revolvers.

Fg (1F) Is a coarse powder normally used in shotgun loads of 12 or 10-gauge and in large-capacity rifle cartridges.

Although these are the major granulation designations, specific powder makers may use additional terminology, such as Goex "Cartridge Grade" (which has granulations between FFg and FFFg) or Swiss "1-1/2 Schuetzen Grade" (which is close to FFg). Two of the major companies that produce and/or import black powder are Goex and Petro Explosives (Elephant and Swiss).

Black powder substitutes should be loaded according to the manufacturer's instructions. At the time of this writing, all black powder substitutes currently available are loaded by volume and not by weight. That is, the correct charge of a black powder substitute will fill the same volume of space that would have been occupied by regular black powder. The metallic cartridge should have no empty space once the powder, wad, lube and bullet have been combined. Substitute powders include Hodgdon's Pyrodex, Hodgdon's Triple 7 (777), Clean Shot, Clear Shot, and American Pioneer Powder.

Manufacturer's that produce black powder cartridges include Old West Scrounger, Dakota Ammo Incorporated (previously known as Cor-Bon), Ten-X Ammunition, and Black Dawge.

Black powder is also messy and corrosive. Though many of the substitutes, such as Hodgdon's Triple 7, produce a powder that seems to be as non-corrosive as smokeless and certainly cleans up as easy, or easier, than smokeless powder, I recommend that a firearm that has been shot with black powder be cleaned the same day it is fired. There are a number of ways that cleaning can be accomplished, and many of them are described in this book. I have found that soap and water works well if you can immerse the revolver parts or the barrel of a double-barrel shotgun in a bucket of soapy water, rinse in hot clean water, dry thoroughly, and then apply a light coat of gun oil or other modern metal preservative. Something else that is easy to use is a non-ammonia window cleaner such as Glass Plus, though many people do use Windex, which does have ammonia in it. Clean the firearm with the window cleaner or a commercial black powder solvent first, wipe dry, and then lightly oil the barrel and moving parts and wipe dry again.

Interestingly enough, when we were preparing this book, we received several responses from some of the cartridge firearms' manufacturers stating that they don't make black powder firearms. Needless to say, we were initially quite surprised. All of the firearms manufacturers we talked to were producing firearms for Western-action shooting, so how could this be? They were producing original or replica firearms that they assumed were only used for smokeless powder. They didn't realize that the Frontier Cartridge Category in the Single Action Shooting Society (SASS) and the Black Powder Duelist category in the National Congress of Old West Shootists (NCOWS) were becoming increasingly popular. In these categories, you shoot cartridges in revolvers, leverguns, and shotguns of the Old West style, but you must use black powder or black powder substitute. When shooting the Frontiersman Category, you are required to use cap-n-ball revolvers as well.

In addition, the popularity of shooting side matches using black powder has been increasing as well. The Plainsman Event is an event that usually has three stages in which you have to use two cap-n-ball sixguns, a double-barrel shotgun, and a single-shot rifle, all using black powder. You could certainly use a muzzleloading rifle and shotgun for this event, but there is usually a number of reloads required, which makes the use of black powder cartridges for these firearms the only way to be competitive. Side matches that include buffalo matches and long-range shooting, such as long-distance levergun using a pistol caliber (examples: .32/20, .38 Special, .357 Magnum, 38/.40, .44/40, .44 Special, .44 Magnum, and .45 Colt.) and long-range levergun using a rifle caliber (examples: .38/55, .40/65, .43 Spanish, .45/70, .45/90, .45/100, .45/110, .45/120 and other original 1800's cartridges) are either required to be shot with black powder or there may be both: black powder and smokeless categories. I have seen competitors shooting in the main match in the Frontier Cartridge Category use black powder in such modern calibers (developed in the 20th century) as the .44 Magnum, .44 Special, .357 Magnum, and .38 Special.

The sport of Black Powder Cartridge Rifle Silhouette (BPCRS) has been around for quite a few years and has seen a continuing increase in the number of participants. This is a sport shot at distances of 200, 300, 375, and 500 meters and requires a period-correct (1800's original or replica) single-shot rifle shooting black powder. A relatively new addition to the sport is levergun silhouette. This may be shot with either smokeless or black powder.

What about hunting? Sure, many of you have heard about hunting with black powder muzzleloading rifles, and there is usually a separate season for it. There has also been a resurgence of hunting with Old West style single-shot rifles such as the Sharps. Some hunters use black powder in the 1886 Winchester shooting a .45/70 or .45/90 for elk, and black powder in the 1866 Winchester or 1894 Marlin with a .45 Colt or .44/40 for deer. It is not only challenging, but adds a feeling of the days gone by to your hunt.

The use of black powder in modern firearms is here to stay and will continue to increase as more competitors see how much fun it can be. Join in on the action and fun. Think about your next match and try to shoot those modern 7-1/2" Colt replicas you have or a pair of new 3rd Generation Colts the old-fashioned way. Make those "smokepoles" smoke!

Why I Enjoy Shooting Black Powder

By: Jim Henley, aka Red Desperado

I enjoy shooting black powder when participating in cowboy action shooting, whether it be cap-n-ball or cartridge, because there is no other sound and feel like the big boom and the buck of a fully-loaded, 255-gr. bullet over 40 grains of FFg in a .45 Colt Peacemaker. To experience the Old West is what I wanted to do, so the best way to do this was to find something that related back to the 1800's.

To me, cowboy action shooting is getting in the theme of the Old West by dressing the part, shooting Old West firearms, and using black powder. After I put on my garb, strap on my guns, and shoot my first shot, I am back in the Old West defending myself from the Indians or the rustlers, or simply putting food on the table. It's the big boom, the buck, and all that smoke that puts me there. I always had an interest in the guns used by the cowboy, even before I started shooting cowboy action. It was not until I had done some damage to my replica Henry rifle by loading too hot of a load with smokeless powder, that I began shooting black powder. This opened up a whole new adventure. Wow, so this is what it was like in the Old West!

Shooting the cap-n-ball revolver is a challenge, trying to make everything work like it should. Pouring the powder, seating the ball, and capping each cylinder gives me a feeling of what they had to go through during the Civil War and in the Old West. Shooting the Henry rifle, the first successful repeating cartridge rifle, is shooting history for me. The old mule ear side-by-side lets me imagine that I am riding shotgun on a stagecoach with this baby across my lap. The '72 Colt Open-Tops, loaded with the .44 Russian, brings about a feeling of change from the cap-n-ball to the cartridge era. The '72 Open-Top was the first Colt production model for cartridges. If one couples these '72s with the '73 Winchester rifle in .44WCF and the '87 Winchester lever-action shotgun (this was John Browning's first design that Winchester patented), one can definitely see things changing. We can now take this one step further, and still stay in the black powder era, by taking a pair of '73 Colt SAAs, a '92 Winchester rifle (another one of John Browning's great inventions), and the dependable hard-working '87 shotgun. It wasn't until just before the turn of the century when smokeless powder began to surface.

I was going to tell you what guns I normally shoot in cowboy action main matches, but that is always a hard decision for me to make because I enjoy shooting all the different types and calibers of guns. I may go out packing '51 Colt Navys, a Henry rifle, and a mule ear side-by-side, or I may be packing a pair of '72 Colt Open-Tops, a '73 Winchester rifle, and a '87 Winchester lever-action shotgun. Then again, you may see me packing nickel-plated 3rd Generation Colt SAAs, a '92 Winchester rifle, and the fun-to-shoot '87 shotgun. I wasn't lying about having a hard time making up my mind, was I?

All these firearms were made for black powder because that's all they had in the 1800's. Shooting black powder in them is a real treat, not only for the guns, but for me as well. It's the real meaning of the smoke wagon. Some say it's the most fun a person can have with their clothes on, and I might have to agree. You can probably tell that I'm a Colt and Winchester fanatic. I am not saying that other companies, such as Remington, LeMat, Spencer, Marlin, etc., did not make good firearms, but I just prefer Colt and Winchester.

Now, after saying all that, I will get down to what's involved with shooting black powder. You hear all kinds of myths about black powder; it's unstable, it could explode, it's too hard to reload, it's too much work to clean up, etc. Yes, black powder is very explosive, but that's what makes it work. You do need to take caution when storing and reloading with black powder, so always store it in a cool, dry place, away from

Red Desperado's firearms for the Frontier Cartridge category: Winchester 1887 lever-action, Winchester 1873 .44-40, and a pair of replica 1872 Open-tops.

any sparks or open flame, and in a magazine made for storing black powder. Most places that sell black powder have magazine plans, so you can make your own, or you can buy one already made from Cabela's. However, these precautions are not much different than what you should be doing with smokeless powders anyhow.

Black powder reloading is a little different than reloading with smokeless powders. With black powder, you need to fill the case making sure there is no air space between the powder charge and the bullet. You should use a soft lead alloy bullet and a bullet lube suitable for black powder. When reloading, you need to stay away from using any plastic containers or metals that will cause static electricity, so do not use plastic powder measures or steel-to-steel parts. However, brass-to-steel and aluminum-to-steel parts are okay. Some people ground themselves, as well as grounding the press, when reloading, which is not a bad idea if you feel the need. All I can tell you is what works for me.

It has been fun experimenting with reloading (the learning curve). To start with, I cast my own two grease-grooved bullets with a 20:1 lead-to-tin alloy, using a Lyman #427098 for the .44s, or the Lyman #454198 for the .45.

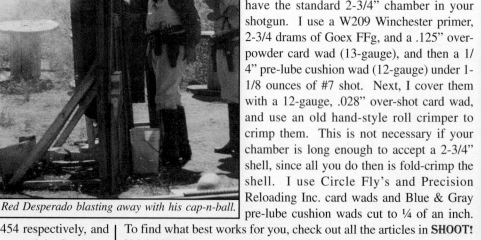

Red Desperado blasting away with his cap-n-ball.

I then size the bullets to .428 or .454 respectively, and lube with SPG bullet lube. I use the Master Caster and the Star Lube sizer from Magma Engineering Co. The next step is preparing the brass. There are no differences here, except that after shooting black powder, I wash my brass in cold water and then add a little citric acid and a squirt of liquid dish detergent. I let them soak for a minute or two, rinse them clean, and then spread them out on a towel to let

them dry overnight, and then tumble polish in the morning. I then spray them with a case lube as required before placing them in the press. Using a Dillon 650 with a Hornady black powder measure filled with Goex FFg set to drop 35 grains through a modified brass case activator and the primer tube filled with Winchester WLP Standard/Magnum large pistol primers, I begin reloading. It is recommended to use a Magnum primer with black powder for a better initiation and cleaner burn. When loading the 12-gauge shotshell, I use once-fired Federal paper hulls cut down to 2-1/2" overall to chamber in my '87. This is not necessary, however, if you have the standard 2-3/4" chamber in your shotgun. I use a W209 Winchester primer, 2-3/4 drams of Goex FFg, and a .125" over-powder card wad (13-gauge), and then a 1/4" pre-lube cushion wad (12-gauge) under 1-1/8 ounces of #7 shot. Next, I cover them with a 12-gauge, .028" over-shot card wad, and use an old hand-style roll crimper to crimp them. This is not necessary if your chamber is long enough to accept a 2-3/4" shell, since all you do then is fold-crimp the shell. I use Circle Fly's and Precision Reloading Inc. card wads and Blue & Gray pre-lube cushion wads cut to ¼ of an inch. To find what best works for you, check out all the articles in **SHOOT! MAGAZINE**, read other books, magazine articles, and ask questions; the same thing you would be doing if you're reloading with smokeless powders.

Cleaning up after shooting black powder is what you make of it. Once you have your firearms seasoned, clean-up is a breeze using just soap and water and the right oil. Here again, there are books

Smokin' the stages with a Winchester 1873 .44-40.

known to thumb-cock my '72 Open-Tops or my '73 SAAs to be competitive in the game. I've used corn meal in a Colt Walker, but found that it's not necessary. Let's face it, it is a big gun, so why not use it to produce a big "boom?"

Cowboy action shooting is a multi-faceted shooting sport in which contestants compete with firearms typical of those used in the taming of the Old West. One aspect of cowboy action shooting is the requirement placed on authentic-period or western-screen dress. So, why not take it one step further by shooting with what was available back in the Old West - black powder, that is. SASS offers two cowboy action shooting main match categories, Frontiersman and Frontier Cartridge. They also have a side match known as The Plainsman. The Frontiersman category requires you to shoot a traditional-style percussion (cap-n-ball) single-action revolver of original manufacture (prior to 1896), or reproductions thereof, limited to .36 caliber or larger shot Duelist-style. One must use black powder in all loads, including rifle, sixgun, or shotgun, and you must use a side-by-side or lever-action shotgun, and any SASS-legal, pistol-caliber rifle is acceptable. In the Frontier Cartridge category, you are required to use a .32 caliber or larger, traditional-style percussion or cartridge, single-action revolver of original manufacture (prior to 1896) or reproductions thereof, using black powder in all loads (rifle, sixgun, or shotgun). You must use a side-by-side or lever-action shotgun, and again, any SASS-legal, pistol-caliber rifle. The Plainsman event requires two .36 caliber or larger, traditional-style percussion revolvers shot Duelist-style, and a SASS-legal single-shot rifle firing a traditional black powder rifle or pistol-caliber cartridge. It requires the use of a side-by-side or lever-action shotgun, and the use of black powder in all loads (rifle, pistol, and shotgun).

For more about what SASS has to offer, see their website at www.sassnet.com or talk to a SASS member. By the way, I also enjoy shooting black powder in other rifles, such as the Trapdoor Springfield in .45-70, and a Sharps rifle in .45-110, as seen in the movie *Quigley Down Under*. These, too, take me back to when the buffalo were plentiful and you needed something large enough and powerful enough to take one of those big beasts down. Such accuracy can be achieved at long ranges with black powder.

So, now that I've addressed the reasons why I enjoy shooting black powder, and some of the myths associated with it, why not come out and join me by using what they used, feeling the real West, and smell the smell - oh, I mean smelling the smoke. They did have showers back in that era, didn't they?

and articles on cleaning black powder that you can check out, but I can only tell you what works best for me. It is recommended to strip all the oil from the gun. With black powder, you do not want to use any petroleum-base oils or hard-type bullet lube. By using a soft lead (20:1) alloy and a suitable black powder bullet lube (SPG), you can maintain accuracy, as well as keep your bore from leading up and the fouling from getting hard. The soft lead will allow the bullet to upset and fill the rifling, which keeps the hot gasses from cutting past the bullet thus causing leading. This bullet upsetting also pushes out the fouling from shot-to-shot, allowing the bullet to engage the rifling for better stabilization, which gives you better accuracy. After swabbing out the bore with a bore mop dampened with water that has a little liquid dish detergent added, wipe clean, and then dry with a tight patch or two. Then oil the bore with a non-petroleum based oil (Ballistol), and wipe off all fouling that is on the gun and in the gun's action, the parts of the action that are exposed. For me, it is not necessary to take the whole action apart, except for once or twice a year or before storing for a long period of time. I do, however, put an aluminum snap cap in the empty cylinder hole when I shoot. This helps keep some of the fouling out of the action of the revolver.

Well, we all know you should clean all your guns after use, regardless if you're using smokeless or black powder, so where's the difference? The difference is that you need to clean all your guns after shooting black powder, but the more you shoot them with black powder, the easier they are to clean. By using the right materials in reloading and cleaning your guns, it is not necessary to clean them between stages.

As stated earlier, shooting black powder for me is getting into the theme of the Old West. It adds the flavor to the sport, the icing on the cake. Yes, you also can be competitive. I may never be a Top Gun World Champion, but I can have a lot of fun trying. I've been

Red Desperado, competing with black powder in a cowboy action match in Jerome, ID.

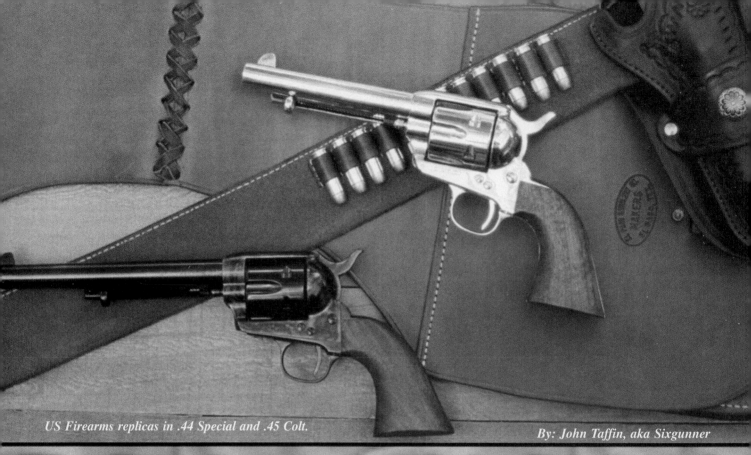

US Firearms replicas in .44 Special and .45 Colt.

By: John Taffin, aka Sixgunner

The Development of the Replica & the Colt Single Action Army

A very wise man once said: "There is nothing new under the sun." With that in mind, we can take a look at the larger picture and say that every single-action revolver ever made is basically a copy of the first truly successful single-action revolver, the Colt Paterson. Colt may have gotten his inspiration for the Paterson while serving as a cabin boy and watching the paddlewheel rotate. However, repeating revolvers go back much further than the 1836 date of the Colt Paterson.

There is a revolver residing in the Tower of London Armories that predates the Paterson by more than 150 years. Now, it does not look like the traditional revolver, but it does have a rotating cylinder that turns 1/6 of a turn each time the hammer holding the flint is cocked. This first "sixgun" was made by John Dante in 1680. By the late 1600's, one Jacques Gorgo had discovered the importance of the forcing cone for a positive transfer of a bullet from cylinder to barrel. By the mid 1700's, the revolving principal was changed from the cylinder to the barrel, and we had the Pepperbox. The Pepperbox made the transition from a single-action flintlock, sometimes with the barrel being rotated by hand, to a double-action percussion revolver. In the 1820's, Elisha Collier began producing both flintlock and percussion revolvers. Geoffrey Boothroyd says in his book, *The Handgun* (1970): "Apparently, an appreciable quantity of Collier arms were sold, but, although few were made on the percussion system, there was no further development, and they do not appear to

have influenced the evolution of the revolver in any decisive manner." At about the same time that Collier patented his idea, Capt. Artemus Wheeler did likewise in America, and Cornelius Coolidge in France. The stage was being set for a true sixgun.

Colt's Paterson was successful, but Colt was not, and the factory was closed. Ten years later, Texas was at war with Mexico and the Texas Rangers/Soldiers needed side arms. Samuel Colt and Samuel Walker put their heads together to improve the relatively fragile and low-powered Paterson. The result was the 1847 Walker, a massive 4-1/2 pound six-shooter firing a .454" caliber ball, that Walker said was good on man or beast out to 200 yards. As good as the Walker was, it was improved one year later as the 1st Model Dragoon appeared, followed rapidly by the 2nd and 3rd Model Dragoons. All of these sixguns were in the 4-pound weight range, so one year after the 3rd Model Dragoon, Colt downsized to a 2-1/2 pound .36 caliber sixgun, the 1851 Navy. With an easily handled sixgun of this size, the day of the gunfighter had arrived. By 1860, Colt was almost able to supply the power of the Dragoon in a sixgun not much larger than the 1851 Navy, the 1860 Army .44.

The Civil War placed the Colt factory on sound financial footing, and they were content to continue to produce the 1860 Army. However, trouble was brewing in Springfield, Massachusetts. The firm of Smith & Wesson had produced a cartridge-firing, seven-shot, tip-up .22 revolver in 1857. Now

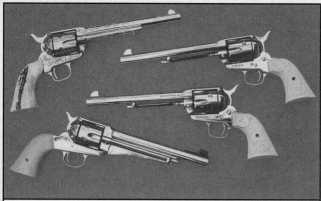

Replica 7-1/2" .44-40s from top left: Model P from Cimarron, a matched pair of Hartford Models from EMF, and a Navy Arms 1875 Remington.

Originally chambered in .44 Henry Rimfire, the 1860 Henry and the 1866 Yellow Boy are now available in replica form chambered in .44-40.

Thanks to Navy Arms, the Model #3 is now back and chambered, as the original, in .44 Russian.

Navy Arms offers the Schofield Model in 3-inch, 5-inch, and 7-inch barrel lengths. Custom grips are by Buffalo Brothers.

they were about to go big bore with a .44 Smith & Wesson American. Colt was caught off guard when this happened in 1869. To add to their problem, Smith & Wesson employed Rollin White, who held the patent for bored-through cylinders. To get around this, Colt first used the Thuer Conversion, which allowed tapered cartridges to be loaded from the front end of the cylinder, and then came the Richards and Richards-Mason Conversions on their 1851 and 1860 percussion revolvers. The back end of the cylinder was cut off, and a conversion ring was added to allow the use of metallic cartridges. By the time the Smith & Wesson patent had run out, Colt had the 1871-72 Open-Top revolver that was originally made as a cartridge-firing revolver, not a conversion.

Meanwhile, Remington was making fairly successful percussion revolvers that differed from the Colt by having a top strap. When Colt submitted their 1871-72 Open-Top for the Army tests, the Army suggested that Colt go back to the drawing board. Did Colt look at the Remington .44 percussion revolver? I don't know, but when the 1873 Model P, the Single Action Army, arrived, it had a Remington-style top strap. Two years later, it appears Remington returned the favor by looking at the Colt Single Action Army before bringing forth their Model 1875. The Ordnance officers who tested the Remington Model of 1875 noted in their report that it essentially did not differ in principal from the Colt, but it was not a patent infringement. It seems like everyone was watching everyone else in those days.

Very early on, European manufacturers, especially in Spain and Belgium, began to replicate the Colt Single Action Army. Frontier Model .44 "Colts" are found marked "ORBEA HERMANOS EIBAR" on the barrel, however some of the more flagrant violations from Europe, often smaller versions in .38 caliber, were actually marked "COLTS PT F A MFG CO HARTFORD CT, USA."

When Colt decided to go into the making of rifles, Winchester decided they would make single-action revolvers. The Colt Single Action Army was originally designed by William Mason. In 1883, Mason designed the Winchester Single Action. The two companies then got together and decided that Colt would make revolvers, and Winchester would make rifles.

The 1st Generation Colt Single Action would be manufactured from 1873 to 1941 with no major design changes, however such things as barrel lettering style, hammer profiles, front sight shape, and the means of holding the base pin in place did change. When production ceased in 1941, nearly 360,000 Model Ps had been made in over 30 different chamberings, with the most popular being .45 Colt, .44-40, .38-40, and .32-20. Colt's official stance was that the Colt Single Action Army was dead and buried, never to be seen again. Sales had been going down for years and they saw no need to resurrect the single-action Army after the war.

Then a strange phenomenon occurred. In the late 1940's, television began to appear around the country. There wasn't much to fill the TV time in those days, and all I vividly remember are old "B" Westerns and wrestling. There were so many western movies that they soon spawned western TV shows that aired on a regular weekly basis. Viewers wanted single-action revolvers like those they saw on these shows. Two companies answered the call. A young gun maker had introduced a .22 semi-automatic pistol in 1949 that was reliable, accurate, and relatively low-priced. This was Bill Ruger's first production arm. Four years later, in 1953, one of the all-time great successes in revolverdom arrived with the Ruger .22 Single-Six. Ruger's .22 is basically a copy of a Colt Single Action Army, with a smaller frame and coil springs. The grip frame remained Colt-sized, it was an immediate success, and it remains tremendously popular 50 years later.

Meanwhile, at the other end of the country, another gun company was founded, Great Western Arms Co. of Los Angeles. Shooters wanted real Colts, but they couldn't get them, so Great Western stepped up to fill the void. The Great Western looked so much like a Colt Single Action Army that they actually used real Colts in the early advertising. I'm not sure exactly when Great Western began, but my memory tells me that I saw the first ads in 1954 when I was a junior in high school. They were smart enough to present John Wayne with an early matched pair, fully-engraved with ivory grips. One of the owners of the company was Audie Murphy. Young Murphy lied about his age to get into World War II, became the most decorated hero of that conflict, and then went on to make Western movies. He may not have been much of an actor, but we didn't care. He was a real genuine hero and could definitely handle a Colt Single Action .45 on the Silver Screen.

In the late 1950's, I bought my first Great Western Single Action. I had good luck with the single-six .22, so I purchased a Great Western .22. That turned out to be a mistake. The 5-1/2" .22 proved to be a really poor shooting sixgun and was definitely out of time. Thirty-five years later, I picked up two more 5-1/2" Great Western .22s, which have proven to be excellent shooters and favorites with the grandkids. In fact, the grandkids and I were just out the other morning shooting the guns. We saved enough money shooting the .22s, that I was able to fill them up with a late breakfast at the Cracker Barrel after we got finished shooting.

Elmer Keith, in the first chapter of his book *Sixguns by Keith* (1955), commented that the test Great Western Single Action that he had received was "very poorly timed, fitted, and showed a total lack of final inspection. The hand was a trifle short, the bolt spring did not have enough bend to lock the bolt with any certainty, the mainspring was twice as strong as necessary, and the trigger pull was about three times as heavy as needed." I think the same guy made his test gun and my .22. Later in his book, Elmer was able to report: "We are happy to report that Great Western has really gotten on the ball and is now cooking on all four burners. They overhauled their design and inspection departments, put in some gunsmiths who knew the score, and are now turning out first-class single-action copies. We have one in 4-3/4" .44 Special, and it is a very fine single-action in every way. It is perfectly timed, sighted, and very accurate. It has performed perfectly with factory loads and our heavy hand loads, and is very accurate at extreme ranges, the real test of any sixgun."

The Great Western Co. was originally owned by a man by the name of Bill Wilson. These guns were totally American-made and are not to be confused with the Hawes Single Actions, which came later. Hy Hunter was an early distributor of Great Westerns, as was EMF, and later he also brought in the German-made J.P. Sauer & Sohn Hawes versions. I have no idea how many Great Western Single Actions were manufactured in the less than ten years they were in business, but it was not unusual to find them at bargain prices ten years ago. However, the prices have tripled, even quadrupled, since then, and they are not all that commonly found at gun shows.

At first glance, Great Western Single Actions look identical to Colt Single Actions with subtle differences in the hammer profile and shape of the trigger guard. They show up on many TV Westerns and are easy to spot when the hammer is cocked. Colts have the firing pin on the hammer, while Great Westerns have a frame-mounted firing pin such as that introduced by the old Christy Gun Works, and picked up by Bill Ruger for use in all of his single-actions. Unlike the Rugers, the Great Westerns have sort of an upside-down, L-shaped hammer.

Great Westerns were made in the three standard barrel lengths: 4-3/4," 5-1/2," and 7-1/2," plus a 12-1/2" Buntline Special. The standard model was a 5-1/2" .45 Colt that sold for $99.50 in 1960, but there was a slight additional charge for other calibers and barrel lengths. In addition to .45 Colt and .22, the Great Western was offered in .38 Special, .44 Special, .357 Magnum, .357 Atomic, and .44 Magnum. The "Atomic" was simply a heavily-loaded .357 Magnum; and believe it or not, the .44 Magnum was on the standard Colt-sized mainframe.

Most of the parts of the Great Western Single Action are interchangeable

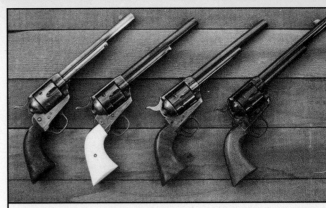

Three generations of Colt .44s compared to AWA's Longhorn .44.

Remington's 1890 Police Model .45 by Cimarron. Custom stocks are by Buffalo Brothers.

Starting with a standard Model P, Cimarron shortened the barrel and changed the backstrap to the 1877 Lightning profile, and the result is the New Thunderer. Custom grips are by Buffalo Brothers.

All the sixguns on the frontier were not Colt Single Actions. The Lightning, the Wells Fargo Schofield, and the Cartridge Conversion all saw service. Custom stocks by Buffalo Brothers.

The sixguns, in replica form, that led to the Colt Single Action Army: the 1860 Army, the Richards Conversion, and the 1871-72 Open-Top. Custom stocks are by Eagle Grips, Dustin Linebaugh, and John Adams.

Many of the 1851 and 1861 Navy Model Colts were converted to cartridge-firing sixguns. Custom stocks are by Ajax.

To celebrate the 125th Anniversary of the Schofield Model in 2000, Smith & Wesson brought it back into production in the original .45 S&W Schofield chambering.

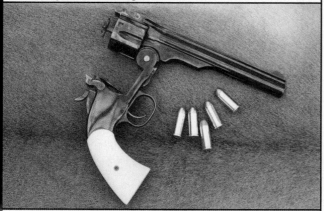

One of the great advantages of the Smith & Wesson Single Action was its break-top operation and simultaneous ejection of all six empty cartridges, followed by easy reloading of new ammunition.

with the Colt Single Action Army except for the hammer, and the hammer, trigger, and bolt screws. The threads on these three screws were changed to help prevent them from loosening as the gun was fired. Two years after the Great Western was introduced, Colt brought back the Single Action Army and, no matter how good the quality had become, Great Western's fate was sealed. They disappeared in the early 1960's.

Great Westerns may have been the first of the modern replicas, however they were not the last, but rather only the beginning. In the late 1950's and early 1960's, such personages as Turner Kirkland of Dixie Gun Works, Val Forgett of Navy Arms, and Boyd Davis of EMF began importing replica firearms. Forgett notes that the first 100 1851 Navy revolvers came from Uberti to Navy Arms in April 1959. That was only the beginning. Today, we have excellent replicas of nearly every sixgun, both percussion and cartridge style, and every lever-action and single-shot rifle from the 19th century. Not only are they available in proliferation, they are extremely close to the originals and still remain relatively low in price; and not only do the above three companies offer quality replicas, they have also been joined by American Western Arms, Cimarron Firearms, and Taylor's and & Co. Mike Harvey of Cimarron has worked especially hard to provide authentic 19th century revolvers.

Forgett says that to date there have been 2,600,000 revolvers and 1,100,000 rifle replicas produced in Italy. These are only some of the choices that today's shooter has: Colt Paterson, Walker, Dragoon, 1851 Navy, 1860 Army, and 1873 Single Action; Remington .36 and .44 percussion, Model 1875, and Model 1890; S&W Schofield and Model #3 Russian; Lemat, Spiller & Burr, Rogers & Spencer, and Starr. In long guns, shooters have these choices: 1860 Henry, 1866, 1873, 1886, and 1892 Winchesters; and the Sharps and Remington, as well as the Springfield Trapdoor Single-Shot.

Replicas today are highly authentic, so much that some have made the assertion that shooters have purchased .45 caliber single-action revolvers thinking they were getting genuine Colt Single Action Armys when, in reality, they were purchasing replicas. Is this really possible? What follows is a list of the obvious similarities and differences between three replicas and three original Colt Single Actions. After examining these listed items one must conclude that for someone to buy a replica thinking it is a genuine Colt, it is obvious that two things must be in place. There must be a totally dishonest seller, matched up with an impossibly naive and supremely uninformed buyer. Eleven attributes of each sixgun were examined:

1) Marking found on the top of the barrel.
2) Marking found on the left side of the barrel.
3) Serial number placement.
4) Style of grips.
5) Finish.
6) Style of cylinder bushing.
7) Style of cylinder pin catch.
8) Finish on hammer.
9) Style of rear sight.
10) Style of front sight.
11) Marking on left side of the mainframe.

The Colt Single Action Army, the Model P, has been in production since 1873 in the following phases: 1st Generation from 1873 to 1941; 2nd Generation from 1956 to 1974; and 3rd Generation from 1976 to the present, with some short periods of non-production. Sometimes they were offered as a standard catalog offering, and other times as a custom shop revolver. All examples from each generation are not identical to each other, as Colt made many changes over the years, including grip style, hammer profile, barrel markings, rear sight notches, etc.

Note: Please refer to the 11 attributes of sixguns previously stated. The #1 attribute will correspond with the #1 for each of the following single-

AWA offers two levels of replica single-actions exemplified by a Longhorn 7-1/2" .44-40 and a Peacekeeper 4-3/4" .45 Colt.

Replacement cylinders from Kirst Kartridge Conversions turns these 1858 Remington cap-n-ball revolvers into cartridge-firing sixguns.

Two original Great Westerns with 7-1/2" and 5-1/2" barrels and Cimarron's Model P fitted with a Great Western grip frame and plastic factory stags.

These replicas cover the development and evolution of the Colt Single Actions: 1851 Dragoon, 1851 Navy, 1860 Army, 1861 Navy, and 1873 Peacemaker.

action sixguns, the #2 attribute will correspond with the #2 for each sixgun, and so on.

Comparing the Single-Action Sixguns:

1st Generation Colt Single Action Army .45 Colt x 4 ¾"

1) Two lines: "COLT'S PATENT F.A MFG CO. / HARTFORD CT. U.S.A."
2) "45 COLT"
3) Three places: bottom of the butt, in front of the trigger guard, and on the main frame in front of the grip frame.
4) Hard rubber, eagle-style, rampant colt with a lightning bolt in his mouth at the top of the grip; American Eagle on the bottom with the head facing right, and E. PLURIBUS UNUM inscribed above the eagle.
5) Finish well-worn on this specimen.
6) Full-length.
7) Spring-loaded catch.
8) Originally case-colored.
9) Pinched V.
10) Blade front sight.
11) Two lines: "PAT SEPT 19 1871. / JULY 2 72 JAN 19. 75." There is also a rampant colt with a lightning bolt in his mouth.

2nd Generation Colt Single Action Army .45 Colt x 4-3/4"

1) One line: "COLT'S PATENT F.A. MFG CO. HARTFORD CT U.S.A."
2) "COLT SINGLE ACTION ARMY .45"
3) On the bottom of the main frame in front of the trigger guard.
4) Hard rubber and checkered with a rampant colt at the top.
5) Standard blue, main frame case-hardened.
6) Full-length.
7) Spring-loaded catch.
8) Blue with polished sides.
9) Square notch.
10) Blade front sight.
11) Two lines: "PAT. SEPT. 19. 1871 / JULY 2. 72 JAN 19.75." There is a rampant colt with a lightning bolt in his mouth.

3rd Generation Colt Single Action Army .45 Colt x 4-3/4"

1) One line: "COLT'S PT F.A. CO HARTFORD CT U.S.A."
2) "COLT SINGLE ACTION ARMY .45"
3) On the bottom of the main frame in front of the trigger guard.
4) Hard rubber, eagle-style, a rampant colt with a lightning bolt in his mouth at the top, eagle at the bottom facing right with E. PLURIBUS UNUM above his head.
5) Bright blue with case-hardened main frame.
6) Collar bushing press-fitted into front of the cylinder.
7) Spring-loaded catch.
8) Blue with polished sides.
9) Square notch.
10) Blade front sight.
11) Two lines: "PAT. SEPT 19.1871 / JULY 2. 72 JAN 19. 75." Also a rampant colt with a lightning bolt in his mouth.

Great Western Frontier Model .45 Colt x 4-3/4 inch, circa 1950's

1) "GREAT WESTERN ARMS CO."
2) "45 Colt" on barrel.
3) On the bottom of the main frame in front of the trigger guard.
4) Plastic imitation staghorn.

5) Standard blue, dark case colors on main frame.
6) Full-length.
7) Spring-loaded catch.
8) Blue with polished sides; frame-mounted firing pin.
9) Pinched V.
10) Blade front sight.
11) None.

Cimarron Model P .45 Colt

1) Two lines: "CIMARRON ARMS CO. / HOUSTON TEXAS USA"
2) "45 COLT"
3) Bottom of the butt, in front of the trigger guard, and bottom of the main frame in front of the trigger guard.
4) Hard rubber with a horse and rider at the top, a Mexican eagle with a snake in his mouth at the bottom.
5) Deep blue with colorful case colors.
6) Full-length.
7) Black powder-style, that is, a screw in from the front of frame.
8) Blue with polished sides.
9) Pinched V.
10) Blade front sight.
11) Two lines: "PAT. SEPT. 19. 1871 / PAT. JULY 2 1872"

American Western Arms Peacekeeper .45 Colt x 4-3/4"

1) One line: "AMERICAN WESTERN ARMS"
2) "PEACEKEEPER .45 COLT"
3) Bottom of the butt, in the front of the trigger guard, and bottom of the main frame in front of the trigger guard.
4) Hard-rubber style grips with a riderless running horse at the top, American eagle at the bottom with his head facing left, and E. PLURIBUS UNUM below the eagle.
5) Deep blue with very colorful case hardening of main frame.
6) Full-length.
7) Spring-loaded catch.
8) Case-hardened hammer.
9) Pinched V.
10) Blade front sight.
11) Two lines: " PAT SEPT. 19 1871— / PAT JULY 2. 1872—"

Today's black powder shooter has a great advantage. Colt Single Action Army Models are still offered by Colt in both .45 Colt and .44-40. It is possible to find original Colt and Smith & Wesson sixguns in good shooting shape at relatively reasonable prices, and probably most important, we can have just about any revolver or rifle in replica form. Sometimes progress really is wonderful. (But not very often!)

In addition to standard models, Cimarron offers the Flat-Top Target in the single-action and Bisley model.

Colt's 12" 2nd Generation Buntline compared to Cimarron's 10" Wyatt Earp.

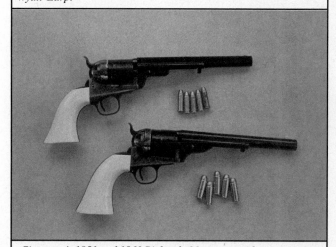

Cimarron's 1851 and 1860 Richards-Mason cartridge conversions with ivory micarta grips expertly fitted by Dustin Linebaugh.

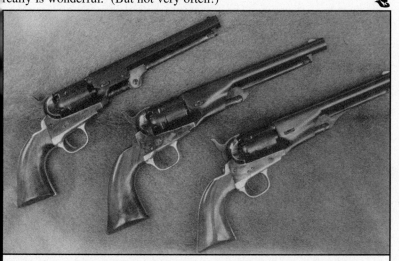

Replicas of the Civil War Era: 1851 Navy, 1860 Army, and 1861 Navy.

Though somewhat resembling the 1858 Remington, Ruger's Old Army is a thoroughly modern and exceptionally efficient and accurate black powder percussion revolver.

The Navy Arms Story

THE DEVELOPMENT OF THE REPLICA

By: Andy Fink, aka Chucky

It's 1959. You watched John Wayne in *Rio Bravo* at the theater last week, and now you just got finished watching an old rerun on TV, *Arizona* with William Holden made in 1940. They used original Henrys, Colts, and Remingtons for this movie. You can still see the sixguns blazing and the black powder billowing. You're excited and want to go out and shoot one of those old cap-n-balls and see that black powder smoke, but where can you get one? You can't afford one of the originals, but maybe there is something out there. You search far and wide without success. You finally find one advertised in *GUNS Magazine*. Yep, that's what you've been looking for! It's a Navy Arms replica of an 1851 Navy .36 caliber cap-n-ball revolver, and it only costs $89.95. You immediately order it, and go down to your local gun store to get a powder flask, some powder, and ball. By the time it arrives, you can barely wait to take it out into the hills behind your old ranch.

That is the story of many a young man with his first replica. The credit of the first replica cap-n-ball revolver produced in volume goes to Navy Arms and Val Forgett. In 1956, Val got off an airplane in Italy after meeting with numerous manufacturers all over Europe. All of them thought he was crazy to try to make replica firearms that could be bought by the general public for a reasonable price. In Italy, Val met Luciano Amadi, who introduced him to two young engineers, Uberti and Gregorelli, who together decided to take a risk with Val. They figured if they could produce and sell a first run order of 500 1851 Navys and 1860 Griswalds to Val, they could at least pay for the tooling. Together, they made the Colt 1851 Navy and the Griswald 1860 revolver, which started a legendary industry. The first Navys came off the production line and were shipped on August 14, 1959 to Navy Arms in Bogota, New Jersey. Val worked out of a small office and figured it would take many months to sell the 100 revolvers that he had just received. He was pleasantly surprised to see that every one sold within 30 days!

At a recent writer's seminar sponsored by Navy Arms, I asked Val Forgett III if he knew who owned serial number 1 of the replica 1851 Navy. He told me that his father, Val Sr., had not even thought of keeping serial number 0001 since he was trying to get every dollar he could to run the business. So, some lucky person out there has a Navy Arms 1851 Navy replica .36 caliber with serial number 0001. I wish it were me!

Val was an ingenious man and felt that there was a significant market in the United States and around the world for replicas that were of good quality, functional, and could be used by the everyday black powder shooter, as well as by the Civil War reenactor and Old West enthusiast. As a member of the North-South Skirmish Association (NSSA), Val was seeing original Civil War guns literally being shot to pieces. The NSSA, in many ways, was the forerunner of the Single Action Shooting Society (SASS). Like SASS, it involved period-correct dressed participants shooting Civil War-era firearms at targets for time against other competitors. Like in SASS, NSSA members shot their guns hard. As a Skirmisher, Val saw that there were many people who wanted to participate in NSSA shoots, but they couldn't afford the cost of an original gun, or were shooting poorly-manufactured original guns that posed a potential danger.

The success of the Navy Arms revolvers was soon followed with additional models, as well as a line of replica Civil War muskets, the first of which was the Zouave rifle. Navy Arms brought to market over a dozen types of Civil War replicas just 18 months after the first revolvers came into the United States. These models included the 1858

Val Forgett shooting Navy Arms' first 1851 Navy - 1959.

Val Forgett during a Civil War reenactment prior to the development of Navy Arms.

Remington revolver, and the 1860 Sheriff's model revolver, as well as percussion and flint dueling pistols, deluxe engraved guns, and gold-inlayed guns. Navy Arms also introduced a full line of accessories, including holsters, belts, bullet moulds, powder flasks, cappers, and target sights. Val even went to RWS in Germany to have them make the original-style winged musket cap!

By the late 1960's, Navy Arms was firmly established as the premiere replica company in the United States. Its color catalog boasted dozens of models of replica black powder firearms, kits, and accessories. Val recognized that the popularity of western movies and TV shows had created a market for his next line of replicas, guns from the Old West. With Aldo Uberti, Val set out to build the Winchester 1866. In the 1960's there were no computers or CAD-automated design systems. Val and Aldo spent many long days in Aldo's workshop at the Uberti factory and hand-made the internal parts on the prototype. Val III relayed a story to me that his father told him about this process. "They would take a part that was too thin, drip weld on it, and then repolish it by hand to get the correct fit and function. Once they got a part to work and hold up under stress, they would give it to Uberti's engineer to draw the part. They would then take the drawing, make another part from its dimension to ensure the tolerances, then proceed with tooling on the part." The first

Val Forgett firing a Civil War cannon during a reenactment.

1866 replicas came out in 1969 and became another instant Navy Arms success story.

Just as he had expanded the replica industry in the 1960's, Val spent the 1970's cementing Navy Arms legacy. He followed the 1866 with the 1873 carbine and rifle, as well as a line of 1873 single-action revolvers and the Henry repeating rifle, which reintroduced the .44-40 caliber to shooters. During the Navy Arms writer's seminar, Val III actually brought with him serial number 0001 of the 1866 carbine in .22, the 1866 Carbine in .38 Special, the 1873 Carbine in .38 Special. and the Henry rifle in .44-40. "By the 1970's, the old man had realized he should keep the first ones," Val III told us. It was an impressive display of replica history that I had the good fortune to both handle and shoot.

Working with the MOD Pattern Room in England, Navy Arms, in conjunction with Parker-Hale Ltd., recreated the Enfield Musket in the 1853, 1858, and 1861 patterns, as well as the Whitworth Confederate sniper rifle and Volunteer target rifle. The actual "pattern" guns, drawings, and gauges that made the original Enfields were used to recreate the guns. Val utilized his connections within the British Government to obtain special permission for this project, and these models began production in the mid-1970's.

When Parker-Hale had financial troubles in the early 1990's, Val

Val Forgett (center) amongst a group of Civil War reenactors.

purchased the black powder division so that production at Navy Arms could continue. As part of the purchase, Navy Arms obtained an original set of inspection gauges for the Enfields made in 1860. The Navy Arms/Parker-Hale Enfields are still made today to these standards and are the finest quality Enfields available. I was able to shoot the Whitworth at the Navy Arms writer's summit, and was able to hit a six-inch bucket off-hand at 168 yards! I can see why Union troops feared the gun in the hands of Confederate snipers!

Wanting to go beyond the normal scope of promoting products, Val set out to show the accuracy and effectiveness of Navy Arms replicas. He used a Navy Arms "Buffalo Hunter" percussion rifle on Safari in Africa. There, he became the first man in the 20th Century to kill the African "Big Five" most dangerous animals (lion, leopard, elephant, rhino, and cape buffalo) with a muzzleloading rifle. Val was given a special award by Safari Club International at their convention in recognition of this feat.

In 1975, Val read that there was an International Muzzle Loading World Championship held each year. He could not believe that the

Val Forgett as a mounted artillery officer in front of his battery of cannon.

United States did not have a team. Val's thoughts were that: "This country was founded by men and women who could out-shoot anyone with a musket." With this in mind, he set out to form a team that would not just be able to compete, but also win and reclaim the United States' status as the home of the best musket shots in the world.

Utilizing his vast resources in the industry, Val assembled a team in less than 12 months. Aside from donating financial resources, Val personally went to the top national black powder shoots held by the NSSA, the National Muzzle Loading Rifle Association (NMLRA), and Levi-Garrett, among others, to recruit the top shooters. He got top coaches to take the time to teach the finer aspects of shooting to team members, and organized uniforms, travel, and other logistics. Just in time for the bicentennial celebration, Val lead the first U.S. team to the World Championships in Versalles, France in the summer of 1976. There, the United States shocked the European black powder establishment by not only winning the overall championship, but setting a new world record in the process! Not content with this, Val continued as the Chairman of the team from 1976-1981, winning all five World Championships held in that time period (a feat unmatched to this day).

In recognition of making the finest replica firearms, Navy Arms' replicas are used by numerous living historical units and government agencies. Among other U.S. historical locations, Navy Arms was chosen to manufacture the firearms and swords that are now on display at the restored Governor's Mansion in Colonial Williamsburg, Virginia.

With the emergence of the popularity of cowboy action shooting

The first Modern replica commercially produced in significant volume was the 1851 Navy from Navy Arms.

in the last 10 years, Val again 'turned his sights' towards recreating guns that would be of the quality to carry the Navy Arms name. Like they had done together for the previous 35 years, Val and Aldo worked together to make the Schofield revolver. As before, they figured out how to make the gun work better than the originals by redesigning the internal parts and making the gun slightly larger to accommodate these internal changes.

Along with Val III, Val Sr. worked with Rossi to improve their 1892 rifles to a level that met the standards he had set since the 1950's. Val's latest project is the Lightning Rifle, which he is working on with Val III and Pierangelo Pedersoli. Pedersoli makes Navy Arms Sharps and Rolling Block rifles, which are absolutely stunning in looks, feel, and accuracy. Unlike his father's toils with hand files and drips of weld, Val III and Pierangelo are designing the Navy Arms Lightning on CAD systems. "The computers make things easier, but there is no difference in the thought process," Val III informed me. "Pierangelo's father (Davide Pedersoli) and my father founded their companies at the same time, so all he and I are doing is carrying on old family traditions."

During the Navy Arms writer's seminar, I asked Val III when the Navy Arms Lightning would be available. He told me that it was on-

A cased set of Remington 1858 replicas from Navy Arms.

schedule for the spring of 2003. I also asked him how he felt about other companies also trying to make a Lightning Rifle. He told me, "It's not a big concern to us. Navy Arms has proven that, for over 45 years, when we come out with a gun, it will work and it will be right."

Val Sr. told his son that in the 1960's and '70's, other replica companies also appeared on the scene attempting to market and sell firearms that he had so painstakingly recreated. "There were dozens of companies that came and went," Val III stated. "Most did not make it for a variety of reasons. Val Sr. ended up buying many of them, including Replica Arms, Classic Arms, and the black powder divisions of Ithaca and Harrington & Richardson, just to name a few. Like before, I expect that the better companies will continue, and the ones that don't keep their promises will fall away."

The result of the last 45 years of work by Val Forgett Sr. is a vast array of Navy Arms products that is difficult for anyone to equal. Their list starts as early as the Brown Bess Muskets used to win our independence from England and winds up with the 1892 Winchester rifle.

In addition to the Lightning, Val III is looking to the future while

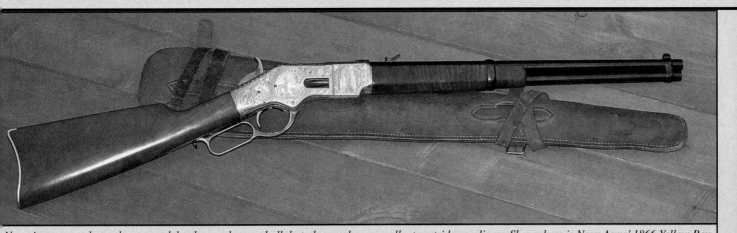

Navy Arms not only produces muzzleloaders and cap-n-ball, but also produces excellent cartridge replicas. Shown here is Navy Arms' 1866 Yellow Boy carbine in .44-40 engraved by Conrad Anderson of Rocktree Enterprises.

still learning from the expertise and experience of his father who still operates the day-to-day business. "When Val Sr. started, there was no replica industry. He created the benchmarks for quality that all our competitors now hold to. Even now, we still feed and function test our rifles to make sure that as few problems make it to the customer as possible. Any company can ship lousy guns out the door, and then fix them later. We want to get those guns fixed before any customer is ever disappointed. My mission now is to raise the standards Val Sr. set, so that shooters can genuinely recognize the difference in Navy Arms products."

Among other things, he is looking toward enhancing their current products by adding items that the cowboy shooter wants,

Val Forgett's son, Val Forgett III, shooting an 1863 C.S. Richmond replica at the Navy Arms Summit meeting in 2002.

such as Wolff springs, full buckhorn sights, and tang sights on all single-shot rifles, while looking toward future products that will peak the shooter's interest. He is also planning on relaunching Replica Arms to cater to the beginning replica shooter. Val III explained: "All the top cowboy action shooters use our rifles, but not everyone can afford them. If I can provide a new shooter with a product that is inexpensive and well-built, I am creating a future Navy Arms customer."

No matter what discipline of replica shooting you do, we all need to give Val Forgett Sr. a big thanks for his lifetime of effort in expanding the firearms industry and wish both Vals continuing success.

The Navy Arms Model 1892 in its various configurations and calibers is one of their most popular Western-action replicas.

Navy Arms' Products

Top Break Revolvers of the Old West
New Model Russian
1875 Schofield (various types)
Single-Action Revolvers of the Old West
1873 Colt SAA (various lengths and calibers)
Bisley Model SAA (various lengths and calibers)
Bisley Model Flat Top Target Model
1873 U.S. Cavalry Model
1895 U.S. Artillery Model
1866 & 1873 Rifles and Carbines (various types)
1892 Rifles and Carbines (various types)
Henry Rifles (various types)
Single Shot Rifles and Carbines
1874 Sharps (various types)
1885 High Wall (various lengths and calibers)
1873 Springfield Cavalry Carbine
No. 2 Creedmoor Target Rifle
Rolling Block (various lengths and calibers)
Colt-Style Percussion Revolvers
1836 Paterson
1847 Walker Dragoon
1851 Navy (various calibers)
1860 Army
Reb Model 1860 (various calibers)
Reb 60 Sheriff's Model (various calibers)
1862 New Police
1862 New Model Pocket Nickel
Solid Frame Percussion Revolvers
1858 New Model Army
Stainless 1858 New Model Army
Brass Frame 1858 New Model Army
Rogers and Spencer Army Model
Spiller and Burr
Le Mat Revolvers (various types)

Civil War Rifles & Carbines –Union
Smith Cavalry Carbine
Smith Artillery Carbine
1859 Sharps Cavalry Carbine
1859 Sharps "Berdan" Rifle
1859 Sharps Infantry Rifle
1863 "Zouave" Rifle
1861 Springfield Rifle
1863 Springfield Rifle
Civil War Rifles & Carbines – Confederacy
1841 Mississippi Rifle (various lengths and calibers)
1863 C.S. Richmond Rifle
Parker-Hale 1853 3-Bd Enfield Musket
Parker-Hale 1858 2-Bd Enfield Musket
Parker-Hale 1861 Musketoon
Parker-Hale Whitworth Rifle
Parker-Hale Volunteer Rifle
J.P. Murray Carbine
Navy Arms Miniatures (various types)
Military Flintlocks
Brown Bess Musket
Brown Bess Carbine
1763 Charleville Musket
1803 Harpers Ferry Rifle
1805 Ferry Pistol
Percussion Caps
Musket Cap
#11 Pistol Cap
Ammo
.41 Rimfire
.32 Rimfire Short
.32 Rimfire Long
Tomahawks (various types)
Bayonets (various types)
Old West Holster ("Mexican Loop" style in various lengths)
Money Belt (replica of Old West "money" cartridge with coin compartment)
"Prairie" Cartridge Belt (exact replica of the canvas belt)
Old West Shotgun Belt (heavy canvas with 12-gauge loops)

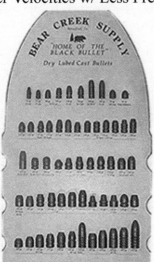
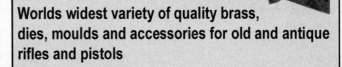
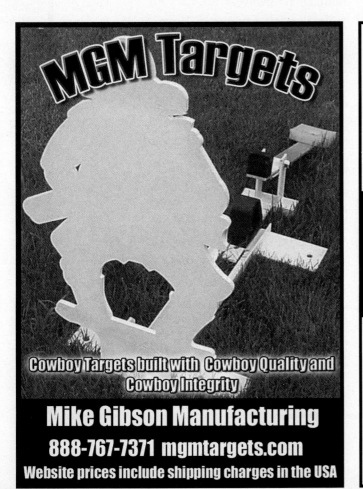

Black Powder and the Old West
Chapter 2
Old West Firearms & Replicas

Black Powder and the Old West
Chapter 2
Old West Firearms
& Replicas

STEVENS'
BOY'S RIFLES

By: Steve Matlock, aka Maddog

Growing up as I did on a small farm west of Boise, Idaho, guns have always been part of my life. At the age of five, I found an old model 1915 Stevens Favorite in our attic. I asked my dad if I could have the Stevens Favorite, and his response was yes, on the condition I never try shooting it. Years before, my uncle tried to shoot out a cleaning patch that was stuck in the barrel, and in the process, two or three bullets became lodged in the bore. A couple of years later, at the age of seven, I figured out that those lead bullets stuck in the bore would melt before it would damage the steel barrel. I heated the barrel and then removed the lead bullets – but that is another story.

That single 1915 Stevens Favorite started my hobby of collecting primarily non-bolt action, single-shot boy's rifles. I have stayed with this hobby for 41 years, and I still enjoy it. The difference between when I was a kid and now is the price of the hobby. My father never discouraged my hobby of collecting guns, even at my young age. I guess Dad thought that if I spent all my money on guns, I would stay out of trouble; he was right. Many young boys and girls started out with these rifles before advancing to a repeater or a semi-auto rifle.

For over 100 years, Stevens' firearms have been an important part of American history. Joshua Stevens founded his company in 1864. The Stevens Arms Company not only made tools, but tip-up pistols and rifles as well. In 1885, Joshua also started making an under-lever falling block that was the forerunner to the Favorite.

In April of 1920, Savage Arms Company purchased the Stevens Arms Company. The Stevens Arms Company became a division of the Savage Arms Corporation, instead of a separate entity, in 1936. Stevens was America's most prolific manufacturer of boy's rifles, and older shooters will remember that many of these rifles were distributed as sales premiums for those individuals selling cards, seeds, or Cloverine salve.

The following is a brief description of the Stevens' boy's rifles:

The #23 Sure Shot, made from 1894 to 1898, had a 20" round barrel with no forend. A weak side brake design, in addition to only being made for four years, makes this a very scarce Stevens.

The #16 Crackshot, made from 1900 to 1913, had a 20" round barrel and a thumb lever-operated rolling block.

The #17 Favorite, made from 1893 to 1939, had an under-lever falling block and was found with round, octagon, or 1/2 round and 1/2 octagon barrels. These rifles were the highest quality and the one with the most variation of all the Stevens' boy's rifles. A change in sights, barrel length, or stock style brought forth new model numbers, such as the #18, #19, #20, #21, and #27.

The #15 Maynard Junior, made from 1902 to 1912, had an 18" part round and part octagon barrel, flat board-type stock, and an under-lever tip-up. It was fashioned and designed after the larger Maynard rifle.

The #65 Little Krag, made from 1903 to 1910, had a 20" round barrel with a peep sight in the rear dovetail. This was Stevens' first bolt-action boy's rifle and was made to meet the demand for a rifle that looked and worked like the, then current, military issue.

The #14 Little Scout, made from 1906 to 1910, had an 18" round barrel, one-piece shapeless flat stock, and a thumb-operated rolling block action. The stock was too thin at the receiver and, as a result, usually ended up broken. It is hard to find a good example of a Little Scout today.

The #14-1/2 Little Scout, made from 1911 to 1941, had a 20" round barrel, two-piece stock, and an exposed

The author, Steve Matlock, proudly displays his collection of Stevens Rifles.

receiver. The #14-1/2 Little Scout had a similar rolling block design to the #14, but it was much stronger.

The #11 Junior, made from 1924 to 1931, had a 20" round barrel and a one-piece stock. It was a lighter and cheaper remake of the #14 Little Scout that had the same stock breakage problems. The #11 Junior was the last lightweight, inexpensive boy's rifle made by the Savage/Stevens Arms Company.

The #12 Marksman, made from 1911 to 1930, had a 22" round barrel and had an under-lever tip-up of much higher quality than the #15 Maynard Junior.

The #26 Crackshot, made from 1912 to 1939, was made in either an 18" or 20" barrel, and had an under-lever falling-block design with a two-piece stock. It was 3rd behind the Favorite and Little Scout #14-1/2 for having the longest production run.

In 1971, Savage Arms Corporation introduced the Model '71 Joshua Stevens' Commemoration Favorite. The demand for a plain shooter was so high that in 1972, Savage introduced the full octagon barrel model '72. A couple of years later, the round barrel model '74 was manufactured and introduced.

In 1999, Savage announced plans to introduce and manufacture a new Favorite Model #30G that sports a barrel that is 1/2 round and 1/2 octagon. I just recently added this model to my collection.

One of the most frequently asked questions is, "When was my Stevens made?" Assembly numbers do not identify Stevens' firearms. Many people think that the assembly numbers are serial numbers, but they are not. The printing on the barrel is the only indication of the time period in which the firearm was manufactured. Some of the higher quality, more expensive models did have serial numbers, but the records to those firearms are lost.

A series of Stevens' boy's rifles.

Identifying marks that show the year a Stevens was made:

1864-1888: "J. Stevens & Co. Chicopee Falls, Mass."

1888-1919: "J. Stevens Arm & Tool Co., Chicopee Falls, Mass. USA" or "J. Stevens A & T Co., Chicopee Falls, Mass. USA"

1919-1942: "J. Stevens Arm & Tool Co., Chicopee Falls, Mass. USA"

THE COLT Thun

The Thunderbolt started as a .44 1860 Army revolver from E.M.F.

"You want a new saddle, Mister?" the telegraph operator asked. "I know a feller selling one cheap. Bad run of cards, you know?"

The Herald man glanced down at the splintered seat of his saddle and shook his head. "I'll keep this one," he said as he handed over his story to be tapped out across the wire.

"What'd you do," the telegrapher asked, "take an axe to it?"

"Something like that," the reporter replied. He looked down once more at the wreck of his saddle and his mind went back to that sinking sandbar on the Arickaree Fork called Beecher's Island.

It was a hot day for late September; so hot that his horse had bloated fast, straining the cinch straps. Lying between the stiffening legs of the dead mare, the Herald man stuffed .44 rimfire rounds into the loading gate of his Winchester as fast as he could. The brass receiver felt slick in his sweaty fingers.

He'd seen plenty of combat during the war, however in those days he'd been an interested, but detached, observer. Both sides were fighting the public relations war as intensely as they fought the war on the battlefield. Journalists were prizes that

derbolt

By: Michael Beliveau,
aka Bottom Dealin' Mike

The Thunderbolt is a compact, sweet-handling six-shooter with all the power of its full-sized 1860 Army bretheren.

The author's 1860 Thunderbolt is modeled after the short-barreled Avenging Angel revolvers.

commanders kept out of harm's way.

The Herald man didn't think the Cheyenne hunkered down on the far bank of the Republican River would feel so protective of his hide. He didn't think they were familiar with the concept of journalistic noncombatants. So he'd been slinging lead as fervently as any blue-trousered trooper.

He loaded four rounds and realized his pockets were empty. The rest of his ammunition was stuffed in the saddlebags on the other side of his bloated mare. He cursed a low fervent stream of invective under his breath. He needed that ammo.

Only a desultory fire was popping from the Cheyenne's weapons on the opposite bank. The Herald man decided it was now or never. He pulled his green river knife and sliced through the cinch.

He called in a low voice to the nearest trooper, "Cover me, Carl, I need some shells."

He leapt to his feet, reaching over the bulk of his horse and grabbing the saddle. He pulled, but 1,500 pounds of dead horsemeat had it pinned. He scrambled over her body and tugged, but it didn't budge.

He heard rifle fire ripping behind him.

"What the heck are you doing?" Carl yelled. His Spencer started banging, shooting a jet of flame from the muzzle that almost blinded the Herald man.

He saw sand fly near his butt as he dropped to a sitting position, grabbed the saddle with both hands, planted his feet on the mare's back, and heaved his body backwards. He flipped over backwards when the saddle jerked free of the mare, tumbling over in the sand as he felt the saddle jerk hard in his hands. He scrambled to his feet, launching himself back into the lee of the horse with a rolling dive.

"You got to be crazy, Mike," Carl yelled at him. "All that for a goll durn saddle!"

"I won this saddle from a British officer back in '63," the Herald man called back. "I ain't about to leave it to some gut-eating heathen."

"Well, I doubt they'd want it now," Carl answered.

The reporter looked at the saddle and started cursing. The leather was ripped and scarred by bullets, and the wooden tree was a splintered mess.

"Here they come!"

The reporter crawled by the tail end of his dead mare, steadied himself, and began to fire as Roman Nose's warriors came splashing across the bright ribbon of water.

"I don't think it's worth fixing, Mister." The telegrapher's voice brought him back to the present with a start.

"I don't like to give up on things too easy," the reporter said with a small smile. "If New York wires back, send it over to the hotel."

Smoke drifted in a golden fog under the oil lamps of the hotel's saloon. The reporter took a long slow pull on his cigar and sent a stream of smoke to join the swirling haze under the rafters. He was sitting with two pair showing and one card still to deal. The only man still in the game was a young miner seated to his left who thought he could fill a flush in hearts on his last card.

"I'm going the limit," he said defiantly. He gave the reporter a hard-eyed look.

"Call," the Herald man said calmly. He flipped a seventh card face up to the prospector, a deuce of clubs, just as a young boy came running up to his table with a sheet of paper.

Without even a glance at the angry prospector, the reporter gave the boy a dime and began to read:

"Good work STOP
Custer acquitted STOP
Rejoining 7th at Ft. Dodge STOP
Go there STOP"

The reporter started to smile. If there was one thing he'd learned during the war it was this - if you wanted to find news, go where Custer was.

"Boys, I'm out," he announced.

"Not with my money you, ain't," the prospector said loudly. His face was flushed and sweaty. "That's my whole poke, mister."

"I said I'm out," the reporter tossed a dollar on the table. "Have a drink on me."

"Why you bottom dealin' son of a…" he clawed for the long-barreled Colt 1860 Army revolver holstered at his waist. He had it halfway clear of the leather when he felt the short barrel of the reporter's revolver grinding hard into the angle of his jaw. He let the reporter pull his sixgun from its sheath and toss it across the room.

"Mister, I'm sure you meant that in a friendly way," the reporter said in a low hard voice. He ground the gun barrel hard into the prospector's jaw bone. "But you weren't smiling, and when a man calls me that, he'd better be grinning like a jack o' lantern."

The reporter jerked hard on the prospector's collar, holding his face within inches of his own. "Now let's see that smile," he growled.

The miner's face jerked in a grotesque grin.

"That's better," the Herald man told him. He pushed him hard by the nape of his neck. "Now get out."

The room was as quiet as a bank vault until the miner

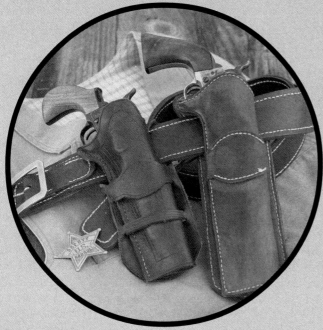

The Thunderbolt's 5-1/2" barrel gives it a decided advantage on the draw over a full-size 1860.

stumbled, shame-faced, out the door. Then the noise started up again as if nothing had happened. From the bar, a tall man, whose hat carried the embroidered crossed-arrow insignia of a civilian scout, grinned and called above the din, "He's right, Mike. You are a bottom dealin' S.O.B!"

The reporter's face lit up with a smile.

"Scout, I never denied it," he answered with a laugh.

He clapped the tall man on the beaded shoulder of his old Civil War cavalry jacket. "Now let's have a drink for old times. I'm headed for Dodge at daybreak."

Back in the fall of 1868, people like Bottom Dealin' Mike appreciated the need for a powerful compact sixgun. As a class, these weapons are called Avenging Angels. Usually, they were made by private gunsmiths who chopped .44 Colt 1860 Army revolvers into more concealable configurations.

I've had a strong desire for one of those cap-n-ball belly guns for a long time. But, I wasn't interested enough to do the radical metal work on the grip assembly that it takes to turn out a classic

Avenging Angel. Those guns typically gave up the plow-handled grips of a standard Colt 1860 in favor of bobbed bird's head grip assemblies. Luckily, that's not a problem anymore.

Single-action sixguns with bird's head grips have become quite popular these days. And backstraps and trigger guards from replica Colt 1851 Navys, 1860 Armys, and 1873 Peacemakers can all interchange because the screw patterns are common between the models. That means bird's head grips made for an SAA will also fit on an 1860 replica.

E.M.F. has two different types of bird's head grip assemblies. The Pinkerton model has a classic bird's head design where the backstrap curves in a clean arc down to the bottom of the trigger guard and the Express model has a recurved bird's head that is reminiscent of the 1877 Thunderer and Lightning double-action revolvers.

My plan was to buy an Express grip assembly and a standard 1860 Army revolver. I'd have bobbed the 1860's barrel down to five inches and repositioned the front sight.

When I explained my plan to Gary Owen at E.M.F., he asked why I didn't just buy an 1860 Army with a five-inch barrel. That guy's a genius. Essentially, the only tool I needed to make my Avenging Angel was a screwdriver. Because of its 1877-style grips, I dubbed my new creation the Colt Thunderbolt.

The short barrel and new grip assembly completely changed the feel and handling of the 1860. It was a change for the better. Standard 1860 grips are never a good fit for me. I can't reach the hammer for cocking without shifting my grip, which then has to shift back for shooting. With the Express grips, my thumb easily reached the hammer, making follow-up shots a lot smoother and a lot faster.

Lately, I've been using the Thunderbolt in side matches at cowboy action matches, and it is a hoot. It's also quite a conversation piece.

I've shot the Thunderbolt with full house loads of 35 grains of Goex FFFg pushing a .451 round ball topped with Bore Butter, but I got better accuracy from the same 28-grain powder charge I've used for years in my 1860 Armys. Groups averaged three to four inches off-hand at 25 yards, which is fine for me. As is usually the case with cap-n-ball sixguns, the Thunderbolt printed almost a foot high at that range. Eventually, I'll make a new front sight to correct that problem, but for now I'm having too much fun shooting my little blaster to head back to the shop.

The modification is simple. The author exchanged the 1860 Army grip assembly with a set from an E.M.F. Express revolver.

The Navy Arms *LeMat*

By: John Taffin,
aka Sixgunner

The Navy Arms LeMat did its best work with Hodgdon's Pyrodex P.

Traditionally-styled frontier revolvers are normally thought of as six-shooters. In fact, Colt labeled the barrels of their Single Action Army and Bisley .44-40 chambered revolvers not with caliber markings, but rather with the words "Frontier Six-Shooter." However, Sam Colt's first revolver, the Paterson, was a five-shooter. Beginning with the 1847 Walker, all full-sized Colt Single Actions, be they cap-n-ball or cartridge firing, were true sixguns.

In recent times, we have found that our government cannot trust us with high-capacity handguns. Personally, I cannot understand why a 20-round magazine is evil and dangerous in the hands of ordinary shooters while two 10-round magazines, which normally work better anyhow, are not. Strange or what? Many may think high-capacity handguns are a recent innovation. Not so. The first high-capacity handgun goes all the way back to the Civil War with a

revolver made for the Confederacy. In fact, quite a few famous Confederate officers preferred the high-capacity "sixgun" known as the LeMat.

Francois LeMat was born in France in 1821, which makes him a contemporary of Samuel Colt. He started out studying for the priesthood. He changed his path, however, and became a doctor, arriving in the United States in 1843. LeMat was a most talented and diverse individual who held patents in several countries on such things as ship's salvage, harbor improvements, cannon ammunition, and revolvers. On a more peaceful note, Dr. LeMat also held several patents on medical instruments.

In 1856, LeMat first patented his Grapeshot revolver. Just prior to the Civil War, LeMat's revolver was ready for production and the governor of Louisiana made LeMat a colonel. LeMat had formed a

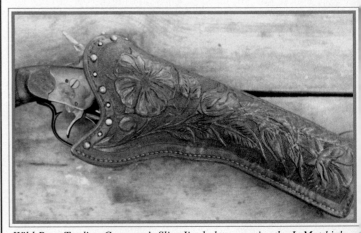

This beautifully-crafted Slim Jim is by Chuck Burrows of Wild Rose Trading Company. It is a true classic holster for a classic revolver.

Wild Rose Trading Company's Slim Jim holster carries the LeMat high on the hip securely, poised for fast draw by anyone whose hands are large and strong enough.

partnership with U.S. Army Major Beauregard, his cousin by marriage. The partnership did not last very long, but Beauregard would carry the LeMat revolver as a general in the Confederate Army. Somewhere around 3000 LeMat revolvers were produced in Paris during the Civil War.

As one would expect with its 10-shot capacity, the LeMat is a large revolver with a weight of 3-½ pounds, heavier than the Colt 1860, but lighter than the Colt Dragoon and Walker. Several variations were made, such as a rimfire and a baby model. Today, if one is in search of a shootable LeMat in good condition, a price tag in the $10,000 range could be expected. Pristine examples, of course, will bring much higher prices. But now, thanks to Navy Arms, modern examples of the LeMat revolver are available for today's shooters.

Navy Arms, long known for providing quality replica firearms for the shooting public in general and cowboy action shooters in particular, offers three modern percussion revolvers of the LeMat pattern, including a Cavalry, Army, and Navy Model. All three are nine-plus-one shooters, with the Cavalry Model having a spur trigger guard and swiveling lanyard ring, the Army Model with a round trigger guard and solid lanyard in the butt, and the Navy Model with the center lever on the back of the hammer to allow firing of the center barrel. Our test gun was the Navy Model.

This is a beautifully-made replica revolver, well-finished with deep bluing and extremely well-fitted walnut grips with excellent checkering. These are faithful copies of the originals, with one exception. A close look reveals a tiny screw on the right side just behind the hammer pivot screw. This is there for a very important reason. The original LeMats, unlike Colt revolvers of the same time, required very precise tuning or they would not work properly. Cylinders would not lock up properly if the gun was out of time and this is exactly the state that I found my test gun to be in. However, by simply turning the adjustment screw which controls the cylinder locking stud engagement so that the cylinder rotates when it should and locks up when it should, I was able to "fine-tune" the LeMat without resorting to a gunsmith's services. Had this addition been on the original LeMats, their production run and popularity might have been much longer and larger.

In order to produce an affordable modern-day LeMat, Val Forgett of Navy Arms combined Old World craftsmanship with modern technology. Many of the parts for the LeMat are investment castings; the cylinders are turned from solid bar steel, as is the barrel. Modern CNC machinery plays a large part in the production of the modern LeMat.

The Navy Arms LeMat revolver loads like any other percussion revolver. First, a measured amount of powder is poured in the front of the cylinder chamber, then a round ball is placed on top of the powder charge and rammed home with the loading lever found on the left-hand side of the barrel. This is a very short stroke lever, so round balls cannot be seated very deeply. Once the powder charge and round balls are placed in each cylinder, appropriate grease (I use that age-old black powder wonder, Crisco) is then placed over the front of the ball filling out the cylinder chamber. I used .451" round balls from Buffalo Bullet Company for the main part of the cylinder and a .65 caliber round ball in the center barrel. Only after all chambers were loaded and greased were the percussion caps, CCI #10, placed on the nipples.

For a powder charge I used a 30-grain volume powder measure. Seven different black powder and five black powder substitutes were used in testing the LeMat. With a 30-grain volume powder measure, muzzle velocities ran from a low of 554 fps to a high of 897 fps.

Is this the first high-capacity handgun? The LeMat is really a ten-gun, holding nine round lead balls around the periphery of the chamber, as well as one .68 caliber round ball or shot load in the center.

Note that by thumbing back the lever on the top of the hammer of the LeMat, the face of the hammer will then contact the center percussion cap to fire the center barrel.

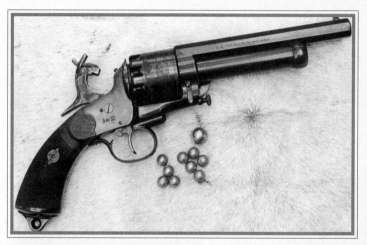

The LeMat is not a tack driver. However, the nine shots will definitely fall under the category of battle accuracy.

Shooting the LeMat was pure pleasure, even with the dirt, grease, grime, and smoke associated with black powder shooting. If you've done it, you know how addictive it can become! If you've never tried it, please do not listen to those who tell you it is not worth the effort. The time required for cleaning is actually less than that required for the normal loading and care of fired brass.

For me, at least without more practice, the LeMat is a two-handed proposition. With a little practice I do not think I would have any problem handling the LeMat with one hand, however. The angle of the grip frame is quite different from the standard Colt Single Action revolvers, coming back rather than down from the mainframe; it is quite comfortable. The hammer is easy to reach and the hammer spur is wide and flat, making it easy to cock. If you are old enough to remember the heyday of TV westerns in the late 1950's, you should remember one series in which the hero carried a LeMat. Don Durant, as Johnny Ringo, was able to fast-draw the LeMat from a special low-riding, spring-clip holster.

The only negative in shooting the LeMat, at least for me, are the sights. The front sight is a large inverted "V" set in a dovetail in the octagon barrel, while the rear sight notch cut in the cocked hammer is very wide. However, at the base of this wide rear sight is a shallow notch that can be used for sighting for more precise shooting, but for me to use it would require a shorter front sight. I believe I could cut my groups in half by altering the sights to suit me and/or playing with powder charges and bullet diameter.

A formidable weapon indeed is the LeMat. Nine .451" round balls and one .648" round ball from the center barrel all delivered on target at a battle distance of 50 feet.

TEST-FIRING THE NAVY ARMS LEMAT BUFFALO BULLET COMPANY .451 RB/CCI #10 PERCUSSION CAPS		
LOAD	MV	GROUP/9 SHOTS 50 FEET
Goex Cartridge	637	3 ½"
Goex FFg	643	4 1/2"
Goex FFFg	793	4 1/4"
Goex Clear Shot FFFg	703	5"
Swiss 2F	731	5 ¾"
Swiss 3F	897	6 ½"
Elephant Brand FFg	554	4 ¾"
Elephant Brand FFFg	623	6 ¼"
Clean Shot FFg	588	6 ¼"
Clean Shot FFFg	811	6"
PYRODEX P	774	3"
PYRODEX Pellet	957	5 7/8"

As is, the LeMat certainly exhibits battle accuracy. If it was 1860 and I was choosing a defensive sixgun, I would take a serious look at not just one, but a pair of LeMats. Having 20 quickly available shots would be hard to ignore!

While test firing the LeMat, I swabbed out the barrel with a patch saturated with Windex after shooting each cylinder. When I was through shooting, I thoroughly sprayed the front and back of the cylinder and down the barrel with Windex and then wiped it down until I got back to the house for formal cleaning. The LeMat breaks down into four parts for easy cleaning by removing the knob at the front of the frame. The revolver is then separated into the mainframe, cylinder, barrel, and center barrel/cylinder pin combination. With black powder solvent, cleanup takes 10 minutes at the most.

As an extra added bonus to test firing the LeMat, Chuck Burrows of Wild Rose Trading Company sent a beautifully hand-carved and brass-spotted Slim Jim holster, common to the time period of the original LeMat. Burrows is a virtual artist in leather and his creation is a true Frontier masterpiece, which, by the way, he crafted from a cardboard outline of the LeMat that I sent him. I recommend him highly for your authentic Old Western leather needs.

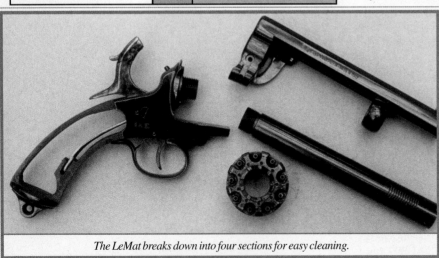

The LeMat breaks down into four sections for easy cleaning.

Those of us living in the West owe an immeasurable amount of gratitude to those that came before us: the explorers, mountain men, trappers, pony express riders, wagon masters, pioneers, ranchers, cowboys, farmers, peace officers, engineers, preachers, missionaries, schoolmarms, and so forth. The West was not easily "won" with many factors involved in the taming. The railroads, the United States Cavalry, the buffalo hunters, the wagon trains, the stagecoach lines, and the telegraph wires, all played an important part. However, the most important part was played by women; women who insisted upon safe towns, schools for their children, and churches to bring faith to the frontier.

Firearms were extremely important in opening up the West. The Hawken rifle, the Colt and Remington percussion sixguns, the Colt the 1911 Colt, and numerous machine guns; and Bill Ruger has single-handedly made and kept revolvers and rifles affordable in our lifetime. B. Tyler Henry accomplished as much, if not more, than all three of these legendary geniuses. He literally changed the concept of rifles as a battle and hunting weapon.

When the Civil War broke out, the troops on both sides were equipped with single-shot muzzle-loading rifles, the same basic design that had been used for over 100 years. By then, rifle barrels were actually rifled, and the flintlock had given way to the percussion cap. However, rifles were still operated the same way - powder down the barrel, followed by a patched ball rammed home by a rod, and then the percussion cap fitted to the nipple. This was state-of-the-art when Henry arrived on the scene.

Winchester Leverguns

By: John Taffin, aka Sixgunner

The most popular chambering in the 1886 Winchester is the .45-70.

Single Action Army, the Springfield Trapdoor, and the Sharps single-shot buffalo rifle, all played their part. But most would agree that the Winchester leverguns were truly "The Guns that Won the West."

THE 1860 HENRY: When one hears the words "firearms design genius," the names that usually come to mind first are John Browning, Samuel Colt, and in our lifetime, Bill Ruger. After handling an original 1860 Henry, as well as shooting the Navy Arms replica, I would rank B. Tyler Henry in this same group; he was a true genius. Sam Colt gave us the first workable revolver; John Browning has many accomplishments, including many of the Winchester leverguns,

There had been previous attempts to come up with self-contained ammunition, however in 1860, Henry received a patent for a rifle firing the first truly successful cartridge consisting of a copper case holding both powder and bullet, with the ignition also contained in the rim-fire case. The .44 Henry round used a bullet originally weighing 216 grains loaded over 26 grains of black powder. The weight of the bullet was soon reduced to 200 grains over the same powder charge for about 1200 fps. The bullets were lubricated to help reduce fouling and with its tubular magazine, the 1860 Henry held so much firepower that it was advertised, "A resolute man, armed

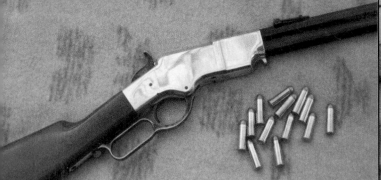

The Navy Arms 1860 Henry is chambered in .44-40 rather than the original .44 Rimfire.

Two great replica leverguns from Navy Arms: the 1873 Winchester and the 1866 Yellow Boy.

with one of these rifles, particularly if on horseback, cannot be captured."

The 1860 Henry was operated with a lever under the receiver, and a tubular magazine that was loaded from the front. A brass follower in the magazine tube was pushed forward until it released the catch that allowed the end of the barrel to swing to the right, exposing the end of the magazine, and allowed cartridges to be dropped down the tube. After the magazine was filled with 15 rounds, the follower was carefully allowed to settle on the nose of the last bullet loaded, and the end of the barrel swung back into place and locked. You can imagine how superior those troops armed with 1860 Henrys felt when their adversaries still had single-shot rifles! The Henry rifle did not have a long history since it was only in production from 1860 to 1866, with somewhere around 13,000 having been produced. Today, thanks to replicas, levergun shooters can enjoy the 1860 once again, chambered not in .44 Rimfire, but in .44-40 Winchester Centerfire, as well as .45 Colt.

THE 1866 YELLOW BOY: In 1866, the Henry was improved with a King's Patent side loading gate, named for Nelson King who followed B. Tyler Henry as Oliver Winchester's shop foreman. This first Winchester, the 1866 Yellow Boy, used the same .44 Rimfire ammunition as the 1860 Henry. However, it was loaded through what has now become the traditional loading gate on the right side of the receiver. The 1866 was also fitted with a wooden forearm. Many

For great black powder shooting, both the 1866 and the 1873 are available from Navy Arms chambered in .44-40.

of the early Colt Single Action Army sixguns, as well as other revolvers, were chambered in .44 Rimfire as a companion sidearm to these leverguns.

Oliver Winchester could certainly pick exceptionally qualified men in the field of firearms. Since the 1866 Yellow Boy was now loaded through a loading gate on the right side of the receiver, it was no longer necessary to put the rifle out of commission, nor even take it off target while reloading. This was a tremendous improvement. Like the 1860, the 1866 lives on in replica form chambered in .44-40, .45 Colt, .38 Special, 38-.40, and .44 Special.

THE MODEL 1873: Seven years later, the 1866 itself would be further improved, first with an iron, and then with a steel receiver to replace the brass frame of the 1860 and 1866 Models. It was chambered in the .44 Winchester Centerfire, also knows as the .44 WCF, or as it is more commonly referred to today, the .44-40, and became the 1873. Five years later, Colt would chamber their Single Action Army in .44-40 for those that wanted a revolver using the same ammunition as their new Winchester.

Mention "The Gun that Won the West," and most people will think of the '73 Winchester. Winchester selected Model '73s that were above average in accuracy and became *One of One hundred* or *One of One thousand* examples at premium prices. The original chambering was joined by the .38 Winchester Centerfire in 1879, and this was followed by the .32 Winchester Centerfire in

A Navy Arms 1860 Henry .44-40 mates well with a Colt 3rd Generation .44-40 and a circa 1879 .44-40 Frontier Six-Shooter.

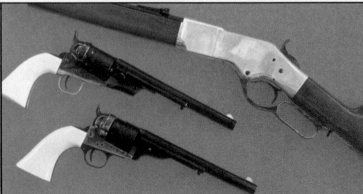

This Navy Arms 1866 chambered in .44 Special will handle the same .44 Colt black powder loads used in the Cimarron Cartridge Conversions.

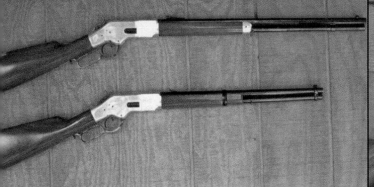

The 1866 Yellow Boy is available in both rifle and carbine versions.

Six years after the introduction of the 1860 Henry, it was improved to become the 1866 Model.

1882. When Colt added these three cartridges to the Colt Single Action Army, it became possible for a shooter of that time to have a sixgun and a saddle gun that chambered the same cartridge. This was a most desirable feature.

THE MODEL 1876: Winchester had the marvelous Model 1873 chambered in .32-20, .38-40, and .44-40. They were great sixgun cartridges, but lacked long-range energy or stopping power for really big game. The next natural step was to scale up the size of the first centerfire Winchester levergun, and the result was the Model 1876. While the 1873 was an easy handling, relatively lightweight little levergun, the Model 1876 was anything but. It was designed for serious big game hunting, and became a favorite of Theodore Roosevelt while he was living in the Dakotas.

Although the 1876 was not quite as powerful as what was to come, it was way above the possibilities of the Model 1873. Its four standard chamberings were: .40-60 (210-gr. bullet at 1480 fps), .45-60 (300-gr. bullet at 1325 fps), .45-75 (300-gr. bullet at 1440 fps), and .50-95 (312-gr. bullet at 1500 fps). Winchester thought about chambering the .45-70 in the Model 1876, but it proved to be too powerful for the toggle-link style action. The most popular chambering was the .45-75, which was not only Roosevelt's choice as a hunting rifle, but was also adopted as the standard levergun by the Royal Canadian Mounted Police.

Today, all Winchester leverguns, except for the Model 1876, are

Four great original Winchester leverguns: 1866 Yellow Boy, Model 1873, Model 1886, and the Model 1892.

offered in one replica form or another. Dare we hope for the offering to eventually be made totally complete by seeing a new version of the Centennial Rifle of 1876?

THE MODEL 1886: John Browning's first levergun design was the large and powerful 1886 Winchester. Way back when I started reading everything I could find about sixguns and rifles, Lucian Cary was the gun editor of *TRUE*. Cary had grown up in my part of the country during the last two decades of the 19th century right over the border in Eastern Oregon. Writing in the late 1940's, Cary said: "The boyish passion for guns will never again be as universal as it was when I was a small boy ...I well remember the summer I spent in the Blue Mountains of eastern Oregon when I was 10 years old. I went trout fishing every day and often hunted grouse with an older boy who had a .22 rifle that he cleaned with boiling water every night - quite properly too in the days of corrosive priming."

"One day a tall, gaunt, bearded man with a pack horse came along the road between our camp and the mountain stream we fished. He carried what seemed to me then to be an enormous rifle. I recognized it as a Winchester and asked what cartridge it shot. 'This,' he said, 'is a forty-five ninety.' I knew even then what that meant. It was a rifle of .45 caliber shooting 90 grains of black powder. To me, who had never fired anything bigger than the .22, that .45-90 was awesome. It was a rifle to shoot grizzly bears with.

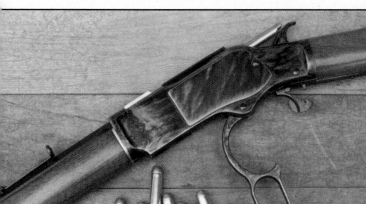

Seven years after the 1866 arrived, it was improved and became the Model 1873.

Winchester's first centerfire levergun, the 1873 Model in .44-40.

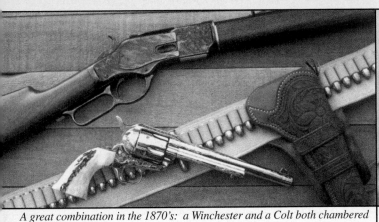

A great combination in the 1870's: a Winchester and a Colt both chambered in .44-40.

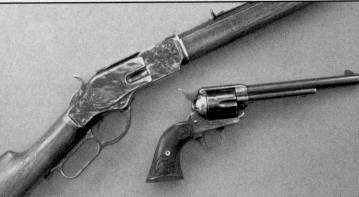

Navy Arms Model 1873 .44-40 and the 3rd Generation Colt Single Action Army .44-40, both set up for black powder use.

It was the kind of rifle I wanted when I was big enough."

The Winchester the old man was carrying was the Model of 1886, perhaps the finest lever-action ever offered by any manufacturer at any time. The Army had adopted the Springfield 1873 Trapdoor in the much more powerful .45-70 cartridge in the same year the Winchester Model 1873 .44-40 came about. It fired a bullet that was more than twice as heavy at the same muzzle velocity. The Winchester leverguns of the 1870's were reliable repeaters, but when compared to the Trapdoor and its big .45, they were not very powerful.

Oliver Winchester's son-in-law wanted to bring forth a more powerful levergun, one that would handle the .45-70. He heard of two brothers living in Utah who were rifle designers. So, Thomas Bennett went to Ogden, met the Browning brothers, and purchased two new rifle designs, one destined to be the 1885 Single Shot and the other the levergun that would become the Model of 1886.

By today's standards, the Winchester 1886 was a huge rifle weighing about nine pounds. Although it was very large, it also had an extremely smooth action that carried over to the miniature 1886 that would come later, the Winchester 1892. The 1886 debuted in the era of black powder cartridges, but would prove to be strong enough that when the transition to smokeless came about, the only change

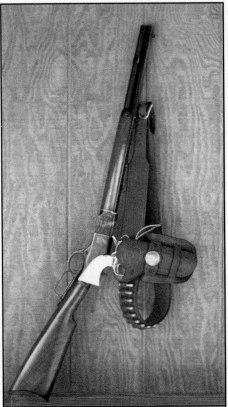

A hard-to-beat combination from the 1800's: a Winchester 1873 and a Colt Single Action Army .45 in leather by San Pedro Saddlery.

necessary was the barrel-to-nickel steel to handle the higher velocities with jacketed bullets. The Model of 1886 would be manufactured for nearly 50 years from 1886 to 1935. During its production run, the 1886 would be made in several versions: full magazine, half magazine, octagonal barrel, round barrel, rifle, and carbine, to name a few.

In addition to the above mentioned .45-90 carried by the old man of Lucian Cary's youth, original chamberings were in .45-70 and .40-82. It was also found in the big 50s, the .50-100 and .50-110, as well as .40-70, .40-60, .38-70, and .38-56. Its last chambering before its demise in 1935 was the smokeless .33 Winchester.

THE MODEL 1892: In the pre-war glory days of "B" Westerns, it was impossible to make a movie without one. The Ringo Kid had one when he met the "Stagecoach." Rooster had one, Lucas had one, and Josh Randall had part of one. Yes, all of these screen heroes had a Winchester Model '92. Who can ever forget the scene in *Stagecoach* (I first saw it on TV when I was nine-years-old) when John Wayne as Ringo twirls his '92 Winchester to stop the stage? Or perhaps the greatest scene ever in any Western was when Rooster Cogburn, with a Colt Single Action Army .45 in his left hand and a freshly twirled .44-40 Winchester in his right hand, yells, "Fill your hand you

Current production firearms, all great for shooting black powder .44-40 loads: a pair of nickel-plated Colt Single Action Armies and a Rossi Model '92.

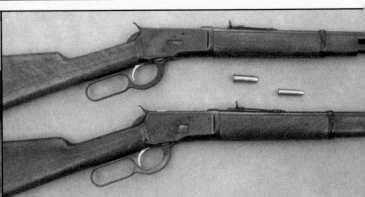

Browning offered the Model '92 chambered in .357 Magnum and .44 Magnum.

Black powder works well in the .44 Special case when used in this 1950's Colt and a Rossi Model '92. Leather by Galco.

Sixgunner shooting the 1860 Henry.

sonnavabitch!" and prepares to meet the Ned Pepper gang single-handedly.

Most of us grew up watching Chuck Connors as *The Rifleman* twirl his large loop lever Model '92 to cock it and then operate it like a semi-automatic on the streets of North Fork. Steve McQueen, as bounty hunter Josh Randall in *Wanted: Dead or Alive*, also carried a bastardized Model '92 with a short barrel and shorter stock. The eye-catching loop lever was there, along with someone's idea of what the little '92 should carry as ammunition as Randall's belt was filled with .45-70 cartridges that would not even come close to fitting the Model '92.

The Winchester Model '92 was made from 1892 to 1931, with some special models lasting right up to World War II and slightly over 1,000,000 units being produced. It was

Replica Model '92s are available in both rifle and carbine.

one of the slickest, no call it *the* slickest, smoothest, easiest-handling levergun ever to come out of Winchester. Winchester's 1873 was mainly chambered for the .44-40, .38-40, and .32-20, easy-shooting cartridges that could also be used in the Colt Single Action Army. The Model 1886 Winchester was chambered for the .45-70 and .45-90. The Model 1892 was simply a miniaturized '86 chambered for the cartridges of the '73. Over its long life, the Model '92 would be made in barrel lengths from 14 to 31 inches, however the 20" carbine model, holding 11 cartridges in its tubular magazine, was pretty much the standard fare.

None were ever made with the large loop lever, this being dreamed up by someone in Hollywood in 1939 for the Duke. It would show up in most of his movies over the next 30 years, as well as in the above-mentioned TV shows. It has no practical value whatsoever, and actually makes the Model 1892 harder to cock at shoulder level.

The Model 1892, which also appeared in .25-20 and .218 Bee, has been out of production for more than 60 years, and trying to find a good one at a reasonable price is not easy. Winchester does have modern '92s made in Japan for them, and Davidson's has had Winchester produce some of these in Special Limited Editions. In the 1950's, many '92s were converted to modern cartridges, first to .357 Magnum, starting with a .25-20 or .32-20, and later to .44 Magnum, using a .38-40 or .44-40 as the base.

Browning combined the best attributes of the 1873 and 1886 to miniaturize the '86, and gave us the Model of 1892. The toggle-link action of the '73 was replaced by the much stronger, double-locking bolts of the '86. The Model 1892 is mostly found chambered in the same cartridges as the Model 1873, .44-40, .38-40, and .32-20.

THE MODEL 1894: Just about the time my interest in firearms began, I remember President Eisenhower being presented with the 2,000,000th Winchester Model '94. What an achievement! Winchester's classic lever-action deer rifle, which began production in 1894, had reached the 2,000,000 mark in slightly less than 60

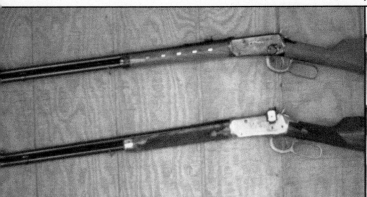

The Winchester Model '94 was chambered in both the black powder .38-55 and smokeless powder .30-30.

100 years separate the Winchester Model 1895 .30-40 Krag and a current .30-06.

Sixgunner shooting the Model 1873.

Two original .38-40s from the turn of the 20th century: Winchester Model 1892 and Colt Bisley Model.

years. Now, 50 years later, Winchester is well past the 7,000,000th Model 1894!

During this high-tech age, the ancient Model 1894 Winchester, with its antiquated lever-action operating system, has reached the 7,000,000 mark. The 1894 Winchester is to long gunners as the Colt Single Action is to sixgunners. Its looks, feel, and performance stir the heart, mind, and soul as no other rifle. Even though it was not yet in existence at the time period depicted by most Western movies, it is still the rifle most seen in countless Western movies. The Colt Single Action and the Winchester rifle Model '92 or Model '94 were indelibly imprinted in the mind of every kid growing up with the B movies of the 1930's and '40's, and the TV Westerns of the 1950's. Perhaps that is why both are still so popular today.

The smokeless powder .30-30 is the caliber most associated with the Model 1894, but it was not the first chambering. In 1894, John Browning's design was brought forth in the black powder cartridges .32-40 and .38-55. Both were later resurrected in modern commemorative 1894's, and the .38-55 is now chambered by Marlin. One year later, in 1895, the legendary .30-30 arrived in smokeless form and the rest, as they say, is history. Along with the .30-30 came the .25-35, a most pleasant-shooting varmint cartridge, and in the right hands, a viable cartridge for even larger game. One of the largest critters to ever fall to the hunter's rifle was a 10-foot, livestock-killing grizzly bear taken in Utah in 1923 by a Model 1894 in .25-35 in the hands of Idahoan Frank Clark. In addition to the .30-30 and .25-35, came the .32 Winchester Special and barrel lengths from 14" (no longer legal) all the way up to 36" on special order. The most popular version of the Model 1894 is the "standard" carbine, or the 20" barrel, full-magazine tube, straight-gripped stock version - the

perfect saddle gun. Early versions are marked .30 W.C.F. for Winchester Center Fire, instead of the .30-30 marking found on all current Model 1894s.

THE MODEL 1895: As a kid growing up, my main hero was not a sports figure, nor a rock star, not even a Western movie star; my man was Theodore Roosevelt. I discovered him by "accident" when a grade-school assignment required us to research and write about a President. I read everything I could find about this remarkable man. I do believe it was his hunting exploits that caught my attention in those prepolitically-correct days of the 1950's. Our school librarian (bless her!) saw to it that we had an extensive collection of hunting books covering everyone from Theodore Roosevelt to Robert Ruark.

As President, Roosevelt carried a personal sidearm rather than trying his best to destroy the 2nd Amendment. This first President of the 20th Century would be a true bridge builder. Jeff Cooper said it best with, "He was an honest-to-God man!" Theodore Roosevelt not only believed in carrying a "big stick," but he also strongly believed in "big medicine." The big medicine he referred to was his favorite rifle for hunting big game, the Winchester Model 1895 in .405 Winchester.

The Model 1895 Winchester is often overshadowed by its predecessors, such as the Model 1873 in .44-40, the Model 1886 .45-70 and .45-90, and the legendary Model 1894 in the equally legendary .30-30. However, the Model 1895 was the first lever-action with a box magazine, allowing the use of the new smokeless powder loads with spire-pointed bullets. All prior Winchester leverguns were tube fed requiring flat-nosed bullets. Pointed bullets are better shaped for long distance shooting, but are dangerous to use in a tubular magazine since there is the possibility that the point of a bullet could set off the

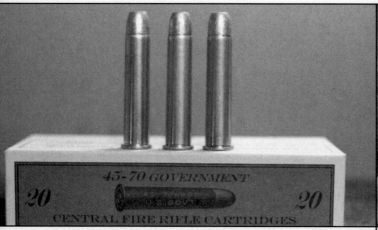

A great cartridge from the 1870's, the .45-70, still lives in leverguns and single-shots.

The first successful levergun, the 1860 Henry. This .44-40 model is by Navy Arms.

The end of the barrel of the 1860 Henry rotates to allow the insertion of cartridges.

The Colt Single Action Frontier Six-Shooter in .44-40 is an original 1879, while the 1860 Henry, also in .44-40, is a replica by Navy Arms.

primer in the cartridge ahead of it as the gun recoils.

The first Model 1895 Winchesters were chambered in the, then modern, smokeless powder loaded .30-40 Krag, and two long-forgotten black powder rounds, the .38-72 and .40-72. Then came the .303 British, the .35 Remington, and TR's favorite, the .405 Winchester. The time period for the advent of the Model 1895 was also the era that the bolt action really began to come into its own with such rifles as the 1892 Krag Jorgensen .30-40 Krag, the Model 1894 6.5 x 55mm Swedish Mauser, the 8mm German Mauser of 1898, and the 1903 Springfield in .30-06. It did not take long for the .30-06 to become "the cartridge," and in 1908, this round, destined to become the number one hunting cartridge choice in this country, was chambered in the Winchester Model 1895.

The 1895 Winchester was designed by Browning mainly to handle the .30-40 Krag cartridge. Given today's loads and bullets of approximately equal weight, the .30-30, which debuted in 1895, achieves a muzzle velocity of 2200 fps, the earlier .30-40 around 2400 fps, and the later .30-06 is rated at 2700 fps. All three of these cartridges arrived within a time frame of about 10 years. It was definitely a great time for cartridge and firearms development, those few years prior to and shortly after the turn of the century, but the black powder era was about to end.

For a more detailed look at the leverguns and loads that won the West, I heartily recommend Mike Venturino's book *Shooting Lever Guns of the Old West*.

Selected Black Powder Loads for Leverguns:
(All weights are by volume)

.45 COLT

Levergun	Bullet/Load	MV/FPS
M1892 20"	Lyman #454190/35-gr. Pyrodex P	840
	Lyman #454190/30-gr. Goex FFFg	720
	Lyman #454190/32-gr. Goex CTG	820
	Lyman 260 Keith/38.5-gr. Goex FFFg	1240
	Oregon Trail 250 RNFP/32-gr. Goex FFg	860
	Oregon Trail 250 RNFP/35-gr. CleanShot	1045

.38-40 (.38 WCF)

Levergun	Bullet/Load	MV/FPS
M1892 20"	OT 180 RNFP/30-gr. Goex FFg	890
	OT 180 RNFP/30-gr. Goex FFFg	1180
	OT 180 RNFP/30-gr. Goex CTG	1215
	OT 180 RNFP/30-gr. Pyrodex P	1210
	OT 180 RNFP/30-gr. Pyro. Select	1140

.44-40 (.44 WCF)

Levergun	Bullet/Load	MV/FPS
M1892 20"	Lyman #427098/36.5-gr. Goex FFFg	1565
	Lyman #427098/36.5-gr. Pyrodex P	1320
	Lyman 200 Cowboy/35-gr. Pyro P	1450
	Lyman 200 Cowboy/35-gr. Goex FFg	1175
	Lyman 200 Cowboy/35-gr. Goex FFFg	1305

.45-70

Levergun	Bullet/Load	MV/FPS
M1886 26"	Lyman 420/ 63-gr. Goex Ctg	1210
	Lyman 420/68-gr. Goex FFg	1470
	Lyman 420/54-gr. Clean Shot	1395
	Lyman 500/65-gr. Elephant FFg	1070
	RCBS 405FN/65-gr. Elephant FFg	1090
	RCBS 405FN/54-gr. Pyrodex RS	1390

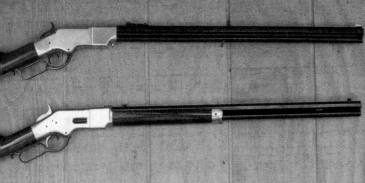

Great leverguns of the 1860's in replica form by Navy Arms: an 1860 Henry and an 1866 Yellow Boy.

Shootists of the 1880's could have a levergun and sixgun chambered in .38-40 just like these replicas from Cimarron.

THE REVOLVING CARBINE

By: Michael Beliveau, aka Bottom Dealin' Mike

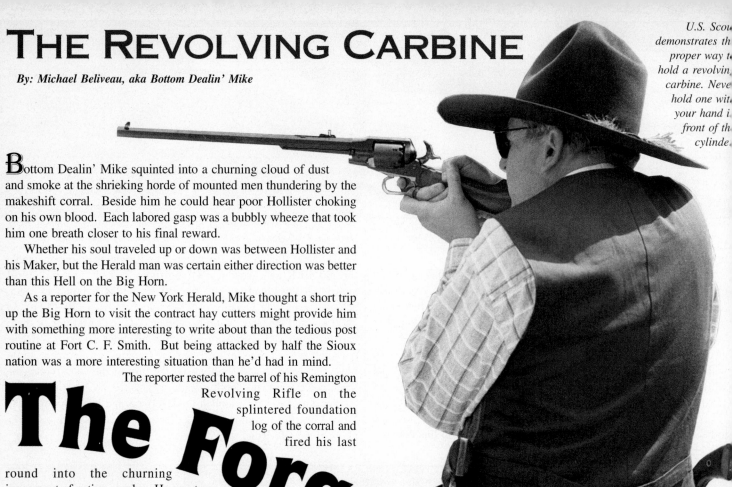

Bottom Dealin' Mike squinted into a churning cloud of dust and smoke at the shrieking horde of mounted men thundering by the makeshift corral. Beside him he could hear poor Hollister choking on his own blood. Each labored gasp was a bubbly wheeze that took him one breath closer to his final reward.

Whether his soul traveled up or down was between Hollister and his Maker, but the Herald man was certain either direction was better than this Hell on the Big Horn.

As a reporter for the New York Herald, Mike thought a short trip up the Big Horn to visit the contract hay cutters might provide him with something more interesting to write about than the tedious post routine at Fort C. F. Smith. But being attacked by half the Sioux nation was a more interesting situation than he'd had in mind.

The reporter rested the barrel of his Remington Revolving Rifle on the splintered foundation log of the corral and fired his last

The Forgotten '66

round into the churning juggernaut of native cavalry. He saw two riders separate from the troop and charge straight towards him. Cursing his luck, he dropped the empty rifle and leapt to his feet. He drew his Remington New Model Army revolver, firing as he rose. But his feet slid out from under him in the slippery ooze of Hollister's blood.

He landed hard on his rump just as a lance flashed through the air where his chest had been a moment before. The pistol was jarred from his hand, but he snatched up Hollister's Winchester Yellow Boy and started firing. He put two rounds into a horse and the third into its rider as he jumped free. Then he heard dry clicks as he jacked the lever and pulled the trigger on an empty gun.

The reporter dropped to his knees, wrestling with the dead weight of Hollister's body to free his cartridge belt.

"They're pulling back," Al Colvin called. "How do we stand?"

"Hollister's dead," the reporter called back over his shoulder.

"So's Sternberg," one of the hay cutters said.

While sliding .44 Henry rounds into the loading gate of the '66 Winchester, the correspondent looked over toward the opening in the corral. He watched two troopers from G Company pull Lt. Sternberg's body to the side of the corral. A thin trail of blood from his shattered skull marked their passage like a line drawn on a map.

The reporter tried to feel sorrow for the lieutenant, but the truth was that pig-headedness and misplaced pride had killed Sternberg as much as a Sioux bullet. Sternberg insisted on standing in the corral opening and "fighting like a man," as he put it. If Sternberg had even a lick of sense, he'd still be alive. He felt more pity for Hollister who just didn't jump for cover fast enough.

"Are you taking Hollister's rifle?"

The reporter looked up at Al Colvin, the head of the contract hay cutters. The big man was standing over him scowling. The reporter turned to the corpse lying in a bloody pool beside him. "Hey, Hollister, you mind if I borrow your gun?" he asked loudly. He waited for a moment, letting the silence hang in the air.

"I don't think he cares, Colvin," the reporter finally remarked in an even voice. "What's it to you?"

"Just askin' is all," Colvin replied. "I guess you changed your mind about that Remington of yours?"

"I guess I did," the reporter answered.

The night before they'd sat around the campfire eating beans cooked with bear ribs and sipping whiskey. The conversation had turned to guns. They'd talked about the new .50-70 Trapdoors issued to the troopers that week and about the Winchesters carried by the civilian hay cutters. The reporter had defended his choice of a cap-n-ball revolving rifle against the good-natured ribbing of the men around the fire.

He'd learned a lot in one day.

"I guess you ain't as dumb as I thought," Colvin remarked with a twisted grin. "Anyway, if you ain't using that Remington, I'd appreciate it if you'd let Zeke use it. He ain't as smart as you yet, so I reckon it'll do him fine."

"I reckon a kick in the pants will do you fine, too," Zeke said hotly. He was ramming a minnie ball down the bore of his Enfield. "I don't need no repeater," he said. "I been carrying this rifle since

Shiloh."

Zeke capped the nipple. "Heck, Al, I got the first injun of the day with this old girl."

"Yeah, and you spent the rest of the day reloading her," Al shot back. "What are you gonna do if they get through that wall, Zeke?" he demanded. "Throw rocks at 'em?"

Al flashed a wicked grin. "Maybe you were thinking of blowing kisses at them, eh?" he said. "Make 'em think you're a winkteh."

"Just give me the danged Remington and rest your jaw," Zeke snapped. "He won't never shut up unless I do what he wants," he said to Mike.

Mike handed Zeke the revolving rifle. "It loads like a belt pistol," the Herald man explained.

"No kidding?" Zeke said sarcastically. "Maybe you can explain how my fly buttons work next."

He sat down and started loading the rifle's chambers with powder and ball. "As if today ain't enough of a trial," he remarked, "now since that milk-sucking lieutenant's gone and got himself killed, ol' Al thinks he's cock of the walk."

"He's doing pretty good so far," the Herald man said. "I'm not complaining."

"Well, of course he's doing good," Zeke said it as if he was talking to a particularly slow-witted child. "He does everything good." He crunched the powder under the last ball and turned the gun to cap the nipples.

"So what's the problem?" the Herald man asked.

Zeke gave him a pitying, sideways look. "You must be an only child," he said.

"Close enough," Mike answered. "The others were babies when I left." He shrugged. "I've been gone a long time."

"Well, there you have it," Zeke said, as if that explained everything. "Al's my older brother," he said. "It ain't possible to like him, and it ain't legal to kill him."

Al walked by and kicked the sole of Zeke's boot. "Here they come again," he jerked his thumb at the wall of the corral. "Out of the north," he said. "Look sharp!"

"Lord, it's going to be a long day," Zeke muttered under his breath.

Back in 1866, the folks running Remington made one of the biggest marketing blunders in the history of marketing blunders. There are people who say timing is everything. If that's true, Remington had nothing going for them in

1866 when they launched their cap-n-ball revolving rifle on the arms market. It was an idea whose time had clearly passed. Not only were cartridge long guns coming in to their own, but to add insult to injury, that same year Winchester unveiled the improved Henry rifle.

The Winchester improved Henry is, of course, now known as the 1866 Winchester. Nicknamed the Yellow Boy because of its bronze gunmetal receiver, the '66 Winchester simply buried the '66 Remington.

It's easy to see why. The 1866 Winchester was a high-capacity, fast shooting, cartridge firing repeater that was easier to load than the original Henry rifle, thanks to the new King's Patented side-mounted loading gate. In contrast, the 1866 Remington was a six-shot cap-n-ball rifle. It was fast shooting, but deathly slow on reloads.

Remington tried to remedy that situation by offering drop-in cartridge cylinders for their rifle in 1868, but it still wasn't a match for the Winchester's popularity. After 13 years of production, Remington had sold less than a thousand of these rifles so they discontinued the model.

If I'd been in Bottom Dealin' Mike's place at the Hayfield fight, I'd have scooped up a Winchester myself. But, luckily, the Sioux aren't likely to attack my little homestead anytime soon. So I can feel free to enjoy my Remington revolving rifle in its modern incarnation.

Uberti builds the only modern replicas of the 1866 Remington revolving rifle, and they've done an outstanding job of recreating these little gems. The only significant difference between the Uberti replica and the originals is in the barrel length. Original '66 Remingtons had either 24 or 28-inch tubes. Occasionally a 26-inch barrel shows up, but they were only available on special orders. Today's replicas have an 18-inch barrel, and they are designated as Remington Revolving carbines by Uberti.

Essentially, these rifles use the same action as the Remington New Model Army revolver. This pistol is often erroneously called the '58 Remington because of the 1858 patent date stamped on it, but calling it the '63 Remington is actually more accurate. At any rate, the action parts on Uberti's replica carbines interchange with parts on their handguns.

If you are familiar with cap-n-ball

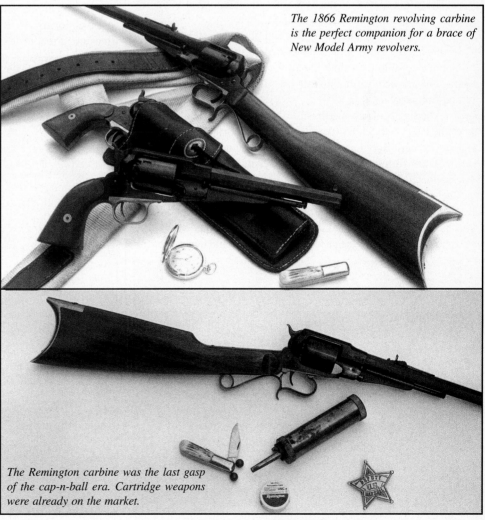

The 1866 Remington revolving carbine is the perfect companion for a brace of New Model Army revolvers.

The Remington carbine was the last gasp of the cap-n-ball era. Cartridge weapons were already on the market.

The Remington carbine is one of the most enjoyable guns you can shoot. It is a stylist's dream.

revolvers, there is little new to learn about the revolving carbine. The loading process is exactly like loading a Remington New Model Army handgun.

You start by pouring a measured charge of black powder into a chamber. I've found that 28 to 30 grains of FFFg grade Goex black powder is more accurate than the 35-grain maximum load. Then you place a .451 diameter round ball over the chamber mouth and ram it home until the powder crunches a bit. Optionally, you can place a lubed felt wad between the powder and ball, though I've personally found them to be of little value.

After loading five of the six chambers, you need to fill the chamber mouths with black powder lubricant. That will keep the fouling soft from shot to shot. This is important both for accuracy and to keep the action from gumming up. I make my lube from a mixture of beeswax and Crisco.

I recommend loading only five chambers for safety, but back in the 19th century they'd have loaded all six and rested the hammer nose in the safety notch. So, when you've greased all five loaded chamber mouths, all that's left to do is cap the nipples and fire away.

Alternately, if cap-n-ball isn't your cup of tea, Kenny Howell of the R&D Gun Shop makes drop-in cylinders that convert these rifles to cartridge guns. The two-piece cylinders are based on the 1868 Remington conversion cylinders except they are chambered for .45 Colt cartridges rather than .46 rimfire rounds. The same drop-in cylinders that you can buy for Uberti replica Remington pistols fit the carbines as well.

When it comes time to fire the revolving carbine, you'll have to hold it differently than a lever gun. You should never get your

hand in front of a revolver's cylinder, especially a cap-n-ball cylinder. There are plenty of documented cases of people losing fingers due to multiple discharges from Colt's cap-n-ball revolving rifles. Also, hot gasses coming out of the barrel cylinder gap can cut your wrist to ribbons. That's the reason Remington designed their rifle without a forearm. You hold it with both hands back on the triggerguard. By tucking your off-elbow tight to your body, you can achieve a rock-steady hold.

In fact, these short rifles handle and shoot very well. I can generally shoot sub two-inch groups off-hand from 25 yards with my '66 Remingtons. And, believe it or not, I use these little gems as my main stage rifles in cowboy action shooting. Because most stages call for more than five rifle rounds, I wear two belt pouches for replacement cylinders. I fire five rounds, pull out the cylinder, and put it into the empty pouch. Then I pull a loaded cylinder from the other pouch, slap it into the carbine, and finish the stage. You can't win a match like that, but the styling is awesome!

For stage use in the cap-n-ball mode, I've developed a couple of tricks to speed up the loading process. Instead of loose black powder, I use preformed Pyrodex Pellets. These are 30-grain equivalents that drop right into the chambers. After the balls are seated, I cover the chamber mouths with precut grease wads. I punch these out of a sheet lube using a bored-out .45 Colt case. These two steps have cut my reloading time in half.

My favorite era of the Old West is the decade from 1866 to 1876. I can team the Remington revolver in cap-n-ball mode with a pair of cap-n-ball sixguns, or I can pop in the R&D cartridge cylinders and mate it to a pair of cartridge conversion revolvers or my 1872 Open Top. Either way, the forgotten '66 gives me a real taste of the Old Frontier.

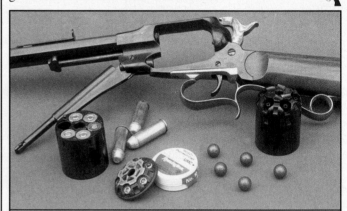

An R&D Gun Shop drop-in cylinder quickly converts the carbine from cap-n-ball to .45 Colt cartridges.

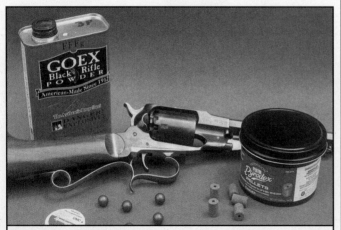

The author appreciates the convenience of Pyrodex pellets for quick reloading during cowboy action matches.

The 1866 Winchester doomed the Remington revolving rifle from the outset. The 1866 Remington was obsolete before it reached the market.

Colt Cartridge Revolvers

By: John Taffin,
aka Sixgunner

Author shooting a 19th century black powder Colt.

It is 1869. You are the president of Colt and feeling mighty good. The Civil War is over and even though Sam Colt died in 1862, the company is on solid footing. That upstart, what was the name? Smith & Wesson, yes that is it, has made a lot of money selling those little rimfire single-actions as concealment weapons, but after the war the demand dropped so far that they couldn't even pay the electric bill (if there had been such a thing as electricity).

Things had not always gone so well for Colt. Samuel Colt had declared bankruptcy even after the Paterson revolver had been such a favorite among the early Texas Rangers. Then came that other war, the one with Mexico, and the company's future was assured. Sam Colt and Texan Sam Walker had put their heads together, and the result was the magnificent Model of 1847, the .44 Walker. Then came the Dragoons, the 1851 Navy, and the 1860 Army.

With the coming of another war, this one pitting brother against brother and father against son, the company was now in great financial straits. The tragedy of the Civil War had proved to be a great asset to Colt. That large Army contract for over 100,000 1860s was money in the bank. Nothing could stop Colt now, and Smith & Wesson would probably disappear.

Just then, that assistant burst into the office. "Mr. President have you seen this?" The upstart firm with the two fellows over at Springfield, that should have been seeking to close their doors, is rumored to be working on a new six-shooter. They had been making those little pip-squeak pistols in .22 and .32 Rimfire, but it was a passing fad; the big bore Colt percussion was the only way to go. "But Mr. President, this time they have a .44 revolver that fires fixed ammunition. What if it catches on? What if the Army gives them a large contract? Where will that leave us?"

Smith & Wesson had their Model #3 .44 before the Civil War, but it would be 1869 before they got it into production. Colt found himself locked out because of the Rollin White patent, and White just happened to work for Smith & Wesson. Colt could have had Rollin White and his patent earlier, but they were not interested at the time. (You can bet they got interested when the U.S. Government ordered 1,000 S&W American .44s!) Now that Smith & Wesson had the patent that allowed for the use of a bored-through cylinder to accept a cartridge case, and although it was due to run out in a few years, what would Colt do until then? The answer came from Thuer, Richards, and Mason.

Colt had several hundred thousand cap-n-ball six-shooters in the field, and also a large stockpile of parts. Colt did not want these to suddenly become obsolete. The first answer was supplied by Alexander Thuer and his patent which turned the back of the cap-n-

The evolution of the Colt Single Action: 1860 Army, Richard-Mason Cartridge Conversion, Model 1871-72 Open-Top, and the Model P.

ball cylinder on a lathe to allow a ring to be slipped over it that held the firing pin. Cartridges were slightly tapered in both .36 and .44 caliber, and they entered the cylinder not from the back, but from the front. The Thuer was not terribly successful, but it was about to be replaced by the C.B. Richards Conversions.

Charles Richards was a Colt employee who came up with the first Colt to feature a loading gate and cartridges that entered the cylinder from the rear. Existing 1851 and 1860 cap-n-ball revolvers had their cylinders shortened and a conversion ring placed at the back end. An ejector rod was then added. Richards Conversions are

Great sixguns from the past: Colt Single Actions chambered in .45 Colt, .44-40, and .32-20.

easy to spot by the ejector-rod housing that stops about one inch in front of the cylinder. Enter William Mason. Mason, a Colt engineer, improved Richards' design by placing the firing pin on the hammer. One can easily spot a Richards-Mason Conversion by the ejector-rod housing that goes all the way to the face of the cylinder.

However, Mason did not stop with his improvement. For as soon as the design was accomplished, Mason set about working on the Open-Top. While the Thuer, Richards, and Richards-Mason were true conversions on existing cap-n-ball revolvers or built from parts at the factory, the 1871-72 Open-Top was Colt's first big bore single-action cartridge-firing revolver. This was not a conversion, but a totally new design with new parts that did not interchange with the percussion models or their conversions.

All original Open-Tops were made in .44 rimfire. When the '72

was submitted to the Army for testing and adoption of a new sidearm, the request came back for a stronger gun in a more powerful chambering. That turned out to be one of the best requests in firearms history. The Army wanted a stronger sixgun, and the result was the solid-frame Colt Single Action Army, still in .44 rimfire. The U.S. Army made one further request, a larger caliber and in centerfire persuasion. That request turned out to be the stuff legends are made of. We cannot credit Samuel Colt with the design as he had died years earlier; instead it came from William Mason, and in 1873 one of the greatest sixguns ever made was introduced.

The prototype may have been in .44 rimfire (some authorities say .44 Russian), but serial number one of the first Colt Single Action Army was offered in the now equally legendary .45 Colt. Basically designed for the military market, the SAA was offered in a barrel length of 7-1/2" to duplicate the feel of the 1851 Navy and 1860

These two 19th century Colts saw service on the Frontier: .44-40 Frontier Six-Shooter, circa 1879; and .45 Colt "US" marked, circa 1881.

Army. It had one-piece walnut stocks and a blued finish, except for the frame and hammer, which were case hardened and colored. The Colt Single Action was soon offered with a shorter 5-1/2" barrel, an easier to pack Artillery Model as opposed to the longer Cavalry Model.

A. C. Gould, writing in 1888, had this to say about the Colt Single Action: "A careful summarizing of the opinions shows that a majority of revolver experts believe that the Colt revolver is not made with such delicacy of parts as some other arms; but it is evident that this very want of delicacy of the parts is much in favor of its adoption by those desiring a revolver powerful, accurate, and less affected by

The fifth most popular chambering in the Colt Single Action was the .41 Long Colt.

Three generations of Colt Single Actions: 1st Generation Model P and Bisley Model, 2nd Generation .45 Colt, and 3rd Generation .44 Special.

exposure to the elements; permitting neglect of care after using, and requiring less attention while using. It is believed that more shots can be fired from the Colt revolver without cleaning, and have it work well, than any other revolver of American make. But with the cleaning found necessary to secure accuracy even with this arm, it seems to demand less attention than other revolvers; accurate shooting has been secured repeatedly, even after firing 100 shots, by simply swabbing out the barrel with a brush or cleaning rod with a cloth drawn through a slot, and without removing the cylinder, which worked well after firing 200 shots." This would definitely explain

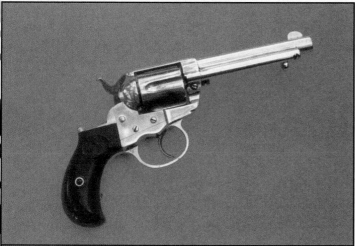

The first successful cartridge-firing double-action revolver was the Colt Model 1877.

one of the reasons that the Colt Single Action Army was more popular than either the Remington or Smith & Wesson. It just kept going, and going, and going.

Colt's standard barrel length for the Model P was 7-1/2" with longer barrels available at an extra $1.00 per inch. These longer-barrelled sixguns are usually referred to as Buntline Specials, with the most famous proponent of the Buntline Special being Wyatt Earp. Hugh O'Brian's TV portrayal of *The Life and Legend of Wyatt Earp* was patterned after the Wyatt Earp from Stuart Lake's 1931 biography *Wyatt Earp, Frontier Marshall*. In fact, Lake served as consultant on the TV series. Lake spent a lot of time with Earp prior to the old lawman's death in Los Angeles in 1929. Lake writes of Earp and the Buntline Special:

"Meanwhile, the fame of Wyatt Earp was spreading beyond the kin of those for whom he solved problems of law and order and the

word of his prowess brought Ned Buntline (E. Z. C. Judson) to Dodge. Buntline's prolific pen furnished lurid tales of life on the plains for consumption by an effete world that dwelt east of the Mississippi River and which, in the seventies, demanded that its portraits of Western characters be done in bloody red. Buntline's outstanding literary achievements had been to make William Cody, a buffalo-hunter, into the renowned 'Buffalo Bill,' and from the exploits of Wyatt Earp and his associates, he now obtained material for hundreds of frontier yarns, few authentic, but many of the bases of fables still current as facts."

He continued to write, "Buntline was so grateful to the Dodge

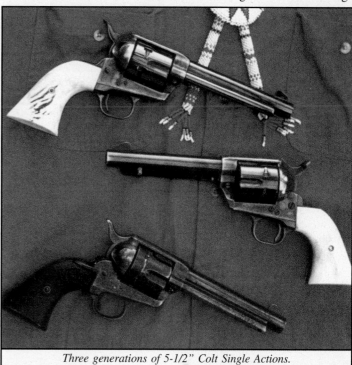

Three generations of 5-1/2" Colt Single Actions.

City peace officers for the color they supplied that he set about arming them as befitted their accomplishments. He sent to the Colt's factory for five special .45 caliber sixguns of regulation single-action style, but with barrels four inches longer than the standard one-foot length, making them sixteen inches over all. Each gun had a demountable walnut rifle stock, with a thumbscrew arrangement to fit the weapon for a shoulder-piece in long range shooting. A buckskin thong slung the stock to belt or saddle-horn when not in use. The walnut butt of

This Model 1877 chambered in .41 Long Colt sent would-be robbers to their graves.

A comparison in size between the Single Action Army and the Model 1877.

each gun had the word "Ned" carved deeply in the wood, and each weapon was accompanied by a hand-tooled holster, modeled for the weapon. The author gave a "Buntline Special," as he called the guns, to Wyatt Earp, Charlie Bassett, Bat Masterson, Bill Tilghman, and Neal Brown. The standard barrel length referred to would be 7-1/2 inches, the original length of the Colt Single Action Army when it appeared in 1873, just three years prior to the Buntline appearing. This was the standard Colt's frontier model .45 caliber, single-action six-shooter with the 7-1/2" barrel, the gun we called 'the Peacemaker'."

Five years later we find Wyatt Earp in Tombstone at the O.K. Corral. What does Lake have to say about it?: "Fast as the two

These 19th century Colts all have one thing in common; they are chambered in .41 Long Colt. A pair of Single Actions, a Bisley Model, a Model 1889, and a Model 1877 Thunderer.

rustlers were getting into action from a start with guns half-drawn, Wyatt Earp was deadlier. Frank McLowery's bullet tore through the skirt of Wyatt's coat on the right, Billy Clanton's ripped the marshal's sleeve, but before either could fire again, Wyatt's Buntline Special roared; the slug struck Frank McLowery squarely in the abdomen, just above his belt buckle."

Lake is not the only one to write of Earp and his Buntline Special. Noted arms collector John S. du Mont adds more information in an article in the April 1955 issue of *The American Rifleman*: "While Ned Buntline would like us to believe that he was the originator of these guns, it is apparent that his first sight of them was at the Colt

exhibit. It is well to bear in mind that Buntline was not always a believer in the strict factual truth where a good story was concerned."

At the other end of the Colt Single Action spectrum, someone came up with the short-barreled 4-3/4" Civilian Model. Many have thought that this idea came from Bat Masterson since he ordered a nickel-plated .45 Colt "...with the barrel even with the ejecting rod." However, history tells us that short-barreled Civilian Models were being delivered at least three years before Masterson placed his order.

Whoever is responsible may be lost, but one of the finest balanced and fastest from the leather sixguns emerged, the 4-3/4" Single Action Army, also known as the Peacemaker, the Hog Leg, and the Equalizer. The gunfighter's weapon had really arrived. A shootist, or shotist if you prefer, was now definitely just as dangerous with his sixgun in the holster as if it were in his hand, perhaps even more so.

The Colt Single Action was carried by gunfighters on both sides

Cimarron's New Thunder, center, is a blending of the Single Action Army and the Lightning Model.

of the law: Jesse James, Cole Younger, Wyatt Earp, Doc Holliday, the list goes on and on. My ultimate hero, Theodore Roosevelt, carried a 7-1/2" Colt Single Action .44-40 as a rancher in the Dakotas. We also know that he carried a concealed sixgun while President, and it may have been his old Colt. In 1916, before heading into Mexico after Pancho Villa, a young Army Lieutenant picked up an ivory-gripped Single Action Army .45 in El Paso. The gun became famous on the hip of General Patton in World War II. It had two notches in the grip from the Mexican campaign. Patton may have decried pearl grips when some reporter called his ivory grips pearl, but several

Colt's first big bore double-action sixgun, the Model 1878 .45 Colt.

The Buntline Special compared with standard single-actions.

decades before, Tom Threepersons carried a 4-3/4" .45 Colt outfitted with pearl grips and used it to great effect. He also designed the world's most famous holster, the Tom Threepersons, to carry it. The first such holster was made by S.D. "Tio Sam" Myres in El Paso, and is now faithfully recreated by El Paso Saddlery.

The career of the infamous team of Bonnie and Clyde was stopped by former Texas Ranger Frank Hamer, whose favorite sixgun was "Old Lucky," a .45 Colt Single Action. Hamer has always been treated unfairly by Hollywood (The movie *Bonnie & Clyde* gives a completely unrealistic portrayal of Hamer), and in actuality he was a real hero, a true "one riot, one Ranger" type of lawman.

The basic design of the action goes back to 1836. The Single

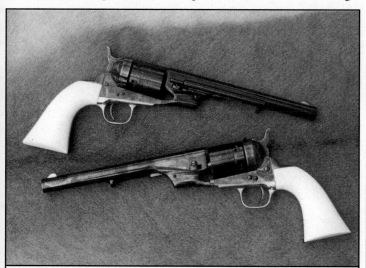

Replicas from Cimarron of the Richards Conversion chambered in .44 Colt.

Action Army itself was introduced 130 years ago, and it still lives today. From 1873 to 1941, more than 357,000 Colt Single Actions in more than 30 calibers were produced. Half of the big sixguns were made in .45 Colt, and half of the rest in .44-40. The next two most popular calibers were .38-40 and .32-20. Long before World War II, however, the Colt was basically a dead design with sales going down, down, down. Even if the coming of hostilities had not occurred forcing a shift to wartime production, the Colt Single Action would probably have been dropped by Hartford.

After the war years, Colt announced that the single-action was dead, and would stay that way. It would be seen no more. But by the

mid 1950's, the new medium of television saturated the airwaves with old Western movies and new Western TV shows, and shooters wanted Colt Single Actions again. The dead Colt was resurrected and the 2nd generation single-action began. Still the same basic gun as the 1873 Peacemaker, the "new" Colt was made of stronger steels and was to be made in only four calibers: .45 Colt, .38 Special, .357 Magnum, and .44 Special.

By the 1970's, the machinery was once again wearing out, and the Colt Single Action was pronounced dead again, only to revive a few short years later with the 3rd generation of the Colt Single Action Army. Two minor changes occurred, however. The hand design was changed for easier assembly, and the cylinder no longer had a full-length bushing, but a button bushing at the front end. It also changed from the original "black powder" screw in the front of the frame to hold the cylinder pin, to a spring-loaded catch, a change that occurred

Sixgunner shooting the 7-1/2" .45 Colt Single Action.

long before World War I. This gives us only three basic changes in the Colt Single Action design in over 130 years. Hammer profiles have changed slightly, the type of lettering on the barrel has changed, and the location of serial numbers has changed, but all these minor variations have nothing to do with the operation of the single-action sixgun itself.

The 3rd Generation Colt Single Action lasted into the late 1980's when the market was flooded with all types of variations as to finish and barrel length, and often second-class examples before the

A comparison of the 1871-72 Open-Top and the Richards Conversion, replicas from Cimarron.

Colt's progress over 13 years: the 1860 Army, the Richards Conversion, the 1871-72 Open-Top, and the Peacemaker.

production was to cease again for the third time. 3rd Generation Colt Single Actions were produced in .45 Colt, .44 Special, .44-40, and .357 Magnum. After being killed off three times one would think that the Colt Single Action would finally be dead and buried; not so. The Colt Single Action 3rd Generation part two still lives. Expensive? Yes, but they are genuine Colt Single Action Armies, and no other single-action can make that statement. Available in both blue case-hardened finish and nickel finish, the Colt Single Actions are still being made in both the chamberings from the 1870's, .45 Colt and .44-40. The .38-40 was offered for a short time, and the .357 Magnum has just recently been added.

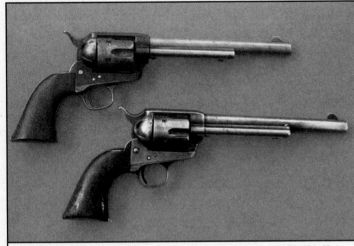

Beautiful black powder sixguns: 1881 .45 Colt and 1879 .44-40.

The Colt Single Action Army is like no other sixgun in its ability to stir heart, soul, and spirit. The mind may tell us that other guns are better for our purposes, but our heart won't accept it. And therein lies the real beauty of a Colt Single Action. The Colt is for campfires and walks in the woods and cowboy shooting and dreaming of days gone by. We may love other sixguns and use them, but only the Colt can totally stir our emotions. My wish, and prayer, and hope is that the grand old Single Action Army may live forever. Pick up a seashell and it is said that one can hear the sea as the shell is placed over the ear. Pick up a Colt Single Action and you can hear the tickling of the ivories in a saloon on Main Street in Dodge City; you can smell wet

cattle as they are driven north from Texas through wind, rain, and dust; you can taste fresh-cooked bacon and beans over a campfire in the mountains of Montana; and you can see the history of a country stretching over a century.

Pull back on the large hammer, sight down the hog wallow trough that serves as a rear sight, and slowly squeeze the trigger. As the gun roars and gently bucks in recoil of a black powder load in .45 Colt or .44-40, you feel the mild but business-like recoil of a heavy bullet as it settles its business with finality. No heavy-kickin' Magnum here, but a payload that has served sixgunners for over 125 years.

Watch a group of Colt Single Action devotees gather and start talking about the big Colt. You can spot 'em easily. They usually wear Stetsons and high-heeled boots, and have a contented look on their faces that no one else can understand. Their eyes mist over as they talk in reverential, almost mystical, tones about the virtues of

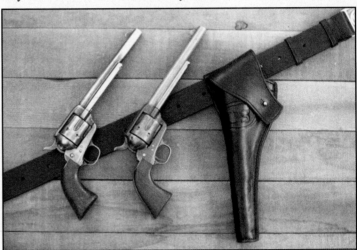

Great 19th century Colts: .44-40 Frontier Six-Shooter, circa 1879; and .45 Colt Cavalry model, circa 1881. Leather is by San Pedro.

the Colt Single Action. Don't expect them to ever change! If you don't understand this, no explanation is possible; if you do, no explanation is necessary.

Sam Colt himself did not believe anyone would ever prefer cartridge-firing sixguns over those they could load themselves. This belief was so entrenched that it stayed with the Colt factory long after Sam's death. This is the reason Colt was caught flat-footed when Smith & Wesson brought forth the first successful cartridge-firing big bore sixgun. Sam also did not believe in double-action

Colt Single Action, circa 1879; author, circa 1939.

Three generations of .44 Colt Single Actions.

sixguns, even though such companies as Deane & Adams and Starr offered double-action percussion revolvers during the Civil War. The new management would not be caught a second time, and as a result, in 1877, Colt offered the first successful double-action cartridge-firing sixguns with the .38 Long Colt Lightning Model and the .41 Long Colt Thunderer Model.

Known officially as the New Double-Action, Self-Cocking, Central-Fire, Six-Shot Revolver, these first double-action Colts would be made from 1877 to 1912. These little sixguns, and they were quite a bit smaller than the Colt Single Action Army, also came from the designing and drawing board of William Mason, and nearly 167,000 would be made before World War I. The most famous names associated with the Model 1877 are Billy the Kid and Doc

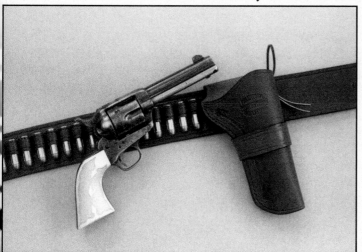

Even though the finish is worn, this .45 Colt has been totally rebuilt by Peacemaker Specialists and is ready for another 100 years of service. Leather by San Pedro Saddlery.

Holliday. Billie Bonney was of very small stature and hands, and certainly found the double-action Model 1877 much easier to work than a Single Action Army, as it was only necessary to pull the trigger to operate.

We often encounter an old sixgun or levergun, and the thought comes to mind 'if only it could talk.' The Model 1877 .41 Long Colt shown in this article can talk, rather the grandson of its original owner can talk. It seemed his grandfather carried this gun at the same time he was preparing to board a train. He received word that there would be an attempt to rob him. He tried to avoid confrontation,

but the two robbers would not be deterred. When it was all over the .41 Long Colt Thunderer had served its owner well, and the two robbers lay dead.

Although it was a double-action or self-cocking revolver, the Model 1877 loaded and unloaded exactly as the single-action by the use of a loading gate and ejector rod. Although the Model 1877 was easy to handle because of its light recoil, neither the .38 Long Colt nor the .41 Long Colt were particularly known as powerful man-stoppers. William Mason took care of this one year later with the introduction of the Model 1878, a Single Action Army sized double-action revolver chambered in .45 Colt. Offered in basic barrel lengths of 4-3/4," 5-1/2," and 7-1/2," the Model 1878 was also known as the Double Action Army or Double Action Frontier Model. When equipped with a large trigger guard for use with heavy gloves, it was the Alaskan or Philippine Model. Chambered in .44-40, it became

Well-worn, but mechanically perfect with good chambers and barrels, this .32-20 single-action and .38-40 Bisley Model still give excellent service.

the Double Action Frontier Six-Shooter. It would also subsequently be chambered in .38-40 and .32-20. It also operated the same as the Model 1877 with a loading gate and an ejector rod.

Model 1878's were owned by such sixgunners as Buffalo Bill and Pawnee Bill. The United States Government purchased 4,600 of the Alaskan Model. The Model 1878 would remain in production until 1905, with slightly over 51,000 being produced. In addition to the four standard calibers, double-action Model 1878's can be found in .44 Russian, .41 Long Colt, .38 Long Colt, .32 Colt, .22 rimfire, and

Although it began as a target model, the Bisley Model found favor with many shooters. This example is chambered in .38-40.

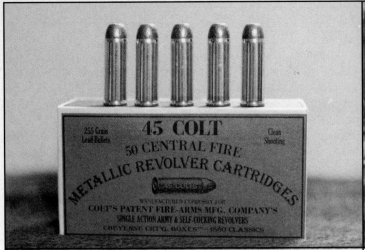

The most popular chambering in the Colt Single Action Army was the .45 Colt.

The Classic Colt Single Action, the 4-3/4" .45 Colt.

three English chamberings: .450, .455, and .476.

Smith & Wesson countered Colt's double-action sixguns by adding the self-cocking feature to their top-break revolvers, with the double-action .44 Russian arriving in 1880. Both the Colt and the Smith & Wesson double-action revolvers were simply their single-action models with a new trigger. This was about to change. Colt introduced the new Navy Double Action Self-Cocking Revolver, the Model of 1889. Not only was this the first double-action revolver with a swing-out cylinder, Colt also introduced the first speed loader, which carried six cartridges that could be loaded all at the same time into the cylinder. There really is nothing new under the sun!

The Model of 1889, as the Model of 1877, was chambered in both .38 Long Colt and .41 Long Colt. It became the first of the Colt .41 frame revolvers, and eventually became the basis for the Colt Official Police, Officer's Model Target, as well as the Python. It was adopted by the Navy in 1889, and when the Army also adopted the new revolver, it became known as the New Army. With a specially rounded grip frame and chambered in .38 Long Colt, it was the Marine Corps Model. It is believed that Theodore Roosevelt carried a Model 1889 chambered in .38 Long Colt during the Spanish-American War.

With the coming of the Model 1889, which would go through several variations over the next decade, Colt had indeed modernized the double-action revolver. All this culminated in the introduction of the New Service in 1897. The era of the black powder revolver was over for Colt.

Colt Single Action Army Production Highlights

The Single Action Army .45 Colt	1873
The Buntline Special	1876
The Frontier Six-Shooter .44-40	1878
Hard Rubber Eagle Grips	1882
Chambered in .38-40 and .32-20	1884
Chambered in .41 Long Colt	1885
First Flat-Top Target Model	1888
Chambered in .44 Russian	1889
Spring-Loaded Travers Cylinder Pin Latch	1892
Bisley Model Introduced	1894
Smokeless Powder Models Introduced	1898
Plain Hard Rubber Grips (No Eagle)	1896
Bisley Model Dropped	1912
Chambered in .44 Special	1913
Chambered in .45 ACP	1924
Chambered in .38 Special	1930
Chambered in .357 Magnum	1935
1st Generation Production Ceases	1941
2nd Generation Arrives	1956
New Frontier Production Begins	1962
2nd Generation Ends at 73,319SA	1975
2nd Generation NF Ends at 7501NF	1975
3rd Generation Begins with 80,000SA	1976
3rd Generation with SA Prefix	1978
3rd Generation NF starts at 04426NF	1979
3rd Generation NF Ends	1983
3rd Generation SXXXXXA	1993

The second most popular chambering in the Colt Single Action Army was the .44-40.

The third most popular chambering in the Colt Single Action Army was the .38-40.

The first double-action revolver from Colt, the 1877 Lightning .38 Long Colt.

The fourth most popular chambering in the Colt Single Action Army was the .32-20.

This Colt Single Action Army .44-40 was beautifully-engraved by Dale Miller and stocked with a ram's horn grip by Paul Persinger.

In 1962, Colt flat-topped the frame, added adjustable sights, and the Single Action Army became the New Frontier.

Cimarron's current Lightning Model (left) compared to an original Colt Lightning (right).

From top to bottom: Pedersoli Creedmoor replica, custom Rolling Block made on original receiver, 1879 Musket, and 1879 Carbine.

The Remington Rolling Block

Black Powder with Rolling Block Rifles, Muskets, and Carbines
By: Andy Fink, aka Chucky

Kapow! Hear the thundering "BOOM," the billowing cloud of white smoke, the smell of the powder, and the feel of the kick of the butt plate against your shoulder. It's an incredible feeling. That's especially true when you also manage to hit what you're aiming at.

The Remington Rolling Block may not be the gun that you think won The West. This is normally reserved for the Colt Peacemaker or the Winchester 1873, but the Remington Rolling Block had a significant impact on taming the frontier and was shipped overseas as a premier military firearm. It also put squirrels, buffalo, deer, and antelope on the supper table. The Rolling Block served as one of the foremost military rifles of the 1870's and 1880's. 22,013 were produced for the U.S. Navy in 1870, and 10,001 were produced for the U.S. Army in 1871. The U.S. military caliber was .50-70 (bullet diameter of .50" with 70 grains of black powder). There were also 314 U.S. military carbines produced.

The No. 1 military and sporting rifle was the most common. The military version had a total of over 1,000,000 produced for both domestic and foreign sales from 1867 to 1888. Barrel lengths varied from 30 to 39 inches, with

Custom Rolling Block in .45-70.

a host of foreign markings such as Chinese, Arabic, Turkish, Spanish, Norwegian, Swedish, Russian, and others.

There were many other versions of the Rolling Block produced. Too numerous to describe, they included carbines, the sporting rifle, the long-range Creedmoor, the mid-range target rifle, a baby carbine in .44-40 (considered very rare), and even a shotgun chambered for

Rolling Block Musket in .43 Spanish.

interchangeable use of 16-gauge brass and 20-gauge paper shotgun shells. Many cartridge types were used in these varieties, especially in the No.1 (1867-1888), and, later, the model No. 5 (1897-1905). These included rimfire calibers of .22 Short, Long, and Long Rifle; .25 Stevens; .25 Long; .38, .38 Long, and .38 Extra Long; .44; and .46. Centerfire calibers included .30-30, .303 British, .30 WCF, .30-40 Krag, 7mm Mauser, 7X57, .32-20, .38-40, .40-50, .40-65, .40-70, .43 Spanish, .43 Egyptian, .43 Turkish, .44-40, .44 S&W, .44 Extra Long, .44-77, .44-90, .44-100, .44-105, .45-60, .45-70, .50-45, and .50-70.

The Rolling Block rifle was not a rifle one would care to pack if on foot all day. However, the carbine was light (7.5 lbs.), easy to carry, fast to mount to the shoulder, and a cavalry man's dream in a single-shot. Accurate out to about 300 yards, it was a formidable firearm. Its one major shortcoming was being a single-shot. When fighting against Indians, the soldiers were often outgunned as

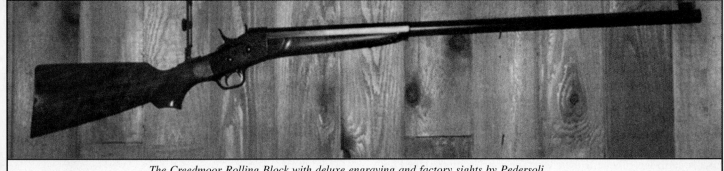

The Creedmoor Rolling Block with deluxe engraving and factory sights by Pedersoli.

the Indians were likely armed with repeating Winchesters in the later years of the 1880's.

To load the single-shot Remington Rolling Block, the hammer is cocked, then the spur on the right side of the block is pulled backwards towards the shooter. This unlocks the block and allows it to "roll" back, providing access to the chamber for loading or cleaning. Once the loaded cartridge is placed in the chamber, the spur on the block is rotated forward and the block locks up. The gun is now ready for firing.

Six different Remington Rolling Blocks (R/B) in two different calibers were used for this article. The first was an engraved Creedmoor replica made by Pedersoli in .45-70 Government. The next three included a customized long-range rifle rebuilt on a Rolling Block receiver in .45-70 Government, an original 1879 R/B musket made for sale to Argentina in .43 Spanish, and a R/B .43 Spanish carbine also manufactured in 1879. The fifth rifle was the new Navy Arms John Bodine, an extremely accurate Rolling Block for long-range (500-1,000 yards). The

Richard McKinney has turned this Remington into beautiful Hawken-style masterpiece that would make J.P. Gemmer himself take notice.

final rifle was the Gemmer Rolling Block. The rifles and the musket provided great shooting, but the carbine was just down right fun. Out to 100 to 150 yards, it is an accurate and powerful rifle.

The Creedmoor

The first rifle to be tested was the R/B Creedmoor reproduction by Pedersoli, which is a beautiful gun. It has a 34-inch, heavy, round

barrel with a diameter of 1 inch. The engraving is superb, and the trigger pull, breaking at five pounds, was acceptable, although not as light as I prefer. Pedersoli did a good job with this rifle. The factory sights are, however, a different story. They are difficult to adjust and hard to see without any windage markings, making the shooting experience more difficult than it used to be.

If this was my rifle (and I would like to have one in my collection), I would have Montana Vintage Arms Company (MVA) long-range vernier sights with a Hadley eyecup and an MVA front globe sight with level installed. That would make this a fine rifle for buffalo hunts, silhouette shooting, or hunting (as long as you don't have to carry it very far since it would be 11.5 pounds).

After spending a frustrating two hours of shooting, in which extensive fouling occurred due to the heat and the sun beating down on the rifle barrel (the shooter and spotter were boiling), we were ready to quit. The chronograph didn't work, primarily due to the location being too close to the muzzle, as well as the heat and blue sky, resulting in poor contrast. We finally managed to get a decent two-round grouping of .5 inches.

Calling it a day, we decided to shoot early the next morning under the shade. By the way, if you are attempting to load a cartridge with a long bullet such as a 532-grain spitzer and the rim hits the hammer and won't go into the chamber, pull the hammer further back while loading allowing it to slide smoothly in. I didn't do this on the

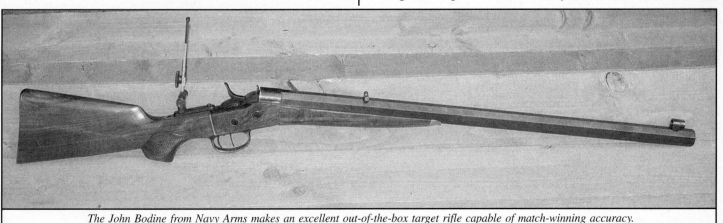

The John Bodine from Navy Arms makes an excellent out-of-the-box target rifle capable of match-winning accuracy.

Creedmoor receiver, and thought there was a problem at first (one of them brain-fade things). Interestingly, I didn't have to do this on the custom R/B discussed later in the article.

The carbine's 17-inch group size was largely due to poor sights and having to aim a good 14 inches below the impact point. Three shots from the carbine actually fell within a four-inch group. The custom Rolling Block provided the best grouping, with four shots falling within 1.25 inches.

Custom Rolling Block

Rolling Block receivers are used for customizing rifles for black powder cartridge silhouette matches. These rifles are designed with heavy barrels, weighing about 12 pounds, and are usually equipped with very expensive rear tang peep sights, with minute-of-angle adjustments for windage and elevation. Front globe styles with replaceable aperture sights that include a level are a must for accuracy. I just acquired a new custom Rolling Block in .45-70 with a Shiellen 34-inch barrel, custom stock, and forearm made by Bill Ward of Twin Falls, Idaho and reblued by Dave Delimont, also of Twin Falls.

Having only a couple of days from the time I received the rifle to the time the test was conducted, I quickly had Dave put on an Axtell, vernier, long-range, tang peep sight. Shapels Gunshop in Boise, Idaho milled the original base off a Lyman globe front sight and had it installed for me.

A number of different powder and bullet combinations were used for testing. The first bullet fired from a clean barrel always had the highest velocity and was always off from the rest of the group! The trigger pull was smooth and also broke at five pounds, much like the Creedmoor, providing the best groups of the day with four shots placed within 1.25 inches. I will definitely use this rifle for buffalo matches, as well as black powder cartridge silhouette.

The No. 1 Military Rifle (Musket)

Although the musket had a very hard trigger pull (11 pounds), it was fun to shoot, and the 36-inch barrel provided the highest velocities during the test. At 100 yards, the point of impact came out at two inches above the sight picture.

The .43 Spanish bullets were all 370-grain, round-nose lead, and came from Buffalo Arms. The first round out of a clean barrel had the highest velocity, and thus a higher impact on the target. Sights were factory military sights, and I used the 100-yard sight setting only. I did notice that the ladder ran out to 1,200 yards, but it was very loose at the top of the ladder and tight at the bottom of the sight ladder.

The No. 1 Military Carbine

The trigger pull of 8-1/2 pounds on the carbine was noticeably less than the musket. The carbine was just plain fun to shoot, and was also easier to handle than any of the others with its 20-1/2" barrel. At 100 yards, the group's impact came out at 14 inches above the sight picture. It may be that either the powder used today is more efficient, or that the bullet is not as heavy as the actual cartridge designed for this particular carbine. The front sight was held in the very bottom of the rear 100-notch sight, and there was not a significant difference in groupings between the rounds loaded with 65 grains of GOEX Cartridge black powder versus those loaded with 70 grains (the old shoulder noticed it though).

The .43 Spanish bullets were all 370 grains and came from Buffalo Arms. Again, the first round out of a clean barrel had the highest velocity, and thus a higher impact on the target. Sights were factory military sights, and the carbine's rear sight was set at 100 yards, although you could flip the sight up and have a 200-yard and 300-yard fixed-sight setting. The Remington Rolling Block carbine is

Carbine with 300-yard sight setting.

Original 1879 Carbine in .43 Spanish and an 1875 Remington Revolver.

Creedmoor Pedersoli with deluxe engraving.

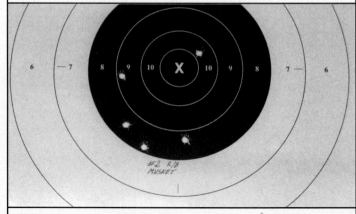

Custom Rolling Block .45-70 2.5-inch group.

very handy, and would make an excellent rifle for the Plainsman event in Western-action shooting.

The Navy Arms John Bodine

The Davide Pedersoli Company of Italy has been building reproductions of the Remington Rolling Block for Navy Arms Co. for almost three decades. For the most part, the Navy Arms/Pedersoli Rolling Blocks have been based upon the Remington No. 1 action, however it is not an exact duplication of the action. They have been built in a variety of configurations from military-style to Creedmoor target rifles. Recently, Navy Arms introduced a new version of the famous Rolling Block named the John Bodine rifle. Col. John Bodine was one of the members of the American team during the famous Long Range Target match of 1874 when the American team defeated the team from Ireland in what became known as the Creedmoor matches. The Navy Arms John Bodine rifle is designed for the exact same purposes for which John Bodine used his Rolling Block, long-range target shooting. This is a well-designed rifle for its intended purpose, too. The rifle is available in .45-70 and .45-90, with a heavy octagon 30" or 32" barrel. The pistol grip butt stock has level comb with no drop and a shotgun buttplate. The forearm has the traditional Remington forend cap, but is made of German silver rather than color-cased iron. Additionally, what sets this model apart from all other Rolling Blocks is that it comes equipped from the factory with double-set triggers. Heretofore, equipping a Rolling Block with double-set triggers was strictly a custom gunsmithing job. The John Bodine is a fine rifle capable of match-winning accuracy and has already proven so in State and National Creedmoor matches.

The Richard McKinney Gemmer Rolling Block

Another style of the Remington Rolling Block rifle was strictly a custom rifle, not by the Remington Custom Shop but by J.P. Gemmer. Gemmer specialized in converting military Sharps rifles into sporting rifles. His specialty was creating a cartridge rifle that had the look and feel of a Hawken rifle. Springfield Trapdoors, Sharps, and Remington Rolling Blocks were all candidates for such conversions. This fine example of a Gemmer Rolling Block was built by Richard McKinney, proprietor of Schuetzen Gun Co. of Drake, CO. The rifle left the Remington factory as a military rifle in the 1800's. In the same manner as J.P. Gemmer, Rich has turned this Remington into beautiful Hawken-style masterpiece that would make J.P. himself sit up and take notice. The rifle is in .45-70 caliber with a 32" Badger barrel. The action has been converted from the "military" style to that of a No. 1 Sporting Rifle, but with the addition of a Hawken trigger guard. At first glance, the overwhelming "Hawken Rifle" appearance almost obscures the fact that the rifle is a Rolling Block. But this dressed up Remington has a style all its own with which few other Rolling Blocks can compare.

Musket Rolling Block .43 Spanish 4.5-inch group.

Reloading

Don't worry about reloading for the Rolling Block, because dies and empty brass can still be found for almost any cartridge from either Old West Scroungers or Buffalo Arms, and the bullets are usually pre-lubed. Lyman produces excellent bullet moulds for almost any old caliber you desire. All black powder loads should be assembled using a drop tube of 26 to 32 inches to allow the powder to settle in the large case. A fiber wad, such as that available from John Walters of Walter's Wads, is then placed on top of the powder followed by the lubed bullet. Crimping is not really necessary as long as the cartridge is used in a single-shot rifle, but I usually prefer a light crimp. Home-cast bullets lubed with SPG or Lyman Black Powder Gold Lube are also common with bullets, and bullet moulds are readily available from a variety of sources, including Buffalo Arms and Old West Scroungers.

Original Remington Rolling Blocks in foreign calibers can still be had today for $300 to $400 from Shotgun News, so grab one today and enjoy the fun. They are more than adequate for either the Frontiersman event at cowboy shoots or Black Powder Cartridge Rifle Silhouette. I guarantee you'll get a lot of interested looks at the range.

The velocities and groups from the four rifles tested were close to what I expected, considering the type of sights used on each. All shots were taken at a distance of 100 yards. The temperature was about 85 degrees with a slight crosswind of about 5-10 mph.

The author and publisher are NOT responsible for the quality of your firearm, your loads, or the loads shown in this article and used in your firearm, or the misuse of such by any person in any way. All loads should be carefully made using full safety procedures for loading firearms. Smokeless powder is NOT recommended in these firearms

Group Comparison at 100 Yards

	Musket	Carbine	Custom R/B	Creedmoor
Caliber	.43 Spanish	.43 Spanish	.45-70	.45-70
Group Size	4.5"	17"	2.25"	3"
Bullet	375 LD RN	375 LD RN	489 gr. Saeco	489 gr. Saeco
Powder	70-gr. GOEX Cart.	65-gr. GOEX Cart.	65-gr. GOEX Cart.	65-gr. GOEX Cart.
# of Shots	5	5	5	5
Velocity	1243 fps	1243 fps	1181 fps	1179 fps
Standard Dev.	25 fps	18 fps	13 fps	13 fps

By: Michael W. Cuber, aka Kid Quick

The Traditions 1860 Army proved to be an exceptional revolver at an affordable price. The deep-blue, rich case colors and mechanical function were all very Colt-like.

Shooting Traditions' 1860 Army

Prior to shooting the Traditions 1860 Army revolver, I must confess to having had little experience with cap-n-ball sixguns. I'd read quite a bit about them, as most people interested in Colt Single Action Armies usually end up doing, but my actual shooting experience amounted to little more than the discharge of six rounds from a Ruger Old Army. I was, however, well aware of the need to have all the chambers of the cap-n-ball sixgun sealed off with either grease or lubricated wads under the projectiles in order to prevent chain fires. As it turned out, this was probably the most important piece of information that I could have known. After obtaining a few Traditions accessories, and carefully reading the instructions that came with the revolver, my first shooting session went off without a hitch. That's when it dawned on me, I'd been missing out on an awful lot of fun!

The fact is that cap-n-ball revolvers are cheap to shoot, and with all of the accessories and components available to us today, these

Velocities recorded by the PACT chronograph were lower than expected, but these low velocities probably contributed to better off-hand shooting.

guns are probably more effective and efficient than ever. The best handgun groups I've ever seen were shot with cap-n-ball revolvers. The same gentleman that shot these groups also hunts with his cap-n-ball sixguns. One of the revolvers this individual uses is an 1860 Army Colt replica. When loaded with a heavy charge of FFFg powder under a Buffalo Bullet conical, this gentleman is able to get complete penetration on broadside shots at whitetail deer and wild hogs. I've deliberately omitted the exact weight of the powder charge this individual uses because it is over the manufacturer's recommendation for the Traditions 1860 revolver. I will state that the charge is the same as that used in the original 1860 .44 caliber revolvers. A hog is a pretty gristly critter to shoot clean through, but the long-barreled cap-n-ball .44 can make it happen. After all, it is results that count, and this gentleman has proven his revolvers to be deadly on game up to 200 lbs.

Black powder and Clean Shot produced very similar groups when fired off-hand at 15 yards.

The Traditions 1860 Army is a very faithful Colt replica. It is certainly one of the better quality reproductions on the market. The revolver I worked with was wonderfully blued and richly case-colored on the receiver. The barrel measured eight inches in length and was squarely cut at the end with a light chamfer for the muzzle crown, the same as original Colt revolvers. Unlike some lesser quality reproductions that use brass extensively, this gun had a two-piece frame with a steel backstrap and brass trigger guard. It also came with a nice simulated ivory one-piece grip. Like the originals, this revolver could be fitted with a shoulder stock, and the metal work and mechanical function looked and felt very Colt-like. In most respects, the Traditions 1860 reminded me of the Colt signature series revolvers released a few years back. When you consider the machine work that is necessary to complete one of these revolvers, it makes you wonder how Traditions can offer them at the prices that they do. While most American companies are turning to employees trained in the use of new materials and cheaper manufacturing techniques, it appears that there is no shortage of craftsmen from the 'Old School' in Italy.

In order to shoot my Traditions 1860, I purchased some Speer .454" diameter round balls, some No.10 CCI percussion caps, and a Traditions plastic powder flask that had a non-removable spout and poured in 33 grains of FFFg powder. The one item that I was not able to find was a suitable lube to seal the chambers. The rifle lubes were all too runny, and the conical bullet lubes too hard, so when I packed the truck for my first range session, a can of Valvoline wheel-bearing grease went with me. Years earlier, I remembered that the Ruger Old Army had been sealed with Crisco and that it had seemed to work satisfactorily. There was a can of Crisco in the kitchen, but I was afraid of what my wife might have said if she had caught me leaving the house with it. I figured that anything Crisco could do, Valvoline could do better. After all, the Valvoline had kept my truck rolling smoothly for years.

Once at the range, I laid the revolver and all of its accessories out on the tailgate of the truck. A cap was placed on each nipple of the revolver and fired to burn up all traces of oil in the cylinders. Then I carefully charged each cylinder with a spout full of Goex FFFg powder. Keeping the revolver pointed up, I rammed a Speer round ball down on each powder charge with the gun's built-in loading lever. Next, it was time to apply the Valvoline. I smeared a dab of the red grease on top of each cylinder and then worked the grease around with a Q-tip. The gun was capped once again and then aimed at a distant milk jug. My 1860 roared to life, and my round ball plowed into the hillside a foot above my target. Re-cocking the revolver, I took aim at the milk jug again but held lower. This time the Speer round ball thumped the jug squarely in the center. Four more shots were placed in the jug before I walked up to inspect it. Not being familiar with these guns, I was humored when I saw a red splotch of Valvoline around each hole in the jug.

My goal during the first range session was to simply familiarize myself with the loading procedures and shooting characteristics of the 1860. On a later range session, I chronographed the 1860 when loaded with black powder and Clean Shot. The actual velocities, recorded eight feet from the muzzle, were hardly what I'd expected. The black powder load produced 613 fps with the Speer .454" round ball, while the Clean Shot load managed to churn up 545 fps with the same projectile. I reflected back on my .45 Colt that produced almost 900 fps with a 255-gr. bullet when loaded with 37 grains of black powder. Obviously, the lack of compression and difference in bullet resistance, coupled with the slightly lighter powder charge, had a significant effect on velocity. Although the velocities were hardly sizzling, the groups that were shot with the Traditions 1860 at 15 yards were excellent. Regardless of which propellant was used, the revolver repeatedly produced groups under two inches for six shots. Undoubtedly, the low velocities and mild recoil helped in producing these groups.

During the second range session, I did notice something that had nothing to do with the Traditions revolver, but may have had some effect on the velocities produced with the Clean Shot. The closed plastic container of Clean Shot had sat on my reloading bench through the winter. When I tried to pour it at the range, I noticed that it was clumpy. The powder also had a greenish-gray tint to it, but I was not sure as to its exact color the first time the container was opened. The can of Goex black powder had also spent the winter on the same bench, yet it showed no signs of clumping or color change. It's hard to say whether or not this is a normal property of Clean Shot, or whether the clumpiness actually had an effect on the velocities that were recorded. Ignition of both powders was very consistent, and there were no misfires of any kind.

After reflecting on my range sessions with the Traditions 1860 Army revolver, I can honestly say that the revolver functioned flawlessly. There was not one thing that could be criticized about the function, fit, or finish of the revolver. It did tend to shoot high, but it is my understanding that the originals were made to do so intentionally as sort of a battle sight zero from point blank to however far the revolver might have been shot. The precision fit, high polish blue, and rich case colors were all very Colt-like, and you would be hard pressed to find a better cap-n-ball sixgun for your money. Traditions even offers a toll free number (1-800-526-9556) to call if you encounter a problem, and detailed instructions for returning your revolver should you experience a mechanical difficulty. These are the kinds of services that define a great company, and I hope that Traditions keeps producing products like the 1860 Army revolver for a long time to come.

Range Test Results:

Load		Speer	Velocity	Group
33-gr. Goex FFFG	.454" round ball		615 fps.	1.75"
30-gr. Clean Shot	.454" round ball		545 fps.	.45"

Note: All groups were fired off-hand from 15 yds. CCI No.10 caps were used. Valvoline wheel bearing grease was used for lube.

The 1847 Colt Walker

By: John Taffin, aka Sixgunner

The first serious .44 caliber fighting handgun, the 4-½ lb. Colt Walker.

In 1830, 16-year-old Sam Colt found himself as a cabin boy on board a ship bound from Boston to Calcutta. A long sea voyage leaves a lot of time for thinking, and apparently Sam had a curious and fertile mind. It is said that he got the idea for a revolving pistol by watching the paddle wheel of the ship. It is a good story, and one of those that if it isn't true, it should be. We do know that he carved a wooden working model of a revolver complete with a rotating cylinder, as this model still exists. He was certainly not the first to come up with the idea of a repeating revolver, but his 1836 Paterson was the first practical pistol using a revolving cylinder, as well as a percussion ignition. Sam Colt received the Paterson patent at the same time that Santa Ana was over-running the defenders at the Alamo.

The Paterson was a five-shot .40 caliber revolver

Armed with a pair of Colt Walkers, any soldier or Texas Ranger was a formidable foe.

with a folding trigger and no trigger guard. It lacked power and was clumsy and poorly balanced; however it was so much more efficient than the single-shot pistols they had been using, that the Texas Rangers took to the long-barreled Texas Paterson immediately. In 1844, Texas Rangers Jack Hays, Sam Walker, and 14 others, all armed with Texas Patersons, fought more than 80 Comanches, killing 33 of them.

The Paterson still exists today in replica form from Navy Arms. It can be bought with or without a loading lever, and in .36 caliber only. With its lack of a trigger guard and the fragile folding trigger, it is not very practical, but it is a very important part of sixgun history.

Just about the time trouble was brewing for the Texicans, the supply of sixguns dried up. By 1845, Congress had annexed the Republic of Texas, making

The 1847 Colt Walker (above) compared to the 1873 Colt Single Action Army (below).

The unlatching of the lever latch on the Walker was a common problem.

war with Mexico a foregone conclusion. The defenders of Texas needed arms. However, four years earlier, Colt had gone bankrupt, and the needed supplier of side arms, sixguns that is, was gone. The Texas Rangers joined the regular Army in 1846 because the Army had two great needs, arms and men. Sam Walker went east looking for volunteers and Colt revolvers. Sam Colt and Sam Walker met, discussed firearms, and pooled their ideas. This resulted in a vastly improved revolver design with features that still exist in single-action sixguns more than 150 years later.

Samuel Hamilton Walker, who was born in 1817, was only a few years younger than Sam Colt. At the age of 19, he entered volunteer service in Maryland against the Creeks, and then went south to Florida to serve as a scout and Indian fighter. In 1842 he went west to Texas and served with General Johnson, and then joined the Texas Rangers the same year. He was known for "daring and gallant feats."

For better balance and security, the fragile folding trigger of the Paterson was replaced by a stationary trigger, which was surrounded by a trigger guard. The small cylinder of the Paterson was enlarged from a five-shot .40 caliber capability to a revolver that could hold six .44 caliber chambers, all of which would accept a full 50-60 grains of black powder. Everything looked great on paper, but even though Colt had the design, he had neither the capital nor the manufacturing facilities. The money came, not from heaven, but from the U.S. Government, as they

provided the funds with orders for 1,000 Walkers. But Colt still had no place to build the big sixguns. Enter Eli Whitney of cotton gin fame with manufacturing facilities. Thus, this transitional model from the Paterson to the Dragoons is also known as the Whitneyville Walker Dragoon.

Sam Walker considered the sixgun that bore his name "effective as a common rifle at 200 yards." It could take down a man or a horse. The Walkers were issued in pairs with Col. Walker receiving his pair just four days before being killed as 250 Texicans battled 1,600 Mexicans. Capt. Walker fell not to a revolver ball, but to a lance on October 9, 1847, with the following report issued on October 20th: "We believe that Capt. Walker, of the rifles, was killed in the affair at Huamantla. Capt. W. left the castle of Perote in command of three companies in advance of Gen. Lane's train. Nine miles south of Puebla he met 900 Mexicans, said to be under the immediate command of Santa Anna. In the charge, Capt. W. received a lance wound entirely through the body, and also lost a leg by a cannon shot. His personal antagonist in the charge, and who lanced him, was a celebrated guerrilla chief; it is said that he had sworn vengeance against Capt. W.; but he, too, fell in the conflict and by Walker's hands, receiving two balls from his revolver."

The 1,000 Walkers were issued to A, B, C, D, and E companies with approximately 220 going to each company, except E, which received only 120 of the new sixguns. One hundred more civilian Walkers were also built. Since Capt. Walker was from C

Sixguns from the middle of the 19th century: Colt Walker, Colt Dragoon, Colt 1851 Navy, Remington Army, and Colt 1860 Army.

Sixgunner shooting the Colt Walker.

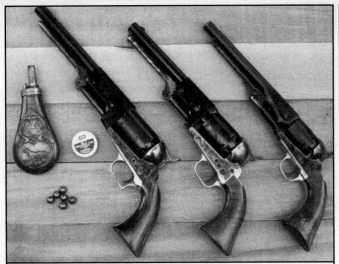

Colt's big cap-n-ball .44s: 1847 Walker, 1850 Dragoon, and 1860 Army.

Company, it is believed by collectors that these were the first to be built. After his death, one of his revolvers, serial #1019, of a pair of special revolvers presented to him by Sam Colt, was returned to Colt and still resides in a museum in Hartford. The war was over in early 1848, Texas was free of Mexico, Sam Walker was dead, and Sam Colt was solidly entrenched as the premier firearms maker. Approximately 15% of the original Walkers still remain.

The Walker, a huge sixgun with a 9" barrel, weighing 4-1/2 pounds plus, would soon be replaced by the slightly smaller and 1/2 pound lighter Dragoon. The awesome power of the Walker would not be surpassed for nearly 90 years. The arrival of the .357 Magnum in 1935 only moved it down to second place. Very few original Walkers survived, however Walker replicas are available from EMF, Navy Arms, Taylor's & Co., and Traditions. Although these are very heavy and cumbersome sixguns, Clint

Colt's first two single-action sixguns, the 1836 Paterson and the 1847 Walker.

Eastwood used a pair of them very effectively in the excellent, and certainly his best, movie *The Outlaw Josie Wales.*

Walkers are normally furnished with one-piece walnut grips, brass backstrap and trigger guard, case coloring on the frame, hammer, and loading lever, and with smooth actions – a truly awesome sixgun! Walkers are normally recommended for use with .457" diameter round balls, but this can be a problem with some of them as seating of .457" round balls can put undue strain on the loading lever, and also raise a burr where the barrel-wedge pin enters the center pin. This makes it very difficult to remove the barrel for cleaning. The steel in these replicas is softer than that found in most American-made sixguns, so a strain such as this should be avoided. In all the Walkers that I have tested, switching to .454" round balls solves the problem.

The Walkers were tested with Goex FFFg and Pyrodex P using the Thompson/Center see-through powder measure. All Pyrodex and black powder loads with these sixguns are measured by volume, not by weight. Walkers seem to do their best work with 55 grains of Goex FFFg and a Speer .454 round ball lubed with a Thompson wad for a muzzle velocity of 1224 fps, or 60 grains of Pyrodex P lubed with Crisco for 1109 fps.

In these days of 11-ounce .357 Magnums made of Scandium, Walkers seem especially heavy. They are, however, a very important part of sixgun history and give a lot of sixgun shooting enjoyment.

1847 Walkers .454" Speer RB Speer #11CAPS

Load	Lube	MV	Groups 5 shots at 50'
50-gr. Goex FFFg	Thompson Wad	1162	2"
55-gr. Goex FFFg	Thompson Wad	1224	2-1/2"
60-gr. Goex FFFg	Crisco	1321	3"
50-gr. Pyrodex P	Thompson Wad	971	3"
55-gr. Pyrodex P	Thompson Wad	1042	2"
60-gr. Pyrodex P	Crisco	1109	1-1/4"

Walkers will shoot!

Remington Revolvers

It is 1863. You have just turned 16 and you are a man at last; a man about to buy your first sixgun. Somewhat reluctantly you enter the local gun shop. You know you are ready for a real sixgun, but will those in the shop understand this? You are not quite sure what you want except you do know that it must be a sixgun that is easy to pack, is powerful, and is quick into action, just in case. Your older brother has one of those new Smith & Wesson Model #1s chambered in that strange little .22 cartridge, but you know with the plans you have for the next few years you need something much larger. That Smith was slick, no doubt about it, but could it really protect a person from either a man or a beast?

The display case is lined with Colt sixguns and a few other makes. The gunsmith shows you a huge sixgun. "This is the Walker Colt. It shoots a .44 round ball and is the most powerful sixgun made. It will never be equalled nor surpassed in power."

You heft it and find that its 4-1/2 pound weight would not be practical for daily use.

"How about this one? It fires the same .44 ball and is a little smaller and lighter." You heft the Colt Dragoon and find it is only a little smaller as it is still a huge sixgun weighing four pounds.

"What about that one?" The gunsmith brings forth a trim sixgun, a Colt 1851 Navy. It feels good and balances well, but you notice the smaller hole in the barrel. It is .36 caliber, and while you will more than likely travel through bear and mountain lion country, you will need a .44 sixgun.

"Don't you have anything that feels like the .36, but shoots the .44?"

The gunsmith reaches under the counter and comes forth with a completely different sixgun. "I just got this one in. It's not a Colt, but rather a Remington. It's in .44 and it weighs about the same as the Navy Colt."

You handle the Remington and you think that this is more like it. The gun even feels sturdier, and although the grip is not quite as comfortable for your large hands as the Colt Dragoon or even the 1851 Navy, you know that this is what you had been looking for.

You strike a deal with the proprietor and he throws in a Slim Jim holster and a wide belt for a couple of dollars more. From this day forth you are a Remington man.

The Remington New Model was available both as an 8" barreled .44 Army and a 6-1/2" barreled .36 Police Model. Colts were more readily available and in a greater profusion of models, but the Remington cap-n-ball sixgun had several advantages over the Colt. The frame of the Remington was solid with a barrel that was permanently screwed into the frame, while the Colt sixguns were all open-top with removable barrels that were held in place by two small pins at the bottom of the front of the frame and a wedge pin that entered the barrel assembly from the side. A town marshal or sheriff who used his sixgun to buffalo drunks would surely opt for this solidly-built Remington.

The Remington also had a better sighting arrangement with a rear sight that has a hog wallow through the top of the frame mated up with an easy to see front sight. The Colt carried a brass front sight, while the rear sight was a notch in the cocked hammer.

*By: John Taffin,
aka Sixgunner*

A pair and a spare from Navy Arms: Two .44s and a .36 Remington Model 1858.

Which of these .44s would you choose? A pair of 1858 Remingtons (top) or Colt's 1860 Armys (bottom)?

The Colt had two great advantages. It was quicker from the leather with its easier to reach hammer and more comfortable grip, and it also would shoot longer without jamming from fouling.

The most famous Remington New Model Army now resides in the Cody, Wyoming Museum. In 1906, Buffalo Bill Cody gave his old ivory-stocked Remington .44 to his ranch foreman with a note on the back of his business card that said: "This old Remington I carried and used for many years in Indian wars and buffalo killing, and it never failed me." Cody's sixgun was #73,293, manufactured in 1864, and may have been one of the nearly 10,000 purchased by Union soldiers at the end of the Civil War.

The history of Remington began in 1816 when Eliphalet Remington built his first rifle barrel. By 1839, it was "E. Remington & Son," which was then changed to "...Sons" in 1845. In 1856, Remington began manufacturing revolvers with the Fordyce Beals designed .31 Pocket Revolver, followed closely by the Rider .31 Double Action Pocket Revolver in 1858. It was also in 1858 that Beals designed the Navy Model Belt Revolver in .36 caliber, which is probably why current replicas are erroneously called Model 1858s. By 1860, these new sixguns were being purchased by those seeking fame and fortune on the other side of the Rockies. The .44 Army Model arrived in 1862, in time for martial use during the Civil War. In July 1861, the Ordnance Department purchased 5,000 Beals Navy Revolvers in .44 Army caliber. The Model 1861 followed later that

year, and the New Model Army arrived in 1863.

After the Civil War, Remington introduced the beautiful little spur-triggered New Model Pocket .31, as well as the New Model Double Action .36 Belt Revolver. Smith & Wesson had introduced the first cartridge-firing revolvers in 1857, and beginning in 1866, Remington followed suit. First came the Rider Pocket Model in .32 Rimfire, and then the Improved New Model Police in .38 Rimfire. One look at the latter and it is easy to see where the inspiration came from for the Ruger Bearcat. It was also during this time that New Model Army revolvers were fitted with cartridge conversion cylinders.

Smith & Wesson brought forth their first big-bore cartridge-firing revolver with the American Model #3 in 1870; Colt followed with the 1871-72 Open-Top and then the Legendary Peacemaker in 1873; and Remington got on board with the Model 1875, with a large contract for the Egyptian government. These "First Model" 1875s were chambered in .44 Remington. By 1878, the .45 Colt and .44-40 arrived in the Model 1875, and then in 1881, 7-1/2" Model 1875s were purchased for the Indian Police. The last batch of 1875s were made with 5-3/4" barrels and in .45 Colt chambering only.

In 1886 E. Remington & Sons declared bankruptcy. However, a new owner rescued the company as Remington Arms. Model 1888 revolvers followed in .44-40 with 5-3/4" barrels, and then two years later the Model 1890 arrived in .44-40 with both barrel lengths. Slightly over 2,000 Model 1890s were produced before production

These original sixguns were used in the Civil War: Remington .44, Colt 1851 Navy .36, and Colt 1860 Army .44.

Navy Arms offers several versions of the 1875 Remington, such as these nickel-plated sixguns chambered in .45 Colt and .44-40.

A man on the frontier was well-armed with a Remington Rolling Block in .45-70 and a Model 1875 in .44-40 or .45 Colt.

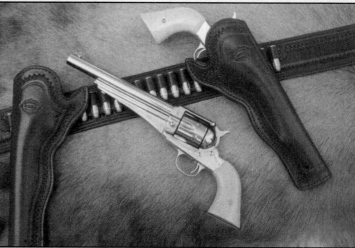

A pair of Slim Jim holsters, such as these from San Pedro Saddlery, are an excellent way to pack a pair of Model Remington 1875s.

closed in 1894.

Original Remingtons in safe shooting condition are difficult to locate and when found can be, as expected, quite expensive. Replica Remington cap-n-ball revolvers are not only easy to find, but thanks to Navy Arms, they are also of excellent quality and relatively inexpensive. They are easy to handle and safe to carry fully loaded (all Remingtons percussion sixguns carry notches between cylinder chambers for the hammer to rest within). Recoil is very mild with both the .44 and .36 caliber sixguns.

Remington percussion sixguns are much easier to prepare for serious shooting than the Colts, as the sights are such that sighting in is relatively easy. Just like the original Remingtons, they are also built to tighter specifications, which may have been an asset to Colt. The Colts kept going and going and going with black powder, while the Remingtons fouled much easier, making operation difficult until they were cleaned. The replica .44 Remingtons I have tried function much better with substitute black powders than the original black powder. The cylinders bind easy with FFFg, but Pyrodex P will eliminate this.

The Navy Arms Deluxe Model is specially tuned with a very tight smooth action, and also carries a barrel with gain-twist rifling for target shooting. It retails for twice as much as the standard model, however it pays its way as groups average less than one inch with this superb model. The best load I have found with this sixgun is 35 grains of Pyrodex P by volume, under a Speer .454" round ball, sealed

with Crisco and ignited by a Remington #10 percussion cap. Velocity is 822 fps, with five shots going into 3/4" at 50 feet. That is excellent performance for a sixgun, cap-n-ball or cartridge, real or replica. The .36 caliber Remington is also a good-shooting sixgun as the results at the end of this article attest.

Shooting results of the Remington replica cap-n-ball sixguns are also located at the end of this article. All loads were assembled using an adjustable volume powder measure, and all Pyrodex loads are by volume, not weight.

At first glance, the Remington single-action Model 1875 looks much like a Colt, but there are several differences. The grip frame of the Remington is part of the main frame resulting in a more solid, and possibly stronger, sixgun. The trigger guard is brass, separate from the main frame, and it does not form part of the front grip strap as on the Colt. The Remington achieves its unique distinctive appearance from a web under the barrel running from the end of the ejector housing to the front of the frame. The cylinder pin also runs all the way to the end of the ejector tube. Quite often "Remingtons" will be seen in western movies, especially those taking place at the time of the Civil War. Nearly all of them are nothing more than Colt Single Actions with the web added by the prop department.

Remington single-actions never even came close to the numbers produced by Smith & Wesson and Colt, with only about 25,000 being manufactured of which 10,000 went to the Egyptian government. The original .44 chambering must have been fairly potent as it carried

Navy Arms' Model 1858 .44 compared with Cimarron's Model 1890.

Navy Arms offers the Model 1858 in both .36 and .44.

An original, and very rare, Remington Model 1888.

Cimarron offers the 1890 Remington chambered in .45 Colt. Grips are by Buffalo Brothers.

a 248-grain bullet over 32 grains of black powder. Smith's .44 Russian, in a shorter case, was loaded with 23 grains of black powder, while Colt's .45 originally packed 40 grains of black powder under a 255-grain bullet. This was later cut back to anywhere from 25 to 35 grains.

Today, an original Remington single-action is rarely seen and quite valuable. However, I've been shooting a pair of Remington sixguns for about 20 years now. They are not expensive originals, but authentic replicas from Navy Arms and EMF. Both Remington single-actions wear 7-1/2" barrels as on the originals, and are beautifully finished in nickel plating. With one Remington sixgun chambered in .45 Colt and the other in .44-40, I have had the opportunity to do a lot of shooting with black powder, as well as more modern loads, for everything from plinking to long-range shooting to varmint hunting to cowboy action shooting.

The 1875 Remington is not quite up to the Colt Single Action as far as 'feel' or balance is concerned. For my hands and fingers, the hammer on the Remington, not riding quite as high as the Colt, is thus not as easy to reach, while the space behind the trigger guard is also slightly smaller and imparts a different feel than that found with a Colt Single Action.

Most .44-40s, at least from Colt, have the same barrel diameter as the .44 Special, namely .426-427 caliber. However, the Remington replica has a barrel that measures .431 inches, so .430-inch bullets are fine for use in the Remington. Oregon Trail offers 200 and 225-grain flat-nosed .44-40 bullets in both .428" and .430" diameters for custom-tailored loads.

Remington made a few changes to their 1875 and brought forth the 1890 Model. The main changes were a standard barrel length of 5-1/2" and better sights, while the web, although still there, was not so pronounced. The sights are much easier to see in the 1890 Model as the sight set-up is now square-notch rear-mated with a blade front, rather than the shallow 'V' rear and pinched blade of the 1875 replicas.

I am constantly amazed at how good Italian replicas shoot, perhaps even better than the originals. It may take some load tinkering, but most that I have encountered in the last two decades have all been excellent shooters.

We have barely scratched the surface of Remington Revolvers. The book *The Guns of Remington* by Howard Madaus is highly recommended for more detailed information, as well as great photos of classic Remington handguns and long guns.

(Ballistic charts listed on next page)

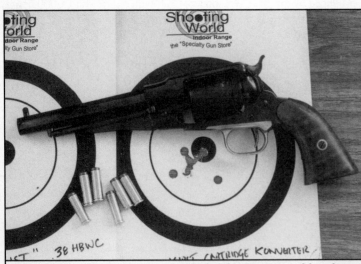

Using the Kirst cartridge-converter cylinder, this Remington .36 performs well with black powder and HBWC .38 cap bullets loaded in .38 Special or .38 Long Colt brass.

A comparison of the Colt Single Action Army with the Remington Model 1890. Both are replicas by Cimarron.

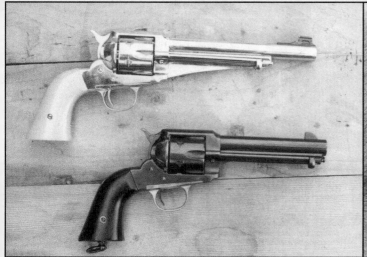

Remington replicas compared: The 1875 and the 1890. Note the bead front sight added to the 1875 for easier sighting.

The Kirst cartridge-converter cylinder is shown with HBWC .38 cap bullets loaded in .38 Special or .38 Long Colt brass.

Navy Arms Deluxe 1858 Remington - .454" Speer RB/Remington #10 Caps

Load	Lube	MV	5 shots at 50 feet
25-gr. Goex FFFg	Thompson Wad	650 fps	2"
30-gr. Goex FFFg	Thompson Wad	752 fps	1-1/4"
35-gr. Goex FFFg	Crisco	948 fps	1-7/8"
40-gr. Goex FFFg	Crisco	1053 fps	1-1/8"
30-gr. Pyrodex P	Thompson Wad	648 fps	1"
35-gr. Pyrodex P	Crisco	822 fps	3/4"
40-gr. Pyrodex P	Crisco	827	1-1/2"

Navy Arms .44-40 Remington 1875 7-1/2"

Bullet	Load	MV	
Lyman #427098 200-gr. FP	35-gr. FFFg	900 fps	

Navy Arms .45 Colt Remington 1875 7-1/2"

Bullet	Load	MV	
Lyman #454424 255-gr. SWC	38.5-gr. FFFg	900 fps	

1858 Remington .36 Police - .375 Speer RB/Remington #10 Percussion Caps

Load	Lube	MV	5 shots at 50 feet
15-gr. FFFg	Ox-Yoke Wad	722 fps	2-1/4"
20-gr. FFFg	Ox-Yoke Wad	805 fps	2-1/8"
25-gr. FFFg	Ox-Yoke Wad	929 fps	2-3/4"
20-gr. Pyrodex P	Ox-Yoke Wad	704 fps	2"
25-gr. Pyrodex P	Ox-Yoke Wad	936 fps	1-7/8"

Remingtons from Navy Arms: .44 Model 1858, .44 Deluxe Model 1858, and Model 1875 .44-40.

Remingtons replicas: Model 1858 .44 and Model 1890 in .45 Colt.

Smith & Wesson Revolvers

By: John Taffin,
aka Sixgunner

Replica Schofields: 5" Wells Fargo, 7" Cavalry, and 3" Hideout.

1869-1899

In all the hundreds upon hundreds of Western movies I have seen, starting with the "B"s at the Saturday matinees in the 1940's, progressing through the same movies being seen in the early days of TV in the late 1940's and early 1950's, to the made-for-television westerns of the late 1950's and early 1960's, it was almost assured that heroes and villains alike would carry a Colt Single Action Army. Many of these sixguns would become as well-known and recognizable as the hero.

There were a few exceptions to the "everyone packs a Colt" rule, however. In the 1940 movie *Arizona*, William Holden used Remington New Model Army .44s. Clint Eastwood also used

Original Smith & Wessons from the 1870's: Schofield Model, a pair of Model #3 Russians, and a New Model #3.

Cartridge Conversion Remingtons in *Pale Rider*. How many instances of Smith & Wessons used in Westerns can you remember? Those that come to mind are Brian Keith as "Dave Blasingame" in *The Westerner*; Robert Culp as "Texas Ranger Hoby Gilman" in *Trackdown*; and Robert Culp again as "the gunsmith" in *Hannie Caulder*. I even recall one continuing instance of a double-action Smith & Wesson Frontier Model being packed, not by the hero, but rather by the sidekick, Nugget, in the *Rocky Lane* movies.

Smith & Wesson revolvers, especially the early single-action revolvers, hold many first-place titles. The first successful cartridge-firing

Standard issue .45 revolvers for the United States Army in 1875 were the Smith & Wesson Schofield and the Colt Single Action Army. Both of these examples saw service with United States Cavalry.

single-action revolver was the Smith & Wesson Model #1 chambered in the then new .22 Rimfire. This seven-shot, tip-up revolver came out in 1857, and was subsequently followed by Models #1-1/2 and 2 chambered in .22 and .32 Rimfire. The first successful sixgun cartridge, the lowly .22, is still the most popular cartridge for both handguns and long guns. Once Smith & Wesson had these little rimfires established, they expected to build a big-bore sixgun. But the coming of war in 1861 put that project on the back burner for a while.

Many believe that the first big-bore cartridge-firing sixgun purchased for the U.S. Army use was the Colt Peacemaker in .45 Colt. Not only was it not the first, it was not even originally chambered in .45 Colt, but rather .44 Russian or .44 Rimfire depending upon which authority one accepts. The first cartridge-firing big-bore sixgun was not marked "COLT" but rather "SMITH & WESSON." Even before the Colt Single Action Army debuted, the U.S. Government had purchased S&W Americans for Army use.

As a teenager growing up in the 1950's (and what a great time that was for kids), I purchased a brand new 2nd Generation 7-1/2" Colt Single Action Army .45. I was even able to buy it on credit at the local gun shop in those pre-plastic days when a 17-year-old could

buy a sixgun with no problem. I soon discovered that I had a neighbor who also loved single-actions. He was quite a bit older than I was, all of about 35, and his single-action sixguns were all of the pre-War type, and they were beautiful. First, of course, was a Colt Single Action that had been expertly converted to a 7-1/2" .44 Special and customized further with an 1860 Colt backstrap,

The apex of Smith & Wesson single-action revolvers was the New Model #3 chambered in .44 Russian.

trigger guard, and grip. It fired only one load, the Keith .44 Special. I have often wondered to this day why Colt, or any other replica manufacturer, has never offered the post-War Single Action Army with an 1860 grip frame. The 1860 parts in this custom .44 Special came from his second sixgun, a .44 1860 Colt cap-n-ball, which now had single-action grip parts.

Both of these were great single-action sixguns, but the most fascinating

sixgun to me was his third single-action. It was also a .44, but not a Colt. In fact, it was a .44 Russian Model #3 Smith & Wesson. Now, at the time, Smith & Wesson had just brought out the magnificent .44 Magnum. They were starting to show up on dealer's shelves, and I had even been able to shoot one at a local shop that had an outside range. Until I saw the Model #3 Russian, I had always thought that Smith & Wesson only made double-action sixguns. After all, Roy, Gene, Hoppy, Red Ryder, the Durango Kid, etc. never carried a Smith & Wesson.

The Smith & Wesson Single Action certainly did not have the marvelous balance of its Colt counterpart, but even as untrained as I was, I could recognize that this was truly a marvelous piece of engineering and much more sophisticated than the Colt. That S&W was so intriguing that I went to the library to try to find some information on Smith & Wessons of the 19th century. However, it was not until Roy Jinks' definitive history of Smith & Wesson (*Smith & Wesson: 1857-1945*) appeared in 1966, followed by *The History of Smith & Wesson* in 1977, did I really learn much about the past of the Single Action Smith & Wesson.

After the Civil War, Colt continued to manufacture the 1851 .36 Navy and 1860 .44 Army as the principle fightin' sixguns for both the civilian and military markets. Smith & Wesson had the

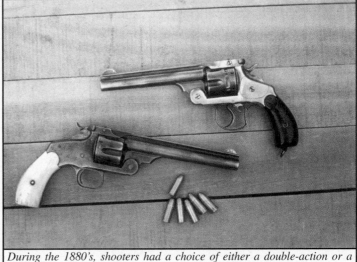

During the 1880's, shooters had a choice of either a double-action or a New Model #3 from Smith & Wesson, both chambered in .44 Russian.

The natural evolution of the Smith & Wesson .44 sixgun style: New Model #3, Double Action, 1950 Target, and the .44 Magnum.

Rollin White patent for bored-through cylinders for revolvers and, as mentioned, did make some small-caliber fixed-ammunition handguns during the War. They were quite popular since they were easily concealed under the officers' tunics. In 1869, Smith & Wesson went big bore with the .44 Smith & Wesson American, a break-top, six-shot single-action. By break-top, or top-break if you prefer, we mean that the S&W Single Actions were hinged at the front of the frame, and the releasing of a latch by the rear sight allowed the barrel and cylinder to rotate downwards 90 degrees.

It would be three years after that first big-bore Smith & Wesson before the Colt Single Action Army, the Model P, or the Peacemaker, would be offered. Even with Smith & Wesson's head start, there is a very important reason why the Colt helped win the West, and every "B" movie hero carried a Colt Single Action Army .45. The Smith & Wesson .44s were mostly sold overseas. Of the 60,000 plus Smith & Wesson Third Model Russian .44s produced from 1874 to 1878, only 13,500 went to the U.S. commercial market. The rest went to Russia, Japan, and Turkey.

The United States Army adopted the stronger .45 Colt Single Action over the more intricate Smith & Wesson, although they had ordered Smith & Wesson Americans before the advent of the Colt Single Action Army. The beautifully accurate .44 Russian.

The following information from *The Standard Catalog of Smith & Wesson* by Jim

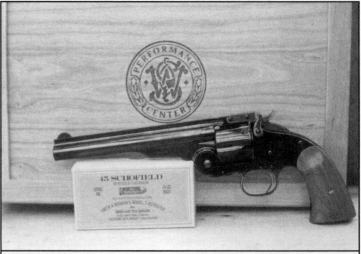

Gripping the Schofield Model.

Supica and Richard Nahas (Krause Publications, 1996; 2nd Ed., 2002) should help remove some of the confusion about the four basic models of the early top-break Smith & Wesson Single Action Model #3s:

1.) S&W Model #3 Americans were made from 1870 to 1874. Features: square butt, smoothly-curved backstrap, top-break latch mounted on the barrel, caliber .44 Rimfire and .44 Russian with a standard 8" barrel.

2.) S&W Model #3 Russians were made from Colt was slower to unload than the automatic ejecting Smith & Wesson, but it also carried a more powerful load and had a solid frame. The first Smith & Wesson Single Action required two hands to operate the latch on the top of the barrel, and was chambered in the less powerful .44 Rimfire, and then 1873 to 1878. Features: round butt with hump on backstrap, a top-break latch mounted on the barrel, .44 Russian with 6-1/2" or 7" barrel standard, and a spur on the trigger guard.

3.) S&W Schofield Models were made from 1875 to 1877. Features: square butt with no hump on backstrap, a top-break latch mounted on the frame, .45 S&W with 7" barrel.

4.) S&W New Model #3s were made from 1878 to 1912. Features: round butt, hump on backstrap, a top-break latch mounted on the barrel, .44 Russian standard plus .38-40 and .44-40, 6-1/2" barrel standard.

The following is one of those stories that, although it isn't true, it certainly ought to be. Many times I have read of the Grand Duke Alexis coming to America and shooting buffalo from horseback with Buffalo Bill Cody. If my memory is correct, I first read about this in grade school. The Duke came over, supposedly, in 1869, had a great time hunting buffalo with both Bill Cody and George Custer, met Gen. Sheridan, was totally enthralled with the Smith & Wesson .44 American, and placed a large order with Smith & Wesson for improved .44s. The story is great, but unfortunately history tells us differently.

The Grand Duke did come over to hunt, but it was in 1872 not 1869. He did hunt with the men mentioned, and during the hunt he carried a Smith & Wesson already

Smith & Wesson offers the Schofield Model through the S&W Performance Center.

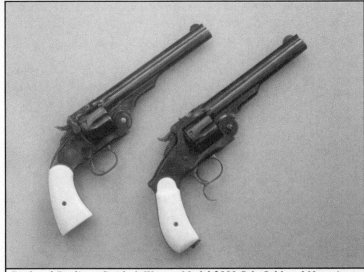

Real and Replica: Smith & Wesson Model 2000 Schofield and Navy Arms Model #3 Russian. Ultra ivory grips by Eagle Grips.

for use, a lanyard ring was added to the butt for security, and a hump was added to the back strap to keep the grip from shifting in the hand when fired. With the arrival of the Third Model, or New Model Russian, the 8-inch barrel was cut to a more convenient 6-1/2 inches.

These old sixguns were magnificent, however it is with the ammunition that the Russians made the most

cartridge case had the same outside diameter. The Russians changed this, however. Now the bullet was made of uniform diameter, the lubrication was placed in grooves in the bullet that were inside the cartridge case, and the cartridge case was crimped into a crimping groove on the bullet. The powder charge was set at a reduced 23 grains, black powder of course, the bullet weight was increased from the 218-grain .44 American to 246 grains (today's .44 Magnum has been standardized at 240-250 grains), and the result was the magnificent .44 Russian. It soon gained a well-deserved reputation for accuracy, and perhaps even more important, the New Model Russian would soon evolve into the New Model #3. This then led to the .44 Special first appearing in the First Model Hand Ejector, the New Century Triple-Lock, which 50 years later, after the Second, Third, and Fourth Model Hand Ejectors, would become Smith & Wesson's greatest revolver and sixgun combination of all time, the .44 Magnum.

chambered in the new .44 Russian. What had actually happened in 1869 was the fact that Smith and Wesson provided one of their new .44 Americans to his Imperial Majesty, the Czar of Russia. The result was a great improvement in the Smith and Wesson .44 American, and a large order was placed with Smith and Wesson for single-action revolvers for his Imperial Majesty's army.

In 1869 Smith & Wesson had produced the first successful big-bore single-action revolver, the Model #3 American .44 six-shot, top-break, automatic-ejecting sixgun. Cartridge cases were made of brass instead of copper, the cases were centerfire instead of rimfire (Americans were also available chambered in the rimfire .44 Henry round), and the .44 Smith & Wesson American cartridge was loaded with 25 gr. of black powder under a 218-gr. bullet with a muzzle velocity of 650 fps. The coming together of Smith and Wesson and the Russians is certainly one of the great events in sixgun and cartridge history as the Russians made major improvements to the American revolver as well as to its ammunition. The First Model Russian was identical to the Smith and Wesson American except for the chambering. With the Second Model Russian, the square stock and grip frame of the American was rounded and diminished in diameter to make it more comfortable

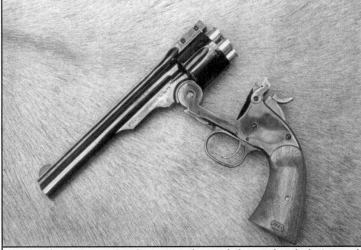

The Smith & Wesson Single Actions featured the top-break design and simultaneous ejection.

significant contribution, a contribution from which we still receive benefits. The .44 Smith & Wesson American, while of centerfire design, was much like the .22 ammunition we still use today. That is, the bullet was of the heel-type with the base of the bullet smaller than the diameter of the rest of the bullet, and this smaller part was inside the cartridge case. This meant that the bullet and the

Original .44 Russian brass was of the folded-head, or balloon, style that was originally used with black powder and has not been seen since before World War II. As has happened with so many of the old frontier cartridges, Starline now offers solid head .44 Russian brass, and dies for reloading the .44 Russian are available from RCBS.

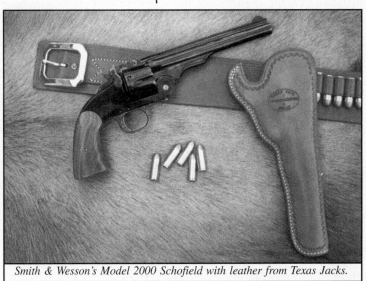

Smith & Wesson's Model 2000 Schofield with leather from Texas Jacks.

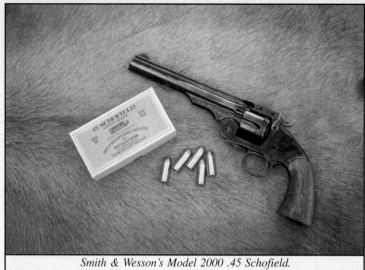

Smith & Wesson's Model 2000 .45 Schofield.

It was my good fortune to recently come up with a shooter quality Model #3 Russian made in 1874 for about half the price of a new Colt Single Action Army. Quite often in the past, different reasons have been advanced as to why the Russians added the spur on the bottom of the trigger guard. It is strange looking, sometimes awkward, and many original owners removed it. Now that I have used the New Model Russian I have discovered that the spur, along with the sights, tells me that the Russians were not gunfighters, but rather marksmen. The sights are tiny and hard to see, requiring concentration, but they are precise. I also found that if I placed my middle finger on the spur when firing the New Model Russian, the result was an incredibly steady hold. With this type of hold it is difficult to reach the hammer for a second shot, but perhaps it was rarely needed.

In 1878 the Russian Model was further improved into what became the New Model #3. The spur was removed from the trigger guard, the butt was rounded, the hump at the top of the backstrap was maintained, and though available in several calibers and barrel lengths, the most prevalent New Models were manufactured in .44 Russian with a 6-1/2" barrel. These beautiful sixguns represent the apex of Smith & Wesson single-action revolvers.

That covers three of the Model #3s, all of which were chambered in what

has proven to be Smith & Wesson's favorite big-bore caliber for 130 years, the .44 that followed the natural evolution from American to Russian to Special to Magnum. The fourth variation on the Model #3, actually an improved American Model Smith & Wesson, was the Schofield.

Major George Schofield of the 10th Cavalry decided to redesign the Smith & Wesson to make it more adaptable

Replica Schofield's from Navy Arms are available in the 7" Cavalry Model and the 5" Wells Fargo Model.

to military use, which in those days meant horseback. Schofield changed the Smith & Wesson opening latch from barrel to frame allowing it to be pushed down with the thumb of the shooting hand rather than opened with the off hand. This allowed one-hand operation, even on horseback. In 1873, a test was set up placing the Schofield Model Smith & Wesson against the Colt Single Action Army. While mounted on a moving horse, the horseman had to empty the sixgun, remove six cartridges from his belt pouch, and reload. It took 26 seconds to unload the Colt, and it was loaded in 60 seconds. The improved Smith & Wesson Schofield took two seconds to unload, and it was loaded in 26 seconds. The Army ordered Schofields.

That was the good news. The bad news was the ammunition or, in some cases, the lack thereof. The Schofield Smith & Wesson was in .45 caliber, not the standard .44 of other Smith & Wesson single-actions. But the cylinder of the Schofield was shorter than that of the Colt .45. The Colt could handle the .45 Smith & Wesson ammunition (the .45 S&W), but the Smith & Wesson would not chamber the longer .45 Colt. When battle units equipped with .45 Schofields received unusable .45 Colt ammunition, a real and dangerous situation existed.

Because the cylinder of the Smith & Wesson #3 frames were shorter than the Colt Single Action, the new cartridge that was brought forth, the .45 Schofield or .45 S&W, was not only shorter, but it also had a wider rim than the .45 Colt. As the Colt Single Action design provided a positive ejection of one cartridge at a time using a rod on the inside of the case and pushing backwards, the Smith & Wesson design required that all six cartridges be ejected at once by the use of an extractor, much like those found on

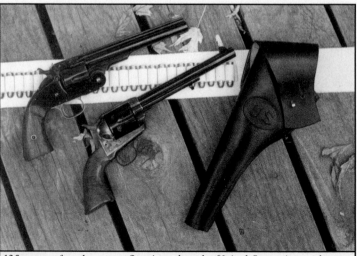

125 years after they were first issued to the United States Army, shooters can still enjoy shooting the .45 Schofield and the .45 Colt.

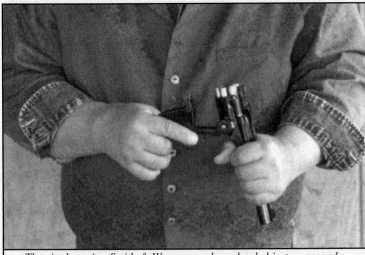

The single-action Smith & Wesson can be unloaded in two seconds.

Action from 1873 to 1900? Today's black powder shooter can solve this problem by using black powder substitutes such as Clean Shot or Triple 7 with an appropriate lube.

The Remington, with its solid frame, was surely a better-designed sixgun than the Colt Single Action with its three-piece frame, back strap, and trigger guard, and the Smith & Wesson Single Action was certainly a more

Smith & Wessons went overseas (the former to Egypt and the latter to Russia and Japan). I have used the Remington, Smith & Wesson, and Colt in replica form, and find that I am always slower with the Remington and Smith & Wesson sixguns. Perhaps this would not be so if I had used them as much as the Colts in my lifetime.

It is always interesting to me to see what contemporary authors thought of the original single-action revolvers. A most interesting book is *Modern American Pistols and Revolvers* written by A. C. Gould and published in 1888. He has this to say about Smith & Wesson sixguns: "It has been my privilege to visit the factory of Smith & Wesson many times, where the greatest freedom was granted me for inspecting the various processes of manufacturing the famous revolvers. The highest mechanical skill is employed; the minutest defect of a part causes it to be rejected; the gauges are super finely constructed, and when a part is fitted to a gauge, it is so perfect that the human eye can scarcely detect the part from the gauge. The barrels, cylinders, and all the small parts are made of the best quality of cast steel, and the framework of Bessemer Steel made at Troy, NY."

today's double-actions. The narrow rim of the .45 Colt of the 1870's did not mate well with the S&W system.

By 1877, the Army had 15,000 Colt Single Actions and 8,000 Smith & Wesson Schofields, however the Schofields were soon dropped from use by the military and sold on the civilian market. Subsequent research by scholars shows that this ammunition supply "problem" may not have been as big of a problem as once thought since the Army apparently tried to order more Schofields in 1878. However, Smith & Wesson was now concentrating on the New Model #3, and Schofields were no longer in production.

Many of the Schofields were cut to 5 inches and nickel-plated for civilian use. Several hundred Schofields were also cut to a barrel length of 5 inches by Wells Fargo and marked "W.F. & CO'S EX." The Schofields may have been dropped by the U.S. Army due to a supply snafu, however there could have been another reason. The Colt, Remington, and Smith & Wesson all competed for the frontier market at a time when all cartridges were loaded with black powder. Anyone that shoots replicas of all three makes with black powder soon discovers that the Colts keep shooting, while the Remingtons and Smith & Wessons often bind up before a full cylinder is fired. Could this have been a contributing factor to the immense popularity of the Colt Single

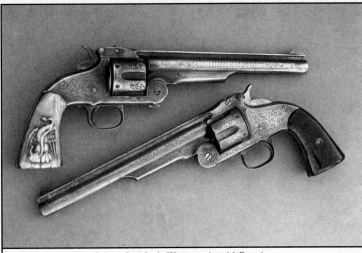

Fancy Smith & Wessons in .44 Russian

sophisticated design with its break-open action that allowed quick loading and unloading. However, the Colt Single Action was the overwhelming choice of most Western sixgunners of the 19th century.

I do believe balance also had a great deal to do with this. Neither the Remington nor the Smith & Wesson could even come close to the near-perfect balance of the old Colt, nor are they as fast from leather as the Peacemaker. Most Colts were also sold in this country; most Remingtons and

"I have closely watched the impressions made upon some of the most skillful mechanics in America when a Smith & Wesson revolver was

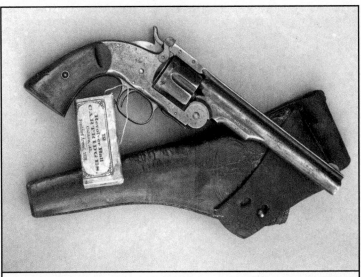

An original Schofield Model .45 that saw service in the United States Cavalry.

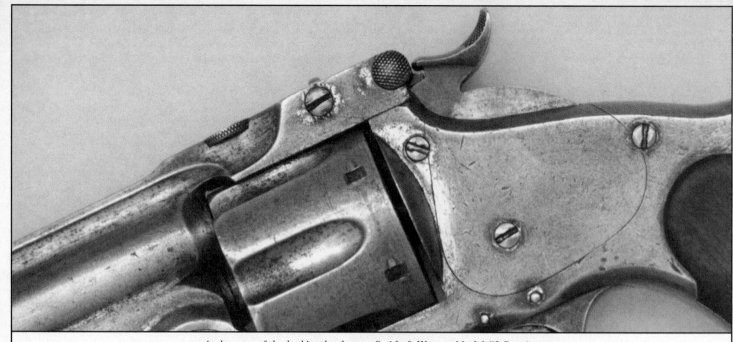

A close-up of the locking latch on a Smith & Wesson Model #3 Russian.

submitted for their inspection. These severest of critics would seem to revel in the pleasure they experienced in seeing such a perfect piece of mechanical work, and unhesitatingly commanded the workmanship in the highest terms."

The old American Model Smith & Wesson revolver was a great favorite with those who knew what weapon to select for reliable work. Many are in use today and highly valued as very accurate weapons; but this model was superseded by a new model Army revolver, which is generally known as the .44 caliber Russian model, the name being given on account of the Russian government purchasing 150,000 of them for her cavalry. This model seems to grow in popularity each year, and many of the best revolver target shooters in America have selected it as their choice of weapon.

Smith & Wesson may have produced a big-bore single-action before Colt, but the Colt was the first to come forth with a workable double-action revolver beginning in 1877. By 1880, Smith & Wesson had a .38 caliber double-action, while the big bores arrived one year later. Smith & Wesson's .44 Double Action First Model chambered in .44 Russian would only be manufactured from 1881 to 1913 with slightly under 54,000 being made. The .44-40 Double Action Frontier,

with slightly over 15,000 in quantity, was offered from 1886 to 1913. Two relatively rare Double Action Smith & Wessons are the Wesson Favorite with about 1,000 being made in .44 Russian, and about 275 double-actions chambered in .38-40. All of the double-action models look basically like a New Model #3 with a double-action trigger added. They still featured the top-break design, however the standard solid-frame Smith & Wesson double-action with a swing-out cylinder would not arrive until the advent of the Military & Police Model in 1899.

Currently, shooters can acquire replicas of the Smith & Wesson Single Actions with both the Schofield and Model #3 being offered by Navy Arms. The Schofield is chambered in .45 Colt and .44-40 with barrel lengths of 7 inches, 5 inches, and 3 inches available, while they Model #3 is offered only with a 7" barrel and in .44 Russian only. Beginning in 2000, the original manufacturer, Smith & Wesson, began offering a 125th year anniversary Model 2000 Schofield. It is still available and is chambered, as the original, only in .45 Schofield.

If it was 1880 and I was choosing a sixgun for serious use, I would have a hard time deciding between a Colt Single Action .45 or a Smith & Wesson .44. Maybe I would do as Jesse James did and buy both.

Still in service with black powder loads only, this Model #3 Russian was manufactured in 1874.

Smith & Wesson Model # 3 Russian (circa 1874) .44 RUSSIAN x 7-1/2"		
Bullet	**Load**	**MV**
Lyman #429483 RN 250		
	20-gr. Goex FFg	623
	20-gr. Goex FFFg	653
	20-gr. Goex CTG	616
	20-gr. Pyrodex P	749
Bullet	**Load**	**MV**
Lyman Cowboy 200		
	20-gr. Goex FFg	633
	20-gr. Goex FFFg	683
	20-gr. Goex CTG	594
	20-gr. Pyrodex P	658
	20-gr. Pyrodex Select	725
Note: All weights are by volume.		

Over 125 years separate these two Smith & Wesson Single Actions: an S&W Model 2000 Schofield and an 1874 Model #3 Russian. Leather is by Black Hills Leather.

Smith & Wesson Schofields: First Model from Navy Arms and a Second Model from Cimarron. Grips are by Buffalo Brothers.

A comparison of the two .45s from the 1870's, a Schofield and a Colt.

The premier cartridge of the Smith & Wesson Single Actions and early Double Actions was the .44 Russian.

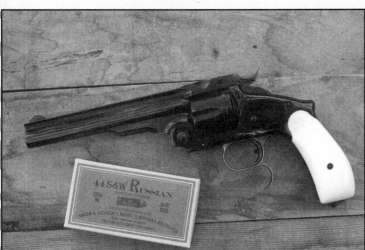

A faithful copy of the Smith & Wesson Model #3 Russian is available from Navy Arms chambered only in .44 Russian. Ultra ivory grips are by Eagle Grips.

Navy Arms Model #3 Russian with Eagle's Ultra ivory grips.

A close-up of the simultaneous ejection feature of all Smith & Wesson Model #3s.

Original Smith &Wessons: 1875 Schofield Model .45 S&W and a New Model #3 .44 Russian.

Note the secure grip afforded by the Model #3 Russian.

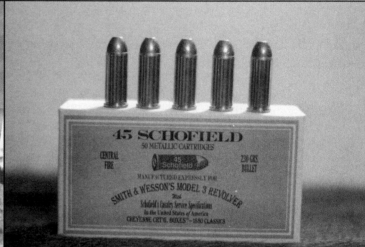

Smith & Wesson's .45 of the 19th century, the .45 Schofield.

Navy Arms' rendition of a Hideout Model Schofield.

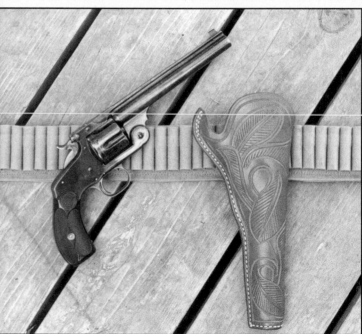

Smith & Wesson's greatest single-action achievement, the New Model #3 .44 Russian. Traditional leather and web belt by El Paso Saddlery.

The Sporting Arms of James H. Bullard

By: G. Scott Jamieson

Photos by: Cody Firearms Museum, E.R. "Ted" Cotton, Robert A. Marshall, Werner List, John Vance, Hampton Williams, and Royal Armouries HM Tower of London

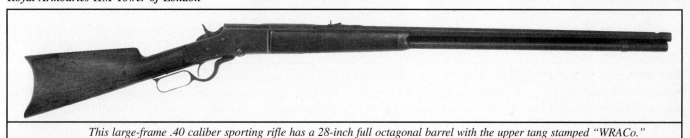

This large-frame .40 caliber sporting rifle has a 28-inch full octagonal barrel with the upper tang stamped "WRACo."

With the appearance of the Bullard large-frame repeater in January of 1883, the world was introduced to a rifle that could claim to be "the smoothest operating lever-action ever made." Not only was it slick in its operation, it could handle the largest cartridges of the day (except for some of the very long cartridges designed for single-shots, with the length of the cartridge being the determining factor, not the powder load). With its plethora of available loadings, including the Bullard proprietary cartridges of .32-40-150, .38-45-190, .40-70-232, .40-75-259, .40-90-300, .45-85-295, and the .50-115-300 (this was the most expensive

met his objectives was #245,700, which was granted on August 16, 1881.

Bullard's repeaters are all based on a falling/rolling block action in combination with a rack and pinion. All pieces, including the breechbolt, were operated by the movement of the lever's pinion. No part of the mechanism acts directly on any other part without the action of a pinned lever or the almost frictionless motion of a locking brace against the hammer. Most repeaters have the breechbolt slamming the hammer into the cocked position; this would never have worked for Bullard. It

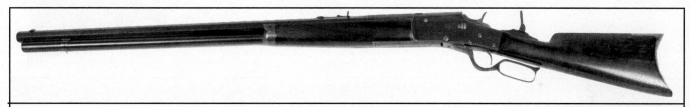

This large-frame .40 caliber sporting rifle also has a 28-inch full octagonal barrel with a crescent steel buttplate. This rifle, in the configuration shown, would have sold new for $35.00 in 1887 without a tang sight.

production cartridge of its time at $90.00 per 1000), the Bullard, in both the repeater and, later, single-shot versions, became very popular with the well-to-do sportsmen of the day seeing use virtually everywhere in the world.

Prior to the establishment of the Bullard Repeating Arms Association, James Bullard was a master mechanic for the Smith & Wesson firm for some five years. During that time he was granted four patents in tandem with Wesson and assigned to the firm for improvements in their revolvers and methods of manufacture. During 1878-1879, he turned his mind to developing a repeating rifle that could safely handle the largest cartridge loadings of the day. His patent for the rifle design that

was his attention to minute detail that contributed to the very high quality of Bullard arms. It may also have been its Achilles heel, for the mechanism was very complex. The author has heard from correspondents over the years relating stories of modern-day gunsmiths "pulling their hair out" when trying to reassemble a repeater! The actual instructions for disassembly and reassembly of a repeater, as written by Robert A. Marshall for this writer's upcoming book, *Bullard Arms II*, take up many pages of text.

After the introduction of the large-frame repeaters (January 1883), small-frame repeaters were introduced to the market in November of 1884, and were chambered in all loadings smaller

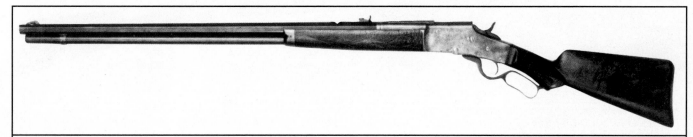

This large-frame .40 caliber sporting rifle has a 28-inch full octagonal barrel with a checkered pistol grip and forearm with a shotgun butt, and a "gutta-percha" buttplate with an elk motif.

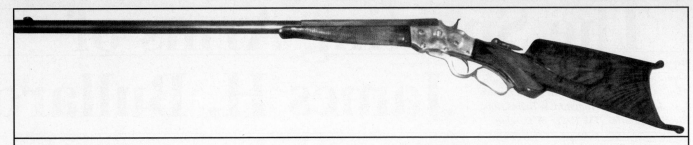

This detachable, interchangeable barrel, single-shot .32-40 caliber target rifle has a part-round, part-octagonal barrel of 28.5 inches, but one can see it has been cut as evidenced by the barrel set-back (the octagonal portion of the barrel should devolve to round at the end of the forearm).

than .40 caliber, with the exception of the .44-40 WCF. This particular offering was dropped from the catalogs quite soon after and, to this writer's knowledge, no factory .44-40 WCF exists, although rumors abound that the Northern Pacific Railway may have purchased rifles in that caliber. In August of 1885, the small-frame (solid-frame) single-shot made its debut, and by January of 1886, the large-frame version of this rifle was tested. In November of 1886, improvements were made to the camming action of the repeater's action by the inclusion of a large breech block, which accounts for some Bullard repeaters being marked "MODEL 1886." This helps us date approximately

shots by a wide margin despite the higher costs involved. By 1888, the company was in trouble financially, but managed to struggle on until January 1891 when the building was sold. The company itself was never sold to any competitor.

The large-frame repeaters encompass serial numbers 1-1500 and 2500-2700, for a total production number of 1700. The small-frame repeaters are numbered from 1501-2000, for a total of 500. The single-shots (all versions) start at 3501 and end at serial number 4100, for a total of 600 rifles. These findings are based on 27 years of research and the logging of almost 470 specific serial numbers. Thus, the Bullard rifle, in any of its

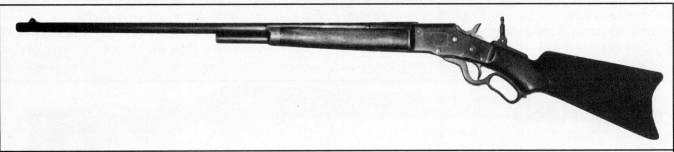

This .38 caliber rifle has a 26-inch part-round, part-octagonal barrel, checkered pistol grip and forearm, and is equipped with a very early Lyman combination tang sight.

when the rifles were sold, as they were not sold in serial number sequence, but assembled and sold largely on demand.

By January of 1887, the first small-frame, detachable, interchangeable barrel single-shots became available, with large frames coming onto the market around April of 1887. This model proved to be popular, with many two and some three-barrel outfits being produced. Around May of 1887, the last sporting rifle innovation was introduced, which was the Bullard Scheutzen model with quickly detachable triggers (from single three-pound pull triggers to double-set triggers), as well as the aforementioned detachable barrels. These versions outsold the solid-frame single-

versions, is one of the most unique and rare production rifles of the "Old West Era," and has a place in any cowboy black powder event.

All Bullard rifles have moderately strong actions, and if checked out by a competent gunsmith and shot with ammunition reloaded to reflect the action's strength, the shooter will be rewarded with a great deal of pleasure, not the least of which will be the commotion and interest engendered by the shooting fraternity when you show up at an event with a *Big Bullard* in your hands.

This .38-45 caliber small-frame sporting repeater has a 26-inch full round barrel. Note that the small-frame repeaters have two receiver inspection plates, unlike the large frames that only have one plate.

This .36 caliber special small-frame sporting repeater has a 24-inch full round barrel, half-magazine, and British proofs sporting a shotgun butt and turkey motif buttplate.

Custom Old Ruger Armys & the Dark Side

By: Terry Nibarger,
aka Red River Drifter

Nothing beats blowing smoke rings into the fog on a cool still morning!

One of the most fun and exciting aspects of cowboy action shooting is watching the black powder shooters practice their art. The only thing more fun is pulling out those flamethrowers yourself, and blasting away into the clouds of smoke that will soon obscure your targets.

Cap-n-ball represents the earliest days recreated in our game. There are many accurate and beautiful reproductions of cap-n-ball handguns on the market today. The problem is that most reproductions are plagued by 1850's and 1860's technology. Of all the cap-n-ball guns in CAS, the Ruger Old Army finds its way to the top of the pile in competitive shooting. I recognize that some folks don't shoot cap-n-ball, or CAS for that matter, to be competitive. But for those that do, reliability is a must. Ruger is known for producing reliable and dependable handguns. The Old Army is no exception.

When I began experimenting with the "Dark Side" of CAS I became extremely frustrated. I was shooting my Colt 1860 Army replicas and was having fits with them. Misfires, caps falling off, and caps falling in the action were the main problems. Several years later, I decided to try it again. I had gone through all the same frustrations and was about to hang it up when a good friend and shooting pard of mine, Hawk Mortimer, loaned me his Ruger Old Armys. Hawk had shot these ROA's in competition for several years, and I knew his problems were few-and-far between. He told me to use them for a few months to see what I thought. I'm sure glad that I did.

I discovered that cap-n-ball does not have to be frustrating. In fact, it can be wonderful! Besides being dependable, the ROA's were very accurate and also as strong as an ox. I knew after my first time out that I had discovered a new love. While working with Hawk's pistols, I realized that, while these were wonderful reliable handguns, they were heavy and really long. I was used to pulling 4-5/8" Colts. These pistols, with their standard 7" barrels and long frames, seemed to take forever to clear leather. They were also slow to move from target to target because of their weight. There are lots of old cap-n-ball pistols around that have been cut down. Shortening these guns to a gun fighting length would be a great improvement. This love affair was about to get serious, and I had to have a pair of my own. I sent Hawk's guns back home, and got my own pair of Old Armys.

From the start these guns were going to be a custom project. I knew what I wanted, but I am not a gunsmith. I also have learned that there is value in quality workmanship. In the past, Larry Crow of Competitive Edge Gunworks has redone two Colt Single Action Armys, and has resurrected a third from the grave. He has also completely gone through my Ruger Vaqueros and has redone them inside and out. Larry is a member of the American Pistolsmith's Guild, which means he is among the best of the best. I sat down with Larry and told him how I pictured the Old Armys because I knew he could make this project happen. I described what I wanted, and left the new unfired pistols in his care.

When I got them back, they were gorgeous! They were exactly what I had described, only better. They wore 5-1/2" Shilen match-grade barrels, were perfectly tapered and smartly balanced, and were topped off with an 11% lapped crown on the muzzle. The outside was a unique satin finish that reduced glare and gave the guns a "worn-nickel finish" look and feel. They wore a pair of rosewood Eagle Gunfighter grips that fit perfectly, and the loading levers were shortened up to match the new barrels. He had even redesigned the loading-lever latch so I could get the cylinders, ramrod, and cylinder pin completely out. I had seen shortened ROA's before, but the removal of the cylinder pin was not possible on those guns. Larry fabricated a loading-lever latch that allowed for a complete removal of those parts for a thorough cleaning. Of course, the actions were smooth and perfectly timed. The interior parts were polished and modified to meet the normal Competitive Edge action job standards. As requested, the only way to tell the guns apart was by looking at the serial number. To say I was pleased with the project is a huge understatement.

I later went by Larry's

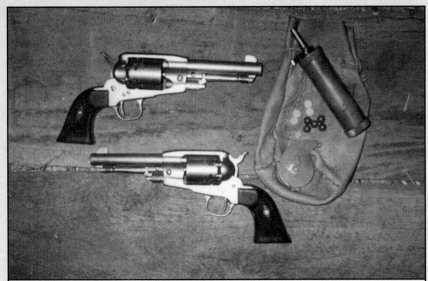
A pair of custom Old Model Ruger Armys with Gunfighter grips from Eagle Grips and powder, ball, wads, and a capper.

it goes quickly. I probably over-clean everything at a match, removing and cleaning nipples every night, but I get the whole pile of guns done in about 45 minutes with Ballistol and water. If I'm shooting cartridge guns, it's about half that time.

After cleaning up the guns, my fingernails may be a little dirty when I go to dinner, but I sure had a blast during the day! Give it a try. As a long-time smokeless shooter, I've got to tell you that it is very easy to get hooked on the "Dark Side." It's a move I've never regretted.

Editors Note:

Red River Drifter won the SASS End of Trail World Champion Frontiersman Category in 2001 and 2002. Lenny McGill also recently released a "how to" video of Red River Drifter covering the basics of black powder loading, equipment, shooting, and clean-up. It should be a great help to those who want to get started in the "Dark Side" of cowboy action shooting.

In addition, Larry Crow of Competitive Edge Gunworks just came out with a series of basic gunsmithing videos. These are designed to show shooters how to disassemble, clean, do some basic tuning, and reassemble most CAS guns.

shop to sight-in the guns. He was very gracious as I tested several loads for accuracy out of the new barrels, and then adjusted the point-of-aim to my specifications. These are the most accurate handguns I own, bar none. I learned a long time ago that you can't outshoot your equipment.

I get many requests for info about the loads I use in these little sweethearts, and it's no secret. I feed them a charge of 25 grains of FFFg black powder. (You must lengthen the ramrod or use a spacer like a .357 bullet to set the ball deeper, as there is room for much more, and I don't use a filler.) I like FFFg because it tends to ignite better than FFg, and it gives you a little more bang when needed for those occasional knock-downs. The charge sits beneath a Wonder Wad from Ox Yoke Originals, and a pure lead .457 ball from Hornady. Remington #10 caps light off the fire. I have been shooting this load for some time now, and only one knock-down has ever gotten away, and that was just because of the angle I was shooting from.

The "Dark Side" is great fun, and not nearly as difficult as most folks think. I think that clean-up is what scares them off. It is easier than smokeless, but unlike smokeless, it must be done. However, once you get the routine down,

Shooting a Winchester '73 with black powder.

Shooting a custom Ruger cap-n-ball.

The shotgun is still a major player in the Frontiersman category.

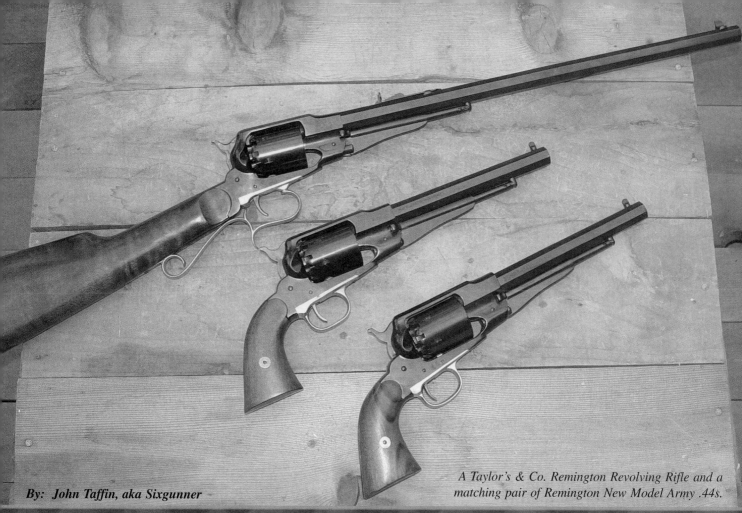

A Taylor's & Co. Remington Revolving Rifle and a matching pair of Remington New Model Army .44s.

By: John Taffin, aka Sixgunner

Taylor's & Co.'s Remington Revolving Rifle

Sam Colt's 1837 Paterson was not the first single-action revolver, but it certainly was the first successful one. Along with the Paterson sixgun, Colt also offered rifles on the same basic pattern. The Model 1837 version was hammerless and had a shield over both the nipples and in front of the cylinder. I assume the shield was to protect the shooter's arms, but it actually causes chain fires, in which firing one chamber would set off one or more other chambers. This hammerless revolving rifle was cocked with the use of a lever in front of the trigger, while the improved 1839 Model had a loading lever under the barrel or on the side. Both guns were offered in several variations, such as rifle, carbine, and even

Taylor's & Co.'s Remington Revolving Rifle and the R&D .45 Colt two-piece cylinder and back plate.

shotgun, with five or more chambers. Colt hoped for a Government contract for these revolving rifles, however that never came to pass.

Sometime in the late 1840's, Colt experimented with a revolving rifle on the Dragoon. The barrel was lengthened and the grip straps changed to accommodate a wooden butt stock. This version, however, never saw production. By 1855, Colt's Model 1855 was available as a rifle or carbine in .36, .40, .44, .50, and .56 calibers. These were true six-shooters, with barrel lengths from 18 to 31 inches in length. A companion shotgun was offered in .60 or .75 bore size. For military use, an 1855 musket was a five-shot .56 caliber rifle that accepted a bayonet on its 38-inch barrel.

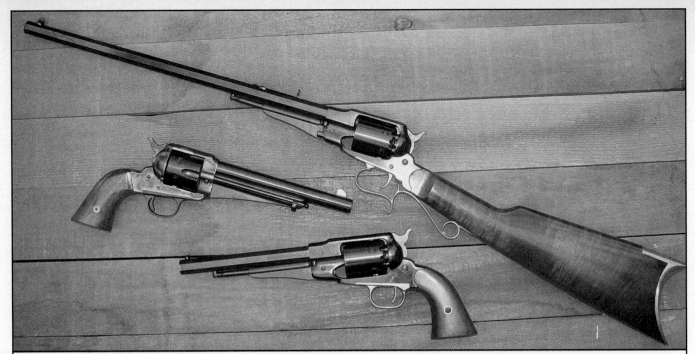

A Taylor's and Co. replica of the Remington Revolving Rifle, shown with the Remington Model 1875 chambered in .45 Colt and the Remington New Model Army .44.

During the Civil War, Berdan's Sharpshooters were equipped with Model 1855s from Colt. In all, the United States Government purchased 7,000 Colt Revolving Rifles. All of these featured a side hammer on the right side of the receiver above the trigger. At the same time the Government was purchasing these revolving rifles, they were staying traditional, as Colt supplied more than 100,000 .58 caliber Springfield Model 1855 single-shot rifles and muskets.

Colt also provided detachable butt stocks for many of their percussion revolvers, especially the .44 caliber Dragoons and 1860 Army Models. Even in replica form, many of these models still have the screw head on both sides of the mainframe and the groove in the bottom of the butt that served to accommodate a removable butt stock. The idea, of course, was to turn a sixgun into a longer-distance carbine. Supposedly, a shooter could extend his effective range by having a butt stock seated into his shoulder. Barrel length remained the same, and one has to wonder just how much more effective the handy packing sixgun became by adding a butt stock.

While Colt was furnishing detachable butt stocks, Remington took a different path. In 1865, using their basic percussion revolver as the platform, Remington straightened the grip straps to become tangs accepting a butt stock, while the barrel was lengthened. With these two operations, Remington's New Model Army Revolver became a rifle. Obviously, this was not one of Remington's most successful designs, as only approximately 2,000 were manufactured, equally divided between .36 and .44 caliber. With the coming of cartridges, many of these were converted to .38 and .46 rimfire beginning in 1866.

There were two inherent problems with the design of the Remington Revolving Rifle. First, there was no forearm for the shooter to grasp with the offside arm. However, this prevented a more serious problem from occurring, as it would be very dangerous for a shooter to have an arm in front of a cylinder. Even if everything worked correctly, the arm could be seriously burned; if things did not go right, a possible chain fire could result and the shooter could end up having a round ball imbedded in his arm. The correct way to hold a Remington Revolving

The R&D .45 Colt Conversion Cylinder adds greatly to the versatility of replica Remington .44s.

The R&D Conversion Cylinder from Taylor's & Co. also works in replica Remington New Model Army .44s.

Rifle when shooting is to place the offhand under the shooting hand. Remington's design even offers a spur on the bottom of the trigger guard for one finger of the offhand to rest upon.

At the same time that Remington was producing revolving rifles, they were also converting their basic sixguns to fire cartridges. From 1866 to the coming of their Model 1875 cartridge-firing revolver, Remington produced over 10,000 cylinders to allow their various percussion revolvers to accept rimfire cartridges.

The advent of so many great lever-action rifles in the 1860's and 1870's effectively killed the idea of a revolving rifle. The leverguns were easier to load, held more rounds, were more powerful, had greater range, were fitted with better sights, and the ammunition was protected from the elements. However, this demise does not prevent the revolving rifle from being a most interesting and intriguing part of history. Original specimens are difficult to locate, are normally very expensive, and usually too valuable to shoot. Now, thanks to replicas, we can own and shoot a revolving rifle.

Taylor's & Co. is known for providing an extensive and diverse line of replica revolvers and rifles for black powder enthusiasts, reenactors, and cowboy action shooters. To this lineup, they have now added the Remington Revolving Rifle. This replica version of the Model 1858 New Model Army .44 is beautifully-finished with a walnut butt stock and brass buttplate and trigger guard, while the rest of the firearm, which is manufactured by Uberti, is deeply blued. The barrel is 18 inches in length, octagon in shape, and features a blade front sight in a dovetail, mated up with a typical lever-action rear sight that is adjustable for elevation by the use of a stepped elevator.

The only problem encountered while shooting Taylor's Remington Revolving Rifle revolved around this rear sight. There was no temper on the leaf itself, so it would not hold elevation. A search through my parts box revealed a rear sight assembly that came off a levergun in the past. This was easily tapped into place on the barrel of the Remington using the dovetail. I would expect future groups fired with this rifle to be smaller because of this addition.

The Remington Revolving Rifle is loaded the same as the 1858 Remington New Model Army .44. That is, a charge is poured into the chamber from the front, a wad, if desired, is placed over the powder charge, and a round ball of the proper size is then placed in the front of the chamber and rammed home by the loading lever under the barrel. Percussion caps are never placed on the nipples at the rear of the cylinder until all chambers are charged and the barrel is pointed in a safe direction. Although the Revolving Rifle loads the same as a companion New Model Army .44, it is a little more awkward to accomplish due to the butt stock and longer barrel.

Shooting the New Model Army Revolving Rifle with black powder, round ball, wad, and cap is a most pleasant experience as recoil is almost non-existent. As with standard charges, using the 140-gr. round ball, muzzle velocities range from 900 to nearly 1200 fps.

To add to the versatility of this little rifle, and to also experience, to some degree, what it was like to shoot the cartridge firing versions of the original revolving rifles, Taylor's & Co. is now providing a conversion cylinder that turns this cap-n-ball

revolving rifle into a six-shot .45 Colt. The cylinder is from R&D Gun Shop, distributed by Taylor's, and is made to fit Uberti-manufactured Model 1858 Remingtons. Cylinders are also available for other manufacturer's replica Remingtons, as well as the Ruger Old Army.

Unlike the Colt Replicas, which often require the wedge pin to be tapped out and the barrel to be removed before the cylinder can be slid off its axis pin, the Remington cylinder is easily removed. Once the loading lever is unlatched and lowered, the cylinder pin can be pulled forward, allowing the cylinder to be released. To replace the cylinder, it is only necessary to slide it back into place (working around the cylinder rotating hand can be a little tricky here), while the base pin is pushed back into the cylinder and the loading lever latched, making the Remington ready to fire once again.

R&D cylinders are made of 4150 steel, while the top plate, which contains six firing pins, is made of 4140. These cylinders are suitable for use in steel-frame sixguns only, with black powder loads or CAS .45 Colt loads as provided by several manufacturers. R&D recommends a maximum velocity of 750 to 850 fps with smokeless powder, and a maximum black powder or black powder equivalent loading volume of 34 grains of FFg.

To load the R&D cylinder, the top plate is removed, the number of desired cartridges are inserted, and the top plate is reinstalled using a pin on the back of the cylinder proper and a corresponding hole in the top plate. The firing pin for the chamber directly to the right of the locking pin is silver in color, so it is always easy to tell which chamber is empty. This prevents the dangerous practice of looking at the front of the cylinder to see where the empty lies. R&D cautions that the cylinder should never be dry-fired, as it will ruin the firing pins.

Installation of the R&D cylinder was a true drop-in fit, with no problems encountered whatsoever. This Taylor's & Co. Remington Revolving Rifle is a most pleasurable shooting rifle, with a definite tie to the 19th century. The addition of the Conversion Cylinder simply adds to the shooting pleasure.

Taylor's & Co.'s Remington 1858 New Model Carbine (Using a Speer .451" round ball with 5 shots at 25 yards)		
Load	Velocity	Accuracy
25 grains of Triple 7 FFFg	1,170 fps	1-1/2"
30 grains of CleanShot FFFg	1,001 fps	2-1/8"
30 grains of Goex FFFg	862 fps	2-1/2"
With the R&D .45 Colt Conversion Cylinder		
Load	Velocity	Accuracy
Black Hills 250 Cowboy Load	825 fps	2-1/8"
UltraMax 250 Cowboy Load	884 fps	2"
3-D 255 Cowboy Load	792 fps	2-1/4"
30 grains of Triple 7 FFg/Oregon Trail 250	888 fps	2-3/4"
Black Dawge 250 Black Powder	1,125 fps	2-1/8"
Cor-Bon 250 Black Powder	845 fps	1-3/4"
Wind River 250 Black Powder	858 fps	2-1/8"

Why Shoot A Colt Lightning Rifle?

By: Lee Anderson, aka Bull Chip

With all the advances in today's manufacturing and shooting technologies, why would one even consider shooting a 100-plus-year-old gun of debatable design using 100-plus-year-old technology in a CAS event? Back then all repeating firearms were in their infancy. They were prone to misfiring, jamming, malfunctions, a short mechanical life, and a host of other irritating, aggravating, and often life-threatening shortcomings. The history of the Old West is vividly punctuated with tales of guns failing at critical times because the engineering and manufacturing processes back then weren't a high science by any stretch of the imagination. The guns designed and produced by these flawed processes haven't somehow magically "healed up" in the last 100 years either. Not to say that shooting one of them isn't satisfying and a lot of fun, because it most certainly is both. It is, however, completely unrealistic to expect one of these guns to perform competitively against modern NC-machined replicas designed with the advantages of many a "hard lesson learned" over the past 100 years.

I'm fairly new to CAS, and have competed for only a couple of years. I'm a life-long Old West history buff and a retired aerospace engineer who has hunted most of my life using many different guns in my 63 years. I'm not new to guns, shooting, manufacturing, or history. I must admit, however, I had never shot black powder until I got into CAS and, I swear, it is addictive. From the start, I knew I was going to try to be as historically authentic in my clothing, guns, and gear as my pocketbook could stand. This meant, if possible, shooting original guns and black powder. Colt's Lightning rifle had always fascinated me, and I managed to acquire a nice original saddle ring carbine in .44-40 caliber. With replicas only recently being offered, if you saw a Lightning for sale prior to the fall of 2002 it was an original. I wanted to go with old guns and black powder for the very same reason that so many hunters today are turning to single-shots, muzzleloaders, and even bows and arrows. I wanted to do it not only because that's the way it was in the past, but also to turn my shooting back into something it had lost. The more variables you remove from any competitive activity, the higher a science it becomes, and eventually the only challenges it presents are quantity (how many) and time (how fast).

Shooting black powder and old guns rapidly shifts you back into a world of many variables, and your primary focus becomes how to effectively do this. Until you learn how to deal with them, worrying about quantity is a wasted effort, and the last thing that concerns you, if at all, is how fast you did it. Shooting a stage "clean" takes on a whole new meaning, and the satisfaction of overcoming the myriad of things that could have gone wrong, but didn't, seeps all the way to your core, just lays there, and sort of glows. How long it took can be unbelievably insignificant. Now, don't assume that because speed isn't high on my list that I have nothing good to say about that aspect of CAS. Today's top shooters

The author's Colt Lightning .44-40 Saddle Ring Carbine sits on one of his own original "Heirlooms in Wood."

absolutely amaze me. They've shaved their moves to a level of efficiency and developed their equipment and shooting to such a precise art that I have trouble believing some of it even when it happens right in front of me. If a fraction of a second is what "cranks you up," then by all means go for it. Old guns and black powder probably wouldn't be the way to go, though. It comes as no surprise to me that my best scores are often less than "competitive." After all, I've chosen to play a competitive game of speed and then, on purpose, saddled myself with a bunch of self-imposed limitations that can only serve to slow me down, such as authentic Old West shooting styles, 100-year-old equipment, and 100-year-old technologies. A note of caution here to those of you hooked on speed. Don't assume that all black powder shooters are automatically out of the running time wise. There is considerable documented evidence to the contrary.

Okay, enough philosophy. Let's get back to that Colt Lightning; you know, the Edsel of the 1880's firearms world. It sure seemed like a good idea at the time. Actually, it still seems like a pretty good idea. So, what happened to it? Why didn't it ever amount to much? Well, I've got a theory on that. No proof whatsoever, but then I haven't heard a better explanation either. I think it involved some Winchester revolvers. You don't see a connection? Ok, let's poke around a little in some "gun history" of the late 1800's. In the 1870's, Winchester started developing a line of revolvers. This is a documented hard fact, and several verified prototypes exist in gun collections today. One of them is a single-action with a very modern "Colt-type" swing-out cylinder. (William Mason, who previously worked for Colt, held the patent, and it seems he also improved the feeding mechanism in Winchester's Model '86 levergun.) Anyway, not a single one of these prototype revolvers ever went into production. This was

Slam firing is not recommended, but is a guaranteed, sure-fire adrenaline rush.

also about the same time that Colt was vigorously promoting the Lightning rifles, the Colt-Burgess lever-action rifle, some side-by-side double rifles, and various shotguns. The SAA military contracts were their financial bread and butter.

Now comes the theory part. Some 50 years ago or so, I can recall sitting in a hunting camp one evening listening to the "old-timers" talk about how when they were younger it was rumored that Winchester management called a meeting with Colt management sometime in the early 1880's. I've heard it a few times since, too. In this undocumented, unsubstantiated, supposed meeting, Winchester is said to have laid their prototype revolvers on the conference table and proposed that if Colt would phase out their long guns, Winchester would not go into the handgun business. Is it possible that they might have also suggested that if Winchester could use the pump-action idea, Colt might make good use of Winchester's swing-out cylinder idea? Both could then focus on processes and markets that each had already developed and established with the advantage of a near monopoly on separate niches in the very lucrative and fast-growing gun market? Nawwwww…no way…couldn't be. Shenanigans like that have always been, and still are, beneath the dignity and beyond the business ethics of large companies in this country; we all know that.

Anyway, if you add up the documented hard facts, it makes sense. Winchester went to a great deal of trouble and expense to develop some excellent prototypes, yet never manufactured a single handgun. At the same time, Colt began to quietly fade completely out of several promising long gun ventures. Winchester already had a very efficient manufacturing process fully developed for long guns and had built a staunch following in the marketplace for them, as had Colt with handguns. In 1893, Winchester introduced their Model '93 slide-action (i.e. pump) shotgun. Smokeless powder pressures exposed

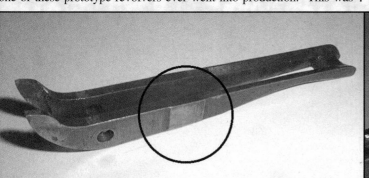

A close-up of the carrier with the friction pad circled.

A properly-adjusted carrier will support the weight of a loaded cartridge. Note the friction pad behind and below the cartridge.

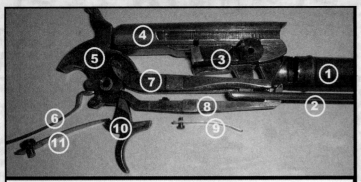

1. Magazine Tube
2. Slide Arm
3. Bolt Lock
4. Bolt
5. Hammer
6. Hammer Spring
7. Carrier
8. Magazine Lever
9. Magazine Lever Spring
10. Trigger
11. Trigger Spring

The approximate position of the Lightning's "innards" inside the frame.

some mechanical weaknesses in it, and after 34,050 guns, its innards were reengineered and the gun emerged as the CAS-beloved Model '97. (A bit of trivia: If you ever come across a '97 below serial number 34,151, it's actually a '93 and is strictly for black powder use.) Is it simply an odd coincidence that the basic mechanical principles of this pump-action shotgun are nearly identical to the Lightning? In fact, except for unlocking the action by pushing the firing pin forward with either the hammer or the finger, Winchester's introductory promotional description of how the Model '93 mechanically functioned is a word-for-word description of exactly how a Lightning functions, right down to all of the safety interlocks. Another odd coincidence, don't you think? The end result of all these odd coincidences was that between 1890 and 1900 Winchester's new pump-action shotgun (a patent once under Colt's control) was a huge success, while Colt's Lightning pump-action rifle quietly died. Colt then introduced their highly successful double-action revolver with a revolutionary swing-out cylinder (a patent once under Winchester's control). Ain't it just grand?

Whatever the case, the Lightning has been the center of countless gun discussions from the day it was introduced in 1885 in the medium-frame version. They were advertised at $16.50 for the 20" carbine and $18.00 for the 26" octagonal-barreled sporting rifle. In 1888, the light-framed .22 caliber and the heavy-framed .38-56-256, .40-60-260, .45-60-300, .45-85-285, and .50-95-300 express versions were introduced at $20.00 each. The only one both practical and acceptable for CAS is the medium-frame, as it only came in the .32-20-100, .38-40-180, and .44-40-200 pistol calibers. Medium-frame production was halted in 1900, so black powder is mandatory for safety reasons.

Does the rifle have inherent design problems? Of course it does. Every repeating rifle on the market back then had design problems. It's documented that the military rejected Winchester leverguns because of their nasty habit of jamming. Is the Lightning mechanism overly complicated and delicate? I don't know. The interaction of the parts in a 1911 ACP is every bit as complex, and it has a comparable number of parts that appear to be just as "delicate," yet it's almost universally considered one of the all-time toughest, durable, and reliable arms anyone has ever produced. I'm still workin' on that question.

Something nobody today will probably ever know is how an original Lightning performed when it was new. If you owned a brand-

new, fresh, out-of-the-box, original Colt Lightning, would you allow some CAS "expert" to put several hundred rounds through it just to test its performance? Neither would I. Those seen in competition today were so neglected, beat up, or worn out to begin with that they weren't of much value to collectors, and they still weren't low-dollar guns. The rifle was never popular enough with shooters in general for gun people or gunsmiths to bother learning much about them. This means that the level of expertise when it comes to repairing, reconditioning, and tuning was never, and still isn't, very high. An SAA, in original like-new condition, isn't up to the demands of today's top speed shooters. Precious few of the new replicas are. Why then should a beat up or worn out old Lightning that's been questionably repaired or tuned be up to the demands? My 1st generation SAA and Lightning both exhibit some of the same inspector stampings, so I assume both were designed, manufactured, and assembled by the same people using the same tools, technologies, procedures, and methods. There were so many SAAs in circulation and they've been popular for so long that gun people have learned to deal with their shortcomings and accept them.

All gun problems are either mechanical or human-caused. The Lightning has a reputation for feeding problems that are pretty much universally blamed on poor design. It's been my experience that poor design often gets blamed for mechanical failures resulting from premature wear due to poor maintenance and/or abuse. Typically, these guns were stuck in a saddle scabbard, stood in a corner, or hung in a barn for months on end (sometimes years) with a fully-loaded magazine. When it was used, only two or three shots were fired. Maybe it got cleaned, and maybe it didn't. Could there be a connection between that and the fact that most feeding problems occur after the first two or three rounds are fired? Magazine springs go "soft" after being compressed for extended periods of time. Typically, any tube magazine gun, old or new, with a weak spring does okay on very slow cycling, but not on fast cycling. A contributing factor to slow feeding is often not keeping the inside of the magazine tube clean and shiny. Black powder residue has always been notorious for hanging up anything that moves in a gun. Are the inevitable feeding problems in a gun with a poorly-maintained, dirty, gritty, and/or corroded magazine tube and a spring weak from abuse an indication of inherent design flaws?

Another feeding problem blamed on poor design concerns the carrier. Once the Lightning forearm moves the bolt a fraction of an inch on the forward stroke, the carrier is not physically restrained. On slow cycling, the carrier often drops before the bolt can "catch"

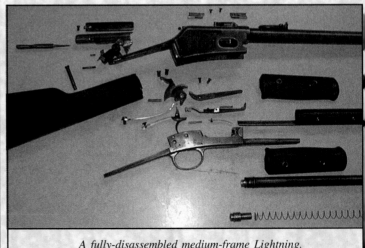

A fully-disassembled medium-frame Lightning.

the cartridge and is usually assumed to be a design flaw. Few seem to be aware that the carrier is not supposed to drop on its own when the bolt is moved forward. There is a quarter-inch square friction pad on the outside of each arm of the carrier. They are to be "sprung" against the inside of the frame just enough to keep the carrier in a raised position under the full weight of a cartridge. If the arm tension is not adequate and the magazine lever is working correctly, the next cartridge in the magazine remains in front of the magazine stop and you simply try to catch the "dropped" cartridge with a faster forward stroke on the next cycle. If the magazine lever gets hung up with black powder residue (or is otherwise faulty), the rim of the next cartridge can move past the magazine stop. It rests against the nose of the cartridge already on the carrier so the rim of this cartridge is clear of the magazine tube. Opening the action raises the loaded carrier, the "loose" cartridge in the magazine is shoved under it and behind the loading gate, and the action is hopelessly jammed open. The shooter, while removing everything through the front of the magazine, usually blames the problem on poor design. Moving the bolt forward simultaneously pushes the cartridge from the carrier into the chamber as it pushes the empty carrier down. As the bolt shuts and the slide "clicks" locked at the end of the forward stroke, the magazine stop at the front of the magazine lever is lowered, and the magazine spring pushes the rim of a new cartridge back against the extension on the bottom front of the bolt. Firing the gun or manually lowering the hammer raises the rear of the magazine lever to unlock the slide. Pulling the slide rearward raises the bolt lock and moves the bolt to the rear pulling the empty casing (or unfired cartridge) from the chamber. The next cartridge is simultaneously pushed onto the carrier by the magazine spring as the bolt moves rearward and ejects the empty casing (or cartridge). As the bolt reaches maximum rearward movement, it raises the carrier placing the next cartridge in a position to be pushed into the chamber by the bolt on the forward stroke of the slide. Should the slide not be moved all the way forward, the bolt cannot lock shut, and therefore the magazine stop on the front of the magazine lever is not lowered and the next cartridge is not released. The gun cannot be fired or the hammer lowered because the rear of the magazine lever is positioned as to block the fully-cocked hammer from being released when the trigger is pulled. This is an intricate, but not complicated, chain of events. Each piece, however, must be of correct form and dimension in order for the timing to be exact.

Again, the Lightning innards are not any different than of the venerable old SAA. One single part often causes a serious jam. It's usually the smallest and simplest piece in the entire gun, such as the 3/16 of an inch in diameter, 1/4 of an inch long pin that retains the firing pin retracting lever in its slot in the bottom of the bolt and is visible when the action is fully open. Should this tiny pin become even a little loose and get jarred out of its hole even a few thousandths of an inch in either direction while the action is open, the gun will be solidly locked open until the pin is returned to its proper position. Have you ever seen an SAA base (cylinder) pin fly out when that one little screw (or the cross-bolt) holding it in the gun came loose? Few people are aware of

1-open...2-stop...3-close...4-fire... Maintaining that cadence under stress isn't easy.

this happening in the Lightning, but many are aware of the same problem occurring in the SAA. So, which one has the design flaw?

The Lightning was never designed to work as fast as the reflexes of a shooter, but the Lightning was designed to work faster than any other repeating rifle on the market at the time. I don't recommend it, but if all you want to do is to send a lot of lead downrange and put on a spectacular show, just position yourself like you would normally shoot it. Then you can sort of crouch forward a little, place the butt of the rifle against the front your hip, hold the trigger back, and jack the slide back and forth with hard, full strokes. The gun fires every time the slide hits the forward end of every stroke. It's called "slam firing." You'd be lucky to hit the side of a barn at 20 feet this way, but it's a sure-fire (no pun intended) way to get everybody's attention, make a lot of noise and smoke in a hurry, and get your adrenaline pumping. It is not proper for SASS competition, and it's really hard on a nice old gun.

The fastest way I've found to safely and consistently shoot the Lightning without abusing the gun is to cycle it in a solid firm manner with a hard stop at each end of the stroke and a slight hesitation between the two. Do it in a smooth and deliberate 1-2-3-4 cadence (open...stop...close...fire) at roughly 1/2 of a second for each of the four actions. That's two seconds per round, or a very respectable 20 seconds for 10 shots. Whether or not you hit the target is a totally unrelated issue. There is a major problem that seems to mysteriously occur only during competition. That smooth disciplined cadence that works so well in practice often falls completely apart under the influence of adrenaline. I've brought up "in its original state" a number of times for a definite purpose. Some things can be done to modify the gun for speed, but they're not the sort of thing that the average shooter would want to attempt at home since most require a good machine shop. Even then the gain is minimal, and I'm not convinced it's worth the effort and expense involved.

Most seem to forget (or choose to ignore) the fact that between 1858 and 1894 Winchester came out with eight similar looking, but internally different, lever-action gun models, each of which was another step in a 36-year-long evolutionary process of improving its strength and reliability. Colt's Lightning was never allowed to evolve beyond its one and only introductory model, so we may never know what its full potential might have been. Even so, a Winchester can still "mess up" and a Lightning is still a neat gun to shoot. So, if you shoot for nostalgia, authenticity, style, show, or just want to be different, a Colt Lightning with black powder is hard to beat. If your mission in life is to knock off a top speed shooter, I'd have to recommend something else. Keep in mind, though, that the new Lightning replicas are only just entering the market. They've never really been put to the test yet, so it remains to be seen just how they'll perform, but let's give 'em a chance. It's pretty certain, though, that one of the following two scenarios will take place. They'll either promote the creation of a whole new pump-action rifle performance knowledge base to give the Lightning a whole new lease on life, or they'll prove that the Lightning really was just an interesting novelty that seemed like a pretty good idea at the time. Dag-nab-it, it still seems like a pretty good idea to me.

In 1866, the U.S. Military introduced a new .50 caliber centerfire cartridge that represented the latest developments in self-contained metallic cartridges. By the end of the war between the states, a foregone conclusion was that muzzleloading rifles were obsolete and a hindrance on the battlefield. The progression of the development of breech loading rifles before and during the war ensured that the replacement for the 1863 Springfield rifled musket would be a breech loader using self-contained metal cartridges. Percussion breech loaders such as Sharps, Smith, and Burnside established the breech loader as a powerful and reliable weapon. Metal cartridge-firing repeating rifles, like the Henry and Spencer, further proved the viability of the breech loader, even though the fire power of these repeaters was largely deemed by the military to be a waste of ammunition. Rimfire cartridges of the day, including those as large as .56 caliber, were lethal, but lacked the stopping power needed for battle beyond short range. What was needed was a cartridge that would exceed the ballistics of the .58 caliber rifled musket, packaged into a compact metal case.

The Great Conversion

An intermediary solution was a short .58 caliber rimfire cartridge used in the 1865 1st Allin Conversion. 1863 Springfield muskets were converted to breech loaders by milling out the top half of the barrel ahead of the breech plug, cutting a chamber, and adding a hinged breech block. This was how the first "Trapdoor" Springfield was created. The concept of a central fire, or centerfire as we now call it, had originated with the Maynard carbine wherein the brass cartridge, although ignited by a percussion cap, had a single center flash hole. All of these developments came together in 1866 when the .50 U.S. Government cartridge, or .50-70, was adopted by the military. The first rifle to be chambered for this new powerful cartridge was the 1866 Springfield, which became known as the 2nd Allin Conversion. The 1866 model was converted from the 1863 musket in the same manner as was the 1865, but it was improved with a centerfire breech block and had the .58 caliber barrel relined to .50 caliber.

The second arm to be converted to accept the .50 caliber cartridge was the 1863 Sharps percussion breech loader. The Sharps Rifle Manufacturing Company received a contract on October 26, 1867 to convert the abundant surplus of carbines left over from the Civil War. The Sharps conversion consisted of relining the .52 cal. barrel to .50 cal. and modifying or replacing the breech block and hammer, as well as other less significant changes. Interestingly enough, if the existing .52 caliber barrels were found to be in good repair and not oversized, they were left "as is" to fire the .50 caliber cartridge in a .52 cal. barrel. Accuracy certainly suffered, but was considered "good 'nuff for government work" back then.

By 1868 and 1869, most of the suitable surplus Civil War arms remaining in the arsenals had been converted to .50-70. In the case of

THE .50-70 GOVERNMENT: AMERICA'S FIRST BIG-BORE CENTERFIRE

By: Kenny Durham,
aka KID Durham

Four rifles chambered for the .50-70 Govt. (top to bottom): 1866 Springfield 2nd Allin Conversion, Remington No. 1 Sporting Rifle (1872), 1885 Winchester, and 1863 Sharps Conversion.

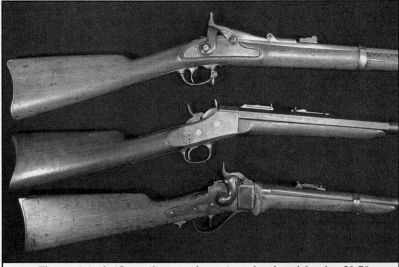

Three original rifles, military and sporting, chambered for the .50-70.

which was followed with a shortened action both in rifle and in the first Trapdoor carbine version in 1870.

From 1866 until 1873, when the Army adopted the .45-70, the .50-70 was the official U.S. Service cartridge. Remington introduced its famous "Rolling Block" around 1867-1868 as the No. 1 Military rifle and carbine-chambered for the .50-70. The U.S. Army showed little interest in the Rolling Block, choosing to devote resources to the Trapdoor models. However, the U.S. Navy and Marines recognized the value of Remington's rifle when combined with the power of the .50-70. So did the New York State Militia, which procured an altered version of the No.1 Military rifle and carbine in .50-70. Even when the U.S. switched to the .45-70 in 1873, New York State choose to keep their .50s in service and did not switch arms until the 1890's when the .30 U.S. Army (.30-40 Krag) was introduced.

Sharps' rifles, the company and private gunsmiths converted civilian-owned percussion Sharps to .50-70, and later to other calibers. In the movie *Quigley Down Under*, Matthew Quigley explains to Marsden that his Sharps has been "converted" to shoot a special metal cartridge. Although fiction, the movie and the rifle are true to history; Quigley's rifle began life as a military percussion breech loader.

New Military Rifle Models for the .50-70

The introduction of newly-made rifle models, both for the military and sporting, established the .50-70 as the standard. For the military, the 1868 Springfield "Trapdoor" was introduced as a new model having a one-piece receiver and breech block into which the barrel was threaded. Surplus 1863 locks, stocks, and a mix of existing and new barrels were utilized from the supply of Civil War muskets in building the 1868 model. In 1869, the Springfield Armory introduced a "Cadet" rifle,

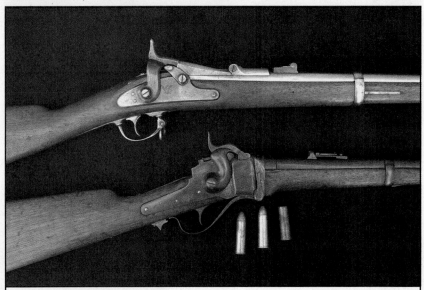

A Civil War rifle and carbine converted to shoot the .50 U.S. Govt. (.50-70).

Sporting Rifles Chambered for the .50-70

The .50-70, great-grandfather of the .30-06, quickly became popular with big game and buffalo hunters.

The Sharps "New Model 1869" and the Remington No.1 Sporting Rifle were the first rifles offered to the general public chambered for the .50-70. In 1872, General George Custer ordered a No.1 Sporting rifle from Remington in .50 caliber, and reported to Remington his extreme satisfaction with the performance of the rifle and the power of the .50-70 cartridge in a letter dated October 5, 1873. In 1872, Sharps introduced a longer version of the .50 caliber cartridge by extending the case length from 1-3/4 inches to 2 inches, allowing the loading of a 500-grain bullet. Also, in 1872, Sharps introduced the "Big 50," which had a case length of 2-1/2 inches. Soon, both Remington and Sharps added many other cartridges in a variety of calibers to their line. But the .50-70, due to its military genesis, remained popular because of the availability of ammunition and on its own merits

1863 Springfield musket converted into the Model 1866 by modifying and fitting the breech with a hinged breech block and relining the .58 caliber barrel to .50 caliber.

1863 Sharps breech-loading percussion carbine converted to fire the .50-70 cartridge. (Carbine courtesy of Bob Benbough.)

were executed. *The average distance at which the 41 antelopes were killed was 250 yards by actual measurement. I rarely obtained a shot at an antelope under 150 yards, while the range extended from that distance up to 630 yards."*

Now, I dare say that General Custer, in all his glory, probably did not get his 630-yard antelope on the first shot, and I rather suspect that more than one of the prairie chickens that the General ground-sluiced may have exploded in a ball of feathers! But surely, the lethality of the .50-70 can't be questioned. The "knockdown" power of a .50 caliber bullet versus the same weight in .45 caliber is substantially more. The ballistically superior .45 (given the same weight) will tend to pass through an animal, leaving it standing in many cases. The "50s" had the reputation of "kicking the slats" from under anything they hit. Such is the case in the photo of Butch Ulsher and Dick Hansen with the buffalo shot with Dick's .50-70 Highwall. One shot from the .50-70

as an efficient cartridge.

The standard loading for the .50-70 was 70 grains of black powder and a 425-gr. bullet; powerful medicine for 1866, and still no slouch today. At first glance, especially when compared to the .45-70, the .50-70 looks fat and stubby and is good for only about 100 yards or so. But don't let looks fool you. Below is an excerpt from the aforementioned letter from General Custer reporting to Remington on his Yellowstone expedition:

"During the three months I carried the rifle referred to on every occasion and the following list exhibits but a portion of the game killed by me: Antelope 41; buffalo 4; elk 4; blacktail deer 4; American deer 3; white wolf 2; geese, prairie chickens, and other feathered game in large numbers. The number of animals killed is not so remarkable as the distance at which the shots

Remington No. 1 Military rifles and carbines in .50-70 saw service with the U.S. Navy, Marines, and the New York State Militia.

dropped the buffalo in its tracks.

Shooting the .50-70 Today

As with other cartridges that were once considered obsolete, the .50-70 is being rediscovered, too. The .50-70, because of the low ballistic coefficient of the 425-gr. bullet, is not the best choice for competing in Black Powder Cartridge Rifle Silhouette matches or target matches. However, a few shooters have ignored these limitations and shoot .50-70s anyway. Why shoot a .50-70 today when there are so many other cartridges? Because it's a great cartridge for hunting and it is just plain fun to shoot! Rifles in .50-70 are harder to find than are .45 caliber chamberings, but Shiloh Rifle Manufacturing, Ballard Rifle Company, and C Sharps Arms all list the .50-70 as one of their standard chamberings. Also, many Springfield Models

Remington No. 1 Sporting rifle .50-70 in original condition. (Rifle courtesy of Lannie Moody.)

Loading the .50-70
Dies, Bullets, and Powder

As with rifles chambered for the .50-70, loading components are hard to find, but easy to obtain. Lyman and RCBS make loading dies and bullet moulds for the .50-70. Cases are available from BELL, correctly head-stamped "50-70 Govt." BELL brass cases are excellent and, with proper care, should last indefinitely. My cases were obtained from Buffalo Arms Co. I also use a Lyman bullet mould #515141, which is a reproduction of the 425-gr. Government bullet. Lyman also makes a 500-grain round-nose, flat-point bullet (# 515142) suitable for the .50-70. RCBS offers a 450-gr. flat-point bullet (#50-450) designed for the .50 caliber lever-action cartridges that works good in the .50-70, too.

The *Lyman Cast Bullet Handbook* provides loading data for the .50-70, listing a variety of powders and Lyman bullets. Accurate Arms Co.,

1885 Winchester "Highwall" with Lyman scope used for testing smokeless and black powder ammunition. (Rifle courtesy of Dr. Richard Hansen.)

1866, 1868, 1869, and 1870 can still be found in excellent shootable condition. My 1866 2nd Allin Conversion is a prime example. I found it at a local gun shop in excellent condition. The bore is like new and it is as accurate as it was the day it left the armory. The same can be said for many Sharps conversions and Remington Military Rolling Blocks. However, prices of the once obsolete originals keep creeping higher and higher. Also, original sporting rifles, such as the Remington No.1 pictured, are still around. Incidentally, two big game animals fell to this particular rifle last year and a buffalo hunt is in the offing. Another option for getting a .50-70 is to have a rifle rebarreled, such as the case with the 1885 Winchester owned by Dick Hansen. The neat compact Highwall equipped with the old Lyman scope is a most formidable hunting rifle out to 200 yards.

Butch Ulsher and Dick Hansen with a buffalo taken with Dick's 1885 Winchester .50-70.

Inc. also provides loading data for the .50-70 using XMP 5744. The powders used in testing were Goex FFg black powder, Pyrodex RS, and Accurate Arms XMP 5744. My schedule unfortunately did not allow time for me to experiment with Hodgdon's new Triple 7 Propellant in FFg equivalent, but doing so is certainly in my future. Hodgdon provides loading guidelines for using Triple 7 in black powder cartridges. As always, black powder is my first choice and most often the best choice to use in these old cartridges. Concerning smokeless powder, Accurate Arms XMP 5744 is an obsolete black powder cartridge shooter's dream come true. XMP 5744 is unlike any other smokeless powder brand because it works great in the .50-70 and many other big-bore, large-capacity cartridges in which using smokeless powder is not recommended.

Loading and shooting an original .50-70 Sharps Carbine.

Author shooting his original 1866 Springfield .50-70 rifle.

black powder and Pyrodex loads only, a 0.030" Walter's Wads fiber wad was used between the powder and bullet. Next, the bullets were seated to the correct depth, and finally, all rounds were given a slight crimp to remove the belling of the case mouth.

At the Range

All four rifles shown in the photo were fired for testing. The Sharps carbine and the Remington Sporting rifle were fired with black powder loads only, using the Lyman 425-gr. bullet. In the 1866 Springfield, black powder and Pyrodex loads were fired using the Lyman 425-gr. bullet. The 1885 Winchester Highwall was used to test all smokeless powder loads and some of the leftover ammunition from the buffalo hunt. The Sharps carbine was fired from the kneeling position at a 100-yard distance, and a

Loading Procedures

When using new brass cases for the first time, as in this instance, the first step was to run them through the sizing die to ensure that they were fully-sized and round, especially in the mouth area. Next, the cases were primed and charged with powder. Using XMP 5744, each charge was weighed. However, with the Goex black powder and Pyrodex loads, the cases were charged from a Lyman 55 black powder measure through the 24" long drop tube supplied with the measure. The measure was set to dispense 65 grains of Goex FFg, which fills the case up to within 0.350" from the mouth. With this much powder, the charge must be compressed approximately 0.220" to allow the bullet to be seated to the correct (desired) depth. In this case, I used the neck-expanding die as a compression die. The same powder measure setting was used with the Pyrodex loads, with the volume being the same as the Goex charge. With the Goex

The .50-70 Govt. (left) and .45-70 Govt. (right) side by side along with their respective bullets.

ten-shot group produced a pattern of fairly evenly-distributed hits over an 11-inch area. Shooting from cross-sticks would no doubt tighten up the group. The Remington, fired from a bench rest, placed five shots into a 3-1/2" wide x 2" high group. This old rifle has a bore that has seen meticulous care over the years. The 1866 Springfield produced good results with the black powder loads, with a five-shot group size that measured 1" vertically, but strung out to 7" horizontally due to some stiff wind. However, the Pyrodex loads produced dismal results. Ten shots were fired at 100 yards, with only eight striking the target, resulting in a group 16" wide x 7" high.

The smokeless powder loads in the Highwall produced excellent hunting-load accuracy, with group sizes running about two inches and under. All of the loads tested were based on the suggested minimum starting loads, as is prudent in any

Springfield 1866 Allin Conversion "Trapdoor" with the dies and components used for loading.

Bell .50-70 brass cases obtained from Buffalo Arms Co.	*Bullets cast from 30:1 (lead:tin): Lyman 425-gr., Lyman 500-gr., and RCBS 450-gr.*

loading situation, especially with vintage rifles. The hunting load that Dick Hansen has developed for his .50-70 Highwall is not only accurate, but a potent pill averaging 1312 fps with the 425-gr. bullet. There is no good reason to push the limits of

velocity and pressure in a vintage rifle. However, in a newly-manufactured rifle chambered for the .50-70, a hunting load in the range of 1300 to 1350 fps is easily achievable. This "grandpa" of a cartridge may be old, but it can pack a real wallop.

See ya at the range!

Load Data

Primer	Powder Charge (grains)	Bullet	Lube	Velocity
Federal 215	Goex FFg 65.0	425-gr. Lyman	SPG	1283
Federal 210	XMP 5744 27.0	425-gr. Lyman	Lyman BP Gold	1169
CCI 200	Pyrodex RS 65.0 (by volume)	425-gr. Lyman	SPG	1143
Federal 210	XMP 5744 25.2	450-gr. RCBS	Reliable #12	1151
Federal 210	XMP 5744 24.0	500-gr. Lyman	Lyman BP Gold	1145

New cases are full-length sized before loading to ensure uniformity.	*Depth gauge used to measure bullet-seating depth, thereby determining the minimum powder level in the case.*

Black powder charge, before (left) and after (right) being compressed (using the neck expanding die) to allow the desired depth for seating the bullet.

The bullets used, carrying a lot of lube, are well-suited for black powder shooting. Lyman Black Powder Gold, Reliable #12, and SPG all gave good results.

A 1-7/8 x 2-3/4 inch group was achieved with a Lyman 500-gr. bullet and XMP 5744.

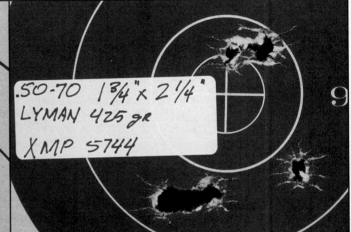

XMP 5744 and a Lyman 425-gr. bullet produced a 5-shot group that measured 1-3/4 x 2-1/4 inches.

Five-shot group from this 1866 Springfield is tight vertically, but spread out horizontally due to wind. The author couldn't resist trying to hit the X-ring with the last cartridge. Lucky?

The RCBS 450-gr. bullet and XMP 5744 powder produced an excellent group only measuring 1-1/8 x 1-7/8 inches center-to-center.

You know how every once and a while, after months and months of nosing around in old hardware stores, gun shops, antique shops, junk shops, and thrift stores (both around home and during every trip you take), you just "happen upon" a real gem? Well, a year or so ago it happened to me! Now, my interest in collecting leans toward U.S. military firearms, swords, knives, and accouterments, but within that field. I really enjoy Civil War (that's the War of Northern Aggression for you Johnnie Rebs) carbines.

So, there I was at a local gun show, wandering around and looking, when I stopped by a close personal friend's table. I stopped mostly just to chew the fat, because he usually doesn't have the kind of neat "stuff" that I am interested in, and when he does it's always "sky high" (I'm really going to get it when he reads this). As we chatted, I happened to glance down and there before my very eyes was the cutest little Civil War carbine you ever did see. Well, maybe cute isn't quite the right word, but it works for me. So, trying to act casual and only mildly interested

that for another story.

After I took my new "toy" home and fondled it a bit, two questions started to form in my mind. "Gee, this is really a neat little firearm, I'd like to find out more about its origins, I wonder how well it will shoot?" This is where those questions took me. From delving into a reprint of the *Baunerman Catalogue of Military Goods* (1927), a copy of *Civil War Guns* by William D. Edwards (1962), and the 8th edition of *Flayderman's Guide to Antique American Firearms and their Value* by Norm Flayderman (2001), I learned the following. My carbine was manufactured by Frank Wesson (yes, he later teamed up with a fellow named Smith) in Worchester, Massachusetts around 1863. It weighs just under six pounds and has a rather unique two-trigger mechanism, with the front "trigger" being the release switch which allows the barrel to tip forward exposing the breech for loading. The octagonal barrel, chambered for the caliber .44 Long Rimfire cartridge, is 24 inches long with a five-land and

A Minor Love Affair with a

By: Bob Benbough, aka Not So Bad Bob

This left-side view of the Wesson action shows the forward "trigger" release mechanism and sling swivel. Even the military carbines had swivels rather than a sling ring.

Frank Wesson Carbine

(which is hard when your heart is pumping fast), I asked, "Hmm, whatcha got there?" He responded, "It's a Wesson Carbine. It belonged to my Dad." After a little more palaver, we got down to the asking price. That is when I knew it was not meant to be; then again, since I'm telling you about the Wesson Carbine, you've probably figured out "the rest of the story." Anyway, we dickered and haggled and I told him about every nick, ding, and rusty spot, while he told me how rare the gun was and how much his dad cherished it. I have to say, we both had a lot of fun over this one, and finally agreed on a price. Naturally, along with the green stuff that changed hands, there were also numerous promises, conditions, and requirements included, but I'll leave

five-groove rifling. This example is a military carbine and has a German silver blade front sight and three-position folding leaf rear sight marked for 100, 200, and 300 yards. Wesson must have had a real hot shot in his marketing department because the .44 rimfire round in a 24-inch barrel is probably not much of a man-stopper at 300 yards. I did, however, find the carbine to be remarkably accurate at 50 yards (but I'll tell you more on that later).

My carbine is of the early First Model, with a rounded-iron frame and forend all forged into one piece. Since it has no extractor, the shooter must extract the spent cartridges using his/her fingers to grip the exposed rim (the breech of the barrel being recessed on each side). Often times, according to my

The Wesson carbine is so lightweight that it handles like a toy. It was reported to have been a favorite of the Indians.

resources, a ramrod also comes in handy, although I haven't had any problems with case extraction. About 4,500 of the military carbine versions were made during the Civil War. One hundred fifty-one were purchased under federal authority shortly after the battle of Gettysburg (early July, 1863) for the state of Ohio, and over 2,000 were supplied to state units from Indiana, Kentucky, Kansas, and Missouri. Wesson rifles continued to be made up until 1888, with total quantities of all types estimated at over 35,000. When I first started researching the ammunition for the Wesson, I thought it was chambered for the .44 flat cartridge (same as was used in the Henry rifle). However, after trying an original round in my carbine (it didn't fit), I discovered that I had more to learn! After checking Frank Barnes' *Cartridges of the World*, I discovered that the round I was looking for was the .44 Long rimfire, which came out around 1860. A number of different rifles, including the Allen & Wheelock, Ballard, Howard, Remington, Robinson, and Wesson, were chambered in this fairly popular round. It was originally loaded with a 220-grain cast bullet and 28 grains of black powder. Barnes claims the .44 Long was a fairly potent short-range cartridge for small to medium game, but was rapidly replaced by the .44-40 WCF after it was introduced in 1873.

The rear sight is a fairly standard three-position folding leaf.

My next question was, "Where in the heck am I going to find brass for this little beauty?" After asking a number of shooting buddies about where to find brass, one of them came up with the answer to my dilemma. While thumbing through a *Dixie* catalog, he found that *Dixie* sold lathe-turned cases for the .44 Long that used .22 blanks inserted into an offset hole in the cartridge base as the primer. My buddy, who felt he needed to return a small favor, sent off for six cases (they're not cheap, my friends), and in short order, I was ready to test fire my baby. I went to my local reloading supply store and picked up a box of .22 rimfire blanks (yeah, I paid for them), and then came back home and started rummaging through all my "stuff" looking for appropriate bullets. First I tried a .44 soft-cast round ball (out of my old muzzleloading stuff) with 27.0 grains of Swiss 1-1/2 and a CCI .22 blank for a primer. I loaded up my six trusty rounds and headed out to the range, threw an aluminum pop can out about 40 paces and took aim offhand, and danged if I didn't hit it! I was impressed. A couple of friends that were with me tried and received the same results. Now, we were ALL impressed. With this for a start, I could hardly wait to see what the gun might do with real bullets.

Now, back to the reloading bench. Another buddy had some cast semi wad cutters for a .41 Magnum that we thought might work. These bullets came out of the mold at about 215 grains, .413 inches in diameter, and looked like they'd really work well. Now, you can imagine how much fun I had digging through all my reloading stuff to find some tools to load a .44 caliber rimfire cartridge. I ended up using a Lyman 310 tool with a .45-70 priming die to seat the blanks in the rear of the case. Then, after experimenting a bit, I loaded 22.0 grains of Goex FFFg powder through a 24-inch drop tube. Next, I put a .030-inch .40 caliber over-powder wad on top of the powder, seated the bullet with about .055 inches of compression using a .45 ACP seating die, and finally put a taper crimp on the case neck with a .303 British seating die. I know it

The bottom of .22 rimfire blanks used to replace the original internal rimfire priming.

Left to right: an original .44 Henry Flat, a modern .44 Long rimfire with round ball projectile, a .41 caliber 215-grain semi-wad cutter, and for comparison reasons only, an original .44 Extra Long rimfire made for the Ballard rifle.

With the barrel tipped forward ready to load, one can note the slight relieved area on the side of the barrel breech to facilitate finger extraction of the spent cartridge case.

sounds weird, but it worked.

Now I was back to the range with my new loads (four rounds, because I had to keep two for photos) to see how well I could do. After putting a target up at 50 yards, I fired one round off the bench, which impacted about eight inches above and an inch to the right of my point of aim. So, I lowered my point of aim about five inches below the black and fired my three remaining rounds. Now, I know this isn't a gun that's going to win any bench rest matches, but for a 139 year-old lightweight carbine using cobbled-up ammo, I was really pleased with a 1-inch group. All of this took a bit of time, but I feel it was time well spent since I now have a much better feel, from actual experience, for what the capabilities are of a weapon that played a role in the war that reunified our country.

By the way, you can bet I'll be looking at other gun shows coming up for another bit of history waiting to be fondled, acquired, researched, and, of course, shot!

Author's four rounds of .44 rimfire shot at 50 yards from the Frank Wesson.

Colt's Cap-n-Ball Revolvers

By: Mike Beliveau, aka Bottom Dealin' Mike

"**A**be Lincoln made men free, but Sam Colt made them equal." There's more than a grain of truth in that old saying. Sam Colt changed the world. Not only did he revolutionize the concept of personal firepower, he also revolutionized the concept of factory production. In England, people were just as interested in Colt's "American system" of production as they were in the guns themselves.

That's quite a legacy for a man whose first company failed, and who was very likely to have ended up as just a footnote in history. If it hadn't been for a combination of lucky breaks, Sam Colt would have ended his life as an obscurity instead of as the most famous gun maker in the world.

Colt's first company was the Patent Arms Manufacturing Company in Paterson, New Jersey.

Colt patented a design for a revolving cylinder that was indexed into alignment with the barrel by a ratchet and was locked into alignment by a bolt. According to legend, Colt's inspiration for this design was a similar arrangement used on a ship's windlass that he'd observed as a midshipman on the brig *Corvo*.

Colt opened the Patent Arms Manufacturing Company in 1836. However, the Paterson Colts didn't sell well. The United States was experiencing a prolonged period of peace that dampened the Army's need for weapons. The Paterson plant was only open for six years, but it laid the ground work for the success that followed. Colt made three types of handguns and two revolving rifle models in the Paterson plant. The belt and holster models were made in .28 and .34 caliber, but the Paterson that ultimately set the stage for Colt's triumph was the holster model, also known as the #5 and the Texas Model.

This was a five-shot, .36 caliber revolver

The sleek 1851 Navy was Colt's second-best seller. It was the most popular Colt among civilians out West.

with a nine-inch barrel. It was a long, sleek pistol with flowing lines and an excellent balance. Like all Paterson Colts, it had no trigger guard. Instead, the trigger folded up into the frame. By cocking the hammer, the trigger would spring into place where it could be pulled to fire the gun. Like all the Colt cap-n-ball designs to follow, the Paterson was an open-top revolver. The barrel assembly was attached to the frame by a wedge that passed through a slot in the base pin, which is called an arbor on Colt cap-n-ball designs. The wedge and arbor assembly made it fairly easy to take the revolver apart for loading or cleaning, but it could be a liability as well.

This was proven when plainsman George Kendall was using a Paterson Colt to hunt buffalo from horseback. As he was galloping beside a big bull, he began firing his Colt into the animal. When Kendall cocked the hammer for his fourth shot, the entire barrel assembly fell off of the gun. He searched the ground and found the barrel, no worse for wear, and after a blacksmith fashioned a new wedge for him, the Paterson was as good as new. Unfortunately, he didn't have buffalo ribs for supper that night.

Despite the occasional embarrassing barrel auto-ejection, it was important that the gun could be taken apart easily since most Patersons had to be disassembled for loading. Of the 1,000 #5 Patersons that were made, only 300 were equipped with loading levers. An extra cylinder was usually sold with the revolver, and the common practice was to carry that spare cylinder fully-loaded so that it could be exchanged quickly when the first cylinder was empty.

General William S. Harney most emphatically stated his views on the necessity of this extra cylinder when he was second-in-command of the 2nd Dragoons during the Second Seminole War in 1836. He was issued 12 Paterson Colts as a trial by the Ordnance Board. Harney, who was later known among the Sioux as Big Chief Who Swears, issued very specific instructions to his troops. "No man can be such a (expletive) fool as not to see the importance of not losing this extra cylinder, for, if lost, you will have only five shots, and when they are gone you will be at the mercy of your enemy. And, if you have lost it, I hope to God he'll kill you. And if he don't, by the (expletive string) I will. The very first one that is lost, the (expletive) idiot that lost it will wish all the (expletive) Indians in Florida had him instead of me."

The Army only purchased a few Patersons, but luckily the young Republic of Texas bought several hundred to equip their Navy. When the Navy was disbanded in 1843, those revolvers were passed on to the Texas Rangers. Nelson Lee, who was a Ranger in the 1840's, said the typical ranger outfit consisted of, "…two or three revolvers and a Bowie knife in his belt, and a short rifle on his arm." Lee served with Capt. John C. (Jack) Hayes in 1845 when they had their most famous fight with the Comanche at the confluence of the Guadeloupe River and Walker's Creek. He said of the battle, "They were 200 in number, and fought well and bravely, but our revolvers, fatal as they were astonishing, put them speedily to flight."

Though historians dispute the number of Comanche involved in the fight, there were a lot of them. And Jack Hayes whipped them soundly at a cost of three rangers killed and four wounded. If the rangers had been armed with single-shot weapons, it might

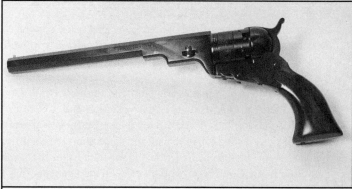

The five-shot, folding-trigger .36 caliber Paterson was the first Colt revolver. The company failed, but sales to Texas lead directly to Colt's future success.

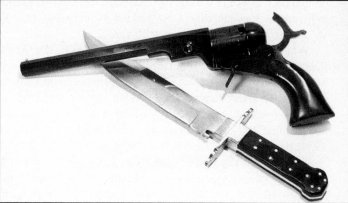

Texas Rangers were typically armed with Colt Paterson revolvers and a Bowie knife.

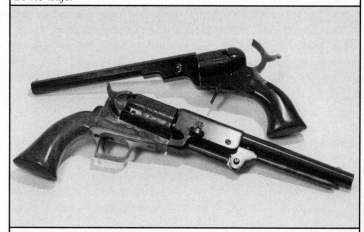

The big .44 caliber Walker at the bottom was designed to improve on weaknesses of the Paterson.

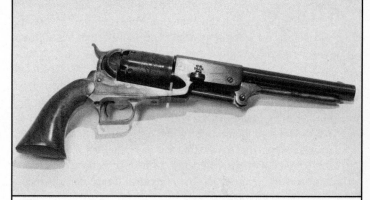

The massive Walker was the most powerful official-issue sidearm ever issued to the U.S. Army.

have been a massacre instead of a victory. That battle convinced Texans that Colt's revolvers were the guns to carry if you were going into harm's way, and that set the stage for Colt's return to the gun business.

Today, Paterson replicas are available through Dixie Gun Works. Pietta in Italy made my Dixie Paterson and it is a dead ringer for the original #5 holster revolver. Because it doesn't have a loading lever, I load it with the same short starter I use for one of my muzzleloading rifles. I've found that the same load I use in my Colt Navys works well with the Paterson; that's a 22-grain charge of FFFg under a .375 diameter round ball topped with my homemade black powder lube. I use Remington No. 10 caps to light the fuse. The Paterson balances very well, though the absence of a trigger guard seems to affect my ability to thumb-cock it smoothly in one-handed shooting, but it easily shoots two to three-inch groups at 15 yards.

When the Mexican War broke out in 1846, the Allen Pepperbox was the most popular personal weapon in the United States. Unlike the Colt design, Allen Pepperboxes didn't have a cylinder and fixed barrel. They had six barrels, all of which rotated around a basepin in double-action mode. For "up close and personal" self-defense these were good tools, but they weren't viable battle weapons.

When the Texas Ranger companies mobilized for the war they wanted revolvers, and the revolvers they wanted were Colts. Almost overnight, the value of used Paterson Colts shot up to $140, and buyers were waiting in line to get them. So, Texas Ranger Captain Sam Walker headed east on a dual mission. First, he had to convince the Army to buy Colt revolvers, and second, he had to convince Sam Colt to get back into the revolver business. Since Colt had to start production from scratch, Walker had some recommendations to improve the Paterson design. The result was the massive Walker Colt, which remains the most powerful, standard-issue sidearm ever adopted by the U.S. Army.

The Walker Colt was a huge weapon. It had a 9" barrel and a 2-7/16" long, six-shot cylinder. Unlike the Paterson, it was chambered for .44 caliber balls backed up by 60 grains of musket powder, making it as powerful as many rifles. Also, unlike the Paterson, it had a fixed trigger protected by a square-backed, brass trigger guard. All of the Walkers were equipped with a loading lever, even though it was the same weak design that first made its appearance on late Patersons.

After Sam Walker received his personal pair of revolvers, he declared that they were as effective as a rifle at 100 yards, and that they were superior to a musket at 200 yards. Of course, that was providing they didn't blow up. Walkers were really too powerful for the metallurgy of the time. Often, that big 60-grain powder charge was more than the iron cylinders could stand.

After the war, John Williamson wrote to the Ordnance Department, "Five companies of discharged Texas Rangers have turned in their arms …These men received less than a year ago 280 of Colt's Patent pistols of which 191 now resort to the U. States. The remainder chiefly bursted in their hands." Capt. Jack Hayes said that for the first few days, the new Colts his men used were continuously bursting. After a few days, the weaker guns were eliminated, and the guns that survived had a better chance of going the distance.

Colt reacted very quickly to the bursting problem. While the

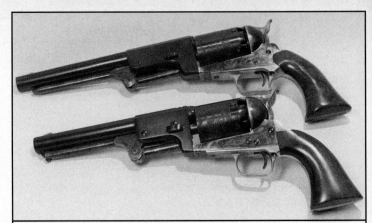
The Dragoon series, like the Third Model Dragoon (bottom), replaced the Walker (top). It was smaller overall than the Walker and held a slightly reduced powder charge.

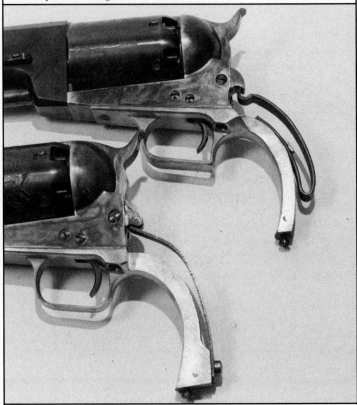
The Dragoon revolvers had a simple leaf mainspring that was more reliable than the V-shaped Walker spring.

All Colt cap-n-ball revolvers are held together by a wedge that passes through the barrel lug and the arbor.

war was in progress, he was already designing the Dragoon series of revolvers. These were to replace the Walkers as the Army's fighting .44 for the next 13 years. Ultimately, there were three Dragoon models. Each model had additional refinements, but they all shared a common basic design. The .44 caliber ball of the Walker was retained, but the cylinder length was reduced, which effectively lowered the maximum powder charge from 60 grains to 50 grains. And, where the Walker cylinders had been made from iron, the Dragoon cylinders were made from low-carbon steel imported from England. Those two changes ended the bursting problem.

The Dragoon's barrel was shortened to 7-1/2 inches, and the weak "T" spring-loading lever catch was abandoned in favor of a spring-loaded catch at the end of the lever. The Dragoon series also abandoned the V-shaped mainspring used in both the Paterson and the Walker in favor of a flat-leaf spring. There were other minor changes during the long production run of the Dragoon series. From 1850 until 1860, the Army bought 1,000 Dragoons every year from Colt, providing a revenue stream that he could rely on as he expanded the company.

Today, only Uberti manufactures replicas of these big-bore blasters, but that wasn't always the case. The now defunct Italian firm of Armi San Marcos made my personal Walker and Third Model Dragoon replicas. They are beautiful guns. The color-case hardening is much richer than I find on the current crop of replicas, and the walnut grips are finely figured.

When I first started shooting my Walker, I used the maximum 60-grain powder charge of FFFg powder. Shooting that load is a pure thrill, but it is very hard on the gun. I battered the wedge of my Walker to the point where it was worthless in less than 50 rounds of full-house loads. Since then, I've standardized on a load of 40 grains of FFg black powder under a .454 diameter round ball for both the Walker and the Dragoon. With this load, both of the big horse pistols can turn in three-inch groups at 15 yards. Both guns hit about a foot high at that range because the sights were calibrated for 100-yard targets. That's not too surprising when you consider that the troops using them expected these handguns to be their primary battle weapons.

After Sam Colt cemented his military sales base with the Dragoon revolvers, he turned to the civilian arena. In 1848, he entered the sub-caliber personal protection market with a short-barreled, five-shot, .31 caliber revolver that came to be called the Baby Dragoon. It was available in three, four, five, or six-inch barrel lengths, and it had no loading lever.

The Baby Dragoon was quickly replaced in the Colt lineup by the all-time best seller among Colt cap-n-ball handguns, the 1849 Colt Pocket Model. The Pocket Model actually appeared in 1850, and it remained in the Colt lineup until 1873. In all, over 325,000 Pocket Models were sold.

My friend Jay Harrell, aka Roughshod, owns a beautiful nickel-plated Pocket Model that is as tight and accurate today as it was the day it left the Colt factory in the mid-1850's. When you handle it, you can see why it was such a big seller. It's light, well-balanced, and small enough to slip easily into your waistband or jacket pocket. This gun was as popular in towns and cities as it was in the gold fields and on the plains.

1850 was a prolific year for Sam Colt. He refined the Dragoon to its final form, and he issued the best-selling revolver in cap-

Colt loading-lever latches evolved from the T-spring catch of the Walker (bottom), through a shallow notch on the Dragoons (top left), and eventually to the deep notch and strong spring on the 1860 Army (top right).

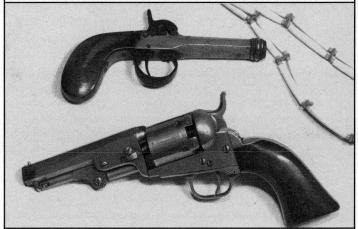

The five-shot 1849 Pocket Pistol was the best-selling cap-n-ball Colt. This nickeled revolver left the Hartford plant in the mid-1850's.

Before the Colt Pocket Model, most concealable pistols were single-shot affairs, like the pistol pictured at the top.

In an effort to get a more powerful hideout gun, many people created Avenging Angels by cutting down full-size revolvers like the .44 caliber 1860 Army at the top.

n-ball history. Then, to top it off, he released the best-known, and perhaps best-loved, cap-n-ball revolver of all time, the Colt 1851 Navy.

This was the sixgun favored by most serious pistoleros of the mid-19th century. Colt's Navy revolver was a six-shot pistol with a 7-1/2 inch octagon barrel that was equipped with a loading lever. The barrel and cylinder were blued steel, the frame was color-case hardened steel, and the trigger guard and back strap were brass. Over the 23 years of its production, the trigger guard went from a square-backed design to the more conventional rounded shape.

The 1851 Navy model was the second best-selling cap-n-ball sixgun in the Colt line. The Hartford plant produced 215,348 Navys by 1873, and another 42,000 were made in London, where the Colt Navy was the first official revolver of the British Army. Unlike the .31 caliber Pocket pistol, the .36 caliber six-shot Navy was considered powerful enough for serious use as a primary fighting weapon. In 1855, the U.S. Army bought 2,150 Colt Navys to supplement the Dragoon revolvers in the mounted service, and the cavalry units put them to good use.

In 1857, Lt. John Hood of the 2nd cavalry was on patrol in southwest Texas. Most of his men were armed with one Navy revolver and a single-shot carbine, but Hood himself was carrying a double-barreled shotgun loaded with buckshot, and a pair of Colt Navys. He needed them when his patrol cut the trail of a Comanche war party. Hood charged his troop straight into the Comanche, fighting them up close and personal, "until all the shots of my [men's] rifles and six shooters were exhausted …if I had had two sixshooters to a man, I would have wounded near all of them."

Because of its light weight and excellent balance, the Colt Navy was a favorite on the civilian market as well. Wild Bill Hickok is possibly the most famous user of the Colt Navy, but he wasn't alone. It was also a big favorite in the west. The famous mountain man and entrepreneur, Uncle Dick Wooten, owned a freight company hauling goods between St. Louis and Santa Fe during the 1850's. He equipped all of his drivers with a single-shot rifle and a pair of Colt Navys, and they used them to good effect during Indian attacks.

Despite service like that, there was a lively debate between the relative merits of the Colt Dragoon and the lighter Navy. Capt. Randolph Marcy summed up the opinion of many cavalry officers. "The Navy pistol, being more light and portable, is more convenient for the belt, but it is very questionable in my mind whether these qualities counterbalance the advantages derived from the greater weight of powder and lead that can be fired from the larger pistol."

In 1860, Colt addressed that concern by making the revolver that many experts consider to be the pinnacle of cap-n-ball design, the 1860 Army model. This .44 caliber six-shooter replaced the Dragoon as the official service revolver, and it became the most-used revolver of the Civil War.

Essentially, the 1860 Army was the marriage of the Dragoon's power with the Navy's balance and light weight. It was a .44 caliber six-shooter built on the .36 caliber Navy frame. Earlier attempts to make a lightweight .44 had centered on efforts to shave metal off the Dragoon revolvers by the fluting cylinders and barrels. The results were ill-balanced, so the attempts were

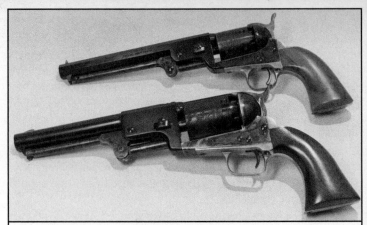
The 1851 Colt Navy (top) and the Third Model Dragoon (bottom) both appeared in 1850.

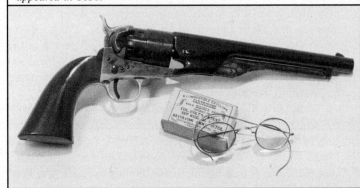
The 1860 Army is considered by some experts to be the best-designed cap-n-ball sixgun ever made.

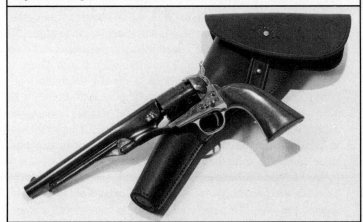
Among Union troops, the 1860 Army was the most-carried revolver of the Civil War.

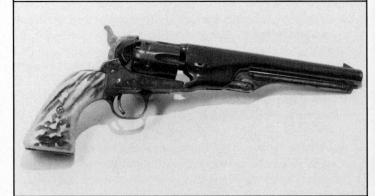
The 1861 Navy was Colt's attempt to modernize the Navy revolver with design features developed for the 1860 Army. Unfortunately, it wasn't a commercial success.

abandoned.

In the late 1850's, advances in steel metallurgy allowed Colt designers to try another approach. They started with a Navy revolver and made the barrel and cylinder big enough to accept .44 caliber balls. They then developed a cylinder that was larger in the front to accommodate the ball, while retaining the same diameter at the rear as a standard Navy cylinder. The eight-inch .44 barrel was streamlined, and the loading lever operated on a rack-and-pinion design rather than a hinge. It was a beautiful pistol. The Colt designers put a longer grip on the Army model, thinking it would be required in order to control the .44 caliber recoil. But, because the frame was the same as a Colt Navy, the Navy grips would also fit the Army revolver, and vice versa. It was a popular modification at the time.

In 1861, Colt applied the streamlined Army barrel design to the .36 caliber Navy. The resulting revolver is considered to be the most graceful Colt cap-n-ball ever built. Unfortunately, it never really caught on with the public. In 12 years, only 38,843 were built. The 1860 Army remained the most popular western sidearm after the Civil War. Cartridge-firing long guns appeared quickly, but the cap-n-ball revolver remained preeminent until the 1870's.

Contrary to popular belief, cap-n-ball revolvers didn't just disappear in 1873 when Colt introduced the Single Action Army cartridge gun. The Army continued to buy and issue cap-n-ball revolvers well into the cartridge era. The last major procurement of model 1860 cap-n-ball revolvers by the Army was an order for 410 pistols placed in 1878, and the final Army order for cap-n-ball 1860s was for four guns in 1880.

In civilian hands, cap-n-ball revolvers continued to provide personal protection long after cartridge handguns became available. In 1878, during the Cheyenne uprising, a Kansas settler wrote that he and his wife forted up in their homestead to drive off a raiding party. "We opened fire on them. My wife with a one-shot gun and I with a cap-n-ball Colt Navy revolver …they immediately left us." Even though they hung on until the end of the 19th century, cap-n-ball revolvers gradually faded from the shooting scene until they came back with a vengeance as replicas in the second half of the 20th century.

I've been shooting replicas of cap-n-ball Colts since 1972. In those 30 years I've acquired replicas of most Colt cap-n-ball models. I'd be hard-pressed to pick a single favorite, but I'm very partial to the big Walker and Dragoons. I have a beautiful, delicately-carved, left-hand, half-flap holster for the Walker made by Jim Barnard of Trailrider Productions, and I have a border-tooled, civilian half-flap, right-hand holster for my Third Dragoon made by Dave Carrico of Carrico Leatherworks. So, I'm able to arm myself with a pair of big-bore blasters for matches, or just for knocking around.

I love those big guns, but as one Westerner said, "A Colt .44 [Dragoon] is a heavy-ish thing to carry around." Because of this, they don't get out as much as my Navies or my Armies. I also have Carrico, civilian half-flap holsters for the Navies and Armies, but I do like them for field use. They hold the gun securely, but they still allow you to get the gun out reasonably quick.

The cap-n-ball revolvers I use most often in matches are a pair of 1860 Armies made by Uberti and sold by Taylor's & Co.

The .44 caliber 1860 Army (bottom) is built on the same basic frame as the .36 Navy (top). The difference is that the front of the cylinder was slightly larger, which necessitated a step-cut in the frame's watertable.

The grip assembly on the 1860 Army is about a half-inch longer than the 1851 Navy to help manage the heavier recoil.

They hit at POA from 15 yards with 30-grain powder charges under Hornady round balls. They are fantastic pistols. For match use, I usually carry them in a set of studded Slim Jim holsters made by Circle Bar-T Leatherworks. They look great, which is half the fun at matches, and they have an authentic design.

For me, personally, I find the history of the West compelling, and Colt's cap-n-ball revolvers are interwoven throughout that history. I've only been able to skim the surface of the Colt cap-n-ball story in this article, but I hope it has kindled your interest in these fine revolvers.

At cowboy action matches, the author likes carrying his Army and Navy revolvers in his Circle Bar-T studded Slim Jim holsters.

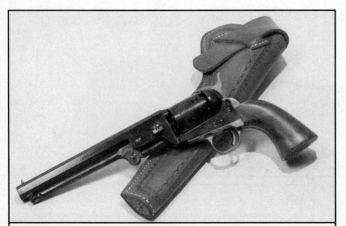

For field use, the author prefers the security of a civilian half-flap holster, like this one from Carrico Leatherworks.

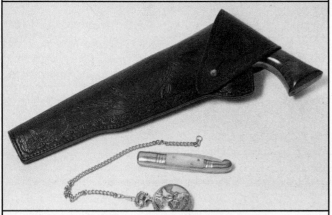

Trailrider's 1847 Walker holster is delicately-carved with a vine and leaf pattern.

Colt's fighting .44s: Walker (top), Third Dragoon (center), and the 1860 Army (bottom).

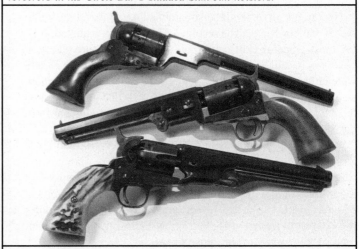

Colt's .36 holster pistols: Paterson (top), 1851 Navy (center), and 1861 Navy (bottom).

The author's son, Rob, takes aim...And fires!

The cap on the 1860 has just exploded.

GREAT SHOOTIN'

COWBOY COMBOS

FROM CIMARRON ARMS
By: Ray Walters, aka Smith n' Jones

When it comes to gun sets for CAS competition, there are usually two trains of thought that dictate what a cowboy carries around in his gun cart. Those two attitudes or philosophies seem to be either about being quick, fast, and smooth, or about nostalgia, looking good, and having fun. Not to say that the two ideas are mutually exclusive, but generally speaking, they don't seem to overlap very often.

As time has gone by and I have had the privilege to shoot literally dozens of different firearms that are suitable for CAS competition (many in SASS-sanctioned shoots), I find that I seem to be gravitating more towards two basic criteria when it comes to making up a set or combination of shootin' irons. The first is to have a rifle and two sixguns that are from, or represent, about the same historical period, and the second is that they be chambered for the same cartridge and that the cartridge is from the same period as the guns themselves.

Now, I know that to meet both of these criteria would be technically impossible, especially if you are considering a rifle of the 1860 Henry or 1866 Yellow Boy type, as these were normally chambered in the .44 Henry Flat rimfire cartridge that has not been commercially available for longer than most any of us have been alive. But, when looking through my rose-colored fantasy glasses, what really works are any of the pre-1890 cartridges, many of which are making strong comebacks thanks to CAS (Cowboy Action Shooting) and BPCRS (Black Powder Cartridge Rifle Silhouette) competitions, in era-correct handguns and rifles like the Henry, the 1866, and the 1873 Winchesters. Now, don't get me wrong. I am not criticizing the '92s, the Marlins, or the '94 Winchesters; it's just that there seems to be something a little mystical and magical about the older-style Winchesters and cartridges, especially when shooting in the black powder categories.

Black Powder. Just the words seem to draw you back to a historical perspective that, while it is in large part fantasy, also has a strong connection to America's shooting roots. There is something about the deep, hollow "ka thump" of a big bore levergun shooting a case full of charcoal that just seems to sound right. Call it living a dream, a fantasy, or whatever you wish, but it is more about shooting in the Old West than any slicked-up .38 "go-fast" sixgun spitting out 100-grain pellets at 400 feet-per-second. Lightning fast? Not likely. Clean and neat? Not hardly. Fun and exciting? In spades!

Now, since I started shooting Frontier Cartridge about a year ago, I have shot only one match with smokeless, and that was one of our local club shoots which sneaked up on me and I found myself without enough pistol, rifle, and shotgun ammo in black powder to participate. Other than that one digression, I have stayed with the smoky stuff and have not regretted it a bit.

Part of my job at **SHOOT! MAGAZINE** is to test not only guns, but ammo, bullets, primers, and powders of all shapes, sizes, and configurations as well. And, I must admit, I find myself really appreciating the user-friendly qualities of many of

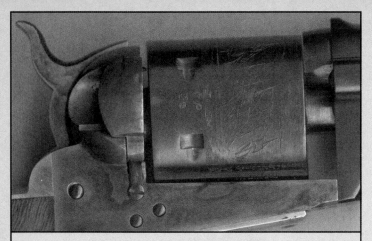

Cimarron's 1872 .44 Colt Open-Top.

Smith n' Jones blasting away with his Cimarron 1860 .44 Colt Conversions.

Three .44s (left to right): .44 Colt, .44 Russian, and .44 four-in-one.

Cimarron's Cowboy Combos: 1866 Yellow Boy, two 1872 Open-Tops, and a pair of 1860 Army Conversions, all shooting the .44 Colt.

the black powder substitutes. I try to bring information to our readers about the various powders that can be used to replace black powder that might convince those who think that black powder is too dirty, messy, or hard to clean up after to give it a try. Many of the new replacements do eliminate or minimize many of the areas of complaints, and that helps encourage shooters to try making "smoke" when they may not do so otherwise.

Having said all of that, I want to tell you about a couple of sets of cowboy guns, actually, two pairs of sixguns and one rifle, that I have had the privilege to test, and which I believe fit just about perfectly into the criteria outlined above. The guns are a pair of Cimarron 7-1/2" 1860 Army Conversions, a pair of Cimarron M-1872 Open-Tops, and a Cimarron M-1866 "Yellow Boy" short rifle, all chambered in .44 caliber. (Actually, we ordered two of the '66s, one for me and one for Chucky, as we both love .44 caliber firearms). All four pistols are .44 Colt caliber and the rifle is .44 Special. What is great about this particular rifle is that it feeds and shoots .44 Colt ammo just as if it was designed to do so.

The accumulation of these guns has happened over a rather extended period of time. The conversions were sent to the office in September of 2001, while the Open-Tops showed up right after Shot Show 2002, and the rifle not long after that. Harvey Lane of Cimarron Arms has been very patient about letting us hold on to this cluster of firearms due to the fact that I let him know that I was wanting to do a series of articles on cowboy-friendly gun combinations. The guns themselves were all shot when they first arrived, and then as sets at regular match-type stages that we set up at the local cowboy range. All of these Cimarron's functioned flawlessly, except for one of the '66s, which would not always eject the .44 Colt empties. After a quick trip to the gun shop, where the extractor slots in the bolt were cut a little deeper, that '66 performed superbly as well.

At the range, I set up a standard CAS scenario and began to run the guns through as if I were at a regular shoot. The guns were all stock, out-of-the-box sixguns with trigger-pull weight and smoothness varying significantly. In spite of this, my runs were satisfactory and left me feeling like I was shooting about as close to the Old West as possible.

The next part of the test was to head for the bench rest to get velocity and accuracy data from a number of black powder, black powder replacements, and a number of smokeless loads. The results were very satisfying, with the Open-Tops coming out on top of the accuracy pile. All the guns were fired from a bench with a sandbag rest. Velocity figures were taken from ten feet away using an Ohler M-35 chronograph. Without a doubt, the black was the most fun to shoot, and all the handguns displayed accuracy that was more than adequate for CAS competition. My personal preference went to the Open-Tops, even though they had the shorter 5-1/2" barrels. They shot a little more accurately and to point-of-aim, and the Cimarron's charcoal-blue finish really set off the brass trigger guards.

The rifle also acquitted itself very well, and in the "short rifle" configuration with a 20-inch octagonal barrel and a brass gunmetal receiver, it was a most attractive long gun. The sights on the '66 were standard ladder/notch style dovetailed into the barrel in front of the receiver, which were, for my aging eyes, quite hard to see, but nothing that a good Lyman or Marbles tang sight wouldn't fix.

As stated earlier, I really like a set of guns that look like they

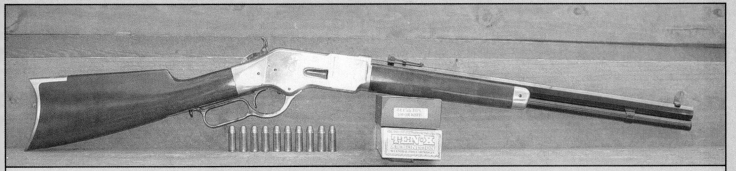

Cimarron's 1866 Yellow Boy Short Rifle in .44 Special also handles the .44 Colt.

belong together and are chambered for one of the old "classic" calibers. The .44 Colt is a very mild-shooting round and one that is available from many commercial manufacturers, including Ten-X (smokeless and black powder) and Black Hills (smokeless only). Other rounds can be fired in the pistols, including .44 Russian and Ten-X's four-in-one.

So, if you're looking for a unique set of cowboy guns that you can have a lot of fun with and just might pull you a little closer to 1872, you should take a look at these shooters in .44 Colt. You won't regret it.

1866 Winchester Short Rifle - Shot at 25 yards		
Load	**Velocity**	**Accuracy**
180-gr. OTBC – HC 18 gr. Goex Cart. ** (**)	775 fps	1.75"
200-gr. Chey-Cast HC 18 gr. Hodgdon's Triple 7 * (*)	955 fps	1.5"
Ten-X 200 gr. BP Factory	995 fps	2.25"
1860 Conversion 7-1/2" - Shot at 14 yards		
Load	**Velocity**	**Accuracy**
200-gr. Chey-Cast BP 22 gr. Elephant FFFg (**)	650 fps	1.3"
200-gr. OTBC- HC 18 gr. Hodgdon's Triple 7 * (*)	800 fps	1.6"
200-gr. Ten-X BP Factory	765 fps	1.75"
1872 Open-Top 5-1/2" - Shot at 14 yards		
Load	**Velocity**	**Accuracy**
200-gr. OTBC- HC 18 gr. Hodgdon's Triple 7 ** (**)	775 fps	1.5"
200-gr. Chey-Cast BP 22 gr. Elephant FFFg (**)	605 fps	1.6"
200-gr. Ten-X BP Factory	655 fps	1.5"

All loads used new Starline brass.
* 1/8 Reliable #12 lube cookie
** 1/8" Chey-Cast lube cookie

(*) Winchester WLP primer
(**) CCI Magnum LP primer
OTBC = Oregon Trail Bullet Company
HC = Hard Cast

The author shooting his Cimarron 1872 Open-Tops in .44 Colt.

A pair of Cimarron 1860 Conversions in .44 Colt.

The Winchester 1887 Shotgun

By: Lee Anderson, aka Bull Chip

The author can attest to the fact that full-charge, 10-gauge recoil is not for the fainthearted.

A .30-30 ON STEROIDS

This title is not a bad description of one of John Moses Browning's well-known contributions to CAS - the Winchester Model '87 lever-action shotgun. I've heard it said that it should've come with a set of wheels and a trailer hitch. I've also been told that it's so ugly it's beautiful (is that possible?). My old 32" barreled 10-guage has been likened to a 20mm cannon, especially when one of those 2-7/8" long solid-brass hulls is levered out of the receiver. That comment isn't as far off as you might think either. The actual inside measurement of those old hulls is 20.75mm. Whatever the nature of the comments, the old girl is guaranteed to attract attention.

I have to tell you, though, it's not easy coming up with a really interesting article on the Model '87. It's big, it's unique, it's tough, it's ugly, and it's reliable; what else is there to say? You just don't hear many debates about its performance, so you can't stir the pot by taking sides. Oh sure, whether or not it is "fast enough" gets bandied about now and then, but that's happened with every gun out there. As is typical of John Browning's guns, it simply doesn't have serious design flaws. Outside of maybe polishing a few surfaces, there is nothing to

modify. What few parts it does have are very robust with no particularly troublesome characteristics. If you unlatch the lever, the action almost falls open. If the lever is simply dropped, the carrier remains lowered, and if it is pushed all the way forward, the carrier is raised. In order to load two rounds, neither round needs to be shoved into the magazine. If the carrier is already down, the first round is simply dropped in the top of the receiver, the second is slipped into the chamber, and the action closed. If the lever was pushed all the way forward, simply push the carrier down with the first round, slip the second round into the chamber, and close the action. In either case, you end up with a round on the carrier, a live round in the chamber, the action closed, and the gun full-cocked. All you need to do is point it, pull the trigger, and work the action to do it again.

The '87 has an extremely short hammer spur, and cocking or lowering the hammer manually can be a little tricky. In some CAS circumstances this could be important time-wise. If called for, four shells are very easily shoved into the magazine through the top of the receiver with a fifth one dropped in on the carrier. You then have the option of either closing the action on the empty

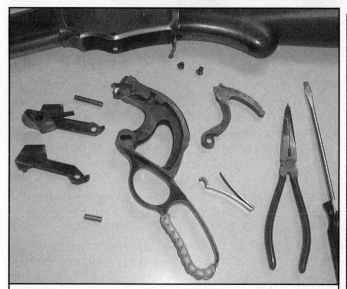

The entire basic "innards" of the Model 1887 Winchester. The trigger and its spring are a separate procedure.

chamber or slipping a sixth round in the chamber and closing the action on a live round with the hammer in full-cock position rendering the gun combat-ready.

The only negative comments I've ever heard are that the barrel is a little long and the hammer spur is a little short. As long as the magazine and its spring are in even fairly good shape, the gun rarely has feeding problems. Closing the action will mechanically drop the carrier. The lowered carrier then releases the next shell from the magazine, which immediately moves onto the carrier before the gun is fired. Should the next shell out of the magazine be sluggish in moving all the way onto the carrier for any reason, the jolt of firing the gun takes care of the problem.

Now is a good time to bring up an often overlooked area of gun hygiene - the inside of the magazine tube. Soft brass shell casings sure do slide a lot easier in a shiny clean magazine than

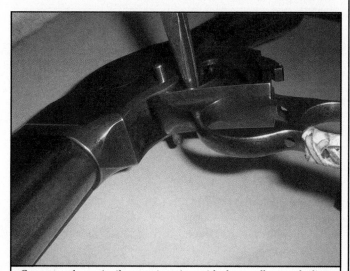

Compress the main (hammer) spring with the needle-nosed pliers while pushing out the pivot pin with the short pin.

in one that has collected several years worth of black powder residue, greasy everyday dirt, a little rust, or some combination of the three.

As robust as these old shotguns are, they do occasionally require disassembly. The '87 is probably one of the simplest repeating arm to take apart. (The same techniques will work on the Tri-Star replica now on the market.) The stock is an independent unit and easily removed by first taking out the blind screw (it goes into, but not through, the lower tang) at the rear of the top tang. The small screw ahead of it secures the trigger spring. The forearm panels, however, must be removed before removing the magazine clamp and unscrewing the magazine tube. Removing all of these items is such a straightforward operation that I see no need to waste space on it. The only thing to remember is that the magazine tube is threaded, not pressed, into the frame.

The gun is almost of a rolling block design. The lever and the breech bolt are a single piece of machined metal as seen in

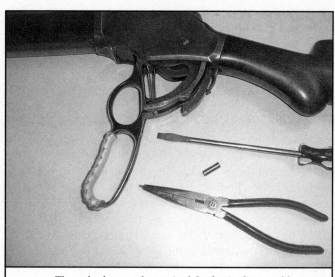

The only three tools required for basic disassembly.

the photo of the disassembled action, and the hammer and hammer spring are nested inside of this piece. The carrier is two separate pieces that fit together around the front of the lever/ breech assembly. The trigger and trigger spring are located at the rear of the receiver frame on a single pin and do not need to be disturbed in order to remove the entire working action from the receiver, as a single subassembly and minimal tools are required to do this. All you need is a properly-fitted screwdriver for the large screws at the lower rear of each side of the frame, a pair of needle-nosed pliers with masking tape-padded jaws, and a 1/4" diameter pin about 7/8" long. That's it! With the action open, the V-shaped leaf-type hammer spring is fully visible. It is the key piece. In some of the photos, you can see that the front of the lower arm of the spring is split into a pair of hooks. They go into a pair of grooves in the pivot pin to keep it from coming out. By squeezing the leaves of the spring together (as close to

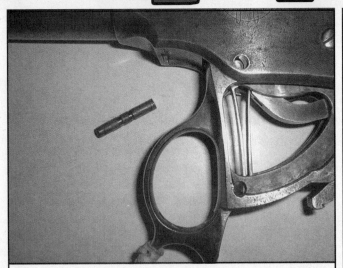

The long, grooved factory pin replaced with the short, non-grooved pin.

the front of the spring as possible) with the needle-nosed pliers, the pivot pin can be pushed out and replaced with the short 1/4" x 7/8" pin. The 1/4" pin is then pushed in to clear the holes on both sides of the frame, and then the compressed hammer spring is released. Remove the two screws located at the lower rear of the frame that retain the arms of the carrier, but do not remove the large screw at the upper right front of the frame because it is the carrier stop and does not need to be removed. The smaller one near it returns the right extractor to its proper position when the action is closed and doesn't need to be removed.

With the gun laying on its side, the entire subassembly, carrier and all, can easily slide out of the bottom of the receiver frame in a single unit. Further disassembly is now easily performed out on the bench. To remove the hammer and hammer spring, compress the hammer spring again and remove the short pivot pin. The shell extractors are removed first by using a sharp point to retract their spring-loaded plungers and then lifting them out. The entire action is easily reassembled in the reverse order

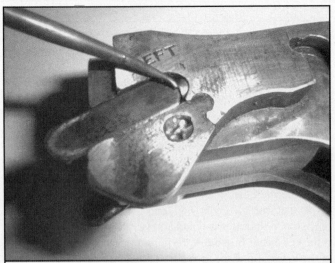

Push the spring-loaded pin that retains the extractor back into its receptacle.

using the short pivot pin, and then by slipping it back into place in the receiver frame. The hammer spring does not need to be compressed; you can simply use your thumb to push out and replace the short pin with the grooved pivot pin. If the right side of the carrier didn't happen to go in under the stop screw, just remove the screw, push the carrier down past it, and replace the screw. The carrier arms are easily accessed and lined up with their respective screw holes through the open top of the receiver. It's not necessary, but a real handy tool is easily fabricated from a piece of 1/2"x 1/8" flat steel at least a couple of inches long, and by using a hacksaw and a file to make a 1/8" wide x 1/2" long slot in one end. After compressing the hammer spring, and before pushing out the pivot pin, just slip the slotted end over both spring leaves to hold it in a compressed state, thereby leaving both hands free.

The '87 was the first lever-action shotgun ever produced in this country. It's strictly a black powder gun and was offered in only 10 and 12-gauge. In 1901, Winchester made some relatively

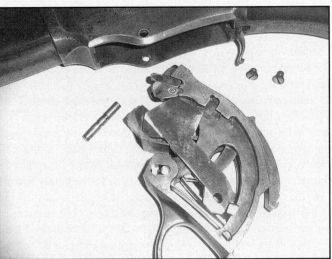

Remove the two short carrier pivot screws and slide the entire subassembly out of the frame in one unit.

minor internal changes to strengthen it, and reissued it as the smokeless powder Model '01 in 10-gauge only since the slide-action Model '97 had pretty much taken over the 12-gauge spotlight by then. A standard 12-gauge '87 came with a full choke and a 30" barrel, but a full-choked 32" barrel was also an option. The 10-gauge was just the opposite. Here's a note of caution if you're going to buy an '87 to shoot. Make sure you check the barrel material closely because Winchester furnished both 3 and 4 blade Damascus barrels on special order. A 20" barreled cylinder bore riot gun was also available in either gauge, so if you happen to come across one with a short barrel, it's not necessarily a hack saw job. In fact, when the courthouse in Tombstone, Arizona was turned into a museum, one of the guns left in the gun rack on the north wall of the county sheriff's office was a 20" barreled Model '87 riot gun, but I couldn't get close enough to tell which gauge.

The 12-gauge was chambered for a 2-5/8" shell, and the 10-gauge for a 2-7/8" shell. The frame of the '87 was case-hardened, and the '01 was blued. The standard stock was plain walnut with a pistol grip, but the same thing in fancy walnut could be bought either plain or checkered at an additional cost. Forearms were never offered in anything except plain uncheckered walnut. Despite the guns "generous" dimensions, they're not particularly heavy. A standard 12-gauge weighs 8 lbs., while a standard 10-gauge weighs 9 lbs. Winchester produced 64,855 of these shotguns between 1887 and 1901.

As I understand it, every now and again one of 'em still shows up taking high-flying Canadian geese up in the northern great plains states. I got to tell ya, it's almost worth the price of one just to watch the expressions on the guys' faces when you show up for a pheasant, quail, or dove hunt with one of these old hand-cannons. Steel shot would be hard enough on the old barrel that I'd hesitate to use it for ducks. For CAS, I prefer to tame down my old 10-gauge with about the same charge as a light 12-gauge, but it still puts on quite a smoke show. Just on sight, an old '87 in either gauge will still command a lot of respect, for sheer size alone if nothing else. Should you, for whatever reason, ever get one of these old thunderers, especially a 10-gauge, loaded up with a magazine full of five solid-brass shells, each filled with a full charge of black powder and 00 buck, you'll be packin' just about as awesome and formidable a beast (at either end!) as you'd ever want to get your hands on. You know, sometimes "how fast" just isn't part of the equation. Man, oh man, you just got to love it!

Lift the extractor out of the bolt. Repeat for the other side.

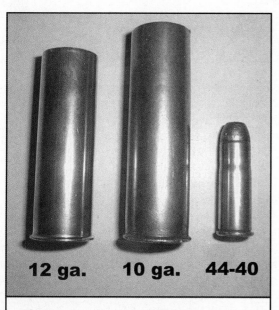

The 10-gauge, 12-gauge, and .44-40 compared.

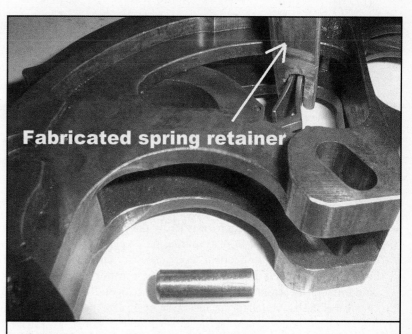

A homemade, slotted retainer for holding the main (hammer) spring in a state of compression is a very handy aid.

Taylor's and Co.'s

By: John Taffin,
aka Sixgunner
Picture provided by:
Bob Benbough,
aka Not So Bad Bob

Spencer Carbine In .45 S&W Schofield

The history of firearms development was changed dramatically on March 6, 1860 when Christopher Spencer received U.S. Patent #27,393. Spencer said, "My invention consists of an improved mode of locking a movable breech of a breech loading firearm whereby it is easily opened and closed and very firmly secured in place during the explosion of the charge. It also consists of certain contrivances for operating in combination with a movable breech for the purpose of withdrawing the cases of the exploded cartridges from the chamber of the barrel, and for conducting new cartridges thereinto from a magazine located in the stock." With those words, we have one of the two first successful repeating rifles using fixed ammunition, the Spencer Repeating Carbine. The other, of course, was the 1860 Henry, which was patented six months later.

The Spencer was a seven-shot, rimfire, lever-action carbine with a tubular magazine in the butt stock. When one pushes down and forward on the lever, which surrounds the trigger, two functions are performed. The fired case is ejected and a new round is fed into the chamber. The hammer must then be cocked before the Spencer is fired. President Abraham Lincoln fired an early Spencer and was duly impressed. The United States Government ordered 10,000 Spencers, with the first guns delivered in December 1862.

I find conflicting information on the chambering of the original Spencers. One source said the original cartridge was a .56-56 with a 350 to 360-gr. bullet over 42 to 45 grains of black powder, while an earlier source cites the cartridge as a .56-52 with a 410-gr. bullet propelled by 40 grains of black powder. We do know that by 1865 nearly 95,000 Spencer Carbines and 12,000 Spencer Rifles had been received by the United States Government. Of course, these rifles went west with the expansion that followed the Civil War and were found on both sides at the Battle of the Little Big Horn. Custer was no stranger to the Spencer as his Michigan Cavalry had received Spencers in early 1863 and used them quite effectively at Gettysburg.

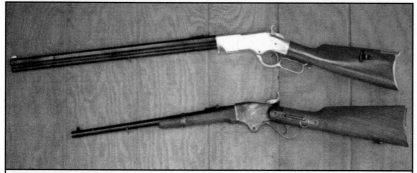

The first two truly successful lever-activated repeating rifles patented in 1860, the 1860 Henry and Spencer.

The original Spencers were loaded one cartridge at a time in the butt stock. Blakeslee's Patented Cartridge Box speeded up the process by providing ten ready-loaded tubes of seven rounds each to allow for faster reloading. Although Spencers would remain in use long after the Civil War, the Spencer Company itself disappeared in 1869. Rimfire ammunition for Spencer leverguns was still being made after World War I.

Spencers are, of course, antiques today and ammunition is difficult, if not nearly impossible to find, and most of us have very little chance of ever shooting an original. However, thanks to Taylor's & Co., new Spencers are

The left and right view of the Taylor's & Co. Spencer.

available for reenactors, cowboy action shooters, and anyone else who simply wants to connect with the 19th century. As are so many other replicas, they have been "modernized" to the point of accepting readily-available ammunition and, in the case of the Spencer, that ammunition is either .44 Russian or .45 Schofield. That alone should tell you that the Spencer does not fall into the category of powerful rifles.

However, put yourself in the place of the riflemen during the 1860's who were used to shooting muzzleloading rifles that required a powder charge to be poured down the barrel, a patched ball rammed down the barrel with a rod, and then a percussion cap placed upon the nipple under the hammer. In less time than it takes to do this, the owner of a Spencer could load seven cartridges in the butt stock and be ready to fire seven rounds by simply working the lever and cocking the hammer. The muzzleloading rifle may have had more power and longer range, but under battle conditions, which one would you choose?

Taylor's & Co.'s Spencer Repeating Carbine is manufactured by Armi Sport of the renowned gun making area of Brescia, Italy. Current models are available in either .44 Russian or .45 Schofield, with a third chambering of a "modernized" .56-50 Spencer being promised, as the

original .56-50 was a tapered rimfire cartridge with a 350-gr. bullet and 45 grains of black powder. The new version will be centerfire and smokeless.

To load the Spencer, the lever must be in the closed position. The thumb then presses the upper end of the magazine base in the butt stock and pushes it 90 degrees to the right. It can then be extracted from the magazine well, and flat-nosed cartridges can be inserted with the bullet entering the well first. After all rounds have been placed in the magazine well, the magazine tube can then be reinserted and rotated 90 degrees to the left and locked into position.

When shooting the Spencer, the lever must be operated with authority all the way to the forward position, and then with like authority, returned to its regular position. If one tries to treat it too gently it may jam. With one smooth operation forward and one smooth operation backwards, the Spencer carbine operates flawlessly.

Several things precluded me from doing any more extensive testing or testing at longer ranges. One problem was snow, another was cold weather, and since I am long past my invincible time of life, both of these factors are extremely important. A third problem is the fact that the sights are for younger eyes, and if I decide to purchase this test rifle, I will use a file to open up the back sight to allow more light through to allow me to see

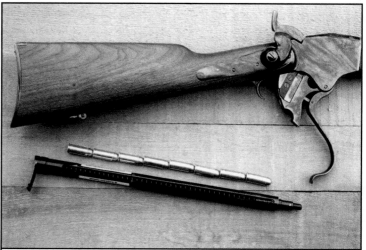

Depending upon bullet length, Taylor's & Co.'s Spencer chambered in .45 Schofield will hold seven or eight rounds. The cartridges are dropped into the butt stock when the spring-loaded tube is removed.

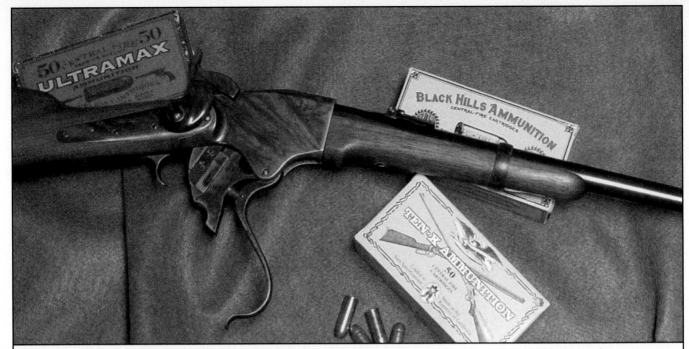

The lever of the Spencer in full-forward position. Notice the hammer is not cocked when the lever is activated.

(L-R) .45 Schofield and original .56-56. Bullets provided by Bob Benbough.

both the front and rear sight.

Taylor's & Co.'s Spencer Carbine seems to be a well-executed and authentic replica. I have never had the opportunity to handle a real Spencer, so I can only compare by the pictures I have seen or examples on display in museums. The wood-to-metal fit on the test gun is excellent, the receiver has brilliant case colors, bluing on the barrel is well carried out, and the wood used in the butt stock and forearm is of excellent quality. The trigger pull is much heavier than what is necessary or desired, and this will also be attended to if I decide to purchase the test rifle.

Not only have I passed my invincible time of life, I am also in the enviable position of having been able to test so many sixguns and leverguns over the past two plus decades that an unintended, negative consequence, is that of my excitability threshold being raised considerably. The Taylor's & Co. Spencer Carbine made it over the threshold and provided a lot of fun shooting. Somehow, as I was operating the Spencer and test-firing, I swore I could hear bugles in the afternoon and hear the playing of *Mine Eyes Have Seen The Glory Of The Coming Of The Lord* and, at the same time, well-off in the distance, the muted sound of *I Wish I Was In Dixie* could also be heard. As I fondled the Spencer I could feel trail dust in my nostrils, hear Longhorns bawling, and even smell bacon and beans cooking over a campfire in the late evening. It takes a quality firearm to be able to do all of this.

With its limited magazine capacity of seven or eight rounds, where does the Spencer Carbine fit into cowboy action shooting? If you are one of the very small percentage of shooters who must win, it doesn't. However, if you are in the category of the other 97% plus who are in the sport to have fun, and at the same time enjoy shooting 19th century firearms, the Spencer dovetails in perfectly. If the stage calls for more than seven shots, one simply takes the time to remove the magazine tube, load three more rounds, and finish the stage. The Spencer definitely fits in with those who shoot cap-n-ball revolvers from the same time period. A pair of 1860 Armys and a Spencer Carbine is about as authentic as one can get shooting with an 1860's persona.

25-yard accuracy of the Spencer. Crude authentic sights are a problem for older eyes.

Taylor's &Co. .45 Schofield Spencer Carbine 6 Shots/25 Yards		
Load	Velocity	Accuracy
Oregon Trail 250 RNFP 25 grains FFg Hodgdon's Triple-7/#12 Cookie	1,050 fps	2-1/4"
Black Dawge .45 Schofield 230 RNFP Black Powder	1,143 fps	1-5/8"

The new and the old: Taylor's & Co. Spencer (top), and an original Spencer in .56-50 caliber (bottom). Original courtesy of Bob Benbough.

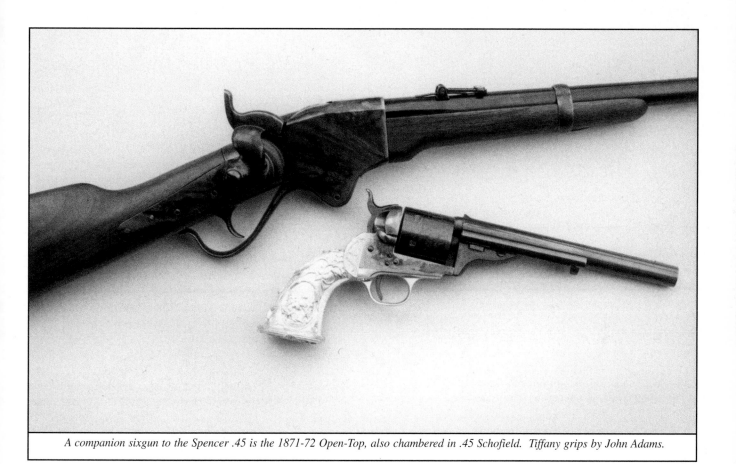

A companion sixgun to the Spencer .45 is the 1871-72 Open-Top, also chambered in .45 Schofield. Tiffany grips by John Adams.

Ladder sight provided on Taylor's and Co.'s Spencer.

Smith n' Jones testing Taylor's & Co.'s Spencer in .45 Schofield.

Spence Wolf and The Old Warrior

By: Kenny Durham,
aka-KID Durham

In 1873, the Army Ordnance Board adopted the new .45-70-405 service cartridge that became known as the .45-70, along with the new model 1873 Springfield "Trapdoor" rifle to fire this powerful cartridge. In 1975, 122 years later, Spence Wolf purchased his first .45-70 Springfield Trapdoor rifle, which he proudly referred to as the "Old Warrior." Like most of us, Spence had some knowledge of Trapdoors and knew that his newly-acquired rifle, equipped with the Buffington sight, was designed for shooting 500-grain bullets with black powder. And, like most of us, that's about all he knew.

Spence acquired some 500-gr. lead bullets, assembled them into black powder cartridges, and headed for the range. His results were dismal, with groups measuring around five feet at 100 yards. He was aware of the history of these old rifles and the accuracy to which they had been fired in the past, so when his rifle and the loads that he had assembled scattered bullets over the place, he was sorely disappointed. Next, Spence tried loading with smokeless powder, but the groups did not improve any to speak of. Believing that whatever accuracy the Old Warrior had once possessed had faded with the passing of the Cavalry, Spence put the rifle away and went on with other projects.

Then, at a gun show in 1988, Spence came across some original .45-70 UMC (military contract black powder ammunition loaded for the Springfield rifle). He purchased 25 or 30 rounds of the old ammunition to play with in the "Old Warrior." To his astonishment, with the UMC ammunition, he put five shots in a group measuring three inches at 100 yards! The old rifle really would shoot after all. Spence knew that the key to accuracy would lie in finding how to craft the ammunition

as it had been in the past. But learning how to recreate the original arsenal loadings would send Spence and his wife, Pat, on a journey with 15 original .45-70 Springfields, lasting three years and consuming many pounds of black powder, lead, and tin. At the end of the journey, Spence and Pat Wolf left for all of us who share their affection for the "Old Warrior" an invaluable resource, a book entitled *Loading Cartridges for the Original .45-70 Springfield Rifle and Carbine*, which was published in 1991. Not until I read the book did I really appreciate the amount of digging and research that the Wolfs had done. Sadly, Spence Wolf's life was cut short by cancer in September 1993. In April of 2000, I had the pleasure of meeting Pat Wolf and learned how she and Spence accumulated the knowledge for writing the book. A few photos, which Spence took during their research, are included in this article. Some of the captions may not what be Spence had intended, but are the best that Mrs. Wolf and I could come up with.

Learning about the Old Warrior

Spence Wolf soon learned that in order to recreate the original arsenal loads for the Trapdoor, he needed a better understanding of the rifle and its overall design and purpose. The Old Warrior is just that, an implement of war. It is not a target rifle or a sporting rifle. It is a weapon with all of the attributes of a rifle having been designed to give the best service under battlefield conditions. Since the sights are calibrated for specific distances, the ammunition must be loaded with the correct bullets and to the correct velocity in order to coincide with the sight settings. Spence's education of Trapdoors broadened as he learned of the different models, arsenal modifications and upgrades to earlier models, and the reasons for such changes. In other words, Spence

One of Wolf's "Old Warriors," a nice 1873 Springfield Rifle (photo by J.S. Wolf).

became an expert on the Trapdoors that most shooters are likely to encounter.

Learning about the Arsenal Ammunition

Spence learned that the ammunition for the .45-70 Trapdoor had undergone many changes over the production period. The .45-70 cartridge was introduced in the era when much development with cartridge design was ongoing. Different alloys of brass and copper were being tested for suitability as cartridge cases. Centerfire primers were replacing rimfire primers in newly-introduced cartridges throughout the industry. Even using centerfire primers, three different types were used in the .45-70 rifle and carbine cartridges. Various methods of cartridge case manufacturing were developing, too. The result was that the ammunition went through several changes from 1873 until 1898 when the last .45-70 cartridges were manufactured at the Frankfort Arsenal. Additionally, many loads developed at the Frankfort Arsenal were contracted out to ammunition manufacturers.

Days of Ammunition Testing

Spence had one goal, and that was to recreate the ammunition as produced by the Government Arsenals in the 1880's. In his own words, "I wanted to discover how to construct the original type of cartridges not tailored to a specific rifle; ammunition that would perform within the accuracy standards of two to four MOA in original three groove barrels with the service sights." Additionally, Spence wanted to show that bullets other than the Government designs, when properly loaded, work well in the Old Warrior. Bullets for gallery practice and hunting are a couple of the variety of bullets available for the .45-70.

While Spence was the one doing most of the load development,

Pat was the technician helping to record all the data. Much of the additional information added to the second edition of the book published in 1996 is due to Pat's knowledge and working alongside Spence.

Recreating the Arsenal Ammunition

Spence's biggest headache developed when he started testing the 405-gr. bullet. He learned that the flat-based 405-gr. bullets used in sporting rifles do not shoot well in the Trapdoor. For Spence, getting acceptable accuracy from 500-gr. bullets had not been too difficult, but the lighter-weight, 405-gr. bullet was giving him fits. Why? The answer lies in the fact that, combined with the oversize bore, the lighter-weight bullet did not provide enough resistance to form a gas seal. Spence discovered that with 405-gr. bullets in the Trapdoor in order for the bullet to properly expand and to shoot accurately, three things were required. The bullet must have a hollow base, must be cast from a soft alloy of lead and tin only, and must be crimped tightly in place by the case mouth.

At the time of Wolf's testing in the late 1980's, no manufacturer was producing an accurate copy of the 405-gr. hollow-base bullet. Spence stated, "I cast a similar (405-gr.) design of modern flat-base bullet in the 40:1 alloy, then lathe-bored the bases to simulate the original bullet cavity. When loaded and fired, these bullets performed to expectations, and I knew I was on the right track." Convinced that he needed a proper mould, Spence sent copies of the original Government drawings of the M1873 bullet to NEI, and they produced a hollow-base, double-cavity mould for Spence. The mould lived up to Spence's expectations and performed well in his tests. Also, at Spence's request, Lee Precision, Inc. began producing a single-

Folded and reinforced head Berdan primed cases (left and right). 1st model solid head boxer primed case (center). (Photo by J.S. Wolf.)

Pat Wolf shooting a great-looking 1884 Trapdoor (photo by J.S. Wolf).

Cut-away photo of the 3-Ball Guard Load (photo by J.S. Wolf).

Target fired by Spence Wolf, details unknown (photo by J.S. Wolf).

cavity, hollow-base M1873 bullet mould as part of their product line. The old-style Lyman 457125 was a close approximation to the 500-grain 1881 bullet, but is no longer so due to changes in the design. Spence, in order to be authentic, ordered copies of the original 1881 design from both NEI and Rapine. He stated that, "Both moulds were made at my request and the bullets used in my tests gave excellent results in the rifle." Saeco also produces the M1881 bullet, which I purchased for my use and testing of Spence's methods.

Many of the changes in the original arsenal loadings were attributable to refinements in the design of the brass case. For example, Spence wrote of the M1882 carbine load, "Similar to the M1873 Carbine load, but loaded in the M1882 pattern case." In this example, it appears that the only difference was the case. Other changes in the arsenal loads involved more significant changes. For instance, of the M1886 Carbine load, Spence wrote, "First loaded in the pattern 1882 case, and then in the pattern 1888 case, the powder charge was about 55 grains. The cartridge length was changed from 2.55 inches to somewhere between 2.42 to 2.45 inches, thus omitting the filler wads, which had caused some accuracy problems in the earlier carbine cartridges. Velocity was 1150 to 1200 fps over the production run period

from 1886 to 1898." In this instance, the brass was changed, the wads eliminated, the bullet seated deeper into the case, and the velocity upped by 50 fps.

Changes in the rifle ammunition presented more radical changes. In 1873, the 405-gr. bullet was standard for both the rifle and carbine. The rifle load consisted of 68 to 72 grains of powder loaded to a velocity of 1350 fps. In 1882, the Arsenal discontinued this load and began producing the 1882 rifle load with the newly introduced 500-grain M1881 bullet. The cartridge was loaded to an overall length of 2.79" to 2.82" and a velocity of 1280 to 1315 fps. Arsenal production was from 1882 to 1888. In 1888, the rifle load was updated by switching to the M1888 pattern case and continued for the next ten years. In 1898, the rifle load was changed to smokeless powder and produced by the Arsenal in limited quantities during the year. Now, given the above-mentioned variety of loads, Spence Wolf had quite a pile to sort through in order to determine just what it was that he wanted to recreate!

Spence settled on recreating five Arsenal loadings, two carbine loads, and three rifle loads. For the Trapdoor carbine, Spence developed loads to duplicate the M1873 and M1882 Arsenal load (the only difference being a change in the case),

Arsenal loads duplicated using Wolf's methods (left to right), M1886 Carbine, M1873 Rifle and 1888 Rifle.

Arsenal bullets: M1873, 405-gr. LEE mould(left), and M1881(left), 500-gr. Saeco mould (right)

M1888 Rifle load fired at 100 yards in 1873 Pedersoli Rifle from Navy Arms.

M1873 Rifle load fired at 100 yards in original 1884 Springfield.

and the aforementioned M1886 carbine load. For the Trapdoor rifle, Spence developed loads to duplicate the M1873, which uses the 405-gr. bullet, the M1882 and M1888, which use the 500-gr. bullet, and the M1889, which also uses the 500-gr. bullet, but with smokeless powder.

For my testing, I chose three Arsenal loads to recreate, the 1873 Rifle, the 1888 Rifle, and the 1886 Carbine. My testing consisted of loading and shooting the ammunition in six Trapdoors, two rifles, three carbines, and an officer's model. In the firearms, however, I took a little bit different tack than Spence had. In the time that has passed since Spence left us, two new Trapdoors have arrived in the form of the 1873 Rifle and Carbine made by Pedersoli. So, in my testing I used an 1884 Springfield Rifle, two 1879 Springfield Carbines, an 1873 Pedersoli Rifle from Navy Arms, an 1873 Pedersoli Carbine from Dixie Gun Works, and an 1875 H&R (Harrington & Richards) Officer's Model. With these six Trapdoors, I had great fun filling the air with smoke.

Case Preparation

One of the steps that is critical to accuracy in recreating the Arsenal loadings is to enlarge the flash holes to 0.096" with a #41 drill bit. Spence learned that ignition problems appeared in 1879 with the 405-grain bullet when the Benet-primed case was replaced with the First Model Solid Head case using a boxer primer. The Benet primer held more priming compound and had two flash holes. By contrast, the new case had a smaller, single-flash hole. To remedy this, the flash hole in the new case was enlarged, thus solving the ignition problem. Wait a minute! What ignition problem? Everything we read tells us that black powder is EASY to ignite. Sure, black powder ignites easily when unconfined or loaded without any compression. But as Spence stated, "When the compressed black powder forms a solid pellet, with each grain tightly interlocked, the problems begin, for the primer flash cannot go up through the charge to ignite the powder quickly." The amount of compression referred to here is significant, in the range of 0.3 to 0.4 inches. Black powder in the Arsenal loads was tightly compressed 120 years ago, just as we do today.

Taking all of the above into consideration, I gathered up a supply of Winchester .45-70 brass. These cases were not new but, in fact, had been fired many times in other rifles. I chose these particular cases because they all needed to be trimmed, which would allow me to trim them to the 2.105" length that Spence specifies in the book. According to Spence, the 2.105-inch length is absolutely necessary to obtain the proper crimp. Spence noted that the W-W case is very similar to the Frankfort

Wolf's M1888 Arsenal load with a 500-gr. Saeco 1881 bullet.

M1886 Carbine load (left), and M1873 Rifle load (right).

Components used in testing Wolf's methods: Federal 215 primers, Winchester cases, and Goex FFg black powder.

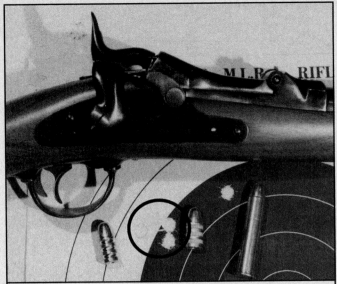

5-shot group of M1886 Carbine loads fired at 100 yards in 1873 Pedersoli Carbine from Dixie.

Arsenal M1888 case. The cases were full-length resized and trimmed to 2.105 inches, while the flash holes were drilled out to 0.096 inches and primed with Federal 215 primers.

Bullets

As mentioned earlier, I acquired a 500-gr. 1881 mould from Saeco, and a Lee Precision 405-gr., hollow-base 1873 mould from Wolf's Western Traders. For my testing, I chose to cast both the 1873 405-gr. bullet and the 1881 500-gr. bullet from 30:1 lead-to-tin alloy. Both bullets are listed at 20:1. However, Spence stated that the ratios of 25:1 or 30:1 will work fine for the 500-gr. bullet. The 405-gr. bullet can work well cast from as soft as 40:1 alloy. However, Spence stated that absolutely no antimony should be present in the alloy. Even if the alloy is soft, the presence of antimony adversely affects the malleability of the alloy, and accuracy will be affected. The bullets were lubed with 50:50 olive oil to bee's wax, which Spence refered to as JSW lube. I have personally used this lube for many years, and it works well as a general-purpose black powder bullet lube.

Loading Dies

Spence discovered that in order to load ammunition that is accurate, the case must be uniformly expanded to the full depth of the seated bullet. The expander plug, furnished with some die sets, is too short and was intended for use with jacketed bullets. The result is that the case neck is expanded only partially, leaving the remaining portion of the neck too small to accept the bullet. Bullets cast from 20:1 alloy or softer, upon entering a case neck that has not been expanded to the correct depth, will be deformed

A variety of Arsenal .45-70 ammunition.

and sized smaller, and accuracy will be lost. One solution is to either make or purchase a longer expander plug for the die. Buffalo Arms Company makes custom expander plugs to fit just about any brand of dies. Another die we will need is a compression die for compressing the powder charge. Finally, although most bullet seating dies are designed to seat and crimp the bullet in one operation, doing so will deform the bullet nose and affect accuracy. Seating and crimping must be accomplished in separate operations, a point about which Spence was very emphatic.

Spence came up with a solution to the die problem, too. He began selling Lee Precision .45-70 die sets, which included an expander plug that would expand the case neck to the depth required when seating the 1873 bullet to the maximum depth required for the M1886 carbine load. Additionally, he included a brass plug for use in the expander die, which turns it into a powder compression die. For convenience, Spence and Pat put together a Lee Precision five-die set that includes a sizing die, expander die, compression die, seating die, and crimping die. Wolf's Western Traders has the Lee Precision two-die set available that includes the expanding die and seating die. If you already

100-yard, 5-shot group with H & R Officers Model using M1886 Carbine loads.

have a standard three-die set, Spence suggests getting the Lee Precision two-die set with the custom expander plug. Special instructions written by Spence are included with the Lee Precision .45-70 dies that explain how to use the expander die and to achieve the vital taper crimp with the seating die. Same as with the bullet mould, special instructions are included with the mould to get the shooter started on the right track.

I used the nominal 55 grains of FFg black powder for the M1886 carbine loading, and 70 grains FFg, by dropping the powder through a 30-inch brass drop tube, for the 1873 and 1888 rifle loadings. Wolf indicated from his testing that, "Goex FFg black powder appeared to give the same velocity and pressure of original loading when the same weight of powder is used." The velocity range for the ammunition that I was trying to duplicate is: 1873 Rifle Load – 1350 fps, 1886 Carbine Load – 1150 to 1200 fps, and 1888 Rifle Load – 1280 to 1315 fps.

M1873 Rifle Cartridge

The M1873 is unique in that the powder is compressed more than in any of the other rifle loadings. The 70-gr. charge, when compressed to the correct depth, measures 0.665" from the case mouth to the top of the charge, which corresponds with the M1873 bullet seating depth. The powder charge has been compressed 0.350 inches, which has transformed the charge from loose powder into a solid pellet of powder grains that interlock. Bullets were carefully seated with the die backed out of the press far enough to ensure that no crimping of the bullet would occur. Next, in a separate press, the loaded cartridge was run up into the Lee Precision seating die with the seating stem removed and the bullet crimped into place. The proper die adjustment was determined by giving the die quarter-turns and running the cartridge up into the die until the inside of the case mouth was firmly against the nose of the bullet without being impressed into the bullet nose. The finished overall length measured 2.52 inches. Spence lists the Arsenal overall length (OAL) as 2.52 to 2.54 inches.

M1886 Carbine Cartridge

In my loading of the M1886 Carbine load, 55 grains of Goex FFg was stacked to a height leaving 0.6 inches of space remaining. The OAL length of the M1886 load is 2.42 to 2.45 inches, requiring approximately 0.73 inches of the 405-gr. bullet to be inside the case. Powder compression is a mere 0.13 inches, and the charge can be compressed with the bullet during seating. Crimping, however, is still a separate operation. Since the bullet in the M1886 load is seated deeper in the case than in the M1873 load, the crimp occurs farther up on the bullet nose. This requires a longer taper to the crimp in order to force the inside of the case mouth firmly against the nose of the bullet.

M1888 Rifle Cartridge

The adoption of M1882-1888 load represented a major change in ammunition. The M1888 was the powerhouse load that gave the Old Warrior its real authority. A 500-gr. bullet moving at 1300 fps packs a wallop. The added weight of the extra 100 grains of lead provided enough resistance that the hollow base could be eliminated. In my loading, the 70-grain powder charge was compressed 0.260 inches. Although this amount of compression is less than the M1873 load, it is a significant amount, and still results in the charge being compressed into a solid pellet with the grains tightly interlocked. Bullets were seated and crimped in separate operations as before. The M1881 bullet is crimped over the leading edge of the front driving band so the case mouth is firmly against the bullet nose.

At the Range

The M1873 rifle loads were fired in the original 1884 Springfield and 1873 Springfield reproduction rifles. Both performed well, but the original Springfield 1884 produced the best group. The velocity of M1873 rifle ammunition averaged 1364 fps in the 1884 rifle and 1378 fps in the 1873 reproduction rifle. At 200 yards, accuracy with the original Springfield was noticeably better than from the reproduction. However, the ammunition performed well and was, in all respects, a good recreation of the M1873 rifle load.

The M1888 ammunition testing was next and, as expected, proved to be more accurate than the M1873 loads. At 100 yards, the 1873 Pedersoli rifle from Navy Arms produced a good ten-shot group. With the factory sights, the rifle printed to the right and high. Velocity from the 1873 reproduction with the M1888 load averaged 1310 fps. The target was moved out to 200 yards and the firing continued. Here is where the original "Old Warrior" really shined with the M1888 load. A 15-shot group, measuring approximately 6 inches, was fired from a bench rest using the "battle" or "skirmish" setting of the Buffington sight. Not a bad group at 200 yards with military service sights.

Finally, the M1886 carbine ammunition was tested in three carbines and in an H&R Officer's Model. Groups were fired at 100 yards only, and a few shots were also taken at the 360-yard steel plate to check the sight settings. The Pedersoli 1873 Trapdoor Carbine from Dixie Gun Works produced a great five-shot group with an M1886 load. Velocity of the M1886 carbine load averaged 1146 fps in the 1879 original and 1140 fps in the Pedersoli Carbine from Dixie. These velocities are right in the ballpark for carbine ammunition.

The Harrington & Richards 1875 Officer's Model was used to test the M1886 carbine load, only to see how the ammunition would perform. The H&R does not have the three-groove Springfield rifling nor military sights. The group produced by the Officer's Model was not a "match winner" group, but certainly verified that the M1886 ammunition loaded by Wolf's methods is accurate and consistent in a variety of rifles.

The final testing of the M1886 Arsenal loading came about as a result of finding an 1879 carbine for sale in a local gun shop. It is an early 1879 model, serial #127031, from the 1880 production. All parts are original and correct, except for the front sight. The bore is in good condition, but the last 1-1/2 inches at the muzzle shows much wear from the cleaning rod. A correct front-sight blade was obtained, and the remaining M1886 ammunition was fired in this carbine. Ironically, this epitomizes what Spence Wolf was trying to accomplish, duplicating the Arsenal loadings so that the ammunition will perform to specifications in ANY Springfield Rifle or Carbine. This "Old Warrior" is a shooter! Next, the buckhorn sight was set for the 360-yard steel plate. The first shot struck low, but the second shot produced the "SPLAT" of a bullet striking steel.

Wolf's research was much more exhaustive than I have been able to describe in this article. Throughout the book, reading conclusions that represented months of research, condensed into a few short sentences and paragraphs, continually astonished me. Spence Wolf accomplished his goal of making the "Old Warrior" perform as it had during the late 1800's. The book that he and Pat published is a valuable resource as a loading manual and as a history book.

Pat Wolf continues to run Wolf's Western Traders, the mail-order business that sells this book, other .45-70 books, and supplies to load the .45-70 ammunition as outlined in the book. Supplies include bullet moulds, loading dies, and custom tools developed by Spence Wolf.

See ya at the range!

A variety of .45-70 bullets from the "collar button," having the same weight as a round ball (left) to the Lyman 457125, weighing over 500-gr. (photo by J.S. Wolf).

The 1877 Sharps

By: Frank Cornell, aka The Mississippi Kid
Photos by: Kenny Durham, aka KID Durham

Arguably, the most aesthetically-pleasing and finely-crafted of the Sharps rifle models made was the 1877, as produced from 1877 through 1880. For those of you not familiar with an 1877 Sharps, I'll describe it for you. It's a trimmer and lighter version of the 1874. The fit and finish of the metal work, as well as the grade of wood used, were normally of much better quality than found on other Sharps models. The hammer and lock plate are considerably smaller and were imported from England. At least three different hammers and several different lock plates are found on original 1877s. Barrels for the 1877s were also imported from England. The action was lightened through several means. The prototype 1877s were simply ground-down 1874 actions, however that didn't reduce enough weight so some redesign was required. The receiver and the breech block are both rounded off, and the receiver sidewalls are thinner than those of the 1874 and are perfectly vertical, versus the slant of the 1874. The breech block was lightened by boring a ½" hole through the lower section, and the tang was narrowed at the location where

it joins the rear of the receiver. The result was an action that was approximately one pound lighter than the 1874 action with a thinner stock through the wrist and an ornamental curl on the end of the pistol grip on several of the '77s.

The action was lightened to allow for a heavier barrel. The 1877 was developed in response to complaints from Creedmoor shooters that the 1874 action was so heavy that it required the use of lightweight barrels, resulting in extreme barrel whip. There was a ten-pound weight limit on Creedmoor guns, so, naturally, it was desired to have as much weight as possible in the barrel. Consequently, the 1877 was originally intended as a Creedmoor rifle and was used at Creedmoor events, as well as at other prominent long-range events of the day.

Another distinguishing feature of the 1877 Sharps was the "Rigby Flat," as found on most specimens. The Rigby Flat was simply a small, flat area approximately 3/8" wide by 2" long on top of the barrel extending from the receiver. Its installation was quite clever as the barrel was dovetailed from the breech

A Sharps 1877 (top) and 1874 (bottom). By removing excess metal and using an English lock, Sharps was able to lighten the action by almost one pound.

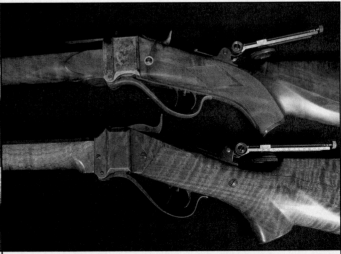

Back side of the actions. The 1877 Sharps contains metal only where needed.

end, and the Rigby Flat was inserted before the barrel was screwed into the action. I was unable to find a written source explaining the purpose of the Rigby Flat. My inquiries into its purpose produced some interesting theories that included a 'sight plane,' a reinforcement piece to help keep the barrel from rising as it heated, and a piece for a barrel wrench to grab. The most plausible explanation came from Carmen Axtell of Axtell Rifle Co. who said, "The Rigby Flat's purpose is purely aesthetic."

The 1877 Sharps had various nicknames and designations. In some factory correspondences, the 1877 was referred to as the "Special" Model 1874. One nickname was the "English Sharps," as its styling was similar to the fine English guns of that time. I would not doubt that the name may have also been applied due to the imported English parts used in its construction. Additionally, many 1877 Sharps were exported to England. Another nickname for the 1877 Sharps was the "Transition Model." The 1877 fell

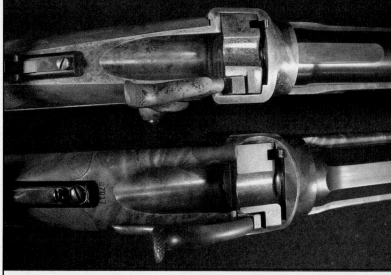

Notice how the area behind the breech block of the 1877 tapers into a long tang (top), while the 1874 remains at full width until the tang (bottom).

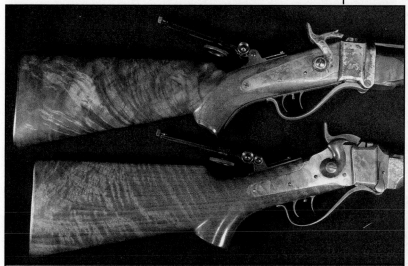

Both Sharps have a unique beauty - the graceful, delicate lines of the "English" 1877 (top) and the rugged massiveness of the 1874 (bottom).

in between the 1874 and the 1878 Borchardt Model Sharps, and was never intended to be a permanent or long-term addition to the Sharps line-up.

Even though the 1877 was intended as a Creedmoor gun, it was offered in various configurations, including the "Lower Grade," Creedmoor, and Long Range Express. The 1877 was offered with practically all the .40 and .45 calibers available from Sharps during the years of its manufacture. According to *Flaydermans*, only about one hundred 1877 Sharps were made. If you add up all the numbers in Frank Seller's book, *The Sharps Rifle*, one could deduce that there was over 200 made. Either number makes an 1877 Sharps a rare item, since decent specimens fetch $20,000 plus, and I have only seen two for sale.

Eventually, like all great guns, someone saw fit to make a reproduction of the 1877 Sharps. Axtell Rifle Company in Sheridan, Montana was the first company that I'm aware of to make a reproduction 1877 Sharps.

Their 1877 Sharps is a fine-looking piece. Axtell builds their actions from 8620 steel castings and offers them in several models with multiple options. The Axtell 1877s start at $2900 for the "Business" model.

Another company offering a high-quality reproduction 1877 Sharps is Classic Rifle Company located in Bend, Oregon. Classic Rifle Company is a custom rifle manufacturer specializing in 1874 and 1877 Sharps. Receivers are built from 8620 steel plate, and the fit, finish, and overall quality of Classic Rifle Company guns is excellent. As Classic Rifle Company is a custom rifle builder, they will provide any option possible. Prices for the Classic Rifle Company 1877 Sharps basic model start at $2250.

C. Sharps Arms of Big Timber, Montana is gearing up for a limited run of 1877 Sharps. A prototype is reported to be on display and is rumored to be the crème de la crème of C. Sharps products. When in production, the C. Sharps 1877 will start at around $5500. Ouch!

The 1877 Sharps was unique to American firearms of its time due to the graceful, almost delicate, design.

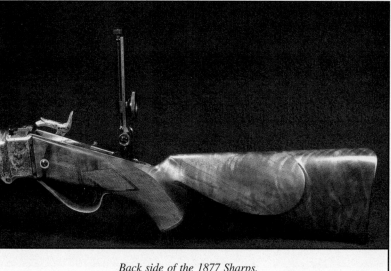

Back side of the 1877 Sharps.

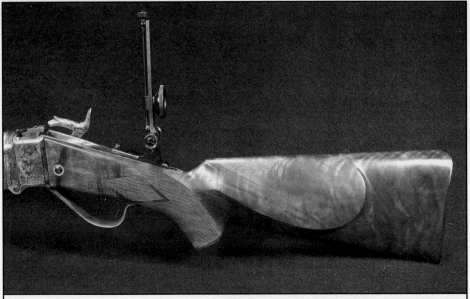

The checkered pistol grip aids in shooting and accents the graceful lines of the '77.

It was built in limited numbers and was not intended to compete with the 1874 models. Very few, if any, 1877 Sharps were used in the field, as the 1874 Sharps was the workhorse of the Sharps line and was built in large quantities for rugged use on the American frontier. While the 1877 Sharps did not have the reputation, character, or impact on history that the 1874 model did, it takes its place as C. Sharps' finest work of craftsmanship.

Color case-hardening is like a fingerprint; no two are alike. This action has an unusual pattern.

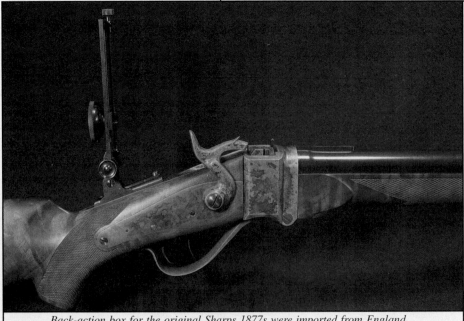

Back-action box for the original Sharps 1877s were imported from England.

Remington's No. 3 Rifle

THE
New Remington Long Range Military Rifle.
(Hepburn Patent.)

By: Kenny Durham, aka KID Durham

This rifle has been pronounced after long and exhaustive tests by the most expert riflemen in the country, as the most perfect Military Rifle under all conditions yet produced. It has also been adopted by the National Rifle Association of America, who recommend it to competitors for the American Team. It has a heavy barrel with our new system of rifling, chambered for a 2 6-10 straight shell, using 75 grs. of quick, clean, moist powder, hard bullet, 520 grs., with our new thick Waterproof patch. This rifle is now used by all the leading riflemen, who pronounce it unequalled.

E. REMINGTON & SONS,
P. .Y.

THE REMINGTON-HEPBURN

In 1880, Remington introduced a new single-shot breech loading rifle as an alternative for the models No.1, No.1-1/2 , and No. 2, all of which were rolling-block actions. The new rifle was simply designated the No. 3, in the same non-descript manner as had been its predecessors. But, just as its predecessors had been dubbed the title Rolling Block, the No. 3 was to become known as the Hepburn. Ironically, the Remington-Hepburn and its competitive equivalent, Winchester's Highwall, were both patented on the same date, October 7, 1879. Patents for both rifle designs were issued to Lewis L. Hepburn and Jonathon M. Browning for their falling-block actions. Remington produced the Hepburn, and Browning produced

The Hepburn and the Highwall were both patented on October 7, 1879.

about 550 rifles before selling the design to Winchester. Interestingly, although Remington had a five-year head start on building and marketing their falling-block rifle, Winchester produced over ten times as many Highwalls as Remington did Hepburns. The total number of Hepburns built was around 12,000 compared to just under 140,000 Highwalls. Undoubtedly, many factors enter into why there was such a disparaging difference between the quantities produced of these rifles, but we will leave that subject for another time.

In the late 1870's, there was a diligent effort on behalf of Sharps and Remington, locked in fierce competition, to build an accurate target rifle having an action of lighter weight than their standard models. The Long Range Target Shooting or Creedmoor Shooting rules, as it were, limited the weight of rifles to 10 lbs. A "Creedmoor" rifle was built to certain specifications that had been adopted during the inaugural match at the Creedmoor Range (Long Island, NY) on June 21, 1873. Range regulations in the "any rifle" category by definition were a rifle weighing no more than ten pounds with a minimum trigger pull of three pounds, and the rifle could not be equipped with set triggers or a telescopic sight. With these limitations, shooters wanted to be able to concentrate the weight in having a heavier barrel and less weight in the action. Sharps accomplished this by streamlining and slimming down the 1874 action and

A Hepburn shooter taking aim during the Quigley Buffalo Match in Forsyth, MT. (Photo courtesy of Ingrid Ruble)

The open breech reveals the compact design.

replacing the massive lock with a slim English lock. The result was the Model 1877 Sharps. Sharps later discontinued the 1877 in favor of the 1878 Sharps, or Borchardt as it became known. Remington had faced this challenge with the addition of the Hepburn to its line of production. Wisely, Remington did not abandon the Rolling Block to produce the No. 3 Hepburn. Remington's later models, the No. 4, 5, and 7, were all Rolling Blocks, and the No. 5 was produced until 1916, surpassing the Hepburn production by nine years.

The Hepburn is, however, a fine rifle with few faults. Unlike Sharps or Highwalls, shooters seem to have distinctly contrasting opinions about Hepburns. They either love them or hate them. Shooters that don't like the Hepburn point out that the stock is farther below the line of the bore than other single-shots, thus making it more prone to torque during recoil. To some, the rifle feels uncomfortable and cumbersome. Others point out that because the breech block slides at 90 degrees to the bore and is operated with a simple side lever, it has no camming action or mechanical advantage to assist in chambering a cartridge. All of this is true, but is of little or no

Original Remington No. 3 "Hepburn" with a new barrel.

significance to a Hepburn aficionado with properly-loaded ammunition, which they are quick to point out.

The positive features of the Hepburn are many, particularly as a target rifle. The action has a short hammer throw, thereby providing a very fast lock time. Also, a Hepburn does not have a half-cock or safety notch in the hammer. Instead, the action incorporates an earlier patented invention of Lewis Hepburn, the rebounding hammer. Additionally, the Hepburn action is incredibly simple. Excluding the firing pin and the extractor, the action has only five moving parts: lever, rocker, breech block, hammer, and trigger. Probably the most appreciated feature of the Hepburn is the minimum amount of movement required to operate the action.

When target shooting from the prone position, subtle changes in body position from shot to shot will affect the location where the bullet strikes the target. When a shift in position is required, several factors come into play, among which is the body angle to the target, the placement of the arms, the grip pressure, and the head position. These factors determine how the rifle moves when in recoil while the bullet is

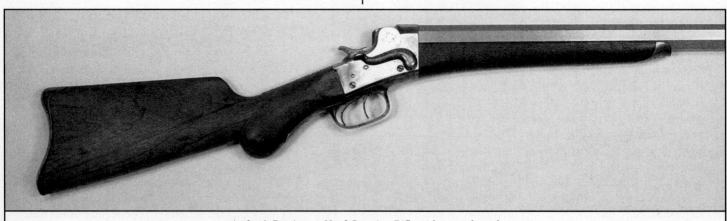

Author's Remington No. 3 Sporting Rifle with a new barrel.

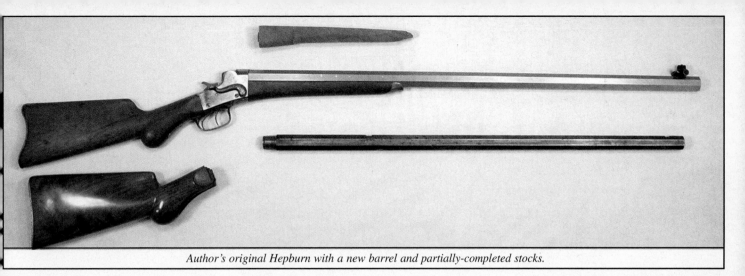

Author's original Hepburn with a new barrel and partially-completed stocks.

traveling down the bore. Rifles operated by means of an under lever most often require that both the rifle and the body be shifted to operate the action, especially if the shooter adopts a very low prone position. The side operating lever of the Hepburn allows the shooter to operate the action with less movement than any other falling block action that comes to mind.

Hepburns were produced in a variety of configurations: Sporting Rifles, Short-Range Target, Creedmoor (Long Range) Target, Light Schuetzen, Long-Range Military Target, High-Power, and the Walker Schuetzen Rifle. The majority of Hepburn rifles that were built were plain Sporting Rifles chambered in .45-70 Government or the Remington .40-2-1/2 (.40-70 straight). The most unusual Hepburn is the Walker Schuetzen, so named for its ornate trigger guard. The Walker trigger guard not only adds a means for steadying the rifle for off-hand shooting, it is also the operating lever. The side lever is missing from the Walker Hepburns.

Today, original Hepburn actions are prized among black powder cartridge shooters and are getting harder to find all the time. Occasionally, though, one will find a Hepburn that may be a candidate for rebuilding. I was fortunate enough to find such a Hepburn at a gun show. It was a Sporting Rifle in .40–2-1/2 that had seen much use. The barrel was worn inside, but is probably still accurate enough for hunting. The butt stock was cracked and both stocks were badly worn. The rifle was disassembled and started down the road to getting turned into a target rifle. First was a new Badger .45 caliber barrel, and then new wood for the rifle. However, I have kept the original

wood and barrel and, in a matter of minutes, my Hepburn Target Rifle can be transformed back into a Plain Sporting Rifle. I encourage anyone who acquires an original Hepburn to keep the original parts with the gun if they choose to rebuild the rifle. Also, I must admit that my Hepburn project remains unfinished, too.

Reproductions of the Hepburn have been produced in the U.S.A. by Okalahoma Territory Arms in Shawnee, Oklahoma and D Z Arms in Oklahoma City. As of this writing, only D Z Arms is still in production. The D Z Arms Hepburns are available as semi-custom rifles as target and long-range rifles, including the Walker Schuetzen Rifle. Plus, D Z builds a left-hand Hepburn just for south paws.

On the target ranges, the Hepburn is still winning matches in black powder cartridge rifle competition. Two prominent Hepburn shooters are Dave Gullo, Proprietor of Buffalo Arms Co., and A.P. "Butch" Ulsher of Butte, MT. Dave has won many Black Powder Cartridge Rifle Silhouette matches, including the 1996 National Championship, with one of his Hepburns. Butch Ulsher has also won many target and silhouette matches with his Hepburn in .45-90, but, without a doubt, his biggest wins have been his back-to-back NRA National Creedmoor Championships in 2001 and 2002. No doubt, this is a feat that would make Lewis Hepburn proud were he alive today. No better tribute to Hepburn could be made than to keep his rifles shooting as they were meant to be.

See ya at the range!

A close-up of D Z Arms reproduction Hepburn, which is also available in a left-hand model.

A short-hammered Hepburn has a fast lock time. Shooter Gene Davids of Idaho Falls, ID is ready to fire.

By: Kenny Durham, aka KID Durham

SIGHTS TO BEHOLD

There are two factors required to shoot a fine rifle accurately. One is, without question, properly-crafted ammunition. The other is good sights. Just as the production of single-shot and lever-action rifles from the late-1800's has flourished, so has the production of sights from the same era. The purpose of this article is to give us you an overview of what sights are available today.

First of all, let me tell you what this article is not about. It is not about who's sights are the best. The "best" sight for one shooter may not be the "best" sight for another shooter. Secondly, not all sights are purchased with the intention of being used for the same purpose. For example, someone building or restoring an original Remington Creedmoor Target Rifle may desire to have authentic Remington front and rear tang sights. On the other hand, a competitive Black Powder Cartridge Rifle Silhouette (BPCRS) shooter may not care about authenticity and may choose whichever sights they feel gives them the most advantage within the rules of the game. One such case in point is when building my wife's CPA Stevens 44 ½ Silhouette rifle, we chose a reproduction of the Stevens front sight. On my CPA

Stevens 44-1/2 Silhouette rifle, I chose a Sharps-style front sight.

Another consideration is price. A top-of-the-line, long-range soule tang sight will cost between $450 and $500. Some shooters, especially younger ones raising a family, cannot afford to lay out that kind of cash. A less expensive sight is their only option. Serviceable sights of reasonable quality are now available. This was not the case only a few short years ago. However, we must remember that we get what we pay for, particularly when buying rifle sights. The cheapest is not always the best, and quality costs extra time to produce. Such things as extremely close tolerances, wear-hardened threads are important because smooth operation adds quality to the product, but cost more to produce.

Bear in mind that this article is, by no means, a complete work on sights. Books could be, and have been for that matter, written on sights solely from one company. For this article, sights were obtained per my request from 11 different companies in order to provide a good cross-section of what is available today. No source or sight maker was intentionally left out, but not all were included. Additionally, when I contacted these companies to ask them to send sights for this writing, I did not specify that

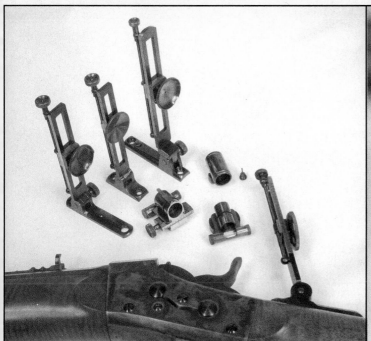

Axtell provides authentic recreations of vernier sights for Winchester (left), Ballard (middle), Sharps (right), and Remington (on rifle). Globe sights are for Sharps' rifles.

Easy-to-read vernier scale set at 0.745.

they send me any certain ones or specify any number of samples. I asked only that they send me a representative example of their sights and that all suppliers would be treated the same regardless of how many examples were sent. Some sent a few, while others sent a lot. Also, two kinds of sights were not included, not because they don't merit attention, but because I had to draw the line somewhere. Those two were receiver-mounted sights and scopes. Finally, you won't find any prices listed for the sights shown here. You can find the name and contact information for each company in the contacts section at the end of the book.

So, on the aforementioned basis, let us explore what sights are available to enhance the accuracy of our favorite Smokepole, in alphabetical order, of course.

Axtell Rifle Company
The Riflesmith - Sheridan, Montana

The Axtell Rifle Co. began producing original-style rifle sights in 1973. At the time, no other company was engaged in producing original-style rifle sights on a production basis. Today, Axtell produces authentic, historically-correct sights for Sharps, Winchester (and Browning), Remington, Ballard, Marlin, Maynard, and Stevens rifles. The sights are precisely-made, more so than were the originals. Not only are the sights of first-rate quality, but great attention has been given in making them historically accurate. For example, the labeling and marking of the staff graduations are done to match the original of each company. The company produces a variety of models for each type of rifle that range from short-range hunting sights to long-range target sights. Front sights are no exception, and the same historically-correct, spirit-level, quality wind gauge front sights are available from Axtell as well. Not all sights from Axtell are off-the-shelf items. Some are special-order and produced only upon request.

Mechanical Accuracy Baldwin Sights
Oklahoma City, Oklahoma

Baldwin's globe front sight with sprit-level shaded in the center of the sight is ideal for bright sun conditions.

Baldwin's reproduction of the original Lyman adjustable eye piece.

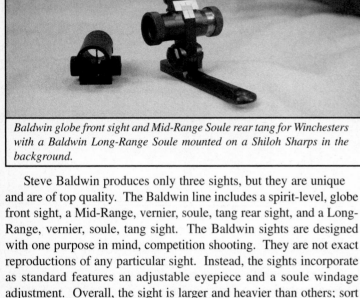

Baldwin globe front sight and Mid-Range Soule rear tang for Winchesters with a Baldwin Long-Range Soule mounted on a Shiloh Sharps in the background.

Target sights from Ballard: long-range wind gauge vernier tang sight for a Ballard rifle beside a plain globe (middle) and a spirit-level, wind gauge, globe front sight (left).

Steve Baldwin produces only three sights, but they are unique and are of top quality. The Baldwin line includes a spirit-level, globe front sight, a Mid-Range, vernier, soule, tang rear sight, and a Long-Range, vernier, soule, tang sight. The Baldwin sights are designed with one purpose in mind, competition shooting. They are not exact reproductions of any particular sight. Instead, the sights incorporate as standard features an adjustable eyepiece and a soule windage adjustment. Overall, the sight is larger and heavier than others; sort of a heavy-duty sight. The Mid-Range sight has 15 minutes of windage adjustment each direction, while the Long-Range sight has 30 minutes of windage adjustment each way. Also, the windage knob is a left-hand thread. The adjustable eyepiece is patterned after the original Lyman and has five apertures. Bases for the Baldwin sights are available for all popular rifles or can be custom-ordered. The Baldwin globe sight is a unique design that features a globe that is about twice the traditional length, and the level is centered in the sight rather than at the rear. These features make the sight ideal for shooting in bright sunlight, thereby minimizing glare. All Baldwin sights are

finished with a black-matte satin finish.

Ballard Rifle, LLC
Cody, Wyoming

Ballard Rifle produces a small line of sights that will cover just about any target shooting situation. For barrel sights, Ballard makes a common blade front and a buckhorn rear sight with elevator. For more precise work, they offer a plain, globe front sight with inserts and a spirit-level wind gauge. The target rear tang sight built by Ballard comes in three models: Schuetzen (short-range), Mid-Range, and Long-Range. The sight is a vernier sight with a wind gauge, meaning that windage adjustment moves the staff not just the eyepiece. The windage adjustment works the same way as a wind gauge front sight. The tang sights from Ballard are available for Sharps, Remington, Winchester, and, of course, Ballard rifles. Additionally, extra sight bases and a Hadley eyecup with different size apertures are available. The Ballard sight is of excellent quality and is precise. I don't believe that it is an exact reproduction of any manufacturer, but it is a well-designed and easy-to-use sight that will withstand the

(Left to right) Lyman's Model 17a globe front sight, a No. 2 tang with target eye disc for a Marlin, and a Model 20 MJT large globe.

Marble's Peep Sight with "click" adjustable windage and elevation. Sights are available for most rifles, such as the original Winchester (left) and Remington Rolling Block (right).

Sights for lever-action rifles from MVA (left to right): Spring-loaded combination rear sight with Marlin base patterned after the original Marble sight and a Model 130 Sporting Tang with Winchester base.

MVA's combination "Beech" front sight, a recreation of the Lyman No. 5.

rigors of competition shooting. The spirit level wind gauge is of the same quality, having a definite "Winchester" appearance.

Lyman Products
Middletown, Connecticut

No review of rifle sights would be complete without including the Lyman Gun Sight Company. Lyman is in its second century of making high-quality rifle sights. Two of Lyman's most popular sights to ever be produced are the Lyman 17a Globe Front Sight and the Lyman No. 2 Tang sight. The three models of the No. 2 are for the Winchester '86 and the '94 and the Marlin lever-actions. They will also fit some single-shot rifles.

Marble Arms
Gladstone, Michigan

Marble Arms is another century-old company that needs no introduction to shooters. Marble still produces a wide variety of high-quality rifle sights.

Long-Range Soule with Hadley eyecup mounted on a custom CPA Stevens 44-1/2 built by Pat Hallinan of Pocatello, ID.

For lever-action and single-shot rifles, Marble Arms produces traditional bead front sights, sporting rear sights, and peep tang sights. The Marble Peep Tang Sight is one of the premier sights available for lever-action rifles. It features both click-adjustable elevation and windage. The sight will also fit some single-shot rifles and comes with three different sized eye discs. Marble furnishes this sight to fit almost any rifle, old or new.

Montana Vintage Arms
Belgrade, Montana

Montana Vintage Arms began producing high-quality rifle sights in 1992. Today MVA is one of the largest manufacturers of period rifle sights. MVA quality is as good as it gets. MVA's sights are a combination of historically-accurate models, while at the same time containing refinem-

ents that improve the products both in durability and service. To describe all of their products here would

Sights from MVA (left to right): Winchester/Stevens Spirit-Level Globe, Long Range Buffalo Soule (with Magnum Hadley eyecup), and combination front sight.

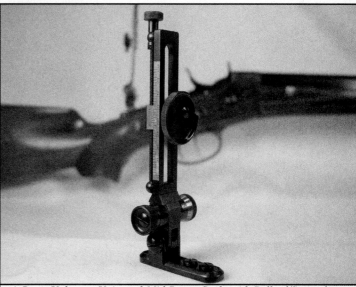

A Parts Unknown Universal Mid-Range Soule with Ballard/Steven base. Both sights include an adjustable eyepiece.

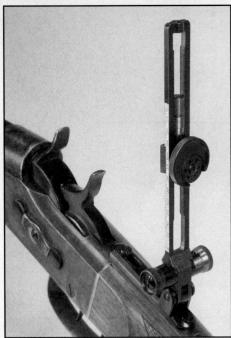

Universal Long-Range Soule patterned "Borchardt" sight for the Sharps 1878 from Parts Unknown.

be impractical. However, we will highlight the most popular MVA sights. To the best of my knowledge, MVA was the first company to reproduce the "Soule" sight. The company produces their Soule in four models: Schuetzen (short-range), Mid-Range, Long-Range, and Long-Range Buffalo. MVA also produces a line of traditional Sharps-style vernier sights and a line of globe front sights that are reproductions of Sharps, Winchester, and Stevens. MVA was also the first company to reproduce the Hadley style eyecup having a variety of aperture sizes. Recently, MVA introduced a large diameter "Magnum" Hadley containing 15 apertures. Another aspect of MVA's products are sights for lever-action rifles. One of the all-time cutest of sights to ever exist is the Lyman No. 5 "Beech" Combination front sight. MVA now produces a reproduction of this sight, and to go along with it, a combination rear sight patterned after the original Marble spring-loaded, quick-release sight. All MVA sight bases are interchangeable. The trademark finish on all MVA sights is a high-polished deep bluing.

Parts Unknown
Winnipeg, Manitoba, Canada

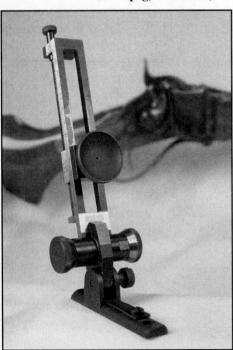

Pedersoli's Long-Range Soule is furnished with some rifles and can also be purchased separately.

Sergio Pustogorodsky produces a variety of sights that include Long-Range, Mid-Range, tang sights for lever-action, and front sights. The Parts Unknown Soule Universal Tang Sights incorporate a system of universal bases and an adjustable detent system that will allow the sights to be mounted on just about any rifle. The universal bases are a "short" to fit Ballard and Stevens rifles and a "long" to fit Sharps, Remington, Winchester, and others. The Long-Range model is patterned after the sight patented by Hugo

Borchardt and furnished on the Sharps Model 1878 or "Borchardt" Sharps, which features a center screw that operates in threads cut into the inside faces of the sight staff thus eliminating the need for a elevating stem screw. Both sides of the staff are calibrated with a vernier scale, thereby making the sight readable from the left or right. The Mid-Range is a traditional-style vernier sight. Additionally, both sights come equipped with an adjustable eye disc containing six apertures. Sights from Parts Unknown are of excellent quality. Standard finish is polished and blued. Sergio is constantly improving and expanding his line of products.

Pedersoli
Italy

The Davide Pedersoli Co. produces sights for many of their rifles. Some of the Pedersoli Sharps and Remington reproductions come equipped with sights from the factory. Additionally, Pedersoli's line of sights are also available separately. Pedersoli produces several vernier tang sights, including a Soule sight. The quality of their Long-Range Soule sight is acceptable, but is not in the same class as the other high-quality sights available. However, the sight does work and is designed to fit a variety of rifles. Although it may be considered an entry-level sight, it is certainly far better than the first tang sight that I bought when I was starting out. I would have been in hog heaven to have had this sight as a starter.

Lee Shaver, Gunsmith
Iantha, Missouri

Gunsmith Lee Shaver has been working on rifle sights for about a year. One of his specialties has been building vernier Soule sights using non-adjustable imported sights as a base. Shooters can send an existing sight to Lee for conversion, or purchase an already converted sight. Recently, Shaver began producing his own line of Mid-Range and Long-Range Vernier Soule sights. Lee's sights are intended to fit the needs of the

Pedersoli's globe front sight is of good quality and includes a variety of apertures.

shooters that either can't afford or do not require the fit, finish, and precision of the most expensive sights. The sights are of good quality and come with a Hadley eyecup as standard equipment. Sight bases are available to fit almost any rifle. Lee also produces front sights and apertures shaped to match each of the silhouette animals.

Shiloh Rifle Manufacturing
Big Timber, Montana

Shiloh produces a small line of sights for their own rifle production, and also makes them available to purchase separately. The sights are reproductions of original Sharps' rifle sights. However, the sights are more of a hunting or sporting-style sight than for target shooting. Shiloh produces front globe sights, semi and full buckhorn rear ladder sights, and a sporting rear tang sight. As with all Shiloh products, the sights are of high quality.

Original-style Sharps globe sights from Shiloh Rifle Manufacturing Co.

A special-order, case-hardened, spirit-level globe from Smith Enterprises - the standard model is blued.

Smith Enterprises
Tempe, Arizona

Ron Smith produces a line of rifle sights for lever-action and single-shot rifles that are very unique amongst the sights available. What makes Ron's sights unique is that they bear the appearance of 1800's-style sights, but incorporate design features that greatly improve the functionality of the sights. Sights from Smith Enterprises include a Sharps-style, spirit-level, globe, front sight, a variety of buckhorn, flip-up, ladder sights, and a long-range tang sight to fit most lever-action rifles. The Long-Range Tang Sight is even more unique among their designs. The amount of elevation adjustment is listed as 0.375 inches, but both sights I tested allowed over 0.500 inches. With this amount of adjustment and the design of the sight, ranges of 400 to 500 yards are possible depending on the caliber. The sight is furnished with two eye discs: a target aperture and a hunting aperture. Sights from Smith Enterprises are of excellent quality.

Whether you are looking for a high-grade competition sight, a replacement for an original sight, or just something through which your tired, aging eyes can line up the front sight on a target, just about anything is available. The only thing we have to remember is which way to turn the knobs!

See ya at the range!

Long-Range Soule from Lee Shaver with an additional base. Rifle in rear bears a Mid-Range sight. Bases are interchangeable and a Hadley eyecup is standard.

Case-hardened, buckhorn, ladder sight with optional "peep" slider.

Smith's Long-Range Tang has an old-fashioned look, but is a modern design.

Great American Classic Sporting Rifle

By: Kenny Durham, aka KID Durham

John Shorb of October Country with an "Old Shaggy" taken with the Great American "Classic" Sporting Rifle.

from October Country Muzzleloading, Inc.

Prior to the development and refinement of the massive British black powder cartridges, and later the Nitro Express cartridges, the large and dangerous game of Africa and India fell at the hands of hunters equipped with muzzleloading arms as large as four bore. Designating the size of a gun by "bore" size has been a European practice since the development of firearms. In America, the same system is used when referring to shotguns, as in 12-gauge or 12-bore, but rarely used when referring to rifles. The "bore" or "gauge" nomenclature is a method of designating the diameter of a barrel by the number of lead balls of the same diameter that can be cast from one pound of lead. Thus 12-gauge or 12-bore means the size of bore of which the weight of 12 balls equals one pound. If we consider that 20-bore equates to .62 caliber, then we can easily understand why U.S. firearms manufacturers chose the inch-measurement based system of caliber nomenclature. Most of the American arms are .58 caliber and smaller.

In 1863, Lt. James Forsyth authored a book entitled *The Sporting Rifle and Its Projectiles,* wherein he described the use of heavy round balls propelled by massive charges of black powder in barrels having extremely slow rates of twist. This was late in the muzzleloading era; and breech loading double rifles of eight and four-bore firing conical bullets were already in use. The breech loading bore-size single and double rifles were direct descendants of the massive muzzleloaders. As cartridge design and ballistics improved, the bore-sized arms gave way to smaller, higher velocity bullets from black powder express cartridges. Ultimately, the black powder gave way to Nitro or smokeless powder that resulted in doubling the energy of many cartridges.

For the hunter who wishes to experience the thrill of taking big game with a bore-sized muzzleloader of the mid-1800's,

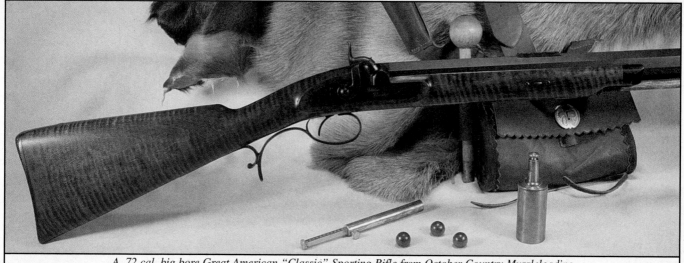
A .72 cal. big bore Great American "Classic" Sporting Rifle from October Country Muzzleloading.

October Country has just the ticket. I had the pleasure of testing a 12-bore (.72 cal) rifle built by John Shorb, President of October Country Muzzleloading, Inc. of Hayden, Idaho. The rifle is the Great American Classic Sporting Rifle and it is a beautiful rifle to behold. The style of the rifle, at least to me, is that of a Hawken, or rather an English-style Hawken rifle. The stock is made of curly maple and is richly-stained with a satin finish, and the overall fit and finish is excellent. It is a massive rifle with a 31-inch barrel, but has very good balance and is not the least bit cumbersome. The patent breech is huge compared to the .54 and .50 caliber percussion rifles we are accustomed to seeing. Also, the rifle is equipped with a musket nipple requiring the use of musket caps, another good idea for a hunting rifle. I have been using musket caps for years on my percussion hunting rifle. The extra fire and potency of musket caps versus size 11 caps is great insurance against misfires, especially in damp weather. Sights are an English three-blade express rear sight and a post/bead front sight. The express sight

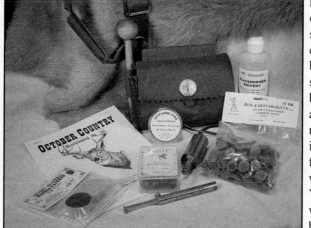
October Country carries a complete line of products for muzzleloaders.

blades are labeled "100," "200," and "300," for settings, but actually calibrate nearer to 100, 150, and 200 yards. The express sight used is designed for a cartridge rifle, and the yardage labels do not apply to round ball trajectories.

Surprisingly, the rifle is not as heavy as I suspected it to be, topping out at 10 pounds. Now, that may sound like a heavy rifle, but considering that the 12-bore round ball weighs 546 grains and the standard charge is 200 grains of Fg black powder, I wasn't any too anxious to be on either end of the rifle. John, in his letter of instructions on loading and caring for the rifle, suggested that I start with a mere 150 grains of powder. Yeah, RIGHT! Like THAT wouldn't kick! Nonetheless, I headed for the range to shoot the most powerful muzzleloader I have ever held in my hands.

I took John's advise and started with 150 grains of Goex Fg, followed with a card wad, then a lube-impregnated fiber wad, and finally the patched round ball. I do have to admit that I walked from the loading table to the shooting bench with some trepidation. Resting the big rifle on

The rifle is equipped with express sights.

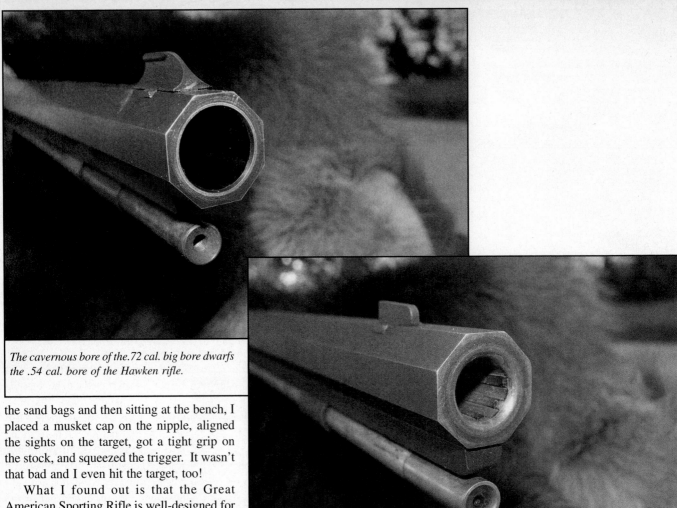

The cavernous bore of the .72 cal. big bore dwarfs the .54 cal. bore of the Hawken rifle.

the sand bags and then sitting at the bench, I placed a musket cap on the nipple, aligned the sights on the target, got a tight grip on the stock, and squeezed the trigger. It wasn't that bad and I even hit the target, too!

What I found out is that the Great American Sporting Rifle is well-designed for its intended use. The rate of twist is 1:104, which is 1 turn in over 8-½ feet. Such a slow rate of twist allows the use of a large powder charge for high velocity, while retaining accuracy. My chronograph, for some reason, would not record the velocity, but Mr. Shorb reports that with a 200 to 220-grain charge, he records velocities in the 1800 to 1900 fps range. Energy at these velocities is about 4,000 ft. lb. But what about recoil? As previously stated, the rifle is well-designed for its use, including minimizing the felt recoil. The stock has a minimum amount of drop, and the wide shotgun butt spreads the force over a wide area. A quick comparison reveals that the recoil from the Great American Sporting Rifle is spread over approximately twice the area as the crescent butt of my .54 Browning Mountain Rifle. However, the recoil from the rifle is still significant. It was not painful, but certainly did rock me back. After shooting 20-some shots of the 150-grain charge, I upped the load to the 200-grain charge that John recommended. Admittedly, the full-charge hunting load fired from a bench rest is a bit punishing, but shooting from a standing or kneeling position, such as one would do when hunting, was fine. From past experience, I know that if a nice bull elk was in the sights, I would not even remember the recoil.

In terms of accuracy, John Shorb reports that his 100-yard groups average about three inches, and 200-yard groups run about eight inches. My groups were not quite that good, not because the rifle is not accurate, but because learning to maintain shot-to-shot consistency with a heavy recoiling rifle takes practice.

The body becomes much more of an integral part of shooting than with other rifles. At 100 yards, my best groups measured about eight inches for five shots. However, four of the five shots were grouped together in about a five-inch, center-to-center spread. With practice and becoming more familiar with the big rifle, groups in the two to three-inch range at 100 yards would be common. Bear in mind that the bullet is almost 3/4" in diameter, which brings us to the next item.

The 12-bore Great American Sporting Rifle (.72 cal.) and the 14-bore Light American Sporting Rifle (.62 cal.) are the "small bores" built by October Country. The real serious "Big Bores" are the 8-bore and the 4-bore (.989 cal.). The 4-bore Heavy Rifle weighs 18 pounds and fires a 1400-gr. round ball (remember, 4 balls per lb. of lead!) atop a powder charge of 300 to 400 grains of Fg black powder. The velocity of this behemoth is about 1300 fps and generates 5,225 ft. lb of energy. John has threatened to send me one of these for testing. I think he's trying to kill me!

October Country Muzzleloading, Inc. carries all the supplies needed to feed and care for their Big Bore Rifles, plus a catalog filled with muzzleloading supplies and equipment for both the traditional and modern muzzleloading shooter.

See ya at the range!

Classic Guns *of the Old West*

By: John Taffin,
aka Sixgunner

Sixgunner in front of the Black's Creek Jail popping off escaping outlaws with his original Winchester Model 1892.

Most of those in my age bracket got their first basic education in the history and use of frontier firearms from the movies, both the wonderful old "B" movies, as well as some great classics made by the likes of John Wayne, Randolph Scott, and even Henry Fonda. It was only as we grew older that we realized how unsafe gun handling was as presented on the silver screen and also how badly history was treated.

As I learned of the time frame of the evolution of single-action sixguns and leverguns, it bothered me greatly to see Colt Single Actions in Civil War movies, and especially to see Winchester leverguns used in any movie from those depicting the war with Mexico forward. Most of the time, the leverguns used were Model '92 Winchesters. The model number denotes the year, and the Old West was pretty well gone by 1892. By then, the buffalo, the stagecoach, and even the gunfighter was a relic of the past.

There were still pockets of relatively rough country left in 1892, especially in the Southwest, and the Model 1892 Winchester filled the bill for survival quite well. At least for a short time, Rangers, both Texas and Arizona style, picked up on the soon to arrive Model 1894 Winchester in the more "modern" .30 Winchester Centerfire, or .30WCF, or as most of us call it, the plain old .30-30. The Winchester

'73 is usually thought of as the "Gun That Won The West," while the Model 1892 gave shooters a much stronger action in the same chamberings.

Many of shootists of the Old West packed a Colt Single Action with a Model 1873 in the same chambering. As the Old West began to disappear, the Model 1873 was often replaced by the Model 1892. Interestingly enough, the .32-20 was very popular in both the Colt Single Action and Bisley Model, as well as the Model 1892 in the 1890's and beyond. Apparently, many felt the larger calibers were no longer as necessary as they had been.

When Oliver Winchester's son-in-law journeyed West in the early 1880's to meet with a young Utah gunsmith by the name of John Browning, neither could have had any idea of the great effect that the meeting would have on rifle production. Winchester got Browning's designs for what would become the 1886 levergun and 1885 Hi-Wall, and in just a few short years, Browning would miniaturize the Model 1886, with the result being the slickest little levergun ever, the Winchester Model 1892.

Who can ever forget the classic scene in *Stagecoach* as John Wayne (Ringo) twirls his large-looped lever Model '92 and stops the coach? Or the greatest scene of all Westerns, when Rooster Cogburn with

Sixgunner's Winchester Model 1892 carbine in .38-40 (.38 WCF).

his '92 in his right hand, Colt Single Action in his left, and teeth clenched around the reins goes forth to meet the Ned Pepper gang in *True Grit*? Sandwiched in between these two, those of us old enough will remember seeing Lucas McCain use his large lever Model '92 to great effect each week in *The Rifleman*. The real star of all of these scenes was the Model '92.

In the past few years, the replica Model 1892 has been imported from Brazil, Italy, and Japan under such names as Browning, Cimarron, EMF, Navy Arms, and Winchester; all well-made, good shootin' leverguns regularly seen at cowboy shootin' matches around the country. One also finds many competitors who have searched the used gun market to come up with authentic Winchester Model 1892s. The real '92s are not cheap, but I have been able to come up with a pair, one for $400 and the other at $600. Check that out against some of the prices of the replicas, especially the replica 1866s and 1873s!

More than one million Winchester Model 1892s were produced from 1892 to 1931, so it should be three times easier to find a Model '92 than a Colt Single Action. The three main chamberings, just as in the Model 1873, were .44 WCF, .38 WCF, and .32 WCF, or as they are better known today, .44-40, .38-40, and .32-20. Two other chamberings are found, the .25-20 and the very rare .218 Bee. During the 1950's, many 1892s were converted to .357 Magnum or .44 Magnum. The originals ended production before the advent of either Magnum, so none were ever produced in these chamberings nor in .45 Colt.

With a 20" barrel, the Model 1892 weighs around six pounds,

and it is an easy handlin' levergun, probably the best ever. In addition to a round-barreled 20" version, as most encountered will be, there are also 24" rifles and 30" muskets with barrels that are round, octagon, or half round/half octagon. Take-down models will also be encountered. Stocks are normally of the straight grip variety of oil-finished walnut. Front sights are usually a post or bead, with the rear sight a buckhorn or semi-buck.

In addition to being a great gun for cowboy action shooting, the Winchester Model 1892 in .38-40 or .44-40 makes a fine close range deer rifle when properly loaded. Older manuals have loads for the .44-40 in the Model '92 that eclipse the .44 Magnum. For turkeys and the like, the .32-20 and .25-20 are just about perfect where their use is allowed by the game laws.

My two Model 1892s are both 20" carbines, one in .32-20 and the other in .38-40. The first cost me $600 and has plenty of character on the outside and a perfect bore. The .38-40, at $400, has been refinished and the bore had some pitting making it a so-so shooter. It has now been rebarreled by gunsmith Keith DeHart using a Douglas barrel of .401" groove diameter and contoured to match the original barrel. Both guns not only shoot like those we dream about, they also reek of nostalgia.

As with most guns we buy, the doors of our minds are then opened for more purchases and more money to be spent. I am on the lookout now for a Model 1892 .44-40, and then a .25-20, and then ......

The Hidden Advocate:
Pocket Pistols
In 19th Century America

By: Michael W. Cuber, aka Kid Quick

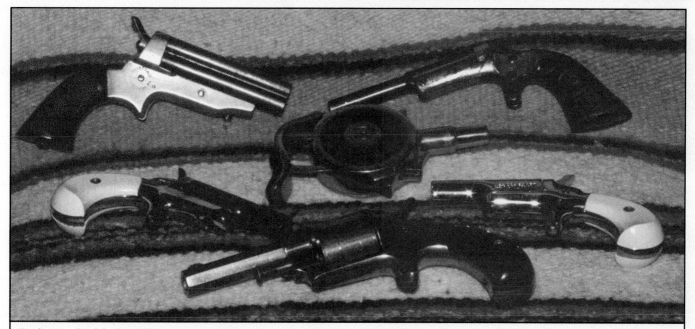

Pocket pistols of the late-1800's came in a variety of makes and models. Featured in the photo is a Sharps Four-Barrel Derringer, a Stevens No. 41 Tip-Up, Two Colt Derringers, a Chicago Palm Pistol, and a Forehand & Wadsworth revolver.

Abraham Lincoln once said that only a fool represents himself in court. At first glance, this statement may seem a little harsh, but the point our former president was trying to make was that everyone is better off with an advocate; that secret weapon that can aid your defense during the most dire moments of circumstance. It is doubtful that our late president's words had any influence on the sale of concealable handguns; however, the concept of a hidden advocate certainly did prove popular with a vast segment of Americans.

Concealable handguns, traditionally referred to as pocket pistols, comprise the most prolifically produced group of firearms ever made. Even today, concealable firearms are the number one seller in gun shops across the country. This has been the case now for almost 150 years. This group of firearms also has the dubious distinction of being one of the most ignored by collectors. Yes, there are a few folks who deal specifically with these types of firearms, and it is a very inexpensive field to get started in, but as a whole, pocket pistols have never generated the same kind of interest as long guns and larger side arms. Pocket pistols generally will not command the kind of prices that other types of firearms frequently do. Despite their general

lack of monetary value, the history of pocket pistols remains one of the most interesting and varied in the firearms industry.

Whether they were called pocket pistols, derringers, suicide specials, or palm pistols, they all had one thing in common, concealability. By being concealable, they gave the individual using them the element of surprise, or drop, on their opponent. This was of great benefit should that individual find him or herself the victim of a felonious act. Unfortunately, sometimes the reverse of this situation would occur, as was the case of our dear President Lincoln. Perhaps no other single event has cast as dark a shadow on a particular type of firearm as did the assassination of President Lincoln. These firearms have been maligned by some ever since this tragic event. What the world will never know is the uncountable number of felonious acts that have been prevented by pocket pistol wielding individuals who were determined to protect themselves and others. It is a point of fact that crime figures rose and then fell sharply between 1850 and the turn of the century. Perhaps it is no coincidence that this was exactly the same period of time that the pocket pistol industry took off like wildfire.

Prior to 1850, if an individual wanted a pocket pistol, they

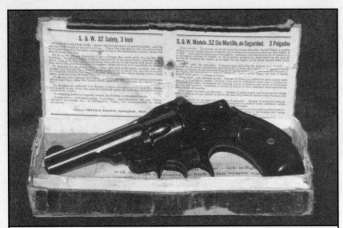

Smith & Wesson .32 caliber Safety Model in its original box. S&W would incorporate hinged barrels on all their models until 1899.

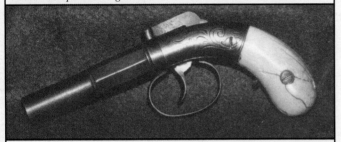

Allen & Thurber single-shot percussion pistol, circa 1849.

This is a beautifully-chromed .32 S&W Safety Model. What a great old-time carry gun!

The S&W .32 Fourth Model was typical of most double-action Smith & Wessons offered during the late-1800's.

This is a .38 caliber Russian Model S&W.

would probably have to satisfy themselves with a pepperbox, a Patterson Colt, or one of Henry Deringers percussion pistols. However, by the 1890's, almost every major arms maker in America was offering some type of concealable handgun. Remington, Marlin, Stevens, Sharps, and even the government's own Springfield Armory was offering pocket pistols. There was also a host of lesser-known manufacturers who produced pistols very similar in design to the products of Smith & Wesson and Colt. Furthermore, there were many manufacturers that marketed their own ingenious and novel designs. One such manufacturer was the Andrew J. Peavey Company, that offered the unique knife pistol. Made in the mid-1860's, this .22 caliber pistol resembled a pocketknife in almost every respect. The A.J. Peavey knife pistol, along with the palm pistols produced by the Chicago Firearms Company and the Minneapolis Firearms Company, would go down in history as some of the most unusual pocket pistols of the late-1800's. In fact, there were so many manufacturers during the latter half of the 19th century that, even today, the products of unknown makers will occasionally surface, as will unmarked guns of foreign manufacturers that were intended for American sales.

While Smith & Wesson and Colt revolvers were the most frequently copied, the name of one man would become virtually synonymous with pocket pistols of all types. This man was Henry Deringer. This association was due, in no small part, to the fact that it was a Henry Percussion Deringer that was found near President Lincoln's seat shortly after he was shot by the assassin, John Wilkes Booth. Regardless of the maker, or the firearm's proper name, if it were small and concealable it would almost invariably be referred to as a Derringer. This association became so prevalent after the president's death that even many of the manufacturers began applying the name to their small handguns; however, most frequently it will be spelled derringer with two R's. Some believe this to simply be a misspelling, but it is the author's belief that the different spelling was used intentionally by the manufacturers to differentiate between their small handguns and the actual products of Henry Deringer. Mr. Deringer's company had managed to survive the transition from percussion cap to self-contained cartridge and was still very much in business with their .22 and .32 caliber pocket pistols as late as 1879. Furthermore, Mr. Deringer had already filed suit, some years before, against a former employee who produced an exact copy of a Deringer percussion pistol under the name A.J. Plate.

Samuel Colt's name was never used, or abused depending upon how you look at it, like Henry Deringer's, but Mr. Colt's products were sorely copied by a variety of competitors. Some, like the Metropolitan Arms Company, went so far as to produce an arm almost indistinguishable from the 1851 Colt, while others like Eli Whitney produced firearms very similar in appearance to Colt's but which used a different internal mechanism in order to avoid infringement upon Samuel Colt's patents. The Whitney two-trigger pocket revolver of 1852, and the ring trigger pocket of 1854, incorporated separate triggers just forward of the firing triggers. After firing a shot, the forward trigger had to be pulled in order to free the manually-turned cylinder. Once a freshly-charged chamber was aligned with the barrel, the firearm could be cocked and fired again. This design was nowhere near as efficient as a Colt, or even a pepperbox, but the Whitney's looked like Colts and this was enough to help them sell. Other companies that produced revolvers very similar in appearance to Colt's were the Bacon Manufacturing Company, the E.A. Prescott Company, the Forehand and Wadsworth Company (formerly Hopkins and Allen), the J.M. Cooper Company, the Nepperhan Firearms Company, the Newbury Firearms Company, and the W.W. Marston Union Arms Company.

While Colt percussion revolvers were being widely copied, two prominent firearms designers joined forces to introduce an efficient self-contained cartridge revolver. These two men were Horrace Smith and Daniel Baird Wesson (Daniel's brother Frank was also a notable firearms designer). Their company, founded in 1852 and restructured in 1857, would go on to become one of the great names in American handguns, Smith & Wesson. Smith & Wesson's self-contained cartridge revolvers gained acceptance from the shooting public almost immediately, and by the mid to late 1860's, there were a variety of manufacturers offering self-contained cartridge revolvers. Previously, it had been Colt revolvers that the other companies had emulated, but after the introduction of the No. 1 First Issue S&W, the product lines of the competitors took on an appearance very similar to the First Issue. Each time Smith & Wesson released a new model, it would be copied, and some of these proved almost as popular as the Smith & Wesson products for a short period of time. Among the S&W copies were the Aetna Arms Pocket Revolver, the American Arms Top Break Revolver, the Connecticut Arms Pocket Revolver, the Marlin 1887 Double Action Revolver, and Philadelphia Deringer's .22 and .32 caliber rimfire revolvers, to name a few. Some, like the Harrington & Richards Top Break, would be produced well into the 20th century. Other revolvers, like Forehand & Wadsworth's and Merwin & Hulbert's, combined the best features of the Colts and Smith & Wessons and went on to become quite popular on their own. The Merwin & Hulbert revolvers were actually produced by Hopkins & Allen before control of the Allen Company was assumed by Ethan Allen's son-in-laws, Sullivan Forehand and Henry Wadsworth.

The practice of selling firearms from one company under different names was not something restricted to Hopkins & Allen. Metropolitan Arms were sold under the name H.E. Demick; Eli Whitney's were sold under the name Eagle Company; James Reid's were sold as James P. Fitch; Bacon Manufacturing Company produced Fitch & Waldo revolvers; and Hero and London pistols were actually factory seconds of Manhattan Arms. Does all this sound confusing? Well, it certainly is, and much of it has only recently been sorted out. Little wonder why some collectors refuse to deal with pocket pistols!

Even though Colt had firmly established itself with percussion revolvers, the company was somewhat slow in entering the fixed cartridge revolver market. When they finally did release their Colt Open Top Pocket Revolver of 1871, they were almost 15 years behind Smith & Wesson's No. 1 First Issue revolver of 1857. There were already a number of inexpensive pocket revolvers on the market, so Colt wisely chose to pursue military contracts for their larger-framed Single Action Army. When Colt finally began producing pocket revolvers in earnest in 1873, they were basically scaled-down versions of the solid-framed S.A.A. Like their larger counterparts, the single-action Colt pocket pistol could still be fired in an emergency with any one of its internal parts broken. If the trigger was broken, the hammer could still be cocked and slipped to fire the weapon. If the cylinder hand was broken, the cylinder could still be indexed manually for shooting, and if the cylinder bolt was broken, the hand could hold the cylinder in alignment with the barrel for shooting. Many older Colts can be found that have been used like this for

French .32-caliber revolver with folding trigger. Like many European pocket pistols, this one is of an unknown manufacturer.

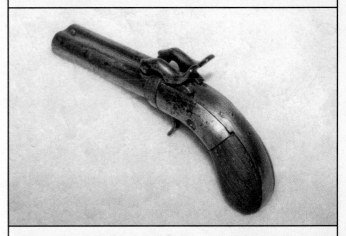

Allen & Thurber double-barrel percussion pistol, circa 1851, in .36 caliber.

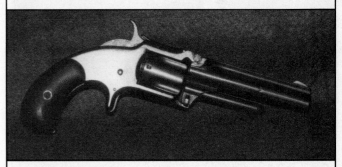

The S&W Third Issue was basically the same as the First Issue, which was highly sought after by Union officers during the Civil War.

The S&W No. 1-1/2 .32 rim was a scaled-up version of the No. 1 .22.

The H&R Young American was typical of many revolvers from the turn of the century. Most followed the lines of S&W and Colt revolvers rather closely.

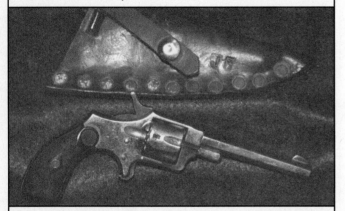

This Hopkins & Allen 1868 revolver with hand-made holster has obviously seen many days of carry usage.

Colt's first Open-Top was a pocket pistol. When Colt introduced this model, they were almost 15 years behind S&W's lead. Colt made up for this with their introduction of the swing-out cylinder in 1889.

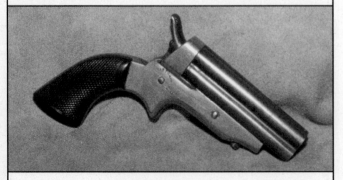

C. Sharps four-barrel derringer, patent 1859, in .32 rimfire.

years. This kind of use will frequently degrade the firearm to the point where it cannot be repaired. This is particularly true of Colts that have been fired repeatedly with broken cylinder bolts. Frequently, these revolvers will exhibit extreme cylinder gaps caused by bullets shaving the edge of the forcing cone as they enter the barrel. Even though it could be done, and was one of Colt's selling points, firing any revolver with broken parts was, and still is, extremely unwise. However, this feature was deemed important by individuals who spent extended periods of time journeying the frontier. New Line Model Colts could be had in a variety of calibers ranging from .22 rimfire up to .41 rimfire. Further development on these designs led to the Colt New House Model of 1880, and the Cop and Thug Model of 1882. The latter pistol actually featured a scene on its grip panels of a cop arresting a thug. In 1889, Colt introduced their first swing-out cylinder revolver. This feature provided for far quicker and easier reloading than previous models that utilized loading gates. The Colt New Pocket of Double Action of 1893 would also incorporate a swing-out cylinder, and was very similar in appearance to most of the double-action revolvers we know today. In fact, most of the design characteristics that can be found on today's revolvers, both double and single-action, originated from Colt pocket revolvers. This holds true even for the products of Smith & Wesson.

Smith & Wesson's first cartridge revolver, the No. 1 First Issue, was unique in that its barrel, when unlocked from the bottom of the frame, tipped up to allow access to the cylinder. Chambered for the self-contained .22 rimfire, this pistol was offered in three different issues from 1857 to 1881. The First Issues featured a slightly-rounded frame ahead of the grip, while the Second Issue featured a recessed, flat-sided frame ahead of the grip. Other than this, both models were virtually identical. The Third Issue featured an improved mechanism and bird's head grip. Even though the first S&W's were hinged on the top of the frame, while later models were hinged on the bottom and latched on top, hinged barrels would be incorporated on all their pistols until 1899. Part of the reason for Smith & Wesson's success, aside from their introducing the first American cartridge revolver, was that their single and double-action revolvers were reliable. As early as the 1830's, there had been attempts to market double-action pistols, but few were successful. Most of these had mechanisms that were very fragile and prone to failure with just a little use. Because of the difficulty in manufacturing these tiny actions and their reliability shortcomings, small single-action, single-shots remained popular even up to the turn of the century. Smith & Wesson played a major role in upgrading and refining new machinery and machining techniques. They were able to make their small revolvers faster and more reliable than anything that had previously been produced.

During the same course of time that Smith & Wesson and Colt were fielding truly efficient single and double-action revolvers, other companies were putting their best foot forward with novel designs of their own. Undoubtedly, credit for the most popular and widely produced of these would have to go to Remington and their Double Derringer. The Double Derringer was produced from 1866 to 1935. Furthermore, copies of this pistol are still being produced today by a variety of manufacturers. Featured in countless Western films, the Double Derringer is the quintessential pocket pistol. Originally chambered for the .41 rimfire, this Remington possessed a good balance of adequate power in a very concealable package. Being easy to load and easy to maintain with its top-hinged barrel, the Double Derringer offered its user two reliable shots. Because this pistol had to be cocked for each of these shots, it was relatively safe for carry in a purse or pocket. Today, copies of this pistol can be seen chambered for everything from .22 short to .410 shotshell. At present, Davis Arms seems to be the most popular manufacturer of these pistols, and, true to tradition, the Davis pistols can be purchased at very reasonable prices. Bond Arms also makes an outstanding .45 Colt derringer.

Even though they have frequently been maligned, pocket pistols will always have a place in society. They are a part of our history and culture. Undoubtedly, as time passes and more research is gathered, the values of the older pocket pistols will increase. We will likely see more replicas of these designs in the future. When you consider all the villainy that can be seen in the world today, the concept of a hidden advocate just makes too much sense to let it slip away.

The modern derringer is depicted by Davis Industries with its .38 Special and has a remarkable resemblance to the old Remington .41 caliber derringers.

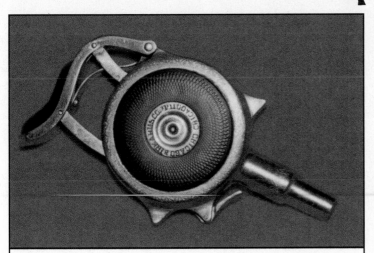

The Chicago Palm Pistol was one of the most unique pistols of the 1890's.

Internal view of the Chicago Palm Pistol showing its rotary chambers.

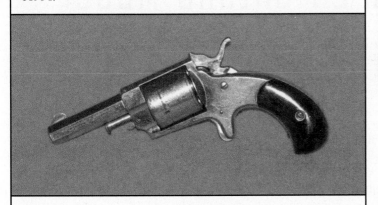

Bulldog .38 rimfire.

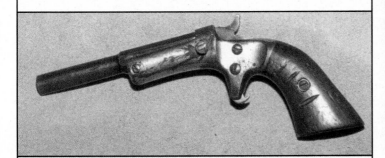

J. Stevens .22 caliber single-shot with three notches on the left grip and two on the right grip.

Smith & Wesson 6-shot, .32 rimfire, three-digit serial number, 1871 reissue.

B
A
L
L
A
R
D

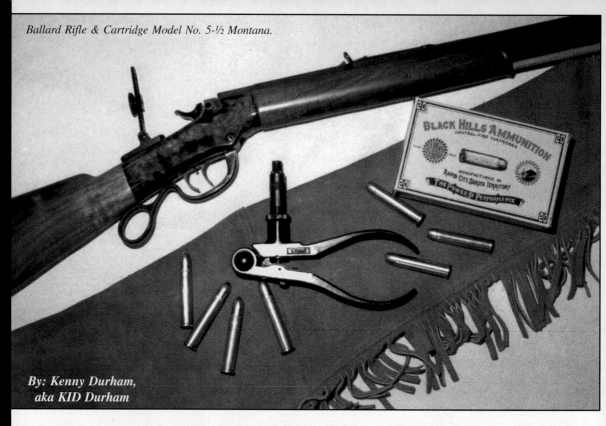

Ballard Rifle & Cartridge Model No. 5-½ Montana.

By: Kenny Durham,
aka KID Durham

Ballard Rifle & Cartridge, LLC
No. 5-1/2 Montana Model

To a rifleman, there is no finer rifle than a well-made single-shot. No matter what era in history the rifle is from, be it an elegant Kentucky flinter from the late 1700's or customized Ruger No. 1 from 2000, single-shot rifles captivate our attention in a manner that no other rifle can. One of the great American single-shot rifles was designed and patented by Charles H. Ballard on November 5, 1861. Subsequently, Ballard patent rights were sold and the rifles were produced by a variety of companies.

The Ballards that most of us recognize today were the Marlin Ballards produced in New Haven, Connecticut, where John Mahlon Marlin made C. H. Ballard patent rifles and metallic cartridge derringers from 1875 to 1880. The following are the succeeding names of the companies: Marlin Firearms Co. - 1880 to 1915, Marlin Arms Corp. - 1915 to 1916, Marlin Rockwell Corp. - 1916 to 1921, and Marlin Firearms Co. - 1921 to date, all at New Haven, Connecticut.

John Marlin took over the redesign and production of the Ballard rifles, which resulted in one of the finest single-shot rifles ever produced. The fine rifles produced by Marlin established the Ballard as the standard for target shooting. In the same sense that Sharps rifles are associated with buffalo hunting, Ballard rifles have become associated with target shooting.

Eighty years ago, in his book *Our Rifles*, Charles Winthrop Sawyer wrote of a particular Ballard rifle. "The specimen shown was the most popular one of the various models issued by the factory, and is true to type. Such specimens are now difficult to secure because Ballard actions were so popular among the target shooting fraternity that the frames were extensively used with barrels of other makes and gunsmith-made special stocks." In other words, Ballard actions were highly prized as the basis for target rifles.

At the same time, Ballard rifles were equally at home in the woods searching for the White Tail Deer, on the plains harvesting great bison herds, in the high meadows stalking the majestic Wapiti, or simply as a boy's first rifle for small game. Ballard models were pro-

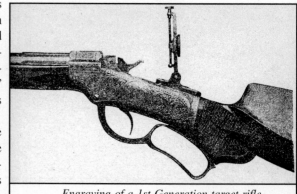

Engraving of a 1st Generation target rifle.

duced in many configurations and calibers to suit any hunting or target-shooting situation. In the late 1800's, the popularity of single-shot rifles diminished in favor of the repeating rifle for hunting. All too often a hunter returning to camp empty-handed would blame his lack of success on having only one shot. Often heard was, " If I'da had a repeater, I'da got em!" Truth is, hunting success is found in a single, well-placed shot, not in the number of cartridges that can be fired in a rifle before reloading. But, fact or myth, single-shot rifles gradually faded from the catalogs of all the major firearms companies as repeating rifles became more powerful and reliable. No longer could a person buy a new Ballard, Highwall, or Hepburn. But times have changed and history is repeating itself.

Would you like to be able to step back in time and order a custom Ballard rifle from the factory? So far, time travel is not possible, but ordering a new Ballard rifle from the factory is! Now, just as 100 years ago, Ballard rifles are being produced at the turn of another century. Ballard Rifle & Cartridge, LLC of Cody, Wyoming acquired the residual rights to the Ballard patent and are producing 2nd Generation Ballard rifles. The 2nd Generation Ballard rifles are not reproductions, but are the real McCoy, in the same models and configurations as were produced in the 1800's. Parts are interchangeable between the new and old rifles and Ballard Rifle & Cartridge also provides repair and restoration service of 1st Generation Ballards, including a factory letter stating the restoration done. The current catalog lists 13 models of Ballard rifles and a host of custom options to suit any shooter.

In May of 2000, at the California State Black Powder Cartridge Rifle Silhouette Championships, Ballard President, Steve Garbe, broke his own national record of 93 x120 by shooting a score of 103 x 120; both records were established with Ballard rifles. Now, we all know that you can't buy a winner and that Steve has won many matches with Sharps, Winchesters, and even Springfield rifles. But, we also know that a shooter can't win with a rifle that won't shoot! So, once again, the Ballard rifles are making their presence known on the target ranges.

While at the California match, I made arrangements with Steve Garbe to have a Ballard rifle sent to SHOOT! Magazine for testing. The rifle that arrived was a model No. 5-½ Montana chambered for the .45-70 Govt. The Montana is the "heavyweight" of the Ballard rifles originally chambered for the .45-110, weighing 14-½ pounds. The No. 5-½ features an under-barrel wiping rod, ring lever, double-set triggers, and a shotgun-style buttstock with a steel buttplate. Rocky Mountain sights are listed in the catalog as standard equipment. The sights installed on the rifle sent for testing were a silver blade front, a semi-buckhorn rear with elevator, and a hunting-style tang rear with windage adjustment.

The overall fit and finish of the rifle is excellent. Wood-to-metal fit is tight and smooth around the wrist of the stock and the buttplate. Stocks are black walnut standard grade as listed in the catalog, but are borderline semi-fancy grade. The grain is tight and dense, which is proper for this heavy rifle. The stock finish appears to be a standard oil finish with the grain properly filled and rubbed to a pleasing satin luster. The amount of finish is adequate, however I would like to see one or two additional coats applied. My preference for stock finish is that 90% is in the wood and the other 10% is on the surface of the wood. I usually add to the finish of any rifle I purchase.

The metal work is also excellent. The barrel is an extra heavy 30" octagon, 1 turn in 18 inch, made by Badger Barrels in Wisconsin. A look through the bore reveals the excellent lapped finish typical of all Badger barrels. Outside, the octagon corners are crisp and sharp with the bluing a rich black that is befitting of this rifle. A brighter polish on this model would detract from the appearance. The action is color case hardened and the colors are deep and rich. A standard feature on Ballard rifles is a lacquer on the action to protect the case colors. Use and exposure to sunlight cause case colors to fade over time. An application of lacquer can prevent or at least slow down the fading. Similarly, lacquering metal is the method by which brass musical instruments are kept bright and shiny. The metal is polished to the desired luster and then sprayed with lacquer. One word of caution with lacquered actions is to avoid using extremely hot water on the lacquered surface. The hot water will dissolve the lacquer! Now, I don't expect anyone to be tossing their Ballard into a tub of boiling water, but IF you use soapy water to clean black powder fouling, make sure the water is cool enough for a baby's behind.

The working of the action of this rifle is smooth and flawless. The double set triggers break with a clean let-off without any creep. I never turned the adjusting screw on the triggers because the set was to my liking as it was. The Ballard differs from all other single-shot rifles due to the design of the breech block. The breech block is a two-piece block consisting of left and right halves. The block is more than just a breech block because it contains not only the firing pin, but the lock mechanism and the triggers as well. All moving parts are inside the breech block, which certainly adds great protection from dust and dirt. Ballards are also known for their fast lock time. Now it was time for testing the accuracy of this rifle.

The Ballard No. 5-½ Montana is designed for bringing down big game at long range. This rifle is meant to consume heavy loads of black powder and long heavy bullets. Somehow, with this rifle, the normal routine of testing factory-loaded ammunition with jacketed bullets was not appealing to me at all. However, one factory load that performs well in every .45-70 that I

A Ballard No. 5-1/2 Montana chambered for the .45-70.

Action and lock are nicely colored with good wood-to-metal fit.

have tested is the 405-gr. flat-point smokeless load from Black Hill Ammunition of Rapid City, SD. Twenty rounds of the Black Hills factory loads were fired from a bench rest at 100 yards. For a final five-shot group, a clean target was posted and deliberate care taken to be as consistent as possible, just as though I were shooting a match. The result was a five-shot group measuring 1-¾" center-to-center of the widest shots, with four shots grouping 1-1/8" center-to-center. It seems that there ALWAYS has to be that one wide shot!

With factory load testing out of the way, it was time for some custom black powder loads tailored just for the 5-½ Montana. Sixty once-fired Black Hills .45-70 cases were fully-sized and checked for length. Two bullets were chosen to use in the rifle, the Saeco 645, weighing 493 grains, and the Lyman Postell, weighing 530 grains. Both bullets were cast from 30:1 alloy, unsized and lubed with SPG. The cases were primed with Federal 215 primers and charged with 70 grains of Goex FFg black powder dropped through a 30-inch drop tube. A Walters 0.060-inch fiber wad was placed in the case and then charged and compressed in a compression die. The bullets were seated to the maximum overall length the rifle chamber would allow, without engraving the front driving band of the bullet into the rifling. The bullet seating depth for both bullets, and therefore the amount of powder compression, had been previously determined by creating a dummy round as detailed in the article titled *Loading Black Powder Cartridges for Single Shot Rifles* also included in this book. These loads were fired from a bench rest at 200 yards. Both loads were accurate and performed well, but in this testing the Lyman Postell bullet proved to be the most accurate, at least with the powder charge and amount of compression used. A different powder and charge could add up to a different result and is where the time consuming effort of working up a load paid off.

After fouling the bore and getting the sights adjusted to hit close to center, a 10-shot group was fired for group size. With factory sights and custom black powder loads, the fired group fell into the two minutes of angle that is a great starting point from which to improve the load. What was intriguing were the five shots that created one hole in the center of the group. The five shots in the center were not fired in succession, but at random, as were the other five shots. The silver blade front sight is not the best for target shooting and had there been an aperture sight in front, the group may have been VERY small. Fifteen of the Lyman Postell rounds were chronographed with the following results: High = 1225 fps, Low = 1207 fps, Avg. = 1214 fps, Extreme spread = 18 fps, and a standard deviation of five. This load is, indeed, a good starting point.

Next, I took the rifle to the silhouette range for a go at the 500-meter rams. I set up a bank of five rams and took a couple sighting

shots to get the right setting. Once the sights were adjusted, I proceeded to knock over all five rams with five shots. This rifle is way over the weight limit for BPCRS, but it sure does a job at 500 meters. I can imagine what it would be like to line the sight up on a nice bull elk about 300 yards away at the edge of the timber.

Ballard rifles are not cheap and likely never have been. Base prices for standard models start at $1850 for a No. 1-½ and top out at $2950 for models No. 4-½ and No. 7. The No. 5-½ Montana lists at $2725. If you wish to build your own Ballard, barreled actions are priced at $1350. All parts are available, which is great when restoring an old Ballard! Ballard Rifle & Cartridge, LLC also sells sights, bullet moulds, and brass for their rifles and other's. You can also learn more about Ballards by logging onto the Ballard web site at www.ballardrifles.com.

See ya at the range!

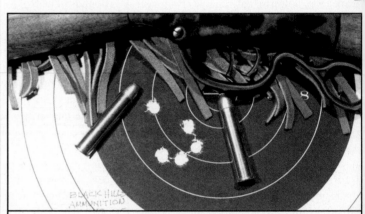
Five-shot group fired at 100 yards with Black Hills factory-loaded ammunition, with smokeless powder and 405-gr. bullets.

10-shot group fired at 200 yards with 530-gr. Lyman Postell bullets over 70 grains of Goex FFg black powder.

Cimarron's 1885

By: Kenny Durham,
aka KID Durham

High Wall Sporting Rifle

On October 7th, 1879, John Moses Browning was issued Patent No. 220,271 for his design of a single-shot, breech-loading rifle. This new falling block rifle was unlike any other being produced in the 1870's. Missing from Browning's design were the large heavy hammer and massive receiver typical of Remington and Sharps rifles. The new rifle had graceful flowing lines in the same manner as did the slender Kentucky Rifles of 100 years earlier. The Browning Single-Shot featured a sleek compact design that was silky smooth to operate with the hammer cocked and ready to fire as the action came into battery. But moreover, the rifle was ruggedly tough; stronger than any other rifle of the day. J.M. Browning & Brothers produced approximately 550 single-shot rifles from 1878 until 1883 when a fateful encounter between one of the Browning rifles and a Winchester salesman changed the course of firearms history. The salesman, intrigued by the unique design, purchased a used Browning Single-shot rifle and sent it to his boss, Oliver Winchester. Upon inspecting the new and innovative design, Winchester sent his son-in-law, T. G. Bennett, to Ogden, Utah, to pursue buying the rights to the graceful single-shot. Bennett, who was also the General Manager of Winchester Repeating Arms, negotiated the acquisition with Browning for the sum of $8000. Once in the hands of Winchester, the internal design was modified significantly for the ease of manufacturing and to improve the functionality of the rifle.

On September 9, 1885, Winchester began producing the Model 1885 which shooters would affectionately dub the "High-Wall" in years to come. By 1920, when production of the High-Wall ceased, some 139,725 rifles had been produced. Today, over a century later, a great number of these rifles are still in use, many in their original condition. After World War II and into the 1960's, thousands of Winchester Single-shot rifles were converted from firing black powder cartridges to small-caliber, high-velocity varmint rifles such as the .219 Donaldson Wasp. Traditional stocks were replaced with Monte

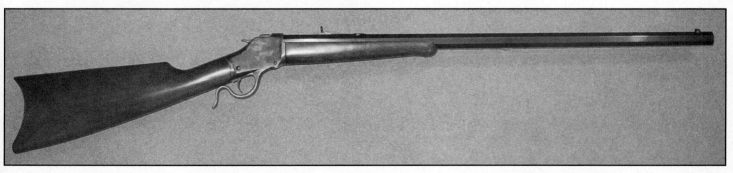

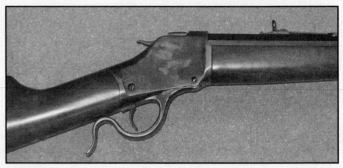

Carlo butt stocks and beavertail forends, but with the rise in popularity of Western-action and Black Powder Cartridge rifle shooting in recent years, many of those "Varmint" Highwalls are once again undergoing another metamorphous. However, this time, the short round small caliber barrels are being replaced with heavy octagon barrels chambered for the all-time favorite black powder cartridges, such as the .38-55, .40-65, .45-70 and .45-90. Additionally, several domestic rifle makers specialize in building custom High-Wall rifles from scratch in a variety of

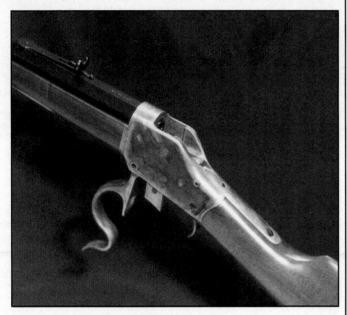

models from sporting, to long-range target, to Schuetzen models. However, these custom recreations of the Winchester Single-shot are produced in a very limited quantity, often requiring a long wait from the time an order is placed until the rifle is in the hands of it's owner.

In recent years, Mike Harvey of Cimarron Firearms Co. has been importing a reproduction of the Winchester 1885 Single Shot made to Cimarron's specifications by the Aldo Uberti & Co. of Italy, and, as in the past, several variations of the 1885 Single Shot are available, along with special orders from the Cimarron custom shop. SHOOT! Magazine received for testing a Cimarron 1885 High Wall Sporting Rifle chambered for the .40-65 Winchester cartridge. This sporting rifle is striking in appearance with a beautifully case-colored action and blued barrel, closely matching the colors and finish of the original Winchesters. The fit and finish of the butt stock and forearm are

good. The Cimarron High-Wall is not an exact reproduction of any model Winchester 1885, but rather a model that "might have" been built by Winchester. Any student of the Winchester Single Shot knows that the prevailing characteristic of the 1885 is the great variation between individual rifles, even within the same models. The Cimarron 1885 is unique in that it contains features from both early and late models of Winchester production. For instance, the Cimarron is the thin side later version of the 1885 and features a coil spring, but bears the crescent butt plate of the 1876 lever-action, as did the early 1885 Winchesters. In addition, the butt plate is of the trapdoor variety and provides access to a five-section brass cleaning rod held in the butt stock, which I don't believe was typical of any original 1885. Another feature of the Cimarron High-Wall is that the hammer remains at half-

cock when the action is closed, whereas the original High Walls were automatically brought to full-cock when the action was brought into battery. The hammer on the Cimarron 1885 must be brought to full-cock manually. This is a great safety feature in my opinion, which makes the rifle a candidate for junior shooters. Also, the trigger is a single trigger that, to my surprise, was very crisp, had no creep, and broke at 3-½ pounds. The rifle carries a 30" full octagon barrel with a twist rate of one turn in sixteen inches to stabilize the long heavy bullets used for black powder cartridge silhouette and long-range target shooting. Standard sights are the traditional Winchester-shaped, blade-

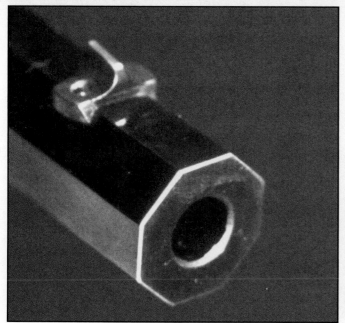

front and semi-buckhorn rear. The upper receiver tang is drilled and tapped with the same hole spacing as used by Winchester for the installation of tang sights. The lower tang is marked with the serial number and the inscription "PAT. OCT 7th 79" just as the original Winchesters were.

The Cimarron High-Wall is offered in four choices of caliber: .38-55 Winchester, .40-65 Winchester, .45-70 Govt., and .45-90 Winchester. Factory ammunition is plentiful for the .38-55 and .45-70, but .40-65 and .45-90 ammunition is strictly a handloading proposition. I am only aware of a couple vendors who offer factory loads for these two cartridges. Therefore, when it came to testing the Cimarron High Wall, I was relegated to "rolling-my-own," so to speak. For testing, I chose to load and shoot black powder ammunition for a couple of reasons. First off, one of the primary reasons for which a shooter might purchase a High-Wall would be to compete in shooting matches, such as black powder cartridge silhouette, mid-range or long-range (Creedmoor) black powder target shooting, and black powder schuetzen matches, all of which require ammunition to be loaded with black powder or Pyrodex. Second, most of the time, with cartridges from the black powder era, it is much easier and quicker to develop an accurate load with black powder than it is with smokeless powder. Many times the first black powder load

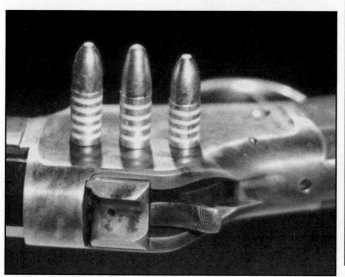

tried in a new rifle, when careful attention is given to bullet fit and seating depth, turns out to be so accurate that a little further tweaking of the load is all that is needed. Such were the results in this case for the Cimarron High Wall as we shall see.

Three bullets were chosen for testing based on how well they fit the bore by inserting the nose in the muzzle - not too loose, not too tight. The bullets were the Saeco #640 cast from 30:1 (lead:tin) and weighing 371 grains, Lyman-Snover cast from 20:1 alloy and weighing 406 grains, and the Saeco # 740 cast

from 30:1 alloy and weighing 413 grains (bullets were weighed with lube grooves filled). Brass cases were Winchester .45-70 cases formed to .40-65 by Buffalo Arms Co. The black powder used was 60 grains of Goex FFg. The powder charge was determined by the amount of powder required to fill the case up to the base of the bullet when the bullet was seated to the maximum allowable overall cartridge length that would chamber in the rifle. Additionally, a little more powder was added so that

LYMAN-SNOVER
1⅝" x 3³⁄₁₆"
100 YDS — 5 SHOTS

SAECO # 640
1⁵⁄₁₆" x 2⅞"
100 YD — 5 SHOTS

with a 0.030" fiber wad placed atop the charge, approximately 0.060" of compression was required to provide the necessary depth for the bullet. The Lyman-Snover and the Saeco #740 bullets, when properly seated to fit the bore, turned out to be at the same depth in the case, and both left one lube groove exposed. The shorter Saeco #640 was seated to the same depth that resulted in a shorter overall length. All test loads were fired from a bench rest at 100 yards using the barrel sights only. The Saeco #740 loads were tried first. Two shots were fired to foul the bore, then a five-shot string was fired. The shots shown in the photo are the first ever fired from this rifle. All three loads produced good and accurate results in the Cimarron. However, the heavier Saeco bullet produced the tightest groups. With seven cartridges left, I posted a clean target and attempted to group all seven shots into the "10" ring. I managed to get four of them

into the center, but put the other three in the "9" ring. My fault, not the rifle's! As I mentioned earlier, when black powder cartridges are properly assembled to fit an individual rifle, this degree of accuracy is to be expected. Outfitted with a globe front sight and a quality vernier tang sight, I would not be the least bit hesitant to enter a black powder cartridge mid-range or silhouette match anywhere with the Cimarron High Wall. The accuracy, weight, and balance of the Cimarron makes it an ideal rifle for hunting, side matches at cowboy shoots, or any of the black powder cartridge rifle events.

See ya at the range!

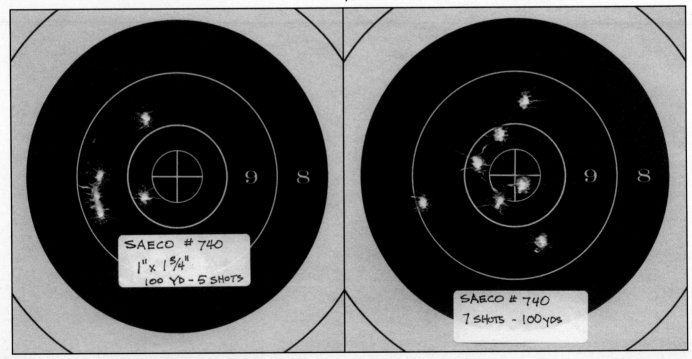

SAECO # 740
1" x 1¾"
100 YD — 5 SHOTS

SAECO # 740
7 SHOTS — 100 YDS

SHARPS, SHARPS, AND MORE SHARPS

By: Kenny Durham, aka KID Durham

Six models of 1874 Sharps pattern rifles (top to bottom): EMF .45-70 Carbine, Navy Arms .45-80 Sporting Rifle, Dixie Gun Works .45-70 Silhouette Rifle, Shiloh .40-65 No. 1 Sporting Rifle, Shiloh .45-100 Long-Range Express, and Pedersoli .45-70 Schuetzen Rifle.

The 1874 Model Sharps in the 21st Century

Recently, at a Black Powder Cartridge Rifle Silhouette match, I noticed an elderly couple standing behind the firing line near the cleaning tables. As I approached the table, upon which rested my gun vise cradling my Shiloh 1874 Sharps No. 1 Sporting Rifle, it became obvious to me that from the gentleman's demeanor he wished to make an inquiry of some sort. I greeted him in a manner to make him feel at ease, upon which he immediately inquired, "Is anyone here shooting a Sharps Buffalo Rifle?" Discerning that he was familiar with the Sharps rifle in name only since he was in "snake-bite" proximity to three Sharps rifles, I smiled and said, "Yes, most of the rifles here are 1874 Sharps." I then went on to explain that the rifles were not original Sharps rifles from the 1800's, but newly-made 1874 pattern rifles or reproductions. I pointed out a variety of Sharps to the couple; rifles of different manufacture, caliber, and configurations. They walked from table to table examining the dozen or so Sharps rifles scattered among the tables. Whether or not the gent would now recognize a model 1874 Sharps is uncertain, but for a few moments on a fall afternoon, he forgot all his worldly cares and indulged himself in the pleasure of enjoying the "legendary" Sharps Buffalo Rifle as so many of us have come to do.

The Model 1874 Sharps is somewhat of a misnomer according to Frank Sellers, author of the book *Sharps Firearms*, which has come to be recognized as the definitive work on the many firearms to bear the name "Sharps." Sellers explains that the action was in production as early as January of 1871, but the designation of it as the model 1874 did not begin until the arrival of the model 1878 "Borchardt." He feels that the company likely felt that a model number designation would be more befitting given the status of the big "side-hammer" rifle than just calling it the "Old Model."

Today, some 120-plus years later, the model 1874 Sharps is as popular as ever. Whether in the hunting fields, at cowboy side matches, buffalo matches, silhouette shooting, or at long-range targets over one-half of a mile away, the big Sharps continues to be the most popular overall single-shot in use. Today, much of the 1874's popularity can be chalked up to nostalgia and the romance of the Old West. But in the late 1860's, when many of the Sharps percussion arms were being converted to shoot powerful metallic cartridges, there was nothing else to compare the Sharps Rifle with. Remington's famous Rolling Block was gaining in popularity, but Sharps had garnered first place in the single-shot race. Ballard rifles were also being produced in some powerful chamberings, but the reputation of Sharps, having

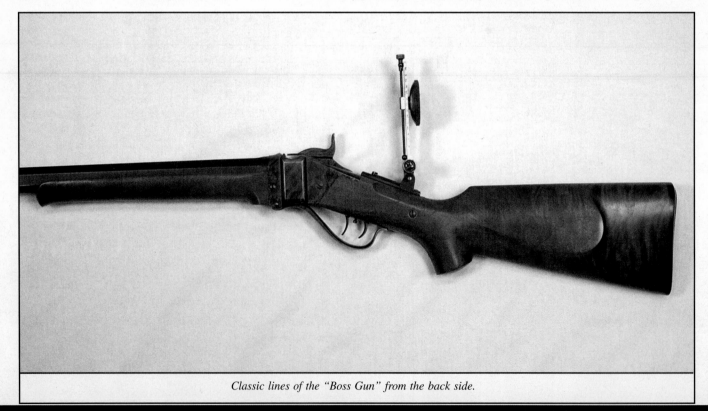

Classic lines of the "Boss Gun" from the back side.

been established by the military, gave them a head start. The Model 1874 Sharps was the culmination of all of the modifications and refinements brought about by the introduction of metallic cartridges and the resulting conversion of thousands of percussion breech loaders. Beginning in 1869, Sharps began serious efforts to corner the civilian sporting rifle market when their military contracts expired. The "New Model 1869" contained some refinements that made for a slimmer and trimmer action, smoother operating, and eliminated the now obsolete percussion priming system. A few additional refinements resulted in the model, which became known as the 1874.

The Sharps Rifle Co. produced the Model 1874 in a variety of configurations. Sporting Rifle, Business Rifle, Military Rifle and Carbine, Schuetzen Rifle, Mid-Range Target, Long-Range Target, and Creedmoor Rifle are some of the configurations. There were others, and a multitude of options from which to choose that blur the distinctions between the 1874 models. In the 1800's, only one company, obviously Sharps Rifle Co.'s, produced the various models of the 1874 Sharps. Today, a dozen or so companies produce rifles patterned after the 1874 Sharps in a mind-boggling variety of configurations, quality, and price ranges. Additionally, there are custom gunsmiths that build 1874 rifles from scratch.

Much of the popularity of the 1874 Sharps today can be traced directly to Wolfgang Droege and the formation of the Shiloh Rifle Company that began producing the 1874 Sharps in the 1970's in Farmingdale, New York. Later, the company was split into two companies: The Shiloh Rifle

A classic example of the 1874 Sharps Long-Range Express in .45 x 2–6/10 (.45-100) from Shiloh Rifle Manufacturing Co. of Big Timber, Montana.

Manufacturing Co. and the C. Sharps Arms Co., both located in Big Timber, Montana. One company retained the "Shiloh" name, while the other, C. Sharps Arms Co., retained the "Old Reliable" trademark. Both C. Sharps Arms and Shiloh Rifle Manufacturing produce semi-custom rifles of equal or better quality than the original Sharps Rifle Company, and the parts are interchangeable with the originals.

Sharps rifles of the 1800's became known as either the "Hartford" or "Bridgeport" Sharps depending upon which plant they were built. Ironically, Shiloh Sharps rifles of the 1900's have become known as either the "Farmingdale" or "Big Timber" Shiloh Sharps. The Shiloh Rifle Manufacturing Co. built the rifle(s) used in the movie *Quigley Down Under*, starring actor Tom Selleck as Matthew Quigley. Although a fictitious character, Matthew Quigley was, without a doubt, the other contributing factor in the current popularity of the 1874 Sharps. Without Shiloh and Quigley, I doubt we would have the variety of manufacturers building the 1874 today. Shiloh Sharps rifles, among black powder cartridge shooters, have almost become synonymous with "original" Sharps rifles. I currently own two Shiloh 1874 Sharps pattern rifles, and the quality and accuracy of these rifles is second to none. The Shiloh Rifle Manufacturing Co. has stayed with the Model 1874 as its sole production. However, Shiloh is in the final stages of putting the 1863 Sharps Percussion breech loader into production.

C. Sharps Arms Co. also produces 1874 Sharps pattern rifles in a variety of configurations. Rifles from C. Sharps are as top quality and accurate as any. I have not owned a C. Sharps version of the 1874, but know shooters who do that are very pleased with the quality of the rifle. One experienced shooter has told me that his C. Sharps 1874 is one of the most accurate rifles he has ever shot. C. Sharps also produces the Model 1875 Sharps, a Sharps design that never actually saw production, and I mention this only because I have fired several of the C. Sharps 1875s and they are fine rifles.

The other major source of 1874 Sharps pattern rifles are those manufactured by firearms makers in Italy and imported by a variety of U.S. companies. Companies such as Armi Sport, IAB, Pedretti & Sons, and Davide Pedersoli produce a multitude of 1874 models. Pedersoli is the company that most shooters recognize as the leader in imported Sharps. American companies, such as Navy Arms Company, Dixie Gun Works, and Cabela's import Pedersoli's various 1874 models, and have contracts with Pedersoli to produce rifles to their own specifications. The Pedersoli Sharps rifles sold by Navy Arms and Dixie Gun Works are used by many shooters in competition across a wide spectrum of events. The Pedersoli 1874 Silhouette model has won many silhouette matches in the hands of good shooters. Taylor's & Co. imports a variety of the 1874 Sharps pattern rifles from Armi Sport that are of good quality as well, and EMF Company imports a line of 1874 Sharps pattern rifle from Italy built to their specifications. Although these rifles might be considered entry-level, they can produce match-winning scores with properly-crafted ammunition.

If these sources aren't enough, there are a few custom rifle builders that turn out only a dozen or so rifles per year. One such builder with whom I am familiar is Richard McKinney, proprietor of Schuetzen Gun Company of Drake, Colorado. I have seen Mr. McKinney's work first hand, and it is first-class all the way with meticulous attention to detail. Finally, there is one remaining alternative to owning an 1874 Sharps. Build your own! This is recommended for only those who are skilled in the art of machining and are very knowledgeable concerning firearms, but several individuals have done so. Retired U.S. Border Patrol Agent Doug Knoell of Santee, California built his own 1874 action from a chunk of steel. It is a unique, one-of-a-kind rifle, just as were many of the original Sharps 1874 rifles.

The different brands of 1874 Sharps listed in this overview vary in price range from about $695 to over $3000 depending on the options. In 1874, the cost of a basic Model 1874 Sporting Rifle was $33.00, a lot of money for those times. Today, the cost of a quality 1874 Sharps pattern rifle is not cheap either, but oh, what fine rifles they are!

See ya at the range!

Black Powder and the Old West
Chapter 3
Ammunition, Reloading & Cleaning

Loading Black Powder Cartridges for Revolvers

*By: Kenny Durham,
aka KID Durham*

In 1980, while working in a neighboring town about two hours from home, I rented a space in a mobile home park, moved in, and prepared to live there during the week and then drive home on the weekends. While I was busy unloading the pickup with my away-from-home belongings, an elderly gentleman greeted me from the mobile home next door. I stopped what I was doing, went over to introduce myself, and as we shook hands, he told me that his name was John Slater. Most evenings after work, I would see John and his wife, Pauline, out in the yard enjoying the early summer weather. One night after a hard day's work of pouring and finishing concrete, my new neighbors invited me to have supper with them.

Inside John's mobile home, one of the first things that caught my eye was a photograph of John Wayne with all of the teenage cowboys from the movie *The Cowboys*. The photo was autographed by John Wayne with something like, "Good luck and enjoy your retirement, John Wayne." The next thing that caught my eye was a big red book on the coffee table titled *Famous Gunfighters*. I picked up the book and opened the cover, only to find greetings and best wishes from several Hollywood stars.

John noticed my obvious curiosity and explained that he had retired from the motion picture industry where he had been a horse wrangler and cowboy stuntman in many Western movies. Turns out that John had also been quite a cowboy, too. He wore a belt with a buckle that had seen much use. Looking closely at the belt buckle, I made out the inscription, "All Around Champion Cowboy - Hoot Gibson Rodeo 1930 – Oklahoma." John had also worked and rodeoed with famous cowboy, actor, and stuntman, Yakima Cannut. Needless to say, dinner was very interesting!

At some point in the conversation the subject turned to talking about guns, and I told John of my interest in black powder and firearms of the 1800's. John mentioned that he was not very knowledgeable

A variety of single-action revolvers in .38 Special/.357 Magnum, .44 Special/.44 Magnum, and .45 Schofield/.45 Colt.

concerning guns. He excused himself from the table and said, "I have something to show you. Have a seat on the couch." He returned shortly with a cartridge belt and holster containing a Colt Single Action. Handing the gun to me he said, "What do you know about this?" I drew the gun from the holster and saw that it was a 1st Generation black powder Colt Single Action Army in .45 caliber. The old revolver showed signs of much use and a fair amount of abuse, and the barrel inside was pretty bad, but still shootable. John told me that the gun had been given to him years ago, but he had never shot it because he was told that black powder ammunition was no longer available. I chuckled and asked John, "Would you like to shoot this gun?" John replied, "Oh, I would love to be able to shoot it!" I told him that when I went home on the weekend I would load up a few shells for him that would be safe to shoot in the old single-action.

Monday evening, when I pulled into the driveway of my home-away-from-home, John

was out of his house and over to mine before I turned the engine off. I handed him a box of .45 Colt ammo loaded with black powder. The 79-year-old gent opened the box like a gleeful kid and examined the cartridges. Before he could say anything, I said, "We can go shoot some of these tonight if you want." A quick shower and a gobbled sandwich later, we were headed for a place to shoot on the outskirts of town. I set up some cans and fired a couple rounds just to make sure the old Colt was okay, and then handed the gun to him. As John squeezed the trigger, the old Colt roared back to life with the rich, full "BOOM" that can only be produced by black powder. He emptied the remaining rounds and we loaded the gun again. John only occasionally hit a tin can, but he didn't really care. For him, the thrill was just getting to fire the old Colt. He shot up most of the box of shells, but saved a few for another time. Late in life, John experienced the joy of shooting black powder for the first time. Whether or not he ever shot the Colt again, I do not know.

When Colt introduced the Single Action Army revolver chambered for the new .45 Colt cartridge, they virtually redefined the handgun in terms of power and functionality. The new revolver was rugged and durable, but retained the balance and feel of the cap-n-ball Colts. The new centerfire cartridge was not only as powerful as any repeating rifle of the day, but for the next 62 years, the .45 Colt would reign as the most powerful handgun cartridge available. Not until 1935 and the introduction of the .357 Magnum, did the .45 Colt slip to 2nd place. Even then, the limitations on the .45 were due to old guns in circulation, not the cartridge. The .357 Magnum held the "most powerful" spot for 21 years when, in 1956, the .44 Magnum stepped into the spotlight. Now, even more powerful cartridges have eclipsed the potent .44 Magnum. Still, revolvers chambered for the .45 Colt, .357 Remington Magnum, and .44 Remington Magnum, each of which were at one time the most powerful handgun cartridges available, are the most popular in cowboy action shooting.

The .357 and .44 Magnums, though products of the modern smokeless era, have roots forever entrenched in black powder history. For this reason, both of these modern cartridges are also excellent for loading with black powder. Perhaps you may have wanted to experiment with some black powder loads for your favorite six-shooter, but have held back because of the different loading methods and uncertainty of shooting black powder in your handguns. We will herein take a look at these three revolver chamberings and how we can load black powder ammunition that is accurate, relatively clean burning, and tailored to the degree of power desired; in other words, black powder revolver cartridges that can be low-velocity loads in the range of 650 fps or full-powerhouse loads that approach the 1,000 fps limit for cowboy action shooting. As we take a look at loading black powder cartridges for six-shooters, realize that the procedures and methods described apply to all black powder revolver cartridges in various other calibers, even though we are focusing on the three aforementioned chamberings.

First, let me state that while I am not a proponent of using reduced black powder loads in repeating rifles, I do not feel the same way about handgun ammunition. The reason for using reduced loads in handguns is not for the "quick recovery" for successive shots or for the win-at-all-cost, squib-load shooters,

.38 Special and .357 Magnum cartridges.

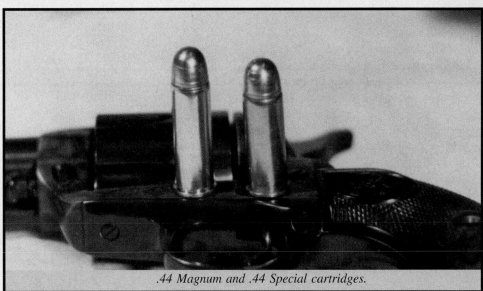

.44 Magnum and .44 Special cartridges.

.45 Schofield and .45 Colt cartridges.

but rather to develop good and accurate handgun shooting. I, along with many others, enjoy shooting .45 Colt ammo with as much black powder as we can cram into the case, but the blast and recoil are substantial. For this very reason, the Army reduced the loading of the .45 Colt from 40 grains to 30 grains of powder, while the "civilian" load was held at 35 grains.

One of the great advantages of using a revolver chambered for .45 Colt, .357 Magnum, or .44 Magnum is that there are shorter cartridges that can be loaded with black powder for reduced loadings. These are the .45 S&W Schofield, the .38 S&W Special, and the .44 S&W Special, all of which can be safely fired in guns chambered for the .45 Colt, .357 Magnum, or .44 Magnum, respectively. In the case of the .357 and .44 Magnums, we can use even shorter cases by using the .38 Long Colt and the .44 S&W Russian. However, these two cases are not nearly as plentiful as the .38 and .44 Specials. Later in this article, we will examine data gathered by utilizing shorter cases and a variety of brands of black powder to vary the velocity of black powder revolver loads.

Bullets and Lube

Original loadings for revolver cartridges of the black powder era, as well as into the 20th century, utilized either a round-nose or conical bullet. For most of my black powder loadings, I stick with the round-nose shape, but the semi-wadcutter designs also work well with black powder. The critical part of a bullet design for black powder is not the shape of the nose, but the amount of lubricant the bullet can carry - the more the better. Many handgun lead bullets, even though designed for smokeless powder, carry sufficient lube to allow for loading with black powder. The role that lubricant plays with the combination of lead bullets and black powder is vital. Black powder residue, or fouling as it is usually termed, is a black sooty coating left in the barrel that is detrimental to accuracy. A proper black powder bullet lube coats the barrel and mixes with the fouling, leaving it soft and easily wiped from the bore after each shot. Without the proper lube, the bore becomes caked with a coating of hard fouling. Two very good black powder bullet lubricants formulated to keep the fouling soft are SPG and Lyman Black Powder Gold.

Black Powder

When loading for revolvers, FFg granulation should be used in .44 and .45 caliber cartridges. There is no great advantage

Bullets used in testing, left to right: .45 cal. RCBS RNFP, .44 cal. Saeco 240 RN, and .38 cal. RCBS 158-gr. RN.

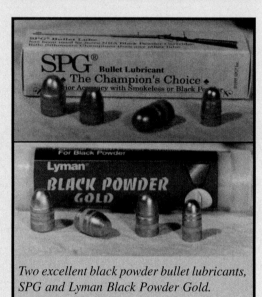

Two excellent black powder bullet lubricants, SPG and Lyman Black Powder Gold.

Bullets with lube ready for loading, left to right: .45 Colt, .44-40, .44 Special/.44 Magnum and .38 Special/.357 Magnum.

A variety of black powders: Swiss, Elephant, and Goex. All three are excellent black powder, each with different burning characteristics, which were used in testing.

to using FFFg in .44 and .45 caliber cartridges, other than to increase the velocity. Also, in some reproductions, I feel it unwise to use FFFg due to the increased pressure from the faster burning powder. This will be explained in further detail later in this article. In .38 caliber cartridges and smaller, FFFg is safe and has long been the norm. The three major brands of black powder available in the United States are Goex, Elephant, and Swiss powder.

Sizing and Priming the Case

Cases should be full-length sized and primed as usual. Magnum primers seem to promote better ignition and cleaner burning of black powder, and while any brand will work, some brands will, no doubt, produce more accurate groups than others. Only by trying a variety of brands will we be able to tell what works the best. CCI brand primers were used for developing all the test data included in this article, with some groups better than others, and they might be improved by trying a different brand of primers. The next step is to expand the case and slightly bell the mouth to accept the bullet.

Loading the Cartridges

For the most part, the procedures for loading black powder cartridges for revolvers are the same as those for loading smokeless black powder revolver cartridges. The significant difference is the method of charging the cases with black powder and ensuring that the case is full. With smokeless powder, a case is almost never filled to capacity. With black powder, the case is ALWAYS filled to capacity. To determine how much black powder to use, we determine the depth to which the bullet will be seated. The easiest way to accomplish this task is to measure the distance from the base of the bullet to the crimping groove. Some bullets do not have a crimping groove and are simply crimped over the front driving band or on the nose. Now we transfer this measurement to a dowel and make a mark around the circumference. The dowel will serve as a depth gauge. Next, we fill the case with a charge of powder and, using our dowel depth gauge, we check the level. We need to adjust the level of the powder so that the index mark on our dowel is even with the case mouth. If the index mark is below the case mouth, then we need to add more powder to ensure that no void or air space is left in the case. Finally, once we have established the correct volume of powder, we can set our measuring device to dispense

Bullets need to be tightly crimped to get the most out of black powder loads. .44 Magnum cartridge shown.

this volume of powder. The measuring device can be as simple as a cartridge case trimmed to length, a muzzleloading style adjustable measure, or a powder measure designed for dispensing black powder, such as the Lyman #55 Black Powder Measure. Do not use modern powder measures designed for smokeless powder, as there is the danger of igniting the black powder from an electrical spark. Whatever means you have of measuring your powder, learn to develop a consistent method of metering and charging the cases. Uniformity during this, and the other steps in loading process, will improve the quality of our ammunition.

Seating and Crimping the Bullet

Cartridges for revolvers have a heavy crimp on the bullet to prevent the bullet from slipping out of the case mouth while the revolver is in recoil. The crimp, however, serves an additional purpose with black powder loads. A heavy crimp on the bullet holds the bullet in the case longer, enhancing the ignition of the powder and allowing the pressure to build in a consistent, uniform manner. What we want to ensure is that our seating and crimping die is adjusted to seat the bullet to the correct depth, and then crimp the mouth tightly into the crimping groove. To properly set our seating die, we will start by setting the die out far enough so that there will be no possibility of crimping the brass. Next, we start a bullet into a case and run the case into the die until we can feel the bullet has been partially seated. Now we withdraw the cartridge and check to see how far we

have seated the bullet. Again, we run the cartridge into the die and seat the bullet deeper. We may need to run the seating stem down some to get the bullet properly seated. Withdrawing the cartridge again, we check the relationship of the case mouth to the crimping groove on the bullet. Once again, we repeat the process until the bullet is seated to the exact depth for the case rim to fold neatly into the crimping groove. Now it is time to adjust the die body to crimp the bullet. We do this by backing out the seating stem so there is no possibility of seating the bullet any deeper into the case. Next, we adjust the seating die clockwise one-quarter turn. We continue the process of adjusting the die in quarter-turn increments and extending the dummy round fully into the die until the bullet is properly crimped. When we are satisfied with the crimp, we tighten the locking ring or nut to secure the die. Finally, with the cartridge in the die, we thread the seating stem down until it is snug on the seated bullet and tighten the locking nut on the stem. We now have the seating die properly adjusted and can seat and crimp the bullets to finish the loading process.

Loading Reduced Black Powder Loads

The data and tables that follow show that by using different brands of black powder and short cases (.38 Special, .44 Special, and .45 Schofield) in the .357 Magnum, .44 Magnum, and .45 Colt, we can tailor black powder loads that range from low to high velocities.

Three Ruger single-action revolvers were used in the testing to gather the data shown. The

revolvers were an original three-screw Blackhawk .357 Magnum with a 6-1/2" barrel, a blued Vaquero .44 Magnum with a 7-1/2" barrel, and a stainless Vaquero .45 Colt with a 7-1/2" barrel. The Rugers were chosen as test guns for two reasons. First, I wanted to maintain uniformity by using revolvers all from the same manufacturer. Second, the Ruger models are the strongest single-action revolvers most commonly used in cowboy-style matches. Suffice it to say that the Ruger single-actions are modern designs built to fire magnum ammunition. Since it is possible to exceed .44 Special and .45 Colt factory-loaded velocities with black powder loads, I wanted to ensure that the guns used for testing were designed for magnum handgun loads. A quick check of the .45 Colt loading data in any current reloading manual will show that a Ruger single-action revolver can be loaded to much higher pressures than the 1873 Colt Peacemaker originals, and reproductions can safely withstand repeated firing.

There are some reproductions in which only mild black powder ammunition should be fired. One example is the 1872 Colt Open Top design chambered for .45 Schofield. In the testing, a .45 Schofield case, loaded with an uncompressed charge of Swiss FFFg that weighed 21.4 grains with a 250-gr. bullet, developed a muzzle velocity of 770 fps. In a separate test, .45 Schofield Black Hills Ammunition factory-

Revolvers used for testing: Top to bottom: 3-screw Blackhawk .357 Magnum, blued Vaquero .44 Magnum, and stainless Vaquero .45 Colt.

.44 Magnum cartridges loaded with Swiss FFg.

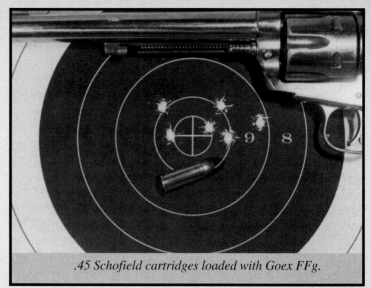

.45 Schofield cartridges loaded with Goex FFg.

loaded smokeless black powder and a 230-gr. bullet averaged 762 fps. In this case, the black powder load exceeded the velocity of the smokeless powder load with a bullet 20 grains heavier. The 1872 open-top design, when chambered for .45 Schofield, has very thin cylinder walls. By adding more powder and compressing the powder charge, we could easily load black powder ammunition, which, in my opinion, would be too powerful for the 1872 Colt design. Just as with any hand-loading situation, the ammunition must not be loaded to exceed the strength of the firearm in which it will be fired, hence the old rule of thumb that only FFg should be loaded in .44 and .45 caliber revolvers. This rule should be followed when loading for original and reproductions of 1800's designs. Black powder is not to be feared, but rather to be respected. The old adage that "one cannot put enough black powder in a gun to blow it up" is nonsense.

For testing, FFg granulation was used in .44 and .45 calibers, and FFFg granulation used in .38 calibers. Elephant and Goex brands were used in the .38 Special and .357 Magnum loads; Elephant, Goex, and Swiss black powder were used in the .44 and .45 caliber loads. The .38 caliber testing had already been completed when the Swiss powder arrived. In all the loading for all six specific calibers, the powder charge was determined by filling the case to where the base of the bullet would be seated, without compressing the powder charge. A Lyman #55 black powder measure was set to throw the volume of powder for each of the six calibers that filled the case up to the base of the bullet. The thrown charges were then weighed, not to be used

as loading data, but as a reference to show that the same volume of black powder can vary according to the manufacturer and lot number.

In the testing for this article, approximately 80 black powder rounds were fired through each of the three revolvers without cleaning. Prior to firing over a chronograph, each revolver was fired with a full cylinder to foul the barrel and chambers. Throughout the testing, all three guns functioned flawlessly without binding up. Now, I must admit that all three revolvers were very dirty by the time I was finished. The black powder fouling, however, did not effect accuracy. In fact, some of the best groups were fired mid-way through the testing. Also, a blow tube was used between five-shot strings to keep the fouling soft. Using a blow tube to keep the fouling soft and moist between shots is a technique borrowed from shooters of black powder cartridge rifles. With the revolver unloaded, a plastic tube was placed in the muzzle and several breaths of moist air blown through the barrel. The revolver was then loaded with five cartridges and fired. The revolver was then unloaded, allowed to cool for a couple of minutes, and the process repeated for the next five-shot string. All groups were fired at 50 feet, standing and using one hand.

Except where noted, all loads used in the testing were minimum loads. The reason is that, unless otherwise noted, none of the powder charges in any of the loads were compressed. Only the minimum volume of powder required to fill the case to the base of the bullet was used. Normally, black powder, when loaded in cartridges, is compressed to enhance the burning characteristics and to increase

.357 Magnum using Goex FFFg.

.44 Magnum cartridges loaded with Goex FFg.

Table 1
.38 Special Data - Federal cases
CCI 550 primers, 158-gr. RN bullet

Load	Velocity	Remarks
17 grains* of Elephant FFFg	690 fps	Min. Vol. Load
15 grains* of Goex FFFg	748 fps	Min. Vol. Load

*Charge determined by volume. Weight shown for reference only.

Table 2
.357 Magnum Data - Black Hills Ammunition cases
CCI 550 primers, 158-gr. RN bullet

Load	Velocity	Remarks
20 grains* of Elephant FFFg	752 fps	Min. Vol. Load
25 grains* of Elephant FFFg	87 fps	Compressed charge
18 grains* of Goex FFFg	813 fps	Min. Vol. Load
20* grains of Goex FFFg	872 fps	Compressed charge

*Charge determined by volume. Weight shown for reference only.

the velocity. However, part of the purpose of this testing was to demonstrate how we can assemble reduced black powder loads if desired without violating the rule that the powder charge must fill the case without leaving any air space.

From the data shown in Tables 1 and 2, we can see that, by varying the components, we can tailor black powder loads for the .357 from low to moderately-high velocity. The loadings shown give us a wide range of velocities, while at the same time maintaining a full case of black powder. In the .38/.357, we can vary the loads from 690 fps to over 870 fps. We could likely exceed 900 fps by using Swiss FFFg, if so desired. Also, note in Table 2 how the velocities of the compressed

Magnum, loaded with a full charge of black powder, is still, by any measure, a magnum handgun.

Making up black powder loads in calibers for which only one case can be used presents a different problem. For example, the .44-40 and .38-40 are bottle-necked cases for which no shorter case can be substituted. Since the short case option exists only with straight-walled cases, our only option for loading reduced-velocity loads is by using an uncompressed charge of a less powerful lot or brand of black powder. For example, in Table 4, the data from the .44 caliber testing indicates that by loading a .44-40 with Elephant FFg, we can assemble loads that produce less velocity than would be produced

Table 3
.44 S&W Special Data – W-W cases
CCI 350 primers, 240-gr. RN bullet

Load	Velocity	Remarks
25 grains* of Elephant FFg	666 fps	Min. Vol. Load
21.4 grains* of Goex FFg	701 fps	Min. Vol. Load
24.4 grains* of Swiss FFg	843 fps	Min. Vol. Load

*Charge determined by volume. Weight shown for reference only.

Table 4
.44 Remington Magnum Data – W-W cases
CCI 350 primers, 240-gr. RN bullet

Load	Velocity	Remarks
32 grains* of Elephant FFg	724 fps	Min. Vol. Load
26.8 grains* of Goex FFg	778 fps	Min. Vol. Load
31 grains* of Swiss FFg	913 fpsn	Min. Vol. Load

*Charge determined by volume. Weight shown for reference only.

charges vary only 3 fps with the same volume of powder, but the charge of Elephant weighed 25 grains compared to only 20 grains of Goex. Another significant variation is the velocity increase that was measured. The same increase in volume for both powders caused the Goex loads to increase by 59 fps, but caused the Elephant loads to increase by 123 fps - twice as much! This is a perfect example of how much the characteristics of black powder vary from brand-to-brand and lot-to-lot.

In the case of the .44 Magnum, the variation in velocity over the range of black powder that was tested was even greater. Table 3 shows that the .44 Special case, loaded with Elephant FFg, exited the muzzle at 666 fps with very mild recoil. On the other hand, in Table 4, the .44 Magnum case, loaded with Swiss FFg, left the muzzle at 913 fps. Recoil with this load is substantial. If we were to load a .44 Magnum case with a compressed load of Swiss FFFg black powder, the velocity would, no doubt, easily exceed 1,000 fps. The .44

for the same volume of the Swiss powder.

Our last example of the data gathered using the .45 Schofield and .45 Colt cartridges confirms the .38 caliber and .44 caliber findings. Actually, the difference experienced with .45 caliber ammunition is even greater and shows the most variation in velocity. Look at the data in Table 6. While all three charges of powder shown for the .45 Colt occupied the same volume, the weight of each charge was different. The charge of Elephant FFg weighed 30 grains, while the same volume of Goex FFg and Swiss FFg weighed 25.4 and 29.5 grains respectively. But notice the difference in velocities. The Elephant powder was the heaviest, yet produced the lowest velocity. The Swiss powder weighed only slightly less than the Elephant, but produced the highest velocity. The same volume of Goex weighed the least of all three charges, but averaged only 60 fps less than did the Swiss powder. Weight is not a true indication of the velocity that black powder can produce.

Table 5
.45 Schofield Data - Black Hills Ammunition cases
CCI 350 primers, 250-gr. RNFP bullet

Load	Velocity	Remarks
23 grains* of Elephant FFg	619 fps	Min. Vol. Load
19.7 grains* of Goex FFg	641 fps	Min. Vol. Load
22.4 grains* of Swiss FFg	714 fps	Min. Vol. Load
21.6 grains* of Swiss FFFg	770 fps	Use in Ruger revolvers only

*Charge determined by volume. Weight shown for reference only.

Table 6
.45 Colt Data – R-P cases
CCI 350 primers, 250-gr. RNFP bullet

Load	Velocity	Remarks
30.0 grains* of Elephant FFg	656 fps	Min. Vol. Load
25.4 grains* of Goex FFg	725 fps	Min. Vol. Load
29.5 grains* of Swiss FFg	785 fps	Min. Vol. Load
38.0 grains** of Goex FFFg	970 fps	Use in Ruger revolvers only

** weighed grains
*Charge determined by volume. Weight shown for reference only.

.45 Schofield cartridges loaded with Swiss FFg.

The data clearly shows why we must use volume rather than weight to determine the powder charge when using black powder. Had we tried to weigh out the same amount of the three different powders, we would have wound up with three different volumes of powder. Again, this is where smokeless powder and black powder are so very different from each other. With smokeless powder, we adjust the powder measure until it dispenses the correct weight as indicated in any loading manual. With black powder, we adjust the powder measure until it dispenses the correct volume of powder to fill the entire case to the base of the bullet.

The .45 Schofield (Table 5), loaded with Elephant FFg, measured 619 fps, which is the lowest velocity recorded throughout the testing. A powerhouse load of Goex FFFg (Table 6), blasted out of the muzzle at 970 fps. That is a variation of over 350 fps between the two loads.

Again, by interpolating the gathered data, we can assume that, in all likelihood, a full load of Swiss FFFg would send a .45 bullet out the muzzle at over 1,000 fps. The old .45 Colt loaded with black powder can still be a magnum handgun round, even by today's standards. With full compressed loads, muzzle blast and recoil are fierce, but manageable with practice. As with any magnum caliber, mastering the .45 Colt with full black powder loads requires hours of practice. It is no great wonder that the Army Ordnance Board reduced the original 40-grain loading to 30 grains in order to tame the bucking .45 Colt.

The final step is the most fun! Whether you have loaded light, medium, or heavy black powder loads for your favorite six-shooter, enter the Traditional Black Powder Frontier Cartridge Category at your next cowboy shoot! See ya at the range!

.45 Colt cartridges loaded with Goex FFg.

LOADING BLACK POWDER SHOTGUN SHELLS

By: Kenny Durham, aka KID Durham

I was six-years-old when I went to a rodeo for the first time. Wow! There were real cowboys riding bucking horses, wrestling steers, and roping calves. My eyes just couldn't take it all in fast enough! A rodeo clown sauntered out into the arena carrying an old shotgun, waving it around and cajoling the audience to watch his antics. When the rodeo action resumed, he stuck the shotgun, muzzle end down, inside his baggy pants. My attention returned to the bucking horses, and I soon forgot all about the clown with the concealed shotgun, as had everyone else in the crowd. Later, the rodeo action was between events and a second clown was performing some stunts in front of the chutes. All at once there was a loud "BOOM" that rattled the whole stadium. At the far end of the arena, a cloud of white smoke hung in the air. The first clown was standing there with the shotgun in his hands grinning from ear-to-ear as all attention focused on him. About the time my heart resumed beating, the shotgun roared back to life again. This time I saw the cloud of white smoke and a bright orange jet of flame blast from the muzzle followed by a second "BOOM." What an awesome sight! I was both terrified and fascinated at the same time. I was also hooked on black powder for life!

Black powder shotguns are like steam locomotives - they make a lot of noise, belch fire, and produce billowing clouds of smoke. Smokeless powder shotgun shells, like diesel locomotives, are very efficient, clean, and functional. But, if I really want to bring a shotgun to life, I just have to shoot it with some black powder shells.

Ever wish you had a black powder shotgun? You might be surprised to find that you do. It doesn't matter whether your shotgun is an original produced in the black powder era or a modern shotgun, because just about any shotgun, even a new one, is still designed for shooting black powder. How is this? The shotgun chamber and the forcing cone are still made the same way they were back in the late 1800's. The forcing cone ensured that the wads would form a tight gas seal in the barrel. When smokeless powder arrived on the scene, it was found that the same chamber and forcing cone arrangement provided the best way to seal the burning gasses behind the wad column. In the 1960's, plastic wads gradually replaced card and fiber wads. The need for a short, quick-tapering forcing cone went away. Today, many competition trap and skeet guns are now made with long, slow-tapering forcing cones or are "back-bored" to eliminate the forcing cone altogether. But, on the inside, the run-of-the-mill shotgun barrel is still made the same way as back in the days of black powder. Old traditions are hard to break and since it works okay, why change things?

Another carryover from the black powder era is the "DRAM EQ" or "Dram Equivalent" designation on a box of shotgun shells. When used in shotguns, black powder has always been measured in the English unit of drams. One dram of black powder is equal to 27.3 grains. Although the dictionary does not indicate so, I think the dram unit, as it relates to black powder, may be thought of more with respect to volume rather than weight, similar to a recipe calling for a teaspoon of sugar. A typical 12-gauge black powder shell may have been loaded with 2-3/4 drams (75 grains) of black powder and 1-1/8 oz. of shot. Such a load would be considered a "light" load. A load consisting of three drams of powder and 1-1/4 oz. shot would be a "medium" load. A variation of the aforementioned load is 3-3/4 drams, approximately 102 grains of black powder, and 1-1/4 oz. of shot. The additional 3/4 dram of powder will increase the muzzle velocity of the 1-1/4 oz. of shot. The listing of the powder charge in drams on the box of shells gave the buyer an indication of the power of the shells. This designation is still used by ammunition manufacturers today. Today's smokeless loads still revert to the old dram unit of weight by the term "dram equivalent." A modern box of shotshells indicating a dram equivalent of 3-3/4 means that the smokeless shells have roughly the same velocity and power as if they were loaded with 3-3/4 drams, or approximately 102 grains of black powder. It is meant to be an indication of equivalent velocity. Actually, I think it's great that shotshells are still linked to black powder. With all this in mind, are you ready to load up some black powder shells for your favorite scattergun?

Solid-brass shotgun shells. Left to right: Winchester 10-gauge x 3 inches, AB&C Co. 10-gauge x 2-11/16 inches, Rem-UMC 12-gauge x 2-1/2 inches, and Alcan 12-gauge x 2-1/2 inches.

A variety of modern shells ideal for reloading with black powder. Left to right: (12- gauge) Federal Gold Medal Paper, Federal Gold Medal Plastic, Remington Premier STS, Winchester AA, and the Remington Game Load. The shells on the right are 20-gauge Remington Premier and Remington Game Load.

Wads suitable for black powder shotgun shells. Left: 0.125" card with 1/2" fiber cushion wad. The white over-shot wad is used only with a roll crimp. Right: Remington RXP plastic wad for hunting load. Note that either choice will provide approximately the same wad column height (separation between powder and shot).

Shotgun Shell Casings

When it comes to cartridge cases for loading black powder shotshells, we have three choices: modern plastic shells, paper shells, and all-brass shells; of these three, the brass shells are the hardest to find. I saw some used brass 12-gauge shells at a gun show priced at $2.75 each. At a local gun store, I also found a new box of Alcan 12-gauge brass shells. The owner is a friend and since I am paying for his son's college education with my gun habit, he sold them to me for $2.75 each, although the box of ten was marked $35.00. I also have a few vintage Winchester and Remington brass shells in 10-gauge and 12-gauge. The 10-gauge shells measure exactly 3 inches long, while the 12-gauge shells are 2-1/2 inches in length. Both use large rifle-size primers. The Alcan 12-gauge shells are also 2-1/2 inches long, but use the Remington size 57 shotgun primer. Remington and Peter's shotgun shells used size 57 primers until sometime in the 1970's when they switched to the now standard 209-size primer. Size 57 primers were commonly available for reloading, but now can only be found randomly at gun shows or stores where someone may have come across a few in a deal. I am fortunate in that I found two cartons of CCI 157 primers in a pawn shop recently. The "157" was CCI's version of the Remington 57 primer. I could have enlarged the primer pockets on my Alcan brass shells to accept the larger 209 primers.

Imported brass shells, which can occasionally be found at stores or gun shows, usually require Berdan primers. However, there is at least one source of new American-made brass shotgun shells. Rocky Mountain Cartridge, LLC of Cody, Wyoming is producing brass shotgun shells in 20-gauge, 16-gauge, 14-gauge, 12-gauge, 10-gauge, and even 8-gauge. Brass shells require larger diameter wads than do plastic or paper shells. The brass case walls are thinner than plastic or paper shotshells, thereby making the inside diameter larger. In the past, wad makers made special sizes of wads to fit brass shells. I have an old box of Alcan wads labeled "For 12 Ga. Brass Shells." The "in-between gauge" size wads are required for use with brass shells; that is, use 11-gauge wads in 12-gauge brass shells. Wads for brass shells are still available and will be discussed later. If you are like me, you'll probably wind up with a couple dozen brass shells to shoot on special occasions, but will use plastic or paper shells most of the time.

When loading plastic shotshells, empties from trap and skeet shooting are a good choice. They are plentiful and have a large capacity, as well as an eight-point star crimp. Once-fired trap and skeet shotgun shells, or "hulls" as they are often referred to, are available at many gun stores. Every trap or skeet club collects and sells once-fired hulls and usually has several brands available for $5.00 to $8.00 per 100. Hunting loads sometimes have a six-point star crimp, which can make it harder to get a good uniform crimp. Also, the low-budget hunting load shells may have a thick base wad that reduces the capacity of the shell. Hulls in 12-gauge are plentiful, however 20-gauge hulls may be harder to find, while empty 16-gauge hulls suitable for loading may be even harder to find. If you are fortunate enough to own a 16-gauge Winchester '97 or double-barrel, you may have to resort to buying loaded shells and saving the empties. Empty paper 10-gauge shells are almost impossible to find, while once-fired plastic 10-gauge empties can sometimes be found at gun stores. At a local store, I found a plastic bag with what must have been 200 once-fired 10-gauge shells for sale.

There are many brands and variations of shells that are suitable for reloading. Perhaps you have been saving empty hulls and already have a supply on hand. Just about any hull will work, however I am only listing a few choices. For me, the easiest hulls to use for black powder are the

Federal Gold Medal Plastic, Winchester AA Trap or Skeet, Remington Premier Trap or Skeet, and the Remington Game Load. The Gold Medal and Remington Game Load hulls have the most capacity simply because the case is straight-walled on the inside. Both the Winchester AA and the Remington Premier shells are tapered inside, which reduces the capacity slightly.

The only thing I dislike about plastic shells is that they were not part of the black powder era. My first few years of hunting were with paper shotgun shells. Even today, the waxy odor of a fired paper shell, still warm from the chamber, brings back a flood of memories of my boyhood hunting days. When it comes to loading black powder shotgun shells, I want the old-fashioned paper hulls!

Where can we find paper hulls in today's plastic era? Believe it or not, Federal Cartridge Co. is still making paper shotgun shells. One of the most popular of all trap loads is the Federal Gold Medal "Paper" Shell. I usually buy several boxes of the paper trap loads and then save the empties for reloading with black powder. Sometimes, the empty paper hulls are available for sale at trap and skeet ranges, too.

Whatever our choice of empties, whether plastic or paper, it is best to have hulls that are all of one brand and style. When using a shotshell loader, mixing brands of shells can cause problems with the adjustment required when seating primers or at the crimp station. Most shotshell loaders require minor adjustments when changing brands of shells.

Powder and Primers

Any shotshell primers will work for black powder. This also applies to brass shells that require a large rifle primer. We are not concerned with accuracy or the other primer characteristics normally associated with rifle shooting. Our only concern is that the primer will ignite the black powder. Since the burning rate of black powder is controlled by the size of granulation, our choices of black powder should be limited to two granulation sizes: Fg and FFg. FFFg burns too fast, creating excessive chamber pressure. You may want to use Fg black powder if you are shooting a vintage 12 or 10-gauge shotgun. For example, if I owned an 1887 Winchester lever-action shotgun in 10-gauge, I would load my shells with Fg. The use of Fg keeps the chamber pressure low and also reduces recoil. Pyrodex RS, the equivalent of FFg, may also be used for loading shotgun shells. Measure Pyrodex by volume only, and make sure you follow the manufacturer's instructions. By volume, 2-3/4 drams of black powder and 1-1/8 oz. of lead shot are equal. For Western-action shooting, a good all-around 12-gauge black powder load is 2-3/4 drams of FFg or Fg black powder and 1-1/8 oz. of size 7-1/2 or size 6 shot. This load requires a wad column height of about 5/8 of an inch depending on your choice of hulls. Two-and-three-quarter drams of black powder weighs approximately 75 grains. The powder can be varied plus or minus five grains either way for ease of establishing the total column height of the powder.

Wads

One-piece plastic wads can be used in black powder shells, but we must find a wad that is the correct length. Plastic wads designed for trap and skeet loads are too long for use with black powder. I have used them at times by cutting out the center section and just using the base and the shot cup. Plastic wads designed for hunting loads may be close to the correct length. However, the shot cup may hold a larger shot charge than desired. The Remington plastic wad pictured has a wad column height slightly shorter than the card and fiber wad next to it. But, the shot cup section of the plastic wad is sized to hold 1-1/4 oz. of lead shot. This may or may not suit our purpose. By varying the powder charge, it is possible to work up a black powder load utilizing a one-piece plastic

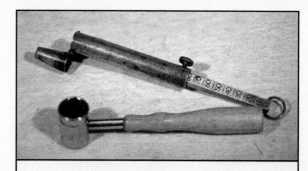

Two ways to measure black powder. Top: Muzzleloading-style adjustable brass measure. Bottom: Lyman-Ideal powder/shot dipper. Both measures are set to 2-3/4 drams (75 grains). Only specific black powder measures should be used. Regular powder measures are not set to measure drams.

Pour the measured black powder charge into a primed shell, and then place a card wad, followed by a cushion wad, into the wad guide. Wads may be seated separately if desired. Operate the lever to seat the wads on the powder charge.

The plastic shell has been filled and the star crimp reformed, so it is ready for the final crimp.

Brass shotgun shells from left to right: Winchester 10-gauge, Rare American Buckle & Cartridge Co. 10-gauge, Rem-UMC 12-gauge, and Alcan 12-gauge. The Alcan shell uses a shotgun primer, while vintage shells use large rifle primers.

Equivalency Chart

Shot Ounces	Black Powder Drams
7/8	2-1/4
1	2-1/2
1-1/8	2-3/4
1-1/4	3
1-3/8	3-1/4
1-1/2	3-1/2
1-5/8	3-1/4

Primer seating tool from a Lee Shotshell Loading Set from late 1960's. A similar tool can be fashioned from a piece of hardwood dowel.

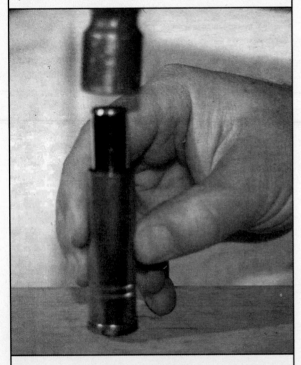

To seat a primer in a brass shell, set a primer face-up on a hard surface, center the shell primer pocket over the primer, insert the dowel, and tap with a hammer until the primer is seated flush with the head of the shell. Finally, pour a measured powder charge into the shell.

wad, wherein the components stack to the correct height to allow a perfect crimp. Another drawback to plastic wads are the long shreds of plastic left in the bore from the wad scraping against the black powder fouling from the previous shot. Rougher barrels are more susceptible to plastic fouling. This build-up of plastic can be a real mess, especially in a tight-choked gun! My preference is for card and fiber wads, but if you wish to use plastic wads, by all means, give them a try. The benefits of a plastic shot cup to protect the shot and produce a good pattern may far outweigh the nuisance of cleaning when it comes to hunting or wing shooting.

Card and fiber wads were the standard in muzzleloading and breech loading shotguns until they were replaced by plastic wads. When card and fiber wads were used in shotgun shells, several thicknesses of each type of wad were available to the hand loader. With such a variety, it was very easy to tailor light, medium, and heavy loads by adjusting the height of the wad column. When using card and fiber wads, you need two kinds and thicknesses with which to build the wad column. We use a hard 0.125" or 0.250" card wad to be placed over the powder, followed by a 3/8" or 1/2" fiber cushion wad. An interesting item to note is that card wads are measured in decimals and fiber cushion wads are measured in fractions of an inch. The card wad acts as the gas seal and the fiber wad cushions the shot for a good pattern.

Sources of card and fiber wads are not nearly as plentiful as they once were. The need for card and fiber wads has never gone away for those of us that also shoot muzzleloading scatterguns. Still, there are a few companies that produce them.

Heavy card wads thicker than 0.125" have enough momentum to "blow a hole" in the pattern. Card wads that are 0.125" thick are sufficient to serve as a gas seal without disturbing the pattern. Now that you have rounded up empty hulls and settled on a choice of wads, you're ready to assemble the components into loaded black powder shotgun shells.

Loading Equipment

Tools for loading black powder shotgun shells may be as simple or as complicated as you desire. A shotshell loader makes the task of loading shotshells easier and faster. However, I will also explain how you can load plastic shotshells with only a punch to knock out the spent primer and a wooden dowel to seat the primers and wads. If you wish to purchase a shotshell loader, there are a variety of models suitable for black powder shells. Used shotshell loaders can be found at pawn shops or stores that take in trades. Prices are generally very reasonable. If you are accustomed to loading shotshells, then you are probably familiar with the characteristics of your loading tool. As for dispensing the black powder, the safest way is to either use an adjustable brass black powder measure or a combination powder and shot dipper.

Now, there are many "rules of thumb" when it comes to black powder shooting. One rule of thumb for black powder shotguns is that the powder charge, wad thickness, and shot charge should all be the same height; in other words, three equal volumes of powder, wad, and shot. Adhering to this rule provides adequate velocity and good patterning qualities in a muzzleloading shotgun. The same applies to loading black powder in shotshells, too, but sometimes we must fudge a little on the wad column. Some old-style powder and shot dippers were dual-marked to indicate "drams" of powder and "ounces" of shot. Simply set the dipper for the desired amount of powder and use the same setting to measure the shot charge. My Lyman-Ideal dipper has the corresponding ounce versus dram settings listed.

But what if you don't have one of these handy dippers? You can make your own. One ounce is equal to 435 grains. Therefore, 1-1/8 oz. is equal to 544 grains. Using your scale, weigh out 544 grains (1-1/8 oz.) of shot. Now, dump the weighed charge of shot into a .45-70 case. If you don't have a .45-70 rifle, buy one! Everyone needs at least one! Next, trim the .45-70 case to the height of the shot. Remember the "rule of thumb" I mentioned? Now we have a combination shot and powder measure for 1-1/8 oz. shot or 2-3/4 drams of black powder.

Loading the Shells

If you are using some sort of shotshell loader, set it up for normal operation leaving the powder hopper empty. Place the shell in the sizing station, operate the lever to resize the brass head, and punch out the spent primer. Next, place the shell in the priming station and seat a new primer. Now, measure the black powder and dump it into the case. Next, place the shell in the charging station. The difference is that your shell is already charged with powder, so all you need to do here is to add the wads and shot. Then, place the card wad and the fiber wad into the wad guide and seat them. Most shotshell loaders have a built-in wad pressure indicator. Use about 40 to 50 pounds of wad pressure to ensure that the wads are firmly seated on the powder. The instructions for your particular press will show you how to adjust the wad pressure. The next step is to drop the shot into the case. This step is where you will discover if your powder and wad column is the correct height or not. If everything is right, the shot will fill to the proper level leaving just enough room for a good crimp. Too low of height and the crimp will fold inward leaving an opening; too much height and the shell won't close. The column height is adjusted by varying the powder charge or the wad column.

Now, move the shell to the station that starts the crimp. This step is important in that it begins the process of folding the shell closed. The crimp starting station has a die to match the six or eight-point folds in the shell you are using. When using paper shells, the crimp starter is smooth inside and only tapers the open shell inward. The word "crimp" is a poor choice because shotshells are not crimped in the conventional sense, but closed by either rolling or folding the opening. However, the closing process is still referred to as crimping. Finally, move the shell to the crimping station and bring the die down over the folded shell to close it. You may have to tinker with the crimp die to get the proper fold depth and a slight taper to the edge of the shell. Examine the shell closely to see that the wad pressure hasn't produced a bulge in the shell. Also, check to see if the loaded shell will chamber in your shotgun, remembering to keep it pointed in a safe direction. If all is well, you're on your way.

Loading Brass Shells

Brass shells are the easiest of all shotgun shells to load because no tools are required, except a way to punch out the old primer and seat a fresh one. As stated earlier, brass shells require different sizes of wads. We must use one gauge size larger wads in brass shotshells. For example, 10-gauge brass shells require 9-gauge wads; 12-gauge take 11-gauge wads, 16-gauge take 15-gauge wads, but 20-gauge brass shells take 18-gauge wads rather than 19-gauge wads. Depending upon the manufacturer, brass shells may use a large rifle primer or a shotshell battery primer. Just about any old punch will drive out the spent primer. For seating the fresh primer, I still use the primer-seating tool that came with my Lee shotshell loading kit that I purchased when I was a teenager. A similar tool can be fashioned from a piece of hardwood dowel for the appropriate gauge. I suggest using about an 8-inch long dowel to add more weight. You will need to bore or carve a cavity in the end of the dowel. This cavity will fit over the brass primer pocket, and when you tap on the dowel, the brass shell will be forced down over the primer without putting any pressure on the primer. To seat a primer in either type of brass shell, we set a primer face up on a hard surface, center the shell primer pocket over the primer, insert the dowel, and tap with a hammer until the primer is seated flush with the head of the shell.

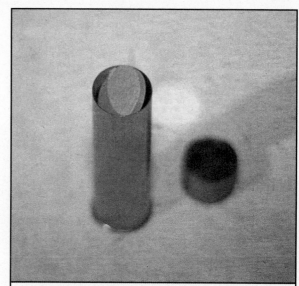

Insert a 0.125" card wad. Card wads are easier to start if inserted at an angle.

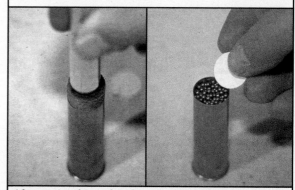

After seating the card wad, insert the cushion wad and push tightly down on the card wad with the dowel. This brass shell, with powder charge and wads in place, is ready for a shot charge. Pour a measured charge of shot into the shell. A homemade dipper can be fashioned from a .45-70 case. Finally, insert an overshot wad.

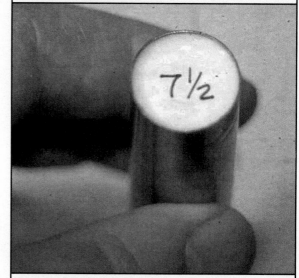

Place two or three drops of Elmer's glue around the edge of the wad. Using your finger, or a similar tool, spread the glue around the inside by rotating the shell. Load data can be written on the wad as was done in the old days, as shown here on the finished brass shell.

Trim the case mouth below the original crimp. A trimmed plastic shell can be loaded with hand tools as though it were a brass shell.

Roll-crimped shells - A Remington factory load and a black powder reload.

A complete set of vintage shotshell loading tools typical of the late-1800's.

Next, measure out the powder charge and pour it into the case. Slide the case from side to side so that the powder is level. Now, start a 0.125" card wad into the shell at an angle. Then, using the dowel, seat the wad on the powder, and follow the card wad with the 1/2" fiber cushion wad. Insert the dowel and push the wad firmly down upon the card wad. You can also apply several pounds of pressure here to add a little compression. Next, pour in a measured charge of shot. Finally, place a 0.030" overshot wad on top of the shot. The total height of all the components should stack up to about 1/32" below the top of the case mouth.

Factory-loaded brass shells were crimped to hold the overshot wad in place. Crimping works fine for a one-time loading, but repeated crimping will work-harden the brass and, after a few loadings, cause the mouth to split. A better alternative for repeated loading is to glue the wad in place. For this, use plain old Elmer's glue. Place two or three drops around the circumference of the wad, and then using your finger or a Q-tip, spread the glue evenly around the inside so that it forms a nice little fillet between the wad and the brass. Set the shell aside to dry. The glue will hold the overshot wad in place through considerable rough handling and leave no residue when fired. You can even write load data on the overshot wad, as was customary with ammunition manufacturers.

Now, recall that I mentioned that there was a way to load plastic shells without any loading tools. There is only one prerequisite. The empties must be of the straight-walled variety, such as Federal brand shells or the Remington Game Load. Additionally, you will need some 12-gauge overshot wads. To prepare the hulls, take a sharp knife and trim off the case mouth below the folds and discard the old crimp. Now you have a plastic case that resembles a brass case. To load plastic shells, simply use the same procedure as outlined for loading brass shells, with the exception that you use standard 12-gauge wads. Finally, glue the overshot wad in place, and you have a finished black powder plastic shell loaded without a shotshell loader.

One more item that appeals to me is the old-fashioned rolled crimp that adorned the mouth of paper shells in days gone by. I recently acquired a roll-crimping tool. Now, just for the fun of it, my black powder paper shells have the look of the old shells, more or less. I'm sure that there are a lot of these old tools around, and with the resurgence of the late 1800's-style of shooting, maybe someone will start producing the shotshell loading tools our grandfathers once used.

After all, our future is in our past! See ya at the range!

Author's Winchester '97 Black Diamond Tournament grade with a variety of black powder reloads.

Maintenance for Black Powder Firearms

Sulfur, Suds, and Black Powder Slurry

By: Michael W. Cuber, aka Kid Quick

All firearms deserve proper maintenance; however, there are some that demand more attention than others, and the most demanding of the bunch are those that utilize black powder. To state the matter simply, black powder arms must be cleaned properly and promptly or they will quickly ruin. Yes, there are bullet lubricants and preservatives on the market that claim to prevent black powder residue from causing rust, and some individuals have had extremely good results for a time, but all black powder residue will cause rust on steel if it is left to sit long enough. Why allow this to happen when a little conscientious effort will prevent it?

Black powder residue consists of a variety of trace chemicals, but it is the salt that causes the majority of the problems in firearms. Potassium nitrate (salt peter) is one of the three main ingredients of black powder, while the other two ingredients are sulfur and charcoal. Anyone who has ever had to render a charge of powder inert in a muzzleloader by dipping the breech end into a bucket of water can testify to the incredible hygroscopic nature of black powder. When the nipple of the muzzleloader is removed and the breech submerged, the black powder dissolves almost instantly into a black slurry. Black powder will dissolve more readily than common table salt, and it is this trait of drawing and holding moisture that causes our problems. Few of us would leave table salt all over our firearms and then set them back in the cabinet, but this is essentially what's happening when a fouled black powder firearm is put away without cleaning.

The patch lubes and preservatives on the market for black powder will inhibit rust to a certain degree, but most of these are only designed to eliminate cleaning in the field. These products will allow the black powder shooter several days out in the field without cleaning, even during inclement weather, but these products are not designed to alleviate cleaning once we've returned home. I've seen .45-70 bores that would begin to show rust within three hours of being fired if no precautions or special lubes were used. These same rifles responded well when they were swabbed with a slightly wet patch in the field and then followed with a dry patch. This would allow the barrels to remain rust free for a couple of days, but without proper cleaning, they would still eventually rust.

The only way rust can be prevented is by removing all traces of salt from the metal surfaces of our firearms. They must be dried completely and then treated with a light preservative. Regardless of action type, our primary concern is the barrel of our black powder firearm. There are several good black powder solvents on the market, such as Hoppe's #9 black powder solvent, and T\C #13 bore cleaner. The real beauty of these solvents is that they come premixed in squeeze-type bottles; however, I've not seen these solvents do anything that could not be accom-

In order to clean the Henry and the '66, '73, and '76 Winchester, side plates were incorporated into their designs. These will need to be removed before the toggle links, bolt, follower, and lever can be cleaned.

When there is no other way to clean except from the muzzle, use a bore guide to prevent damage to the muzzle's crown.

plished with plain old soap and water. There are a variety of formulas, which all of us have probably heard of, such as those that use a few drops of lemon juice, ammonia, or hydrogen peroxide. All of these may work, but be careful about using ammonia because it eats brass, and in some cases I've heard of it producing poisonous gases when mixed with other chemicals. I've never used anything other than good old hot water and soap. Maybe this is because it's what we used in the military before we would put our weapons away in the armory. In any case, when our weapons were dried and treated with a light preservative, they seemed impervious to corrosion.

Regardless of the cleaning solution you choose, you'll need a good heavy rod to clean black powder long guns. The skimpy rods used for modern centerfire rifles tend to bend too easily when pushing the large brushes and jags used for most black powder guns. Also, you'll have to use an adapter on the end of the skimpy rod most of the time1. Kleen-Bore Inc. offers an excellent western-style kit for firearms .38

The Western Gun Cleaning Kit from Kleen-Bore features a heavy-duty brass rod and everything necessary to clean firearms .38 caliber and larger.

caliber and larger. The heavy-duty brass rod that comes with this kit features a laminated wood handle that swivels on the rod. This rod is so precision-machined that it feels like a one-piece rod even though it is sectioned, and it is long enough to clean musket barrels up to 36 inches in length. The Kleen-Bore kit also comes with an assortment of brushes and jags to accommodate just about any cleaning job. When you're finished using your Kleen-Bore kit, the heavy rod, accessories, patches, and solvent can be rolled back up in the leather pouch that comes with the kit.

Another solution, and one that quite a few black powder cartridge shooters have caught on to, is to buy a surplus .50 caliber machine. gun. cleaning rod. These rods are not quite as nice as the ones from Kleen-Bore, but they are sufficiently stout and will handle large brushes without the need for an adapter. One trick I've seen a couple of silhouette shooters pull off is to use the .50 caliber brush in their .45-70s between stages. While other competitors are busy scrubbing their barrels repeatedly with wet and

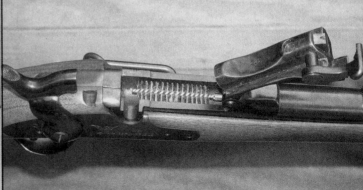

Firearms are not the only items requiring cleaning after being used with black powder. These cartridges need to be soaked in a bucket of soapy water to loosen the fouling on them. After soaking, swab them out and let them dry on a dish towel, but only with the wife's permission, of course.

Black powder fouling has a tendency to creep around cartridges and into the action of single-shots like on this Trapdoor.

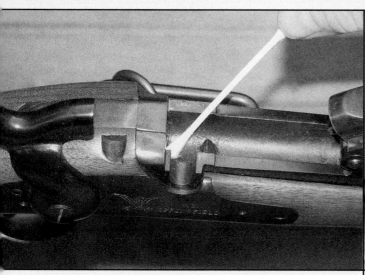

Q-tips are handy for cleaning the fouling out of hard-to-reach nooks and crannies.

The recess for the rim is another area where black powder fouling frequently accumulates.

dry patches, the competitor with a .50 caliber brush simply needs to muscle the tight brush through once and then follow up with a tight patch. If you can start the brush from the breech end, most of the fouling will be pushed out of the muzzle on the first pass. The .50 caliber brush clears fouling fast and really works!

Once the match or hunt is over and you've returned home, it's time to break out the black powder solvent, or soap and water, and get rid of that blackish-gray crud coating your barrel. Because of the mess and rotten-egg smell, it's sometimes nice to do this before you leave the field or range. If you're single, you don't usually have to worry about this. You really need nothing more than your

In this photo the rod has been inserted and the patch installed from the breech end so that the fouling will be pulled out towards the muzzle and not pushed into the action.

rod and patches for the soap and water work. A brush will become heavily fouled in short order if used in a wet bore. It is also a good idea to wring the patches out before inserting them in the bore. This will prevent excess water from getting into the action. Try to start the wet patches from the breech end and remove them at the muzzle end rather than dragging them back through the chamber wet with a load of fouling. If you are unable to clean from the breech end, place some patches inside the action so that they can catch fouling and moisture that might otherwise find their way into the action. If I have to clean from the muzzle, I like to use a bore guide to prevent damage to the muzzle's crown. It also helps

Be sure to always clean the breech face of black powder single-shots. If they are not cleaned, the breech face will become pitted over time.

Most military muskets come with their own one-piece cleaning rod, such as this one from a Remington Rolling Block.

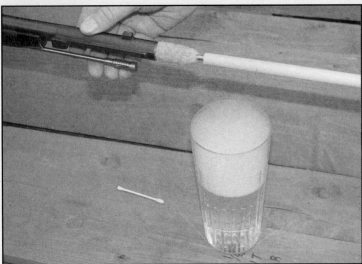

There are a variety of good solvents on the market, but they won't do anything that cannot be accomplished by using good old soap and water. Always dry parts thoroughly after using soap and water, and then treat them with a light preservative.

The take-down lever/pivot pin visible at the bottom of this photo has been removed so that the falling block of a Sharps could be removed for cleaning.

to elevate the butt of the firearm some and reverse the patch before it clears the chamber. This helps keep everything in the barrel and will prevent your cleaning solution from running into the action. One other option that works very well is to place an empty cartridge case of the correct caliber in the chamber and close the action part way. Push your first wet patch through the bore from the muzzle and all the way to the brass. The partially closed action will safely keep the brass from being pushed out of the chamber where it will collect the patch, cleaning solution, and fouling neatly inside protecting the action from the solids and moisture on the patch. Simply discard the brass, contents and all, and then finish the cleaning process.

Once the fouling has been completely dissolved, it's time to dry

Shotguns also foul, particularly around the breech face. If neglected, a shotgun might become hard to close, or spent shells may become difficult to extract. These are two of the most common failures that can be seen on the range.

the bore thoroughly with two or three clean patches. After it has been dried, you can apply one of the many good preservative oils that are on the market. Better yet, you can break out a brush and bore solvent, like regular Hoppe's #9, and give the barrel the once over like a more modern firearm. The brush will help "season" the barrel, and if you use a regular solvent like Hoppe's, Shooter's Choice, or Kleen-Bore Copper Cutter, you will not need to apply a preservative once the barrel has been dried. If you shoot a particular firearm frequently, this method will alleviate the hassle of having to remove the preservative prior to shooting.

Even though our barrels are clean, we don't want to put our shooting irons away just yet. Using Q-tips or pipe cleaners, we need to remove any

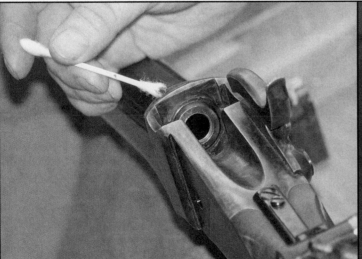

Fouling will accumulate in the channels of the falling block as it has on this Sharps replica.

The area immediately surrounding the chamber is another place where fouling will accumulate.

When working with a break-open type shotgun, always make sure that the locking lug and extractor are clean and in good working order.

There are a variety of cleaning products on the market that will assist in the maintenance of black powder firearms. A few of the more popular ones are shown here.

residue or spillover from every nook and cranny of our firearm's actions. I don't know whether or not the person who invented Q-tips was a shooter, but he or she sure does deserve some kind of shooting award for all the Q-tips that have been used by shooters over the years. The beauty of the Q-tip is that it has two ends; one end can be used with our solvent, or soap and water, while the other end is saved for drying. These cotton-tipped sticks are not only great for cleaning, but they can also be used to apply oil or cold blue to parts that are hard to reach. They also work great for cleaning the inside of cartridge cases that have been used with black powder. I like to dump my empties in the sink with the dishes to dissolve the residue. Then after removing them from the water, I'll swab them out and place them on a dish towel to

Anyone familiar with cap-n-ball revolvers is no stranger to the cleaning process.

dry. Unfortunately, I've not been able to convince my wife that this should be considered a normal part of our dish washing routine.

If you happen to be working with a muzzleloader, pay particular attention to the residue that builds up around the nipple and hammer. Frequently, unseen residue will build up in the cup of the hammer, or it will accumulate between the side plate and barrel. It's not a bad idea to occasionally remove the side plate and carefully clean the delicate lock arrangement of the muzzleloader. This will ensure reliable function of the set triggers, hammers, mainsprings, and trigger sears. Also, when cleaning a muzzleloader, always remove the nipple from the barrel. This will allow you to thoroughly clean and dry the nipple and flash hole, both of which are critical for reliable ignition.

The cylinder can be placed into a bucket of hot soapy water and cleaned with a short rod and brush, and on a Colt, the barrel could also be placed into the bucket. The author prefers to clean the frame of black powder revolvers with wet and dry patches, followed by Q-tips and pipe cleaners. Fouling must first be dissolved and then the part thoroughly dried in order to prevent rust.

To get crud out of hard-to-reach spots, use a solvent such as Birchwood Casey Gun Scrubber. Once the part has been dried of solvent, it can be hit with a shot of Sheath Rust Preventative.

Muzzleloaders are not the only firearms with problem areas. On most black powder cartridge single-shots, a certain amount of residue always manages to get around the cartridge where it adheres to the breech face. If we're dealing with a Rolling Block or a Trapdoor, this residue is easy enough to remove; however, if we're dealing with a falling block, we may have to do some disassembly in order to clean the breech. If you don't think this is necessary, note the pitting in the breech face the next time you pick up an old Rolling Block. This pitting could have been prevented if the residue that caused it had been wiped away after shooting.

To remove the falling block from a Sharps type rifle, first make sure that the rifle is unloaded, and then bring the hammer to half cock and break the under lever open partially. Next, depress the locking detent ahead of the small lever/pivot pin located on the bottom right side of the action. (Note: this is assuming that you are grasping the firearm as you would normally with the muzzle pointing away from you.) Swing the lever in a forward arc until its tip is pointing down at the ground. Now, with your hand cupped under the falling block and its linkage, pull the small lever/pivot pin free from the receiver. The breech block, underlever, linkage, and extractor can now be withdrawn from the bottom of the receiver. Try to remember the positions of these parts so that they can be reassembled easily after being cleaned. Besides the breech face, you will notice that residue also likes to collect around the extractor. Also, pay attention to the area immediatly surrounding the chamber because it is another place that residue will collect.

To reassemble the Sharps action, simply reverse the order in which the breech block and extractor were removed. When

Don't forget to make sure that the nipples and flash holes are dry and free of excess oil on the cap-n-ball sixguns.

you've lined up the hole for the under lever with the hole in the receiver, you can reinsert the small lever/pivot pin. Remember that this pin must also pass through the extractor, so be careful while aligning these parts. Once the pin is in place, the lever can be rotated back up and over the detent, and you're finished with the reassembly.

Perhaps the dirtiest action type that anyone will ever have to deal with are those on the Henry and the '66, '73, and '76 Winchester lever-actions. When these guns are shot, black powder residue goes everywhere! Fortunately, the rifles and carbines that utilize this action type were manufactured with cleaning in mind. All have side plates, which are easily removed to facilitate cleaning of the toggle links, bolt, follower, and lever (please refer to the article *Maintenance for the Lever Action Rifle* in the Oct/Nov 2000 issue of SHOOT! MAGAZINE for more information). On the Henry and '66 Winchester, the side plates are mortised in place and must be driven downward with a light tap from either a wooden or plastic mallet. On the '73 and '76, the side plates will have a lip on the front that holds onto the receiver, while the rear of the plate is inlayed to precisely fit the hole in the receiver under the plate. Resist the temptation to pry this plate up from the rear. Instead, lightly tap on it with your wood or plastic mallet. The plate should fall out or at least pop up so you can get a hold of it with your fingers.

Other firearms that can get really dirty are cap-n-ball sixguns.

Fortunately, these were also designed with ease of cleaning in mind. To clean a black powder revolver, you will need to remove the cylinder, which, of course, should be unloaded. On Colt-type revolvers, the barrel will have to be removed first by removing the wedge pin above the loading ram. You can use the loading ram to help push the barrel from the grip frame, but be careful not to mar the front of the cylinder. A thin strip of plastic or wood under the ram will prevent damage to the cylinder face. Once the barrel has been removed and the revolver brought to half cock, the cylinder can be removed from the base pin. You don't want to get the revolver's grips wet, but all other parts can be placeed in a bucket of warm soapy water. The barrel and cylinder can be scrubbed with a short rod while in the bucket. This keeps all the fouling and slurry that you create contained, and the water can be changed to rinse the parts before they are dried. I prefer not to submerge the grip frame, but some folks do. Instead, I like to clean the outside with wet and dry patches, while using Q-tips and pipe cleaners to clean the hard-to-reach area around the hand and bolt stop. One product that works well on action parts that you don't want to submerse is the Birchwood Casey Gun Scrubber. Propelled by aerosol, this solvent can be blasted into the most hard-to-reach areas of a firearm. If you have access to compressed air, you can blow the solvent out using an air chuck, and then blast the parts with a shot of Birchwood Casey Sheath Rust Preventative. Be careful not to get oil on your grips. If you do, they may become oil-soaked and prone to cracking and discoloration. Before reassembling your cap-n-ball sixgun, make sure that the areas around the nipples are clean and that there's no fouling or excess oil in the flash holes of the cylinder. A clean used toothbrush is sometimes helpful in cleaning around the nipples.

The last firearm that should be mentioned is the black powder shotgun. These firearms can be cleaned using the same techniques used for rifles and revolvers. On break-open shotguns, it may be beneficial to remove the barrel, or barrels, for cleaning. Besides this, pay close attention to the breech area of the shotgun, particularly the breech face, rim recess area, extractor, and the locking lug surfaces. Fouling left in these areas can cause stiff closing and faulty extraction of spent shells, two of the most common malfunctions seen on the firing line.

Please remember that all black powder fouling must be dealt with in the same manner regardless of where it is found. It must first be dissolved. Then the part in question must be thoroughly dried and treated with a preservative. This is what makes keeping a black powder firearm clean and in good working order such a challenge. If you are a competitor that shoots black powder week after week without a glitch, you're already well aware of what it takes to keep your equipment in order. From a collectors standpoint, the firearms designed to utilize black powder, particularly black powder cartridge guns, are some of the most valuable guns on today's market. When properly maintained, these firearms should be available for future generations to enjoy.

Black Powder and Black Powder Substitutes

By: John Taffin,
aka Sixgunner

Black powder shooters today have a great range of powder to select from, both authentic black powder and black powder substitutes. For testing the .45 Colt, we had at our disposal ten black powder brands and granulations and six black powder substitutes. Which one to use? This is often decided for us by what powder our own particular gun shop happens to stock. However, this situation is changing for the better as gun shops are offering a greater variation of black powder and black powder substitutes. In fact, one local shop, which did not even offer black powder five years ago, now offers several variations of both black powder and substitutes.

You'll notice from the results using 16 different types of powder, but always the same load by volume, that it is possible to vary muzzle velocities by more than 300 fps. Black powder must always be used slightly compressed, so instead of trying to come up with reduced loads, it is possible to simply change powder if lower muzzle velocities and less recoil is desired; and at the other end of the spectrum, it is also easy to see which powders give the highest muzzle velocities.

The latest black powder substitute is Hodgdon's Triple 7. As with all other black powder or black powder substitutes, Triple 7 is loaded by VOLUME, not by WEIGHT, using an adjustable black powder measure. I use it to set my Lyman black powder measure, and then load as any other powder. All the loads listed below are by volume. To duplicate black powder velocities, Hodgdon recommends that the load of Triple 7 be reduced by 15%. Hodgdon also warns that cartridge loads should have a loading density of 100%, with compression not to exceed 1/10 of an inch. Wads of cardboard or polyethylene up to .030" may be used, however they warn against using any kind of filler to come up with reduced loads. All of the loads below were assembled without wads or filler of any kind.

We have experimented using a grease cookie in .45 Colt loads and come to the conclusion that it is not necessary to minimize barrel fouling or to maintain accuracy, however it is a great help in sixguns with tight tolerances such as Smith & Wesson and Remington replicas. Colt replicas just keep going, and going, and going, whether a grease cookie is used or not. All sixgun cartridge loads assembled with Triple 7 used the FFg granulation.

While no wad was used with any of the sixgun cartridge loads, the Ox-Yoke wad was part of every load assembled in percussion or cap-n-ball revolvers. The use of Triple 7 made the operation of the tight-fitting revolvers, such as the Remington, very easy, and the Triple 7 shot so cleanly that the same patch was used to swab the barrels of four different sixguns.

All black powder sixguns, whether they are of the cartridge or cap-n-ball persuasion, and also whether black powder or a black powder substitute is used, should be cleaned fairly quickly after shooting. I prefer to do it the same day I shoot them simply to have it done. How quickly black powder guns must be cleaned depends a lot upon the climate in each particular part of the country. The more humid the weather, the quicker the firearm should be cleaned. Black powder substitutes give more leeway, and Triple 7 is no exception to this, however clean-up is so easy that one does not tend to put it off.

(Ballistic information continued next page)

(Continued from previous page)

EMF's 1860 Army with Speer's .451" round ball and 40 grains of Clear Shot for 990 fps produced this grouping.

This group was produced by EMF's 1858 Remington with Speer's .454" round ball and 40 grains of Swiss FFFg.

One of the rarest of the Civil War era sixguns is represented by Navy Arms' Rogers & Spencer. Here it was shot with 20 grains of Triple 7 and Speer's .451" round ball.

.45 Colt					
Bullet: Lyman #454190 sized to .454" - **Lube:** Lyman Black Powder Gold					
Load: Black Powder Volume Measure of 30 Grains					
Ruger 7-1/2" Old Army	**MV**	**Group***	**Cimarron 7-1/2" Vaquero Model P**	**MV**	**Group***
Goex Ctg	782	1-1/2"	Goex Ctg	771	1"
Goex FFg	792	7/8"	Goex FFg	770	7/8"
Goex FFFg	895	1"	Goex FFFg	878	1-1/8"
Elephant FFg	769	1-1/4"	Elephant FFg	755	1"
Elephant FFFg	818	1-3/8"	Elephant FFFg	810	7/8"
KIK FFg	770	2-1/8"	KIK FFg	760	2-1/8"
Swiss FFg	930	1-1/8"	Swiss FFg	902	1-3/8"
Swiss FFFg	999	7/8"	Swiss FFFg	985	1-1/8"
Wano FFg	663	2"	Wano FFg	654	1-1/2"
Wano FFFg	733	1-3/8"	Wano FFFg	708	1-1/2"
Goex Clear Shot	899	7/8"	Goex Clear Shot	875	1-1/8"
Pyrodex P	895	1"	Pyrodex P	893	1"
Pyrodex RS Select	858	1-1/8"	Pyrodex RS Select	857	7/8"
Pyrodex Pellet	998	1"	Pyrodex Pellet	969	7/8"
Hodgdon Triple 7 FFg	947	1-1/4"	Hodgdon Triple 7 FFg	943	1-1/2"
Clean Shot FFg	764	1"	Clean Shot FFg	750	1-3/8"
Clean Shot FFFg	810	1-1/2"	Clean Shot FFFg	794	1-1/2"
Five shots at 50 feet.					

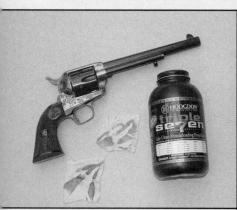

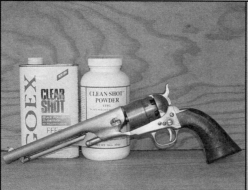

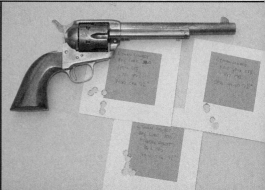

These two patches were run through the barrel of the Cimarron Model P .45 Colt after 25 rounds using Triple 7 and a reliable #12 grease cookie, as well as shooting 25 rounds without the cookie.

Two black powder substitutes that work well in replica cap-n-ball revolvers are Clear Shot and Clean Shot.

Black powder doesn't shoot accurately? These three groups were shot with the CFA 7-1/2" .44-40 using Lyman's cowboy bullet lubed with Lyman's BPG (Black Powder Gold), Goex CTG, and Pyrodex P. Today's black powder shooters have a veritable supermarket of sixguns and powders to choose from.

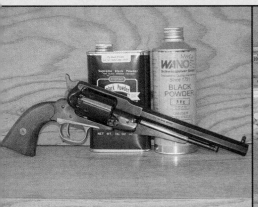

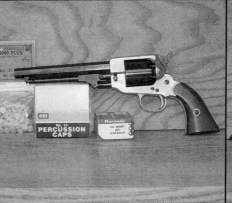

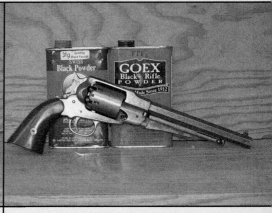

Navy Arms' Model 1858 with Elephant Brand and Wano black powder.

Yes, there are other .36s besides the Remington and the Colt. This is Navy Arms' rendition of a Spiller & Burr.

EMF's Remington Model 1858 with Swiss and Goex FFFg.

Hodgdon's Triple 7 FFg/Sixgun Cartridge Loads		
.45 Colt/ 30-gr./Oregon Trail 250		
Sixgun	**MV**	**Group***
CFA 7-1/2" .45 Colt	943	1-3/4"
EMF 1875 Remington 7-1/2" .45 Colt	854	2-5/8"
EMF 1890 Remington 5-3/4" .45 Colt	827	2-5/8"
.45 Schofield/ 25-gr./Oregon Trail 250		
Sixgun	**MV**	**Group***
CFA 7-1/2" .45 Colt	673	2-1/8"
EMF 1875 Remington 7-1/2" .45 Colt	751	2-1/8"
EMF 1890 Remington 5-3/4" .45 Colt	675	2-1/8"
.44-40/ 30-gr./Oregon Trail 200		
Sixgun	**MV**	**Group***
CFA 7-1/2" .44-40	998	1-1/2"
.38-40/ 30-gr./Oregon Trail 180		
Ten Round Groups For .38-40		
Sixgun	**MV**	**Group***
CFA 7-1/2" .38-40 #1	907	3"
CFA 7-1/2" .38-40 #2	911	2-3/4"
EMF 7-1/2" .38-40	918	3-1/8"
*Five shots at 50 feet - CFA = Cimarron Firearms		

...yrodex is available both in powder and pellet ...rm, both of which work well in Ruger's Old Army.

Another oldie, this 1881 U.S. Cavalry Colt uses black powder loads only.

Powder flask, caps, and conical bullets with Ruger's Old Army spells successful black powder shooting.

This sixgun may look old, but in reality, it is a new, antique-finished .44-40 from Cimarron. It works well with Hodgdon's Triple 7.

This 3rd Generation Colt Single Action Army 7-1/2" .44-40 has been given an antique finish by Peacemaker Specialists to match up with black powder from KIK and Wano.

Oregon Trail 250 using 30 grains of Clear Shot.

Various groups shooting 25 rounds with the .45 Colt without cleaning: Lachmiller 255 using Lyman BPG lube and 30 grains of Clear Shot.

Percussion Revolvers

EMF Colt 1860 Army "Antique Finish"
.451" Speer RD Ball/Ox-Yoke Wad/CCI #11 Percussion Cap

Load	MV	Group*
20-gr. Hodgdon's Triple 7 FFFg	779	2"
25-gr. Hodgdon's Triple 7 FFFg	943	1-1/2"
30-gr. Hodgdon's Triple 7 FFFg	1035	2"

EMF Remington 1858 "Antique Finish"
.454" Speer RD Ball/Ox-Yoke Wad/CCI #10 Percussion Cap

Load	MV	Group*
25-gr. Hodgdon's Triple 7 FFFg	1017	1-1/2"
30-gr. Hodgdon's Triple 7 FFFg	1070	1-1/2"

Navy Arms Remington 1858
.451" Speer RD Ball/Ox-Yoke Wad/ CCI #11 Percussion Cap

Load	MV	Group*
25-gr. Hodgdon's Triple 7 FFFg	921	2"
30-gr. Hodgdon's Triple 7 FFFg	1043	1-3/8"

Navy Arms 1847 Walker
.454" Speer RD Ball/Ox-Yoke Wad/ CCI #11 Percussion Cap

Load	MV	Group*
40-gr. Hodgdon's Triple 7 FFFg	1175	2"
45-gr. Hodgdon's Triple 7 FFFg	1252	2-1/4"
50-gr. Hodgdon's Triple 7 FFFg	1291	1-3/8"

Navy Arms Rogers & Spencer
.451" Speer RD Ball/Ox-Yoke Wad/ CCI #10 Percussion Cap

Load	MV	Group*
20-gr. Hodgdon's Triple 7 FFFg	912	1-1/2"
25-gr. Hodgdon's Triple 7 FFFg	1043	2-1/4"
30-gr. Hodgdon's Triple 7 FFFg	1215	2"

Navy Arms .36 Spiller & Burr
.375" Hornady RD Ball/Ox-Yoke Wad/CCI #11 Percussion Cap

Load	MV	Group*
20-gr. Hodgdon's Triple 7 FFFg	990	2"
25-gr. Hodgdon's Triple 7 FFFg	1014	2-3/8"

Traditions 1847 Walker "Texas Ranger"
.454" Speer RD Ball/Ox-Yoke Wad/CCI #11 Percussion Cap

Load	MV	Group*
45-gr. Hodgdon's Triple 7 FFFg	1218	2-1/2"
50-gr. Hodgdon's Triple 7 FFFg	1234	2"

Ruger Old Army
.457 Speer RD Ball/Ox-Yoke Wad/CCI #11 Percussion Cap

Load	MV	Group*
30-gr. Hodgdon's Triple 7 FFFg	866	2-1/4"
35-gr. Hodgdon's Triple 7 FFFg	1031	2"
40-gr. Hodgdon's Triple 7 FFFg	1167	1-1/2"

*Groups are five shots at 50 feet

Selected Loads for Other Sixgun Cartridges

.44 Russian/USFA SAA 7-1/2"

Bullet	Load	MV	Group
Lyman #429383 250 RN	20-gr. Goex FFg	693	2"
	20-gr. Goex FFFg	745	1-5/8"
	20-gr. Goex CTG	656	2"
	20-gr. Pyrodex P	775	1-1/4"
	20-gr. Pyrodex SLCT	740	1-3/8"
Bullet	**Load**	**MV**	**Group**
Lyman #429667 240 FN	20-gr. Goex FFg	675	2-1/4"
	20-gr. Goex FFFg	724	1-7/8"
	20-gr. Goex CTG	660	1-3/4"
	20-gr. Pyrodex P	775	1-3/4"
	20-gr. Pyrodex SLCT	726	2"

.44 Special/USFA SAA 7-1/2"

Bullet	Load	MV	Group
Lyman #429383 250 RN	26-gr. Goex FFg	769	1-3/4"
	26-gr. Goex FFFg	823	1-7/8"
	26-gr. Goex CTG	697	1-1/4"
	26-gr. Pyrodex P	839	1-3/4"
	26-gr. Pyrodex SLCT	811	1-1/2"
Bullet	**Load**	**MV**	**Group**
Lyman #429667 240FN	26-gr. Goex FFg	747	2"
	26-gr. Goex FFFg	784	2"
	26-gr. Goex CTG	711	2-1/4"
	26-gr. Pyrodex P	802	2"
	26-gr. Pyrodex SLCT	775	1-1/8"

.44-40 (.44WCF)/USFA SAA 7-1/2"

Bullet	Load	MV	Group
Lyman #427666 200 FN	35-gr. Goex FFg	811	1"
	35-gr. Goex FFFg	870	2"
	35-gr. Goex CTG	716	2"
	35-gr. Wano FFg	898	2-1/8"
	35-gr. Pyrodex P	965	1-3/4"
	35-gr. Pyrodex SLCT	846	2"
Bullet	**Load**	**MV**	**Group**
Oregon Trail 200 RNFP .429"	33-gr. Triple 7 FFg	998	1-1/2"

.45 Schofield/USFA SAA 7-1/2"

Bullet	Load	MV	Group
Lyman #452664 250 FN	25-gr. Goex FFg	737	2"
	25-gr. Goex FFFg	805	1-1/2"
	25-gr. Goex CTG	717	1-7/8"
	25-gr. Pyrodex P	791	1-1/2"
	25-gr. Pyrodex SLCT	766	1-1/2"

All powder charges are by volume, not by weight.
All groups are five shots at 50 feet.

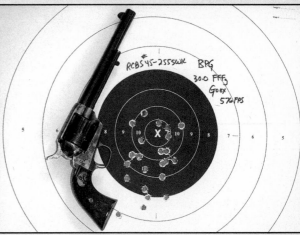

RCBS 255 using Lyman BPG lube and 30 grains of Goex FFFg.

Lyman #454190 using Lyman BPG lube and 33 grains of Goex CTG

Oregon Trail 250 using 33 grains of Triple 7 with a Reliable #12 grease cookie.

Oregon Trail 250 using 33 grains of Triple 7, but this time with no cookie.

Some of the accessories that make black powder percussion shooting more enjoyable: a brass ramrod, nipple wrenches, powder dispensers, powder measures, various-sized spouts, a plunger-operated greaser, and a percussion cap dispenser.

These two old originals, an 1879 Frontier Six-Shooter and an 1881 Cavalry Colt, should only be used with black powder.

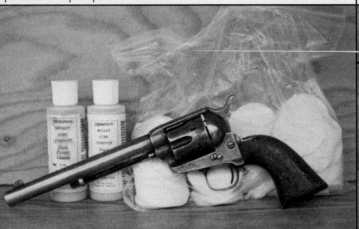

Thompson's Bullet Lube offers a complete line of both shooting and cleaning supplies to keep this 1879 Colt Frontier Six-Shooter well-maintained and shooting.

EMF's Remington's and Hodgdon's Triple 7 result in good groups.

Triple 7 with Navy Arms' 1847 Walker and 1858 Remington.

Lyman's black powder measure and drop tube for safely loading black powder cartridges.

Goex offers a complete line of black powder with FFFg best-suited for sixgun cartridges.

Triple 7 and the results with Ruger's Old Army.

Triple 7 and full-house loads in Cimarron's Model P .45 Colt.

Triple 7 gives excellent results in EMF's 1858 Remington.

Various black powder loads through the US Firearms' .44-40 4-3/4" single-action.

Colt Single Actions made prior to 1900 should only be used with black powder.

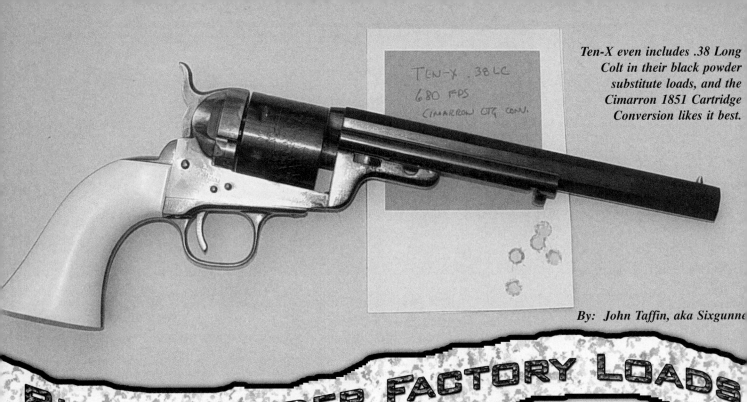

TEN-X .38 LC
680 FPS
CIMARRON CTG CONV.

By: John Taffin, aka Sixgunne

Ten-X even includes .38 Long Colt in their black powder substitute loads, and the Cimarron 1851 Cartridge Conversion likes it best.

BLACK POWDER FACTORY LOADS

A few short years ago, it was very difficult to find factory-loaded black powder or black powder substitute cartridges. Thanks to cowboy action shooting, all that has changed and we now have several companies offering shooters their choice of cartridges loaded with black powder or with black powder substitutes, such as Clean Shot. Four of those companies are Black Dawge, Cor-Bon, Wind River, and Ten-X. Cor-Bon and Ten-X's loads are assembled with Clean Shot, while the other two are strictly purists going with black powder all the way. This gives shooters a choice of true authenticity or the black powder feel with less fouling and easier clean up.

COR-BON has offered some of the best hunting and defensive ammunition available, and has now recently added "black powder" loads for the .45 Colt, .45 Schofield, .44-40, .38 Special, and even

12-gauge shotgun shells. Loaded with Clean Shot, Cor-Bon's loads will normally shoot in most sixguns without swabbing or cleaning, while shooting dozens upon dozens of rounds. However, the Smith & Wesson Model #3s, Schofields, and Remington 1875 and 1890 models may require attention between cylinderfuls to keep them operating. My solution to this is to simply squirt Windex at both the front and rear of the cylinder without removing it from the frame. Windex is cheap and seems to cut the fouling very quickly.

BLACK DAWGE CARTRIDGE COMPANY offers genuine authentic black powder loads using black powder, wads, and SPG lube. They also offer bullets for shooters who prefer to load their own, and they will also load them using customer-supplied cases. Black Dawge's loads are authentic in more ways than one. They not only use black powder, but they also provide full-power 1870's-style loads. Both their .45 Colt with a 250-grain bullet and the .44-40 200-grain bullet clock out in the 990 fps class using sixguns with 7-1/2"

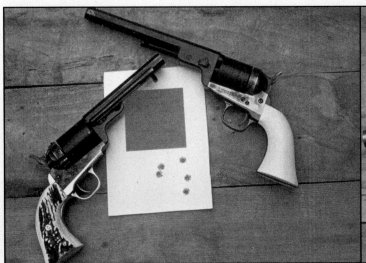

Black Dawge's .38 Special load performs well in Cimarron's cartridge conversions.

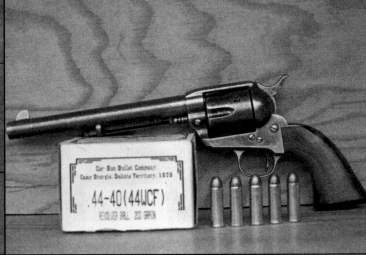

Cimarron's "antiqued" Model P and Cor-Bon's .44-40 black powder match up well together.

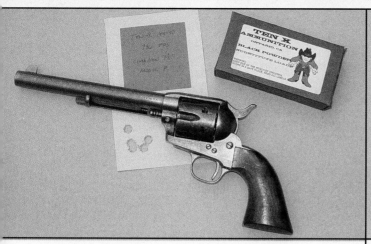

An excellent sixgun and an excellent load. Cimarron's Model P .44-40 with Ten-X 200 RNFP black powder substitute loading.

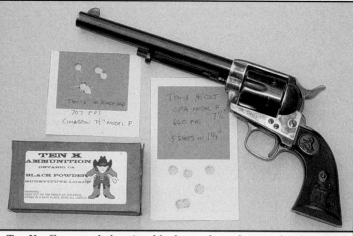

Ten-X offers good-shooting black powder substitute loads in both .45 Schofield (200 grains at 707 fps), and .45 Colt (250 grains at 660 fps). This sixgun is Cimarron's 7-1/2" Model P.

arrels, while the 180-grain .38-40 load hits 1030 fps with the same arrel length. I did some shooting with the full power .45 Colt using 7–1/2" Cimarron Model P at long-range to see if one really could ive an account of himself if caught out in the open without a rifle. Using a full-sized silhouette target, found I could easily head shoot t 50 yards; consistently body shoot t 100 yards; and at 200 yards I ould come close enough to keep hem pinned down. The cavalry oldier was not at a great isadvantage when armed only ith a 7-1/2" Colt Single Action rmy.

In addition to the above loads, Black Dawge offers black powder oads in .38 Special, .44 Russian, 44 Special, .44 Magnum, .45 chofield, and rifle loadings of .38-5, .40-65, .45-70, .45-90, and .45-00, plus 12-gauge shotgun shells. WIND RIVER uses cast bullets t a 20:1 lead-to-tin ratio with all cartridges loaded with Goex FFg lack powder. For testing, we had black powder loads in .45 Colt,

Black Dawge's black powder load for the .45 Colt duplicates the original 40-gr. loading of the 1870's.

.44-40, .38-40, .44 Special, and .38 Special. By the time you read this, they should have bullets available for reloaders. The original Military .45 Colt Black Powder load was 40 grains. It has not been easy to verify this, however in A.C. Gould's book *American Pistols and Revolvers* published in 1888, the author does state that apparently this load was too much for the pony soldiers so it was lowered to 30 grains, while the civilian load became 35 grains.

Wind River's .45 Colt loading is more along the lines of the later military loading of 30 grains. I also used this load on targets at 50 and 100 yards with the same results, that is, head shots and body shots being relatively easy to accomplish at these distances.

TEN-X is a complete supplier of 19th century cartridges in both smokeless and black powder versions. For black powder shooters, they not only offer sixgun cartridges, but levergun

Cor-Bon's .45 Colt and .45 Schofield fired from Cimarron's 7-1/2" Model P.

Cimarron's 10-inch "Wyatt Earp" stays on target with factory black powder loads.

This beautifully-engraved Cimarron Model P likes Wind River's .44-40 black powder load.

Black Dawge's .38-40 load and Cimarron's 7-1/2" Model P.

and single-shot cartridges loaded to black powder levels as well. For those shooting Ruger Vaqueros in the new fangled Magnums, the .357 and .44, Ten-X also offers a black powder loading of these rounds. We tested Ten-X black powder loads in .45 Colt, .45 Schofield, .44-40, .38-40, .44 Russian, .44 Colt, and .38 Long Colt. All loads shot exceptionally well.

All the loads supplied by the four companies were fired in a variety of sixguns. It made for several days of enjoyable shooting, and several afternoons of not so enjoyable cleaning. More than a dozen sixguns from Cimarron, EMF, and Navy Arms were tested supplying the following results.

.45 Colt:			
Sixgun	Load	MV	Group*
CFA 7-1/2"	Cor-Bon 250	715	1-3/8"
	Black Dawge 250	964	1-3/4"
	Black Dawge (Red.) 250	725	1-3/4"
	Wind River 250	759	2-1/8"
	Ten-X 250	660	1-1/4"
CFA 10"	Cor-Bon 250	767	1-1/2"
	Black Dawge 250	1049	2-1/4"
	Black Dawge (Red.) 250	719	1-1/2"
	Wind River 250	766	1-1/2"
EMF 1875 7-1/2"	Cor-Bon 250	720	2-3/4"
	Black Dawge 250	1013	2-3/8"
	Black Dawge (Red.) 250	708	2-1/8"
	Wind River 250	775	2-3/8"
EMF 1890 5-3/4"	Cor-Bon 250	715	2-1/8"
	Black Dawge 250	953	2-1/2"
	Black Dawge (Red.) 250	680	2-3/4"
	Wind River 250	705	2-1/2"

.45 Schofield (.45 S&W)			
Sixgun	Load	MV	Group*
CFA 7-1/2" .45	Black Dawge 230	979	2-1/4"
	Cor-Bon 200	728	1-7/8"
	Ten-X 200	707	1-1/8"

.44 Russian			
Sixgun	Load	MV	Group*
CFA 4-3/4" .44 SPL	Black Dawge 200	773	2-3/8"
	Ten-X 200	684	1-3/4"

.44 Colt			
Sixgun	Load	MV	Group*
CFA CTG CONV 8"	Ten-X 200	708	1-1/2"

.44 Special			
Sixgun	Load	MV	Group*
CFA 4-3/4"	Wind River 200	701	2-1/8"

.38 Long Colt			
Sixgun	Load	MV	Group*
CFA CTG CONV 7-1/2"	Ten-X 128	680	1-1/8"

.44-40 Winchester (.44 WCF)			
Sixgun	Load	MV	Group*
CFA 7-1/2"	Cor-Bon 200	795	2-7/8"
	Black Dawge 200	990	2-3/4"
	Wind River 200	845	2-1/2"
	Ten-X 200	736	3/4"
EMF 7-1/2"	Cor-Bon 200	794	2-5/8"
	Black Dawge 200	973	3-1/8"
	Wind River 200	815	2-5/8"
NA 1875	Cor-Bon 200	Too Long For Cylinder	
	Black Dawge 200	930	1-3/4"
	Wind River 200	818	1-3/4"

.38-40 (.38 Winchester Centerfire)			
Sixgun	Load	MV	Group*
EMF 7-1/2"	Black Dawge 180	1033	2"
	Wind River 180	858	2"
	Ten-X 180	776	1-1/2"
CFA 7-1/2" #1	Black Dawge 180	1072	2-1/4"
	Wind River 180	817	2"
CFA 7-1/2" #2	Black Dawge 180	1028	1-3/4"
	Wind River 180	848	1-3/4"

.38 Special			
Sixgun	Load	MV	Group
CFA CTG CONV 5-1/2"	Black Dawge 140	820	2-1/4"
	Black Dawge 158	798	2-1/4"
	Cor-Bon 158	656	1-3/4"
	Wind River 125	690	1-3/4"
	Wind River 160	603	2"
CFA CTG CONV 7-1/2"	Black Dawge 140	872	1-1/2"
	Black Dawge 158	844	2-1/2"
	Cor-Bon 158	708	2-1/2"
	Wind River 125	726	2"
	Wind River 160	646	2-3/4"

*Five shots at 50 feet
NA = Navy Arms
CFA = Cimarron Firearms
CTG CONV = Cartridge Conversion

LOADING BLACK POWDER CARTRIDGES

By: Kenny Durham,
aka KID Durham

for Single Shot Rifles

During the 1988 Presidential election campaign, former President Richard Nixon was a guest on one of the television news magazine programs. When asked about the Democrat's ability to conduct foreign policy, former President Nixon stated, "The Democrats know very little about foreign policy and what they do know is wrong!" This same statement could be paraphrased to apply to conventional smokeless powder reloading by stating that, "Smokeless powder shooters know very little about loading black powder cartridges, and what they do know is wrong!" The statement may be valid for the simple reason that, while in the process of loading black powder cartridges, we use the same type of brass cases, primers, bullets, loading scales, and loading dies, the techniques are very different.

Many of the fine-tuning processes required to produce target accuracy in modern high-powered rifle ammunition are either of little value or incorrect when it comes to loading black powder cartridges. The truth of this is found in the burning characteristics of black powder. Smokeless powder is a progressive burner and can be compared to a NASA rocket launch where the rocket gains velocity as the propellant burns. In a rifle barrel, this all happens very fast. The smokeless powder burns, starting the bullet to move down the bore attaining maximum velocity as the propellant fuel is consumed. In contrast, black powder burns all at once and blasts the bullet through the barrel. It is more complicated than this example, but visualize a baseball being thrown as representing smokeless powder, as opposed to a baseball being hit with a bat to represent black powder. Both methods of propelling the baseball will cause the ball to travel through the air at the same speed and for the same distance. However, the way in which the force is applied to the baseball, or bullet in our case, is why different methods of loading must be used when loading black powder cartridges.

As an example, I will be discussing the .45-70 Government cartridge. The .45-70 is the most widely used and easiest black powder cartridge to load, and has been in continuous production by ammunition makers for over 130 years. Its long-time popularity is attributable to the .45-70 being adopted as the U.S. military round in 1873. Firearms manufacturers back then, just as in the 20th century, quickly produced rifles chambered for military cartridges. The same trend continued on to the .30-40 Krag, .30-06, .308 Winchester, and currently the 5.56mm or .223 Remington. Due to the popularity of the .45-70 and its military genesis, more components are available for reloading it than any other black powder cartridge.

Since I will be discussing how to load .45-70 ammunition for a single-shot rifle, the cartridges will be tailored for long-range shooting at 200 yards and beyond. The reason for this is simply that the most popular shooting activities today involving black powder cartridge, such as single-shot rifles, cartridge rifle silhouette matches, long-range and Creedmoor target shooting, and long-range steel gong or buffalo shoots. The basic rules for producing accurate black powder

These Winchester .45-70 factory-loaded cartridges with 70 grains of FFg and a 500-gr. bullet are probably from the early 1900's.

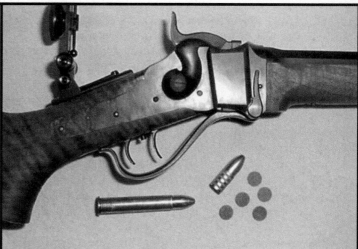

1874 Shiloh Sharps in .45-90 with a Soule tang sight from Montana Vintage Arms.

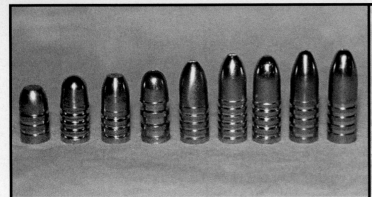

Black powder bullets from left to right: RCBS 45-325 FN, Lyman 457124 385-gr., Ohaus 45-385 F 400-gr., Original Winchester .45 Gov. 400-gr., Saeco #645 490-gr., Saeco #745 530-gr., NEI 458-520 520-gr., Lyman Postell 457132 CV, and Steve Brooks custom mold 540-gr.

Two similar bullet types. The one on the left is for smokeless powder, while the one next to it is for black powder. The bullets on the right are the same as the other two, but the groves are filled with lube.

ammunition are actually very simple:

1. Match the bullet to the barrel.
2. Match the case to the chamber.
3. Determine the proper bullet seating depth for your rifle.
4. Fill the case full of black powder.
5. Seat the bullet.

1. Match the Bullet to the Barrel

First, your bullet must be designed for black powder. Do not even consider using copper-jacketed bullets with black powder or Pyrodex. They just don't work. The only jacketed bullets that work with black powder are paper-patched bullets. Paper-patched bullets were the forerunners of the copper-jacketed bullets and were very popular in the late 1800's for hunting and target shooting. For this project, you are only going to use bullets with grooves for lubricant. Lead bullets designed for black powder usually have anywhere from three to six grooves to hold plenty of bullet lube, whereas lead bullets designed for use with smokeless powder may have only one large lube groove. For black powder, the lube not only prevents barrel leading, but mixes with the black powder residue leaving it soft and easily wiped out by the next bullet as it passes through the bore. Lube for a black powder bullet is usually a combination of bee's wax and some type of natural, non-petroleum based oil with other additives to enhance the properties. The standard for the last several years has been SPG lube, however there are several other good bullet lubes available made exclusively for black powder, such as Lyman's Black Powder Gold. You can make your own, but it's best to start with a proven product.

The rate of twist of your rifle barrel is the next consideration in choosing a bullet. The twist rate of rifles chambered for .45-70 varies from 1 turn in 22 inches to 1 turn in 18, or even 16, inches. The faster the rate of twist, the longer and heavier the bullet can be in order to be stabilized. A good rule of thumb is for 1 in 22 twist, use no heavier than a 405-grain bullet; for 1 in 20 twist, use no heavier than a 500-grain bullet; and for 1 in 18 twist, limit your bullets to about 540 grains in a .45-70. Bullets longer and heavier than 540 grains are impractical to use in a .45-70 because of the limited powder capacity. Bullets heavier than 540 grains should only be used in the longer .45 caliber cases such as .45-90, .45-100, or even larger capacity cases. This does not mean that you are limited to only one bullet length and weight in your rifle, but merely an indication of what may produce the best accuracy for your rifle. For example, my 1884 Springfield Trapdoor shoots very well with 500-grain, round-nose bullets even though it has a 1 in 22-inch twist.

The third consideration when choosing a bullet is its diameter. The nominal diameter for .45 caliber rifles is a bore diameter of 0.450 inch and a groove diameter of 0.458 inch. However, rifle barrels vary from manufacturer to manufacturer, and vintage rifles may have oversized bores. Another reason for variance in barrel diameters is due to industry changes that occur over time and attempts to standardize calibers. For instance, the popular .40-70 cartridge chambered by Sharps, Winchester, and Remington varied in groove diameter from 0.406 to 0.410 inch. Today, .40 caliber barrels usually have a 0.410-inch groove diameter. If you rush out and purchase a

Bullets filled with lube. From left to right, Lyman 385 RN, Winchester Original .45 Gov., Lyman #457658 480-gr., RCBS 45-405 FN, and RCBS 45-500 FN. The two RCBS gas-check bullets on the right are good black powder bullets, but not legal for most competition shooting.

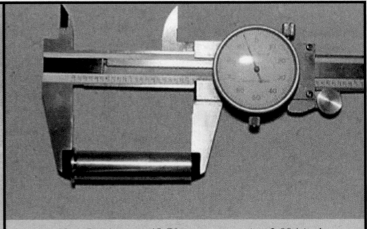

New Remington .45-70 case measuring 2.094 inches.

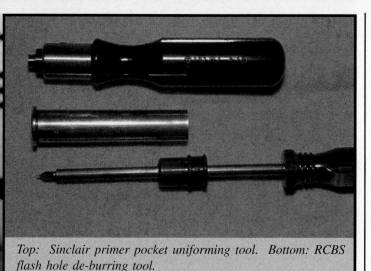

Top: Sinclair primer pocket uniforming tool. Bottom: RCBS flash hole de-burring tool.

new 0.410 bullet mold for your original .40-70 1885 Winchester Highwall, you may find that you can't get the bullets into the chamber. Conversely, you may find that your original .45-70 may have a groove diameter of 0.460 or greater, requiring a bullet larger than the standard 0.458 inch to produce accurate groups.

To determine your barrel's bore and groove diameters, you must "slug" the barrel by driving a soft, pure-lead slug through the barrel, after which you can use a micrometer or dial calipers to carefully determine the dimensions. For all practical purposes, this applies mainly to original vintage rifles. The reproductions by most manufacturers currently are 0.450 bore and 0.458 groove for .45 calibers. However, this is not always the case and bore dimensions do vary. So before ordering a custom mold, be certain of the bore dimensions.

Most .45 caliber rifle bullets and molds available today fall within plus or minus one thousandth of an inch of these dimensions. Swaged and cast-lead bullets are available from various vendors and can be ordered pre-lubed with SPG or Lyman's Black Powder Gold lube. There is no shortage of bullet molds as they are available from Lyman, RCBS, and Saeco, as well as custom makers such as Hoch molds, Steve Brooks, and Paul Jones to name a few.

2. Match the Case to the Chamber

For the best accuracy, cases need to match the chamber in the rifle as closely as possible. When buying brass, it is good to buy 100 or more empty cases of the same lot to help ensure more uniformity between cases. All new cases should be run through the sizing die, and then the neck-expanding die should be set so that it will expand the case neck without belling the case mouth. This sizing and expanding

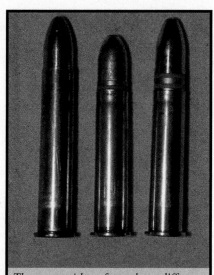

Three cartridges from three different rifles, each of which requires a different bullet seating depth. From left to right, .45-90 for Shiloh Sharps, .45-70 for Dixie Sharps, and .45-70 for Remington Hepburn.

of the cases is the first step in working and shaping the brass so it is round and uniform.

Now the new cases need to be trimmed to a uniform length. Cases can either be trimmed now, or trimmed after they have been fire-formed in a specific chamber. If trimmed before they go through the initial firing process, they will be slightly shorter than the trimmed length after firing. However, this slight shortening will have no, or only minimal, effect for most rifles. In the case of an oversized sloppy chamber, you should trim after the initial firing.

The nominal case length for .45-70 is 2.10 inches. Chambers in most rifles are probably slightly longer by a few thousandths of an inch. For the utmost accuracy, it is best to have the cases the same length as the chamber, however having them 0.005 or 0.010 of an inch shorter is perfectly acceptable. It is most important that cases be of uniform length. Always remember, consistency of all components and procedures is the key to accurate ammunition.

Another important step is to deburr the inside of the flash hole with a tool available specifically for that purpose. This ensures that

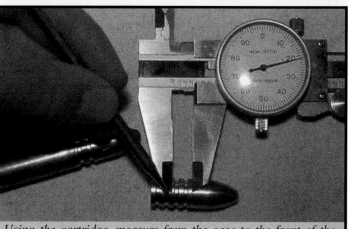

Using the cartridge, measure from the case to the front of the first driving band.

no burr is left from the broaching of the flash hole and leaves it round with a uniform chamfer in each case. Finally, using a case-chamfering tool both inside and outside removes any sharp edges at the case mouth. At this point, cases should be ready to load. There are additional steps that may improve accuracy, such as making sure the rim thickness, the flash-hole diameter, the primer pocket depth, and the case wall thickness near the case mouth are uniform. These additional procedures are reserved for troublesome rifles that are extremely finicky about ammunition.

3. Determine the Proper Bullet Seating Depth

To determine the depth to seat the bullet for your rifle, run one of the cases into the expanding die, belling the mouth ever so slightly. This should be just enough to start a bullet into the case. Next, start a bullet into the case and seat it to about half of the seating depth. Now, carefully slip this test round into the chamber until it stops. Of course, it will not fit as the bullet is out too far, but you will see how much further the bullet needs to be seated for the round to be fully chambered. Now, remove the round and run it up into the seating die and seat the bullet slightly deeper, and then try it in the chamber again. The cartridge should enter the chamber further than before. Repeating the process and continue seating the bullet deeper until the cartridge will enter the chamber and you are able to close the breech. Once this seating depth is determined, adjust the seating die stem to seat the bullet slightly deeper. About a half or a full turn on the stem should do it. You have just determined the maximum overall

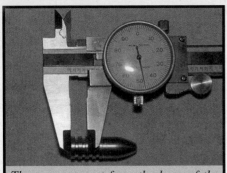

The measurement from the base of the bullet to the mark from the previous measurement.

length of a finished round for an individual rifle.

Why the extra turn? The reason for this additional depth is to allow room for the fouling buildup where the rifling starts. Loaded cartridges that chamber in a clean barrel may be too long and will not chamber in a rifle that has been fired several times unless a few thousandths of an inch allowance is provided. The bullet may be seated deeper if desired. Many times during a match, I have witnessed shooters who could not get a round far enough into the chamber to close the breech because the slight fouling buildup prevented them from placing the cartridge that last 1/16 of an inch or so into the chamber.

Now we are ready to seat primers in all the cases. The primers should be fully seated in the pocket, but never with so much force that the primer is deformed. Doing so can cause inconsistent ignition and degrade accuracy.

4. Filling the Case With Black Powder

When choosing gun powder, granulation choices should be limited to Fg, FFg, or cartridge grade. As a rule, FFFg granulation burns too fast for .40 and .45 calibers. The two most common brands available are Goex and Elephant. Black powder imported from Switzerland is becoming popular among target shooters, too. However, the Swiss powder has different granulation designations and is about twice the price of Goex or Elephant. Once the brand and granulation is chosen, you can determine the powder charge.

Actually, the powder charge was determined in the last step when you were establishing the bullet seating depth. The major difference between loading black powder and smokeless powder is that while smokeless powder rarely fills the cartridge case to capacity, black powder always fills it to capacity. Black powder also burns cleaner and more consistently when slightly compressed.

To determine capacity: 1.) Measure the length of the bullet exposed from the case mouth to the tip edge of the first driving band or to the tip of the bullet. 2.) Now transfer that measurement to another bullet and scribe a mark on the bullet. 3.) Next, measure

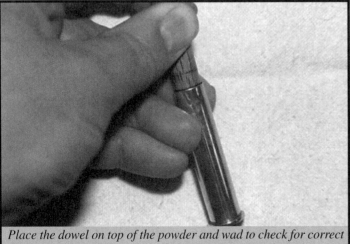

Place the dowel on top of the powder and wad to check for correct bullet seating depth.

from the base of the bullet up to the mark. This measurement is the amount of the bullet that is seated inside the case. 4.) Finally, transfer this measurement to a short piece of wooden dowel by making a mark around the circumference of the dowel. The dowel will serve as a gauge to measure the powder depth allowing you to fill the case with powder just up to where you think the powder level is going to be. Place the dowel in the case on top of the powder. If the mark falls below the case mouth, add more powder until the mark on the dowel is even with, or slightly above, the mouth. When the mark is even with, or slightly above, the case mouth, you have determined the correct powder charge by the volume of powder.

Notice that I used the term volume and not weight. The reason for this is that if you use a different granulation or brand, or even a different lot of the same brand of powder that is used, the weight of this volume will vary. That is why you must always determine the "volume" of powder to use first, and then you must use "weight" to

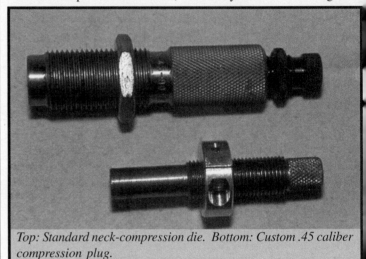

Top: Standard neck-compression die. Bottom: Custom .45 caliber compression plug.

measure each charge as long as you use the same powder. You can figure out a method to measure the powder for each round in the loading process. You can weigh each individual charge, use a brass muzzle loading style volumetric measure, or use a powder measure, such as Lyman 55, specifically designed to safely dispense black powder. Even a .45-70 case shortened to the proper length will serve as a powder measure.

The next step is to apply some compression to the powder charge so it is tightly packed into the case. The compression will help the powder burn cleaner and more uniformly. The easiest way to compress the powder is by dropping the powder through a 24" to 30" long brass or aluminum tube. This is because the powder stacks to a considerably lower height when dropped through a tube than when just dumped into the case. If a drop tube is used, then it needs to also be used when determining the powder charge. The powder charge may be compressed by the act of seating the bullet, but if excessive pressure is applied, it will deform the bullet. Additionally, a special compression die with a plug of the correct size can be purchased. The powder charge can be varied a few grains by the amount of compression that is applied. Slowly pouring the powder through a drop tube may provide all the compression that is needed for the load. On the other hand, you may discover that by increasing the powder charge, and with some additional compression, the load performs even better. This is where the fine-tuning part of working up a load comes into play. For example, my 500-meter ram load is the volume of powder that weighs 63 grains for this specific lot of Goex Cartridge Grade black powder. The powder is dropped through

The wad is seated and the powder charge is compressed and ready for the bullet.

a 30" brass tube with a 0.030" thick wad on top of the powder charge, and then compressed an additional 0.092" in a compression die. Some powders require different compression that can vary from almost no compression to 0.250 of an inch or more. Whatever amount of compression you apply, the finished height of the compressed powder column, including the wad thickness, should be at the level where the base of the bullet will be seated. No more, no less! There must never be any vacant air space or void in a black powder cartridge as this can cause chamber ringing or other possible damage.

The next-to-the-last step is to place a wad on top of the powder charge. The purpose of the wad is to protect the base of the bullet from the hot gasses produced during combustion, in other words, a gas check. I insert the wad prior to compressing the powder charge, but some shooters prefer to compress the charge before they seat the wad with the bullet. Commercial standard black powder ammunition in the 1800's was not loaded with a wad between the powder charge and the bullet, but target ammunition was. Experimentation will determine if a wad helps improve accuracy. Suffice it to say that most target shooters use wads.

Wads are made from all sorts of material varying from 0.030" to about 0.060." They can be cut from stiff cardboard such as tablet backing, shirt boxes, or manila folders. Milk cartons also make excellent wads and are my second choice for wad material, but my first choice is the vegetable fiber material that is purchased from Buffalo Arms Company. Vegetable fiber material is similar to very heavy brown wrapping paper and is available in 0.03" and 0.06" of thickness. Many shooters are using polypropylene wads with good success, but I prefer natural fiber materials. Pre-cut wads can be purchased from either material in various thicknesses for about $20 per 1000. If one desires to cut their own wads, wad punches are available from any supplier of black powder cartridge components.

5. Seat the bullet

The final step is to seat the bullet carefully into the case. The seating die should already be adjusted from the test round we created to determine the bullet seating depth. However, you may find that you need to adjust the die body to remove the bell mouth or to crimp the bullet. If you adjust the die, then you will also need to adjust the seating stem. It is not necessary to crimp the bullets in place for single-shot rifles. When seating a bullet, it is important that the seating stem fits the nose of the bullet. Die makers have several shapes of seating stems to fit almost any bullet. To seat the bullet, gently place the bullet in the case without putting any lateral pressure on it. Gently run the case up into the seating die and seat the bullet. It should be a smooth, almost slick, silky feeling when the bullet slides into the case, with very little resistance. If you experience a

bumpy, jerky, or tight-fitting resistance, then your case neck needs to be expanded more to match the bullet diameter. Usually 0.002" is about right, and most .45-70 dies are furnished with a 0.456" expander stem.

Now it is time to check the finished round. Is the bullet seated fully on the powder charge? Did the seating process deform the bullet at all? Has the bell mouth been straightened back out? If you are satisfied with the finished cartridge, it is time to see if it will chamber in the rifle. While opening the breech, slide the cartridge into the chamber. It should glide right in, but may have to be gently pushed the last few thousandths of an inch. Depending upon the model of rifle and the safety considerations, try closing the breech. Care is needed here! Some actions are ready to fire as soon as the breech is closed. You don't want any holes in the wall or anything else! The breech should close easily. If it doesn't, don't force it! Extract the round and try to determine what is causing the problem. However, you should not have a problem if you have followed all the steps described.

Fine Tuning for Best Accuracy

Once you have loaded and fired these cases in the selected rifle, you will have cartridges that are perfectly fitted to that rifle. These cases become unique in that they will fit that rifle better than any other rifle out there. When you are ready to load them again, you will not need to full-length size them unless you choose to. To neck-size the cases, back the sizing die out until only the area where the bullet is seated is sized by the sizing operation.

There is an almost endless list of things you can experiment with to fine-tune your load. Perhaps an increase or decrease in bullet diameter will improve the group. Or you can try a different bullet, or the same bullet cast from a different alloy. Sometimes, a change in primers will tighten up a group or even out the velocity spread. Also, as already mentioned, you may vary the powder charge and the amount of compression to tighten up a group, too. A final item to examine is the amount of neck tension on the bullet. Maybe a larger neck expander plug is in order. Using a chronograph to measure the muzzle velocity and standard deviation will give you a good indication of how consistent your loads are.

My basic rule is to keep the process as simple as possible. If a load produces good results, don't tinker with it. The goal is to load up and have fun shooting the black powder ammo. Keeping good records of the shooting and the conditions at the time can be invaluable if a problem develops when a certain condition is encountered. The fine-tuning process is reserved for loads that need further improvement. By using the steps outlined above, you will be able to get the utmost accuracy out of your black powder cartridge rifle.

See you at the range!

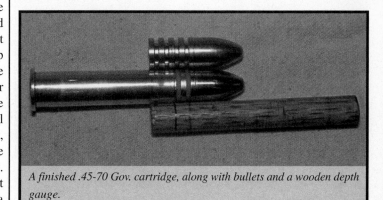

A finished .45-70 Gov. cartridge, along with bullets and a wooden depth gauge.

The first "modern" cartridge using inside lubricated bullets was the .44 Russian in the Model #3 Smith & Wesson in 1871.

Old West Cartridges
for Sixguns and Leverguns

By: John Taffin, aka Sixgunner

The time from the end of the Civil War until the turn of the century was one of great activity for the development of both sixguns and leverguns, even single-shots for that matter. All of these firearms were originally designed for black powder use. Some made the transition to smokeless powder very easily, while others withered and died. The great interest in black powder shooting that has arisen, especially in the last couple decades, has resurrected several dead cartridges and pumped new life into many that were barely hanging on. In my lifetime, the .45 Colt and the .45-70 Springfield have both been pronounced dead so many times I lost count. Instead of being buried, they have been rediscovered and are two of the most popular chamberings in the early years of the 21st century.

We will look at both sixgun and levergun cartridges by

The legendary .45 Colt originated as the Colt Single Action Army in 1873.

traveling two different roads. For the sixgun cartridges, we'll take a look at them in chronological order, mostly at those that are still in use today. The tracing of levergun cartridges will be accomplished by looking at the Winchester leverguns from 1860 to 1895. There were other leverguns, even pump guns using black powder cartridges, but by looking just at

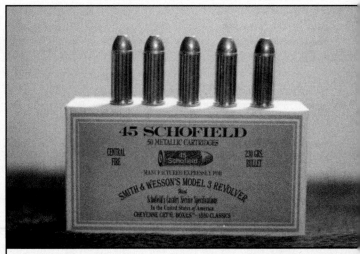

In 1875, Smith & Wesson introduced the Schofield Model in .45 S&W.

Winchesters, we will cover most of the field. Again, we will mostly look at those still in use, or at least those for which ammunition can be tailored, by starting with the .45-70, or basic .45, brass.

The proliferation of cartridges during this time period can easily be seen by looking through *Cartridges of the World, 9th Ed*, edited by Mic McPherson. There are more than 60 pages in this massive and useful volume of obsolete cartridges alone. Three other books that provide valuable information for black powder cartridges, all by Mike Venturino, are *Shooting Colt Single Actions*, *Shooting Sixguns of the Old West*, and *Shooting Lever Guns of the Old West*. Mike's fourth book on shooting single-shots has

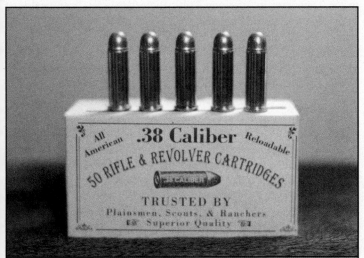
The first double-action Colt was the 1877 Lightning chambered in .38 Long Colt.

just been published as well. All of these books should be on the shelf of anyone who shoots black powder.

Black Powder Sixgun Cartridges

THE .44 SMITH & WESSON AMERICAN (1869)

Smith & Wesson introduced the first cartridge-firing revolver in 1857 with the Model #1 chambered in .22. Their plans to bring forth a larger caliber sixgun were interrupted by the Civil War, however in 1869, the first Model #3 arrived chambered in the .44 S&W American. To derive this cartridge, Smith & Wesson simply enlarged their .22 to .44 and changed from rimfire to centerfire. They maintained the same basic projectile design by utilizing a two-step or heel bullet in their new .44. As a result, the cartridge itself is the same outside diameter as the bullet. Usable brass for shooting an original .44 S&W can be made from .41 Magnum brass.

THE .44 RUSSIAN (1871)

The .44 Russian is our oldest surviving frontier centerfire sixgun cartridge. When the Russians took a look at the .44 S&W American from Smith & Wesson, they made one very significant change in the ammunition. As mentioned, the .44 American featured a heel-type bullet at .434" in diameter that was the same outside dimension as

The Winchester 1873 .44-40 was then followed by the .38-40.

the cartridge case. To accommodate the Russian's request, and to also come up with the standard cartridge case/bullet design that still exists today, the bullet was changed to fit inside the new .44 Russian case, resulting in a bullet of about .428" in diameter.

Somewhere around 250,000 .44 Russians from S&W went to the Czarist government. However, it would be the New Model #3 that would make a great reputation for the .44 Russian in this country. The .44 Russian New Model #3 was smaller and trimmer than the Russian Model and no longer carried the strange hook on the bottom of the trigger guard. It would become the target shooter's favorite in the 1880's.

The last .44 Russian chambered sixgun was made prior to World War II, but the cartridge is alive once again thanks to Starline Brass and Black Hills Ammunition. The original .44 Russian loading consisted of 23 grains of black powder in balloon-head brass for around 750 fps muzzle velocity. With today's components in old-style balloon-head brass, this load, with a 240-grain bullet, yields from 765 to 800 fps from a 7-1/2" barrel depending upon whether

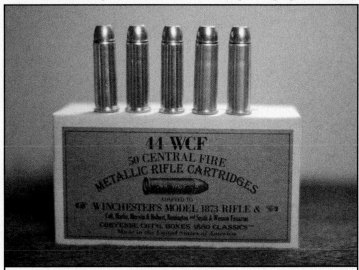
Winchester first chambered their Model 1873 levergun in .44-40. Colt added this chambering to the single-action Army in 1878.

one uses FFg or FFFg black powder. Starline's brass is, of course, modern solid-head style and requires less powder for the same results.

THE .44 COLT (1870)

Colt was caught off guard with the introduction of Smith & Wesson's cartridge-firing .44 in the age of the percussion revolver, but not for long. Colt soon began to offer conversions on their percussion sixguns. The 1860 Army was a most popular revolver for conversion to cartridge firing. Mike Venturino, in his excellent book *Shooting Sixguns of the Old West*, shares the fact that the .44 Colt was brought forth to chamber in the converted 1860 revolvers. He has pulled bullets from some of the original cartridges, reprimed the brass, and used 21 grains of Goex FFg black powder for the propellant, achieving a muzzle velocity of approximately 750 fps with the 210-grain bullet.

The bullet used in the .44 Colt was a heel-type bullet, the same as used in the .44 S&W American. This style of bullet had a base that was smaller in diameter than the rest of the bullet. The two-step bullet had the base inside the case, while the main part of the bullet body had the same outside diameter as the cartridge case. This allowed the original barrel to be used in 1860 Cartridge

The .44-40 and .38-40 was followed by the .32-20 in the early 1880's.

Conversions. These bullets were not lubed in the conventional way, but rather had a hollow base that accepted a lubed disk.

The .44 Colt, which was originally only offered in the 1860 Colt Cartridge Conversion (the 1871-72 Open-Top was chambered in .44 Henry Rimfire), is back, once again, and to keep things simpler today, the .44 Colt is made the same as the .44 Russian/.44 Special/.44 Magnum with a bullet that fits inside the case. Actually, the current .44 Colt has a cartridge case that is longer then the .44 Russian, but shorter than the .44 Special. The cylinders on the 1860 Army are smaller in diameter than the Colt Single Action, so the rims of the standard .44 Russian or .44 Special overlap when placed in the cylinder. To counteract this, the rims of the new .44 Colt are smaller in diameter than the .44 Russian. The Russian can be used in .44 Colt sixguns, but can only be placed in every other chamber. The .44 Colt round can be used in any sixgun chambered for .44 Special.

THE .38 LONG COLT (1871)

The .38 Long Colt is another one of those old cartridges that were originally loaded with heel-type bullets. The first guns chambered with heel-type bullets were the Colt New Line Pocket Revolvers with a spur trigger and a five-shot cylinder. With the coming of the cartridge conversions, it was only natural to chamber the .36 caliber cap-n-ball sixguns, the 1851 Navy, the 1861 Navy, and the 1862 New Police in .38 Long Colt.

When Colt brought forth their first double-action sixgun in 1877,

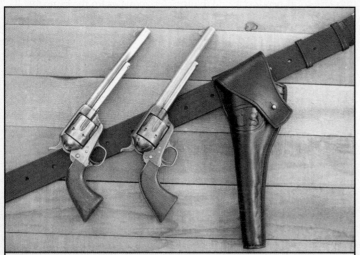

Black Powder Only! A 7-1/2" .44 WCF Colt Frontier Six-Shooter, circa 1879, and a U.S. marked 7-1/2" Cavalry .45 Colt, circa 1881, still live using black powder. Leather by San Pedro Saddlery.

the Lightning Model was chambered in .38 Long Colt as a companion to the Thunderer in .41 Long Colt. With the switch from heel-type bullets to bullets inside the case, the .38 Long Colt was manufactured with a .357" diameter bullet, the same as used in the later .38 Special, and much later .357 Magnum. With the advent of the .38 Special in 1899, the .38 Long Colt was sent into oblivion. Today, however, Starline Brass offers brand-new .38 Long Colt brass. With an 1851 Navy Cartridge Conversion, such as offered in replica form, standard size 150 to 158-grain bullets work fine with 17 grains of FFFg giving muzzle velocities of around 700 fps. If one chooses to fit a conversion cylinder to a percussion 1851 sixgun while using 148-gr. hollow-base lead bullets, they will expand to fit the rifling of the larger bore.

THE .45 COLT (1873)

The .45 Colt is certainly one of the greatest revolver cartridges of all time, perhaps THE greatest. Consider this: In old original sixguns or current replicas, it can be used with 30 to 40 grains of black powder for traditional shooting, or in the proper sixguns, such as custom five-shooters, it can be loaded up with 350 to 360-grain bullets, and

These two Colts, a .32-20 Model P 4-3/4" and a .38-40 Bisley Model, were made at the turn of the century. They are safe with the use of smokeless powder, but are more spiritually pleasing with black powder.

nip at the heels of the mighty .454 Casull, all this from a cartridge case that is more than 125 years old. The Colt Single Action Army .45 Colt was the first choice of many gunfighters, cowboys, Texas Rangers, the U.S. Cavalry, etc. The .45 was the #1 most powerful sixgun cartridge until the advent of the .357 Magnum more than six decades later. The original .45 Colt loading consisted of a 255-grain bullet over 40 grains of black powder for over 900 fps, an awesome load even today. Apparently it was too much, as it was soon cut back to 30 grains for military use and 35 grains for civilian use. Using today's solid-head brass, these loads in a 7-1/2" barreled sixgun give 775 to 800 fps with the 30-grain charge depending upon the powder granulation used, and 875 to 920 with the 35-grain charge. When loaded in the old folded-head or balloon-head brass that had more capacity, 40 grains of FFg yields 1030 fps. Traditional as it may be, it does not detract from its awesome power.

THE .45 SCHOFIELD (1875)

The Model #3 single-actions from Smith & Wesson were all of the break-top design requiring two hands to operate. Major Schofield adapted the Smith & Wesson Model #3 to better serve the purpose of the military by making two significant changes. Instead of being chambered in .44 Russian, the Schofield Model was changed to a .45. However, a problem existed in that the S&W cylinder was too

Another sixgun for black powder loads only, a Smith & Wesson Model #3 .44 Russian from 1874.

short to accept the .45 Colt round. So, Schofield not only improved the Smith & Wesson top-break single-action by redesigning the latch to allow it to be operated with one hand, but he also came up with a shorter .45, the .45 S&W, or .45 Schofield. In its original loading, the .45 Schofield carried 28 grains of black powder. Using a 255-gr. bullet and balloon-head brass with today's components, I acquired 880 fps with this load in a 7-1/2" barreled sixgun. So, this was no light load by any means. Today, shooters have access to brand new brass from Starline. Using 25 grains of black powder or black powder substitute and a 250 to 255-grain bullet will yield velocities from 700-800 fps depending upon the powder chosen, as well as the granulation.

THE .41 LONG COLT (1877):

Originally, the .41 Long Colt had a bullet whose outside diameter was the same as the cartridge case. When it was modernized and loaded with a bullet that would fit inside the case, the bullet came out at a diameter of .386 inches, while the bore diameter was around .403 inches. That is not a marriage made in heaven! To make it work, two things were necessary. The bullet had to be pure lead to expand to seal the bore, and the base had to be hollow to aid in this expansion.

The original loading of the .41 Long Colt was a blunt-nosed 200-grain bullet that was a better man stopper than today's standard .38 Special. No one wanted to be shot with any round, of course, but the

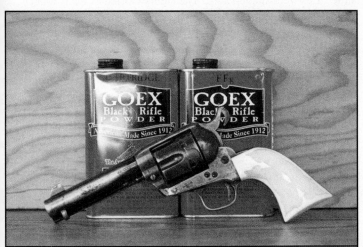

This original Colt Single Action Army bears the scars of 100 years of use, however it has been completely rebuilt on the inside and has been stocked with old ivory by Peacemaker Specialists.

.41 was dreaded because the bullet often picked up a lot of dirt and crud, which was left in the body to rapidly speed infection. A man was much better off to be shot with a .44 or .45 that missed vital organs and penetrated completely than to have a .41 lodged in his body.

The .41 Long Colt was mainly found chambered in the 1877 Thunderer double-action sixgun from Colt that was the favorite of Billy the Kid. It was also the fifth most popular chambering in the Single Action Army behind (in order) the .45 Colt, .44-40, .38-40, and .32-20. With black powder loads and the hollow-base bullet, the .41 Long Colt does right at 700 fps.

THE .44-40 (1877)

Sometime between 1871-1873, both Colt and Winchester were at work to "modernize" the sixgun and levergun. Colt's contribution was the Single Action Army in .45 Colt, while Winchester brought forth a new levergun, the first chambered in a centerfire cartridge. The Model 1873 and the .44 Winchester Centerfire, also knows as the .44 WCF or .44-40, would soon lay a very strong claim to being the gun and cartridge that won the west. The sixgun was the tool of

Cimarron's 7-1/2" Model P .45 Colt takes us back to the 1880's using loads tailored with black powder or Pyrodex.

the gunfighter and lawman, but the rifle was every man's weapon. When Colt chambered the Single Action Army in .44-40 in 1877, those on the frontier who lived by the gun could have a sixgun and levergun chambered for the same cartridge. By the time the 1890's had ended, this was pretty passé. However, in the last 10 years, we have seen a large migration back to sixguns and leverguns chambered for the same cartridge, and not just among black powder shooters. The combination makes a whole lot of sense to a whole lot of shooters.

The .44-40 was not a true .44, but closer to a .42, and it carried a full charge of 40 grains of black powder. With today's components in old balloon-head brass, 40 grains of FFFg, and a 205-grain Lyman bullet, it clocks out at 1100 fps from a 7-1/2" barreled sixgun and close to 1400 fps from a levergun. This may not look like much alongside the Magnum mania that has corralled so many bolt-action rifles, however I would not want to count all the game that has fallen to this load over the past 125-plus years.

THE .38-40 (1884)

No one really knows the reason behind the .38-40. Perhaps Winchester simply wanted a flatter-shooting, lighter-recoiling cartridge for the Model 1873. The .38-40 is simply the .44-40 necked down to a .38, actually .40, caliber. With a 180-grain bullet, it was found to be flatter shooting than the .44, and was a powerful but easy-shooting load in the Colt Single Action Army. It was first

This 7-1/2" Colt Single Action Army is 125 years old and still shooting well.

chambered in the Winchester 1873 around 1880, and then in the Colt Single Action in 1884.

Some have said that the .38-40 was really a .40-38, with the first number denoting the actual caliber and the second the number of grains of powder. This, however, is only surmise, with no facts to back it up. The name .38-40 is certainly less confusing than if they had named it .40-38. Most believe that the original loading for the .38-40 was a full charge of 40 grains of black powder under a 180-grain lead bullet. With today's components in old-style balloon-head brass, these loads clock out at well over 1,000 fps from a sixgun.

THE .32-20 (1884)

Another of the great sixgun/levergun cartridges, the .32-20 was the varmint chambering for the 1873 Winchester, and a natural for an easy-shooting cartridge in the Colt Single Action Army. The .32-20 was part of a trio of sixgun cartridges, along with the .38-40 and .44-40, from Winchester that were first offered in the Model 1873 levergun. Although it was the fourth most popular chambering in the Colt Single Action, the .32-20 would be the most popular chambering in the Bisley Model. The reason is simple. The Bisley, with its target-style grip frame, hammer, and trigger, was more conducive to deliberate shooting than fast draw work, and the .32-20 was a fine varmint cartridge, an easy-shooting defense load, and, in skilled hands, was also used to take deer-size and larger game. The use of 18 to 19 grains of black powder or black powder substitute and a 100-grain bullet will give a very pleasant shooting 700-800 fps.

The Black Powder Cartridges of Winchester Leverguns

1860 HENRY .44 RIMFIRE

In 1860, Henry received a patent for a rifle firing the first truly successful big-bore cartridge consisting of a copper case holding both the powder and bullet, and with the ignition also contained in the rimfire case. The .44 Henry round used a bullet that was originally 216 grains over 26 grains of black powder. The weight of the bullet was shortly reduced to 200 grains over the same powder charge for about 1200 fps. The bullets were lubricated to help reduce fouling, and with its tubular magazine, the 1860 Henry held so much firepower that it was advertised that, "A resolute man, armed with one of these rifles, particularly if on horseback, cannot be captured."

One of the main reasons for this last statement is the unbelievable firepower of the Henry. Up to that point in history, battle rifles were single-shots. The Henry carried as many as 17 rounds in its tubular magazine, which loaded from the front.

Rimfire cartridges may be long gone, but a black powder shooter can have a replica, an excellent replica I might add, 1860 Henry chambered in the reloadable .44-40, or even .45 Colt. More than 140 years after B. Tyler Henry patented the first truly successful levergun, thousands of them are being fired all over the country with centerfire ammunition and black powder.

THE 1866 YELLOW BOY .44 RIMFIRE

The .44 Henry was a great rifle, and was improved shortly after its birth. Production of the 1860 Henry lasted only from 1860 to 1866, with somewhere around 13,000 having been produced. In 1866, the Henry was improved with the King's Patent, named for Nelson King, who followed B. Tyler Henry as Oliver Winchester's shop foreman. This first official Winchester, the 1866 Yellow Boy, used the same .44 rimfire ammunition, but it was now loaded through King's patented loading gate on the right side of the receiver. No longer was it necessary to put the rifle out of commission, or even take it off target, while reloading. As with the 1860 Henry, excellent replicas of the 1866 Yellow Boy are also available chambered in .38-40, .44-40, and .45 Colt, as well as those two upstart cartridges from the end of the black powder era, the .38 Special and the .44 Special, both of which, in all probability, began life as black powder cartridges in 1899 and 1907 respectively.

THE MODEL 1873

We have already mentioned the Model 1873 in conjunction with sixguns as its three centerfire cartridge chamberings of the .44 WCF, .38 WCF, and .32 WCF were all adaptable to sixgun use. The Model 1873 still exists in replica form in all three chamberings, and makes an excellent choice for the black powder shooter.

THE MODEL 1876

A somewhat larger version of the Model 1873, the Winchester 1876, introduced at the Centennial Celebration in Philadelphia, was chambered in .40-60, .45-60, .45-75, and .50-95. The first loading, the .40-60, is only slightly more powerful than the .44-40 of the Winchester 1873, however it was a favorite of Theodore Roosevelt for hunting deer and antelope, and it was this chambering in the 1876 that he used to capture the boat thieves. The .40-60 featured a 210-grain lead bullet at around 1500 fps with 60 grains of black powder. Brass can be made for the .40-60 from the .45-70 brass.

Although the 1876 was larger than the 1873, it still was not enough to handle the .45-70 of the Springfield Trapdoor. Instead, it was chambered in the .45-60 with a 300-grain lead bullet at around 1300 fps with 60 grains of black powder, while the .45-75 was a fatter bottleneck cartridge using a 350-grain lead bullet at around 1450 fps. This was Theodore Roosevelt's choice for Old Ephraim. The former can be made from .45-70 brass, while .45-75 brass is available under the Bertram brand. The powerhouse of the 1876 Winchester was the .50-95 using a 300-grain bullet at close to 1600 fps, which made it more powerful than the .50-70 Government. Brass for the .50-95 is also available from Bertram.

To date, we can have replica leverguns of the 1860, 1866, 1873, and 1892. The 1886 and the 1895 are both offered from time to time under the Browning or USRAC banner. One big hole in the replica supply is the Model 1876. I keep hearing rumors that we will see an 1876, and I not only hope this is true, but that it will also be available in the original chamberings, at least the .45-75 and the .50-95.

THE MODEL 1886

John Browning's first levergun design for Winchester was the Model 1886. It is a great rifle that will handle the heaviest of the modern .45-70 loads. It is, without a doubt, the strongest traditional levergun ever manufactured. In addition to the legendary .45-70, for which current 1886s are still chambered, the 1886 was chambered in nine black powder rounds plus the smokeless .33 Winchester before the originals ended production in 1935.

Of the original chamberings, the most popular and most useful for today's black powder shooter are the .38-56, with a 270-grain bullet at 1400 fps; the .40-65, with a 250-grain bullet at 1500 fps (both of which can be formed from .45-70 brass); the .45-70, with a 405-grain bullet at 1200-1300 fps; the .45-90

Express, with a 300-grain bullet at 1500 fps; and the .50-110, with a 300-grain bullet at 1700 fps. Brass for the .45-90 and the .50-110 is available from Starline.

THE MODEL 1892

We could easily argue that the Winchester Model 1892, a scaled-down 1886 also designed by John Browning, is just about the handiest saddle gun ever devised by man. Although chambered in the same three original cartridges as the Model 1873, namely .44 WCF, .38 WCF, and .32 WCF, it has a much stronger action. Today's replicas are offered in .44-40, .45 Colt, .44 Magnum, and .357 Magnum (both of the latter two work just fine with black powder). The .38-40 and .32-20 should be available in 2003. The 1892 in its original state was also chambered in a fourth cartridge, the .25-20, which is simply the .32-20 necked down. It would not anger me in the least to see a replica chambered for this handy little small-game cartridge.

THE MODEL 1894

Mention the Model 1894 and one immediately thinks of the .30-30. This most legendary cartridge did not come about until 1895 when it was introduced as a smokeless powder cartridge. The original chamberings for the Model 1894 were the .32-40 and .38-55. The .38-55 has benefited from a renaissance of sorts, since it was chambered in several Winchester Model '94 commemoratives, and is now offered by Marlin in the Model 336. This is a grand old cartridge that is easy to shoot with a 255-grain bullet at around 1200-1300 fps. Brass is available from Starline, and Oregon Trail Bullet Co. has added an excellent plain-based lead bullet in various diameters to suit individual rifles. Brass for the .32-40 can be made from .38-55, but it will be slightly shorter than the standard and is available from Buffalo Arms Co.

THE MODEL 1895

The two most well-known chamberings of the Model 1895 are the .30-06 and the .405 Winchester (Theodore Roosevelt's "Big Medicine"), both of which have been revived and chambered in current production 1895s. Both of these began life as smokeless powder cartridges, however the first chamberings for the box magazine Model 1895 were the smokeless .30-40 Krag and two black powder rounds, the .38-72 and the .40-72. If one should be lucky enough to come up with an original 1895 in either of these two chamberings, both of these cartridges are available from Bertram Brass. The .38-72 uses a bullet around 270 grains at 1450 fps, while the 280-grain bullet of the .40-72 can be driven to over 1500 fps with black powder.

Today's black powder shooter of sixguns and leverguns has a veritable supermarket of guns and equipment from which to choose. In addition to the many originals that are still in great shooting shape, we can choose from a long list of replica firearms. On the sixgun side of the list, we have cartridge conversions, as well as replicas of the Colt Single Action Army, S&W Schofield and Model #3 Russian, and Remington Models 1875 and 1890. All models of leverguns exist except for the Model 1876, which I hope will be resurrected. For shooting these firearms, companies such as Oregon Trail Bullets, Meister Bullets, and AA, LTD offer a long list of cast bullets, or one can cast their own with molds from RCBS, Lyman, NEI, and several others. The last time I checked, I had access to black powder from Goex, Wano, KIK, Elephant, and Swiss, as well as black powder substitutes such as Clear Shot, Clean Shot, Pyrodex, and Triple Seven. It is a great black powder world out there!

I think a lot of shooters would like to try the Black Powder Cartridge Category in cowboy action shooting. It looks like fun, the guns go "BOOM" instead of "poof," there's smoke everywhere, and it looks more authentic as well. However, shooters are afraid of the voodoo incantations required to use the "holy" black. Every "Dark Lord of the Soot" seems to know "THE" secret way of making gunpowder work, and each insists you do it his way or go directly to heck, do not pass go, and do not collect $200. If one reads ten books about black powder, they'll get ten different recipes; some with grease cookies made from rancid unicorn grease, bullets made on an out-of-production mould of lead and unobtanium in a precisely 20:1 mix that you've moulded yourself by the dark of the moon, and homemade bullet lube (or expensive commercial bullet lube). You can't use your usual progressive reloader or your commercially-lubed bullets either. It all sounds very complicated and expensive, it smells like sulfur, and most people decide it isn't worth it, so they stick to one of the smokeless categories.

However, the "Soot Lords" are hiding the facts. If you use the black powder substitute Clean Shot, shooting in the Black Powder Cartridge Category is only slightly more difficult than shooting smokeless. According to the folks at Clean Shot, "Clean Shot Powder is a pyrotechnic composition that is best described as replica black powder. It does not contain nitro-cellulose, nor is it a smokeless propellant. It is a propellant designed for use in percussion and black powder cartridge arms found by a competent gunsmith to be in good shootable condition. Clean Shot Powder is not black powder, but it does smoke. It is classified by the Department of Transportation as a flammable solid in limited quantities and can be shipped by most common carriers." (To that I add, "Boy, does it smoke.") No voodoo incantations or prayers to the dark lords are required. Here's how.

Loading

You can load Clean Shot on your normal progressive reloader. Before you start, degrease it thoroughly wherever the powder will be in contact; otherwise, it'll gum up where it touches old bullets, case lube, etc. You'll probably need to insert the rifle powder measure for full-house loads in the bigger cartridges, but stick with the same commercially-available (cheap) bullets you've been using with smokeless lube. In fact, Clean Shot says you don't need any lube at all because Clean Shot makes its own lube! SPG-lubed bullets will result in fouling with Clean Shot.

No Case Lube

Do not lube your cases, because the case lube will stick to Clean Shot and gum up the works. If you load bottlenecked cases, such as .44-40 or .38-40, and you're using a progressive press, run them through the sizing/decapping die while the other dies are removed, and then tumble them to remove the case lube. If you're using a Dillon Press, this is easy because one can take two tool heads, put the sizing/decapping die in one, and the rest in the other. Yes, this is a pain compared to smokeless, but only with those cartridges, the more common .38s and .45s are easy (especially the .38s).

Don't try to match black powder loads by weight. Clean Shot is lighter than black powder, so just try to match the volume. Twenty-one or so grains by weight of FFg Clean Shot will fill a .45 Colt case, so don't try to stuff 37 grains in there because you'll never make it.

For initial loads, plan on filling the cartridge with powder, leaving enough room for the bullet. A dowel makes a convenient tool to adjust this. Mark off the length of the bullet less 1/16 of an inch, and

Using Clean Shot in the Black Powder Cartridge Category

By: Captain George Baylor

T. X. Clean Shot, using Clean Shot powder, makes a lot of smoke with a Navy Arms Schofield shooting .45 Colt loads.

adjust the powder charge until the dowel goes that far down. Remember, it doesn't matter what it weighs, but you might want to weigh it so you can duplicate it later. Black powder charges must fill the cases and leave no air space. Black powder substitutes, such as Clean Shot, are not quite as touchy as to leaving any air space, though it is still recommended that no air space be left within the cartridge case. Some of the black powder substitutes do not provide as consistent of burning rates as regular black powder, and thus the standard deviation in their velocities will be higher.

Light Loads

Are full charge .45s taking your arm off? Do you already have a collection of .45s? Do you not want to spend thousands going to .38? Well, I've got good news for you; reduced loads with Clean Shot are okay. A shooter can cut back five grains at a time until he/she is happy. Fifteen grains, plus or minus (by weight), and a 200-grain bullet in .45 Colt will make a good CAS load. Just make sure that you fill the space with Caulk Backer Rod, a round foam rod obtained at a hardware store, which comes in 3/8" diameters for .44 caliber weapons, and 1/2" for .45 calibers. Cut the rod into the lengths needed to fill the case completely, and then compress with the bullet. I made a jig to cut sections using an X-Acto knife. If one of the "Soot Lords" objects to your "wimpy loads," remind him that in the 19th century, the U.S. Army considered the full charge .45 Colt load too hot, and that there was a target load called the .45 Revolver with about 10 gr. of powder behind a 200-gr. bullet at 650 fps. Duplicating the load mentioned above makes a pleasant shooting load for rifle and pistol. If he's still complaining, ask him to stand downrange and play catch. If you're shooting .38s and they're too hot, try .38 Long Colts. If you're shooting .32-20s and they're too hot, well, you're on your own.

By the way, I use FFFg only in my percussion pistols, not in cartridges. All of my cartridges get FFg. FFFg meters better than FFg, but FFg gives plenty of velocity for CAS usage. If you want more velocity, you can use FFFg, but it isn't necessary for CAS.

Regular Primers

You can use magnum pistol primers, but you don't have to when using Clean Shot because it does NOT require them.

Dillon Press Note

You can load .45 Schofield (correctly called .45 S&W, but both Starline and Black Hills call it .45 Schofield) cases in .45 Colt dies by readjusting everything. I use a separate tool head and set of dies for the Schofield cases to eliminate the adjusting. All .45 cases should get a strong roll crimp in all cases, smokeless or smokey. Unless you have a genuine S&W Schofield, there's no reason to use Schofield cases. You can get reasonable velocities by using the Caulk Backer Rod filler in .45 Colt cases, and you won't have to deal with two different kinds of cases when reloading, assuming your rifle is .45 Colt.

Shotgun Loads

You'll need to reload, so a $50 Lee Load All will do to start with. I, however, wore mine out and moved to a Mec 9000G to gain more speed. The suggested load for this 12-gauge uses Winchester AA Hulls, Winchester Red AA Wads, WAA12R 1-1/8 oz. #7-1/2 shot, 50 grains of FFg Clean Shot by volume (41 grains by weight), and Federal 209A Primers. Lately, I've

To create reduced loads using Clean Shot, the Caulk Backer Rod is used as a filler. Pre-cut sections are inserted into the case at the bullet seating station of this Dillon XL650. Note the sections of Caulk Backer Rod in the bullet tray.

Use the bullet upside-down to compress the Caulk Backer Rod, but don't leave the bullet like that.

Now the bullet is fully-seated, which further compresses the Caulk Backer Rod and the Clean Shot powder, resulting in very consistent light loads.

The use of Dillon's Powder Check die is highly recommended since high, low, or missing charges are caught with this. This shows a perfect charge.

When finished, empty the powder measure back into the Clean Shot container and seal tightly, since unfired Clean Shot is hygroscopic.

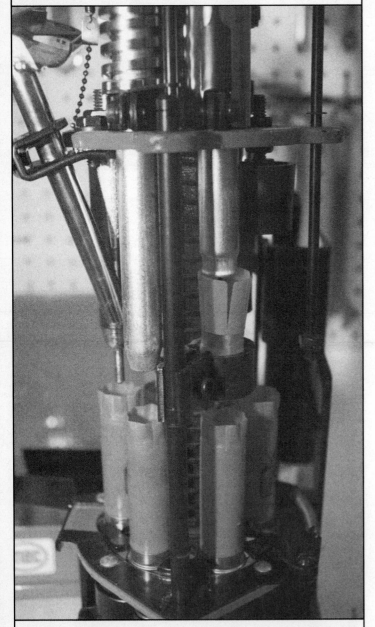

Captain Baylor uses a Mec 9000G to load shot shells, using Clean Shot just like smokeless.

switched to 1-1/4 oz. of shot. Recoil is still low, but if I hit the knock-down, it goes down.

Using local prices, a box of reused hulls cost me $4.58, or $6.58 for a box of fresh hulls. Compared to about a dollar per round for commercially-available Clean Shot rounds, that's pretty good and not much worse than buying smokeless shells by the case. Black powder loading is almost like loading smokeless, except for daily clean-up.

Clean-up After Loading

When you finish loading, empty the powder measure (pistol, rifle, and shotgun), and put the Clean Shot back in the original container and seal it. No partially-completed rounds should be left open, because unfired Clean Shot is hygroscopic so it absorbs water. Flakes left out will be blobs in a few days in a humid climate, and it will also corrode the steel parts of your reloading system. So, blow the powder measure out with compressed air, and then blow any powder dust off the loader.

Shooting

You'll have fun shooting black powder not only because there is more smoke and noise than you have had before, but you'll also receive attention from other shooters and spectators. Clean Shot doesn't smell as bad as black powder, but Chanel isn't coming out with Eau De Clean Shot anytime soon. The first thing you'll notice is that the unprotected brass will turn black and corrode after shooting. As soon as you unload your pistols and retrieve your rifle brass, dump the brass into a jug of water and vinegar. When you get home, rinse the jug out with clear water two or three times, pour the brass out, let them dry, and then tumble them as usual.

If you find that some rounds have corroded because they got missed, submerse them completely in full strength ZEP All-Purpose Cleaner overnight. When they look shiny and clean, take them out, rinse them thoroughly with water, and let them dry in a wire mesh basket so the water won't stain them. Putting the tray in the sun to dry quickly or in the oven at 230 degrees will help them dry without watermarks or discoloration, and then tumble them clean as usual. CLR or ZEP Calcium, Lime, and Rust remover will make the brass shiny and clean almost instantly, but it costs considerably more so I reserve it for problem "children." Also make sure that you wear rubber gloves when using it.

Gun Cleaning

To clean your gun, spray Windex with vinegar (not ammonia), which is available at Home Depot, on the gun and down the bore, and then run a Bore Snake through the chambers and bores. Spray your lubricant of choice full-strength on the last foot of the Bore Snake; usually one pass will do it. Next, spray the rest of the gun with Windex/vinegar, scrub as necessary with a toothbrush, and then DRY THE GUN by blow drying with compressed air or heat drying with a hair dryer. Now wipe down the gun with lubricant, so it will be ready to store. I do not spend anymore time cleaning when using black powder than with smokeless. I shoot revolvers with very little lube, generally just the base pin, and not much more on the rifle. I can go an entire day's match without cleaning, and have experimentally gone 12 stages without cleaning. I clean shotgun chambers as often as I would if shooting smokeless when in competition.

No Special Lubes Needed

I've tried several lubricants with Clean Shot, but most black powder shooters swear by Ballistol. If you're going to use real

Captain Baylor firing his Marlin Cowboy Limited using full-charge .45 Colt Clean Shot loads.

black powder some of the time, you probably want to use Ballistol, but Break Free CLP and Rem Oil from Remington have proven very effective for me. The only rust problems I've encountered were when I failed to dry the gun after using water/Ballistol (10:1 mix). Consequently, I don't use water when I use Ballistol now. Instead, I coat the outside of the guns liberally with Break Free before storing them in the safe, and always place them in a gun sock. The trick is to coat everything with a rust protectant - inside and outside.

I have experimentally left my guns uncleaned, but sprayed with Ballistol, Rem Oil, or Break Free after shooting for one, two, five, seven, and 14 days without corrosion. I don't leave brass pieces unclean for very long, however, which brings us to how to care for a Winchester '73.

Winchester '73 Tips

The Winchester '73 has a brass shell lifter, and Clean Shot discolors brass, so what should one do? When you finish shooting, bathe the shell lifter in Windex with vinegar and then in lubricant. When you get home, disassemble the '73 so that you can remove the shell lifter. Immerse it in full-strength ZEP All-Purpose Cleaner, clean your other guns, clean the disassembled '73, and then check on the shell lifter. If it's all shiny and bright, take it out, rinse in water, Brasso as needed, lube, and then reassemble. If it still has stains, leave it there a bit longer, overnight if needed. If you don't get all the stains off and can't wait, go ahead. You're not hurting anything but the looks of your gun, which you can work on later. CLR or ZEP Calcium, Lime, and Rust remover, used full-strength, will take just about anything off brass, but make sure to keep it far away from blued parts.

Shotgun Cleaning

The shotgun is the hardest to clean because plastic wads will melt and coat the bores. However, that will come off with either a good bore brush or by using a Bore Snake several times. I just spray Windex/vinegar down the bore and run the Bore Snake until it's clean. As an alternative to the Bore Snake, you can take a paper towel, saturate it with your cleaning solution, wad it up, and shove it through the barrel from the chamber end using a cleaning rod. Usually, once per barrel is enough. The rest of the gun is cleaned and oiled like the revolvers and rifle.

See, that wasn't so hard, was it? Oh, one more thing: try not to laugh when the timer operator starts the timer and then runs upwind.

Hodgdon's Triple 7 black powder substitute shown with an antique Smith & Wesson .45 Schofield and a current production model .45 Schofield. Together they make a great team.

By: Ray Walters, aka Smith n' Jones

BLACK POWDER AND THE 1875 S&W SCHOFIELD

The two best-known American military cartridge revolvers of the late-19th century were, without a doubt, the Colt Model 1873 single-action army revolver (SAA) and the Smith & Wesson #3 Model 1875, often referred to as the Schofield. The history of these two great arms has been ruminated over time and time again, and interesting reading it is. However, for purposes of brevity, we will look only at the Smith & Wesson Schofield model, and more specifically, the latest version of that great sixgun that is once again being produced by Smith & Wesson.

A couple of years ago, we started hearing rumors that Smith & Wesson was planning on reintroducing, on a limited basis, the Schofield Cavalry Model in the era-correct .45 S&W

Buffalo Creek's Reliable #12 black powder bullet lube.

Schofield cartridge. At Shot Show 2000, Chucky and I had the opportunity to meet with Roy Jinks from Smith & Wesson to hear first-hand how the #3 Schofield project came to be. Our meeting was extremely enlightening and informative, and Chucky and I came away anxiously anticipating the arrival of this newest

offering from S&W; the first in decades for the single-action shooter and Western-action shooting fan. After meeting with Tom Kelly, who was to be our contact with Smith & Wesson, we were assured that SHOOT! MAGAZINE would be on the list to receive one of the new Schofields for testing and evaluation.

In the fall of 2001, we received a phone call from Smith & Wesson that our #3 was on the way. When we picked it up, there was a scramble to see who was going to have the honor of doing the test-lucky me! I found myself in possession of a classic firearm that was of new production and by the original manufacturer; something that does not happen very often in the firearms industry.

Through the spring and summer of 2002, I took the Schofield out and put a few rounds through it, but due to all of the other irons in the fire (no pun intended), there was never time do the testing. In fact, it is because of this book that the #3 finally got its day at the range and, indeed, the reason for the focus of this article.

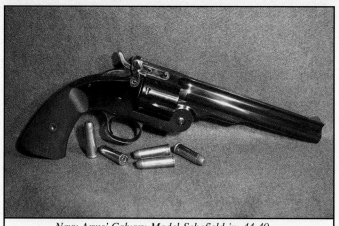

Navy Arms' Calvary Model Schofield in .44-40.

It seems that some months back when Chucky was talking with Tom Kelly about the Schofield and our upcoming book, he mentioned the fact that I was planning on testing the gun, not only with a variety of smokeless loads, as is our normal process, but that I was going to do some tests with black powder and black powder substitutes for possible inclusion in *Black Powder and the Old West*. To this, Chucky was told, "Don't waste your time shooting any form of black powder because the new Schofield is built with such close tolerances, specifically between the cylinder and the forcing cone, that the black powder fouling will cause the gun to bind up in no time at all." When Chucky told me this, it came as more of a challenge than a warning. You see, I had been doing quite a bit of black powder and black powder replacement testing over the summer and had come up with some loads that shot unbelievably clean, leaving minimal residue and fouling. And, because this was a firearm that was originally designed to shoot black powder, I had to see if there was a combination that would function in the new #3 and give the CAS Frontier Cartridge Category shooter an opportunity to use it in regular competition.

As I talked with several other shooters, including Sixgunner, I came to find out that black powder fouling had always been a problem with the Schofield, and was one of the reasons that it was not as well received by the military as the Colt SAA. Even the current Schofield replica models made in Italy and imported by a number of companies were somewhat "cranky" about shooting black powder. Even more so was the new production Smith & Wesson, as those tolerances have been tightened up to make the gun more efficient with smokeless powder.

The Fix

We CAS shooters who choose to dabble in the "Black Arts" (black powder and its substitutes) are living at a wonderful time because there are several black powder substitutes that provide most of what black powder does so well and, in most cases, eliminates much of what shooters don't like about the "real stuff," namely residue, fouling, and clean-up problems. Now, this fouling stuff has more to do with clean-up problems than with anything else. Most of what is problematic about charcoal-based powder is easily dealt with by following the same guidelines that our forefathers used over 100 years ago. Still, the problem of residue fouling that prevents moving parts from working as they should is certainly one that many of the new replacement powders can improve.

The first of the successful replacement powders was Hodgdon's

Pyrodex series of powders that changed the way a lot of shooters looked at black powder shooting. In more recent years, we have seen other names come on the market, including Clean Shot, Clear Shot, American Pioneer Powder, and Hodgdon's latest offering, Triple 7. Most of these powders were developed to try to minimize the amount of fouling left in firearms, thereby making "black powder" shooting more user-friendly.

The next improvement that we saw was the introduction of a couple of new lubes, which, when used in conjunction with the "cleaner" black substitutes, has done wonders for the fouled gun problems. While there are any number of great, time-proven lubes on the market, including SPG and Lyman's Black Gold, these latest lubes seem to be different in that they are somewhat harder and have more of a tendency to "stay put" in the lube grooves of a bullet when in their packing containers. They also seem to work better in "lube cookie" form than most of the softer lubes due to having a higher melting point (usually around 170 degrees), and are not as prone to melting and contaminating the powder charge even when the temperature goes up and no wad is used.

The point of all this is that when challenged with the warning that the new Schofield would not work with black powder or black substitutes, I immediately started putting together some .45 Schofield loads using a variety of hard-cast bullets, powders (both black powder and substitutes), primers, and lubes. What I discovered was that the new Schofield could be fired repeatedly without "gumming up" when the right combination of powder and lube was used. Changing the primers and the weight of the bullets, however, did not seem to affect the functioning of the gun. The loads that I found would work in the Smith & Wesson are not, in all likelihood, the only ones that will function therein, but I know they worked very well, and were suitably accurate to boot.

So, if I could find a load or loads that functioned well in the new Smith & Wesson Schofield, the same type of loads will probably work in any of your sixguns that you may be having fouling problems with. Even such problems as sticky cylinder base pins that don't want to come out of your SAAs after a couple of stages can be cured by the correct use of the right lube. And, perhaps, the most important point of this discussion is that a cowboy can go to a shoot and use what is arguably one of the finest firearms that has come out by Smith & Wesson in years in the Frontier Cartridge Category.

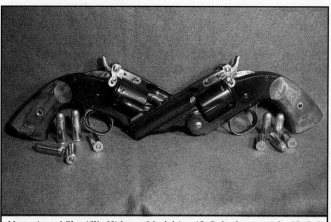

Navy Arms' Sheriff's Hideout Model in .45 Colt shown with .45 Colt cartridges (left) and .45 Schofield cartridges (right).

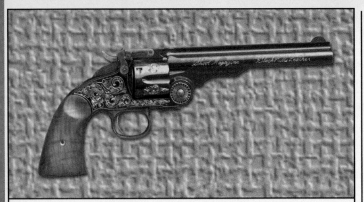

Smith & Wesson's .45 Schofield is currently produced in S&W's Performance Center. The firearm shown was provided by S&W and was engraved by Jim Downing, aka The Gun Engraver.

The loads that I used with success all utilized a hard-cast bullet, factory-lubed with the usual hard, nearly plastic, colored lube that most manufacturers use today. Several were tested, and all performed adequately. Most were in the 200-grain weight range, and the powder charges ranged from 18 to 21 grains by volume. Criteria for powder-charge volume was figured by using a full case, less the area, taken up by the bullet below the crimp groove and the thickness of the lube cookie (usually 1/16 of an inch). Little or no compression of the powder charge was utilized while making sure that there was no air space between the bullet and powder. In most of the loads, a lube cookie was used instead of the more traditional lube-in-the-grooves method. The only reason for this was that I could find few commercially-lubed bullets which utilized the two lubes that I was testing. The one exception was the 250-grain RNFP produced by Chey-Cast Bullets in Cheyenne, Wyoming. This fledgling bullet manufacturing company also produces one of the lubes that was used throughout this test.

As I stated before, there are probably other lube and powder combinations that will work, but I know from testing that these do. In fact, I tried several of the more standard bullet/lube combinations (standard-lubed bullets) with replacement powders and none of them functioned for more than six shots.

While there are a lot of mixed emotions about using black powder lubes in "cookie" form, my experience with this project is that the system works very well and left me with very few negatives to detract from the positive results. A couple of items that were obviously on the negative side are that you expend considerably more time reloading and that you use a considerably greater amount of lube when going the "cookie" route. Additionally, the space taken up by the lube cookie is space that would normally hold additional powder, thereby giving lower velocities. On the other hand, that extra lube blowing through the gun is what helps keep the fouling to a minimum and the gun running smooth.

The loads that I shot successfully through the Smith & Wesson, as well as a pair of Navy Arms Sheriff's models and a Navy Arms Cavalry model, were all lubed with either Buffalo Creek Supply's Reliable #12 or Chey-Cast black powder lube. These are very similar lubes with a high melting point and a solid, waxy texture. The "cookies" were cut using a case of the appropriate caliber with the rim end cut off. The lube was melted in one of my wife's glass cookie pans and allowed to cool until hard. Thickness was determined on a, more or less, "guesstimation" process, trying to keep the thickness between 1/8 and 1/16 of an inch.

The black powder substitutes that worked the best, in fact the only two that performed satisfactorily in the S&W Schofield, were Hodgdon's Triple 7 and American Pioneer Powder FFFg (also known as Clean Shot). Both propellants, when used with one of the above-mentioned lube "cookies," worked well. The test was a very simple one - fire 50 rounds as fast as they could be loaded and fired without fouling the cylinder to where it would not turn freely.

Using my Lyman #55 black powder measure, I charged the Starline brass, primed with Winchester WLP primers with the appropriate amount of powder, set a cookie on the powder, and seated the bullet using Redding's Competition seating die. The rounds were then crimped with the Redding standard crimp die. A small test sample of each powder type was also loaded without a cookie for comparison purposes. Typically, the highest number of rounds that could be fired without the lube cookie was six. With a cookie of either Reliable #12 or Chey-Cast BP lube, I was able to fire 50 rounds of each and still had a relatively free-turning cylinder. Velocities ran around the 675-750 fps range. Loads made up of a variety of "real" black powder, with and without cookies, suffered the same fate as the replica powders, only allowing about 5-6 rounds before the cylinder would bind. One interesting point was that the black powder factory load that is being produced by Wally Wenzel of Black Dawge Cartridge Ammunition Company managed to burn clean enough to nearly get through three cylinders full (13 rounds) before the cylinder became sticky. The loads that Wally puts together are his own special recipe using real black powder, usually Goex, and averaged 940 fps through the S&W.

Conclusion

The only conclusion that I have come up with is that the additional lube that is forced down the barrel when using a higher melting point lube cookie keeps the resultant fouling so soft that the next bullet can easily blow it right out. When I shot at Trailhead in Columbus, Texas in 2002, I used Hodgdon's Triple 7 and Reliable #12 loads in my handguns and Clean Shot and Chey-Cast lube loads in my .44/40 rifle, and shot the entire 12 stages without cleaning any of my guns. When I ran a Windex-soaked patch down each barrel after the shoot was over, they actually came out cleaner than if I had been using TiteGroup smokeless --go figure. However you look at it, these new lubes and black powder replacement powders will go a long way towards making the Frontier Cartridge Category a lot more pleasurable for the average shooter. Try these combinations, as well as some of your own, and see if dabbling in the "Black Arts" isn't a lot easier than you thought.

Smith n' Jones shooting S&W's current production .45 Schofield.

Up In Smoke!

By: Daniel Alley, aka Big Pete

Melted beeswax and olive oil lube and bullets.

.38 Special bullets being pulled from beeswax/olive oil lube.

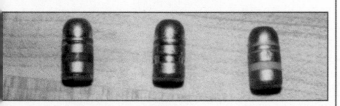

.38 Special 158-gr. RNFP bullets. Left to Right: factory lube, no lube, and beeswax/olive oil lube.

I am pretty much locked into the "modern" class in cowboy action shooting. Due to limited funds and a certain amount of dedication to the manufacturer, I'm shooting a pair of Ruger Blackhawks in .38/.357. Good solid guns, they can take whatever I throw at them, whether it be low-powered cowboy loads or some rompin' full-out .357 loads.

But after about a year of cowboy action shooting and watching other folks shooting other styles in other classes, I wondered what it would be like to shoot black powder. As I said, I can't compete in any class but "modern," but the clubs I shoot with are a pretty fun-loving bunch and don't much care what you shoot as long as it's safe and easy on their steel.

So, I got to thinking (that was the tough part), why not? Why not shoot black powder out of my .38s? Yeah, why not?

Every black powder shooter I talked to said, "Why, ya just fill up the case 'n stick a bullet in." Well, it ain't quite that simple, but darn near!

What you need are a few winter days with the ammo closet already filled up with cowboy loads and a desire to get out of the house and away from the TV.

The first thing you have to deal with is the fact that petroleum-based lubricants do not get along with black powder. As I already had a few thousand cast bullets around, I had to do a bit of thinking again. What to do with all that smokeless lube on all those bullets? It's petroleum-based lube, right? Well, soak 'em in some petroleum! Any solvent that will clean the grease off of your auto parts will clean the lube off of your bullets. Some will leave more residue than others. My choice, probably the worst choice, was the quickest at the time. Please be very careful if you do this at home. But then you are already a very careful reloader, right? A few minutes in a coffee can filled with a couple of cups of gasoline took off all the lube and left almost no residue. A couple of cups of gasoline will work for several hundred bullets and is easy to send off to your local recycler when you're done. Just ask the boys at the auto shop on the corner.

After all that experimenting with solvents and worrying about the gasoline, I found out that my cast bullet supplier will make a batch of cast bullets without any lube any time I ask! They're good folks and really support the cowboy action shooting clubs in the area. You just call and they make up a batch of bullets for you!

If you live in the Northern Nevada area, you're really in luck. You won't believe what a deal you get if you can pick the bullets up at the source - contact Western Nevada Bullets.

OK. You've got all that nasty smokeless lube off of your bullets, now what do you do?

All the old books I've read say the old timers made their own lube out of a 50-50 mix of beeswax and peanut oil. Well, the peanut oil is no problem; you can get it at the grocery store. I use olive oil as well. The beeswax, now that might be a problem. But any craft store that has candle making supplies probably has beeswax as well. Don't use the paraffin you'll find there; it's petroleum-based. The beeswax will be more expensive than you thought, but it goes a long way. Five dollars worth will make enough lube, when mixed with the oil, for hundreds, if not thousands, of bullets!

OK. Got that beeswax and a bottle of olive or peanut oil. Now comes the part you gotta be careful about. DO NOT, repeat DO NOT, use any of your wife's cooking utensils for the next step! Go to a second-hand shop or buy a new one, but DO NOT use one of your wife's pots for this next step!

Put the beeswax into a pot and melt it on the stove on low heat. When it's liquid, add approximately the same amount of olive or peanut oil to the pot. Turn the burner off and let it cool. When cool, your bullet lube will come out of the pan in a nice big cake.

Home-made powder dipper using a .45-70 cartridge.

Ready to lube some bullets now! Be sure to use the same pot you bought at the second-hand store for this step, too! Put the pot on the stove with low heat. Stand up a few bullets in the bottom of the pot. The amount of bullets that will fit will be decided by what caliber you're shooting. Add a few pieces of your lube at a time. Let 'em melt and keep adding until the level of the liquid lube is just over the last lube groove on the bullets. Got enough lube in? Turn off the heat and take a break.

This next step will require some experimentation and experience. The temperature of your lube at the time you pull the bullets out is fairly critical - too hot, and you've got a big glob of semisolid lube on the end of your bullet. Too cold, and no lube sticks to the bullets at all! Just right, and you have a perfectly-lubed bullet.

I use a pair of pliers to pull the bullets out of the lube, as my fingers get pretty well "lubed" themselves, and the bullets are still pretty warm at this point.

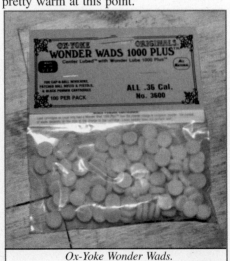

Ox-Yoke Wonder Wads.

OK. You've got some bullets lubed up and ready to go, and you've picked out some empty cases you want to use for this experiment.

All the reading I've done says to use magnum primers because the black powder is harder to light off when using standard primers. So, I've never used anything but magnum primers, and every cartridge goes off.

Filling the cases may take some experimentation as well. I have made my own powder dippers out of old cartridge cases in the same caliber I'm loading. Don't use your usual powder measure as it may build up static electricity. Not a good thing with black powder around! With a bit of brazing rod and some solder, you can make a powder dipper easily. For .38 Special I used a Dremel tool to cut approximately .2" of length off the case to be used as a dipper. This gives you about 19 grains of FFG powder by weight, and will appear to fill the cases to the top. When I have a loading block filled with charged cases, I give the whole thing a little shake and the powder settles down into the cases quite a bit.

Some of the folks in the clubs I shoot with that load black powder cartridges don't use a patch under the bullet, and some do. I do, but I can't give a technical reason why. It's just the way it was done in the "old days." For a patch in my .38 Special black powder loads, I use a cardboard wad cut from soda or beer 12-pack cases. It measures about .002" in thickness. The "Ox- Yoke" lubed wads in .36 caliber are a bit too big for the .38 Special cases, but they will work. Their .32 caliber wads seem to be a better choice, as they don't shave off as much material in your bullet-seating die.

To cut my cardboard wads, I use the 3/8" punch from a Snap-On Tools punch kit (kit #PGH8A). I'm sure the whole kit is expensive, but the single punch isn't. It was less than $3.00! I had to order it, but what the heck, it was worth the wait! It cuts a wad of about .37" in diameter; just slightly too big, but it works. I place the wad on the case just before seating the bullet. This is faster than pushing it down into the case with a pencil, though it does cause the rare bulged case. When that happens, I salvage what I can and move on. I do not wait until a match to see if the case will chamber.

I use the bullet-seating die to compress the powder in the cases. It is the moderate compression that black powder needs to burn efficiently and seems to work well.

What I've read says you don't need to crimp your cases when using black powder, but my seating die does it for me, and I suspect that the crimp doesn't hurt when I load them in my '94.

And there you have it! You've just loaded up some of Big Pete's ".36-20" black powder loads! Now you're ready for some real smoke

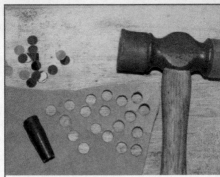

Snap-On Tools gasket punch and cardboard material are great tools to make wads.

and noise!

I can already hear some of you whining about cleaning your guns after shooting black powder. "It's so much work." "It makes so much mess." "It's so smelly." Well, you got me on the smelly part. But it's actually easier than cleaning the guns after shooting smokeless powder and doesn't involve the dangerous solvents. Just plain old hot soapy water will do. And before you start whining about getting water into the works of your prized old shooting irons (you don't get the solvent down into the works, do you?), use the same precautions, and the water won't get down in there either! And no excuses now - you gotta clean 'em the same day you shoot 'em! And you've got to be quick about drying the bore and the other parts you clean with soap and water. I run a couple of dry patches down the bore and wipe off everything with a dry towel, then hit them with a hair dryer or portable heater to make sure I got it all. For a lube, I use TC "Bore Butter." It does a great job of keeping everything lubed and rust free, and it smells great, too! When I'm done with the bucket of soapy water, I toss my brass in and let them soak for a day or so.

There. That wasn't all that difficult, was it? It will be worth it at the next match when your "weenie" .38s give out with a huge black powder "BOOM" and that big cloud of aromatic smoke floats downwind!

Home-made powder dipper, .38 Special caliber.

SHOTGUN MAINTENANCE

By: Michael W. Cuber,
aka Kid Quick

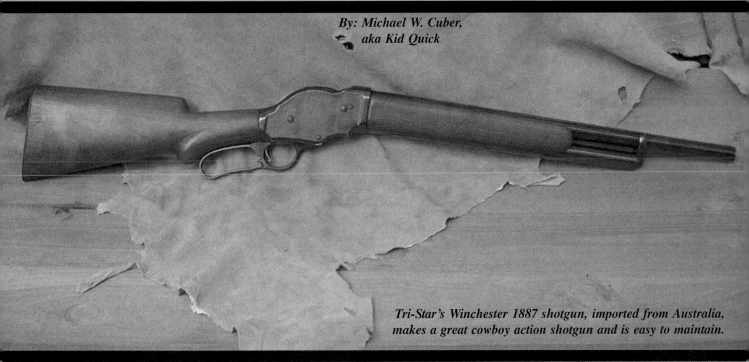

Tri-Star's Winchester 1887 shotgun, imported from Australia,
makes a great cowboy action shotgun and is easy to maintain.

Western-action shooters take a great deal of pride in their firearms. We embellish our single-action revolvers with handsome grips, maybe some engraving, and, of course, the actions have to be smooth. We dote on our rifles as well, customizing them with engraving and fancy walnut. Frequently, we send them to gunsmiths to have their actions slicked up or their triggers adjusted to break-like glass. Of course, once we've invested this kind of time and effort in our firearms, we usually do our best to take care of them. In a way, our firearms say something about who we are, and most of the time it is our revolvers and rifles that will become the most personalized. These are the guns that we fondle and contemplate long after the match is over, while the firearm that is the most in need of this attention is neglected. This neglected member of our battery is usually the shotgun, and the reason for this neglect is something we may never fully understand. When a group of shooters was asked why this is so frequently the case, the only thing that one of them could come up with was, "I'd probably take better care of it if it had rifling in the barrel!" Whatever the reason, the smooth bore is just not as endearing to most of us as our rifles and revolvers are. Whether they are side-by-side, pump, or lever-action, our shotguns are frequently the oldest and most fragile firearms that we own. To prevent failures on the firing line and to get the most out of them, our shotguns need more than a few drops of oil when we can't break them open anymore—they need specialized care and maintenance.

Each action type has its own peculiarities and maintenance requirements, and most of these requirements are pretty easy to fulfill. In most cases, a little preventive maintenance now can prevent a trip to the gunsmith in the future. This is particularly true of the Model '97 Winchester and its replicas, like those imported by

Interstate Arms. The Model '97 is, undoubtedly, a proven performer and has withstood the test of time; however, their actions do wear out, particularly if their locking mechanisms are not lubricated properly. If your '97 does wear out, the only thing a gunsmith is going to be able to do is read your '97 its last rites. The cartridge lifter/bolt lock of the '97 locks on the receiver. When the locking surfaces become worn and rounded due to lack of lubrication, your Model '97 is dead! To a lesser degree, this is also true of side-by-side shotguns, which utilize inclined planes that bear against lugs located between the chambers. When the locking lever's inclined surface wears out, the action becomes sloppy and the gun is said to be "off face." There are a variety of factors which will contribute to this wear, such as slamming the action closed and pushing the lever manually past the spot where it comes to rest on normal closing. Unlike the Model '97, a worn out side-by-side can be brought back to life by building the locking surfaces up with weld and machining them back to a proper fit. This is expensive work, especially if the locking parts have to be heat-treated again. To keep your side-by-side from wearing excessively, make sure that the locking lugs are always lubricated, and when closing your shotgun, let the locking lever gently slap against the side of your thumb. This provides a measure of buffering for the inclined plane of the locking mechanism, and the lever will close as far as it needs to when your thumb is lifted. Assuming that your side-by-side is like-new and of quality manufacturer, its locking mechanism, at least, should last a lifetime if so treated. After a while, catching the lever with your thumb will become reflexive and a natural part of your shotgun handling procedure.

The two chief concerns with original and replica Model 97's are

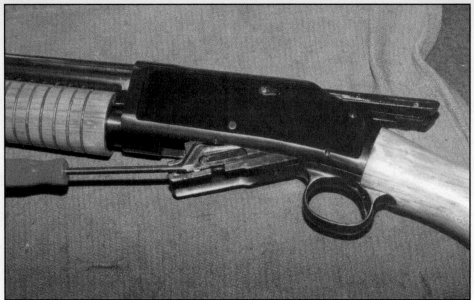

The locking spring on the cartridge lifter of the '97 must be sharp to prevent wear to the inside of the receiver. A dab of grease on this part is also a good idea.

may come a time when your '97 requires the replacement of a major part. In most cases, it will be best to leave this work in the hands of a qualified gunsmith. The general consensus among gunsmiths is that the '97 and its replicas are difficult guns to work on. To begin disassembly, your gunsmith will need to remove the butt-stock, which is retained by a hidden bolt that can be accessed by removing the butt-plate. Once the stock has been removed, the small screw next to the hammer will need to be removed so that the cartridge lifter retaining pin can be drifted out of the receiver. The next step will be the removal of the trigger group. This assembly is held in place by a cross-pin and the small stop-screw just ahead of the cross-pin. The

head-space and lock-up. On the take-down models, head-space is determined by a washer that fits between the barrel and the threaded take-down block. These washers come in a variety of thicknesses and are becoming increasingly rare. When the head-space is good, wear can, again, be prevented by keeping the locking surfaces of the bolt and cartridge lifter lubricated with grease. The action's overall lock-up while cocked is achieved by the long square spring (at least it should be square) that can be seen on the left side of the cartridge lifter when the action is open. This spring must have full travel and its outer surface must be square. If it becomes rounded, it will round the edge of the locking recess on the inside of the receiver. When this happens, the gun will not lock up solidly and the slide handle will want to come back by itself on firing. Because we're dealing with the inside of the receiver, it's extremely difficult to build these surfaces up with weld and machine them like we did with our side-by-side, and if it were possible to do so, the receiver would need to be reheat-treated. What we have to do is keep the locking spring from rounding in the first place. If it is beginning to round on the corners, it can be restored by gently prying it up and then carefully stoning it square again with a medium sharpening stone. The spring can be pried up and held in place with a small screw driver. Be careful not to bend it too far or break it. The spring will flex a little though, and this will actually restore some of its necessary travel. Once you have the edges square again, apply a dab of grease to the entire top part of the spring. Also, make sure that the locking recess on the inside to the receiver is free of carbon and grit. This procedure will go a long way in preventing wear to the inside of the receiver, and is one of the more important maintenance procedures that can be done for Model '97 shotguns.

Even with the best of care, there

gun will need to be elevated off the bench to drift out this cross-pin. Brownells offers bench blocks specifically for this purpose. When the screw and cross-pin are removed, the trigger group can be driven out. When the trigger group comes out, it will come out in pieces—this is because there was only one pin holding it all together in the first place. (Note: in order to reassemble and install the trigger group, a slave pin will have to be made. This pin will hold the trigger group together temporarily while the assembly is being reinstalled. When the original pin is pressed back in place, the slave pin will be dislodged and should fall free from the receiver.) The cartridge lifter can be removed by cocking the hammer and pressing the slide release. In most cases, the cartridge lifter will drop right out. To remove the bolt, your gunsmith will remove the screw which is visible in the front of the bolt when viewed through the ejection port. When this screw is removed, the slide hook can be removed from the bottom of the bolt, and the rest of the assembly can be slid back out of the receiver. To reassemble, your gunsmith will reverse this order, and herein lies the difficulty with '97s. Almost every part in your '97 will have to be held in place

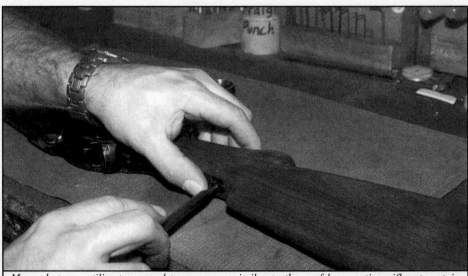

Many shotguns utilize tangs and tang screws, similar to those of lever-action rifles, to retain their butt-stocks, and this Model '87 is no exception.

Once the tang screw has been removed, the butt-stock can be pulled free of the receiver.

and slide the buttstock off the tang, then remove the forearm pieces. When these pieces are removed, be careful to note the two bushings that can be found between the magazine tube and barrel. The retaining screws for the forearm goes through these bushings, which are necessary to prevent the forearm pieces from sliding around. Once these pieces have been removed, the barrel band can be removed, along with the magazine end cap, follower spring, and follower. Be careful when you remove the retaining screw on the end cap. You may want to cup your hand over the end cap as it is being removed because it will be under spring tension. Once the magazine's internal parts have been removed, you may unscrew the tube

somehow, as the retaining pins and screws are reinstalled.

One of the more unique beasts that a shotgun shooter may encounter is the Model 1887 Winchester. Designed by John Moses Browning, this lever-action smooth bore is a tribute to the machinist's art. Occasionally, original Winchesters can be found; however, if you're not lucky enough to find an original, don't despair. Presently, Tristar is importing a very well-made replica from Australia. Unlike our '97 Winchesters, the 1887 Winchester is very easy to disassemble. Remember, regardless of action type, neither the author nor Shoot! Magazine can assume any responsibility for the work you chose to do on your firearms. Before disassembling any firearm, be sure that it is unloaded. To begin disassembly of the Model '87, remove the tang screw

Be careful not to lose the bushings between the forearm pieces of the '87. These prevent the forearm from sliding up and down when the retaining screws are in place.

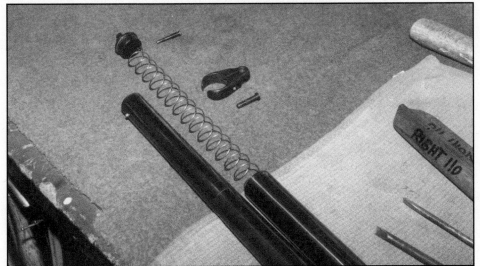

Whether you are disassembling an '87 or '97, be sure to cup the magazine end cap with your hand when you remove its retaining screw. The end cap will be under spring tension.

itself from the receiver. Next, you will remove the side plate carrier pivot screws from both sides of the receiver. The removal of these will free the two-piece carrier. Using a pair of medium-size needle nose pliers, compress the main spring that is visible when the lever is down. The main spring's ends act as retainers for the lever/bolt pivot pin. When the main spring is compressed, it can be withdrawn. This will free the lever pivot pin which, when removed, will allow the complete removal of the bolt and lever assembly. The only other parts that you may, or may not, want to remove are the trigger return spring and the lever latch spring.

To reassemble, you will simply reverse this order. The only part that you may have difficulty with is the leg attached to the center of the hammer. This leg, or strut, must go inside the underside of the bolt. If it is not positioned in its proper place, the bolt and lever assembly will not go back into the receiver. Even though the '87 has few internal parts, its internal workings are a marvel of engineering and design. If you ever get the chance to take a look inside an '87, take a minute to study its parts and then consider the genius of Mr. Browning. Most will agree; the '87 is one impressive shotgun!

Of the three types of shotguns mentioned thus far, those of the side-by-side configuration are generally the most delicate and the most frequently seen by gunsmiths. Side-by-side shotguns will normally be of either the box-lock or side-lock variety, and these

To remove the two-piece shell carrier of the '87, it will be necessary to remove the side plate carrier pivot screws from both sides of the receiver.

This photo shows the compressed mainspring of the lever bolt assembly being withdrawn. The ends of this spring retain the pivot pin for the lever and bolt.

action and lifting the breech end of the barrels up and away from the receiver and butt-stock assembly. This is as far as disassembly will need to go for most general cleaning purposes; however, if you find it necessary to replace an internal part and feel like tackling the job yourself, further disassembly will be required. Normally, you will need to remove the butt-stock in order to get into the action, and most of the time you will need to remove the trigger guard first to accomplish this. Remove the screw from the end of the trigger guard, then lift up the end from the inletting in the stock. While the tail of the trigger guard is clear, the trigger guard can be unscrewed from the forward part of the action. The butt-stock may be attached by one of two possible ways. On older shotguns, it will generally be by a tang and tang screws similar to those found on most lever-action rifles. If the stock is

two action types are quite different from one another. Futhermore, depending upon their age and maker, guns of the side-lock persuasion may have either internal or exposed hammers. Side-lock guns are designed to be easily disassembled and maintained, while box-locks can be difficult for even a seasoned gunsmith. Currently, good examples of both action types are being offered by EAA, Tristar, and Stoeger. Before disassembling any side-by-side, make sure that the firearm is unloaded. After checking your firearm, remove the forearm from the barrels by depressing its locking button or by lifting its locking lever, and cantilevering the forearm down and away from the barrels and action. Once the forearm has been removed, the barrels can be detached by opening the

After the mainspring has been removed, the pivot pin can be easily drifted out to free the lever/bolt assembly.

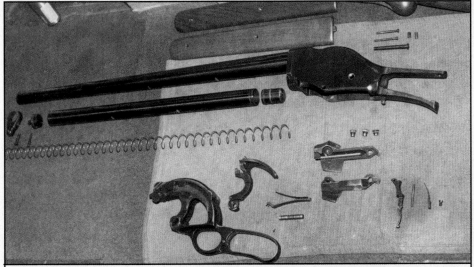

Even though it has few parts, the '87 lever-action is a tribute to the machinist's art. It's no surprise that it was invented by John Moses Browning.

group to the action. By drifting out this pin, the triggers can be removed and the stock can be removed from the action.

Side-lock actions are generally the easiest to work on because they come apart in four major assemblies: the trigger group, two side plates with locks, and the receiver body. Box-lock actions are an entirely different story. On these, the triggers may be attached by pins or screws, and may or may not be part of an integral assembly. Often times, the triggers will be holding the internal hammers at full-cock and when the trigger assembly is removed, the hammers will slam forward—sometimes even past their normal position when decocked. Frequently,

not held in place by a tang, it is probably held in place by a hidden bolt that runs through the stock. If you remove your shotgun's tang screws and suspect that the butt-stock is retained by a hidden bolt, carefully remove the butt-plate or recoil pad. This will allow access to the retaining bolt, which can normally be removed with a large screw driver. Once the bolt has been removed, the action can be pulled forward off the stock. As a rule of thumb, most box-locks with internal hammers use the hidden bolt in the stock, while most side-locks use a tang and tang screws to retain the butt-stock. Also, on side-locks it will be necessary to remove the side plates, which are inletted into the stock in order to gain access to the retaining pin that holds the trigger

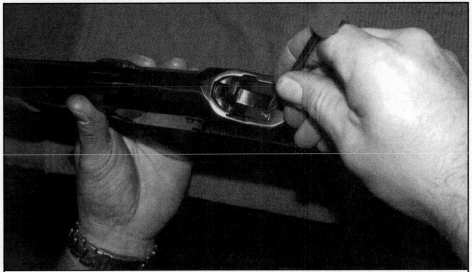

To remove the cartridge lifter of the '97 pump gun, your gunsmith will need to remove the retaining screw next to the hammer. This screw holds the cartridge lifter's pivot pin in place. Even after this pin is removed, it will be necessary to remove the trigger group before the cartridge lifter can be taken out.

the hammers will be under considerable spring tension. The removal and installation of these parts may require the use of slave pins and specialty tools depending upon the model of shotgun being worked on. Again, depending upon the make and model of your shotgun, you might be better off leaving it in the hands of a qualified gunsmith. If you are unsure as to what type of shotgun you have, or are curious about what type of maladies you might expect, ask a gunsmith. Most are normally very willing to share the knowledge they've accumulated from working on numerous firearms.

One thing that any action type will benefit from while it is disassembled is proper lubrication, and a very effective technique was recently passed on by a local gunsmith. You will need a spray

The cartridge lifter stop screw of the '97 will need to be removed to facilitate removal of the trigger group. When the retaining pin for the trigger assembly, located behind the stop screw, is removed and the trigger guard drifted out, the trigger assembly will fall out in pieces. (Note: a slave pin will be required to reassemble and install these parts.)

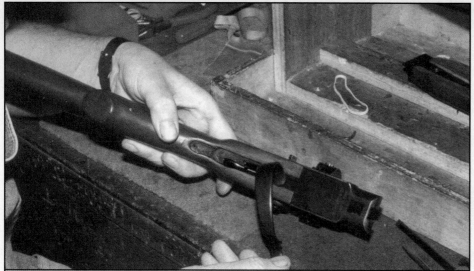

Most of the time, disassembly of the side-by-side will begin with the removal of the butt-stock, but sometimes it will first be necessary to remove the trigger guard. Like many shotguns, this one's trigger guard features a threaded shaft which is screwed into the receiver.

splitting down the center. If the forearm is not too rough on the inside, it should be an easy matter to pull the rag free. Some of the more frequent problems encountered by gunsmiths working with side-by-sides are locks that are worn, sear surfaces that wear because of improper hardening, firing pins that gall and stick in receivers (this is normally caused by dry firing without snap caps), and cracked stocks. Most of the time, all of these, except the problems caused by improper hardening, can be prevented with a little maintenance. In fact, the same holds true for all the other types of shotguns we've addressed.

Regardless of the type of shotgun you own, it should be cleaned after every use. At minimum, you should

lubricant such as G-96 and an air hose. While the action is separated from the stock, liberally spray lubricant into its internal workings, then blast the excess free with compressed air. The air will spread the lubricant into the hard-to-reach areas of the action. If you happen to be working with a side-lock, treat each major assembly in the same manner. This is a very effective means of lubricating your action without getting the stock pieces oil-soaked. To reassemble your shotgun, simply reverse the order in which it was disassembled. When it comes time to reinstall your shotgun's forearm, try placing a rag between it and the barrels before it is snapped into place. This will cushion the forearm as it slaps the barrels and will prevent it from cracking and

Some side-by-sides have hidden tang screws under their levers. To get at these, you'll have to hold the lever over with your thumb.

As the gunsmith removes this action from the stock, you can see much of the delicate inletting. Having a side lock restocked can be a costly venture.

run a bore mop with a light oil or bore cleaner like BreakFree through the barrel or barrels before you put your shotgun away. Preferably, you should run a solvent-soaked brush through the bore, followed by a dry mop or patch. Shooter's Choice is one of the few solvents advertised to remove plastic wad fouling and is a good choice for shotguns. Also, Kleen Bore makes a very practical and economical shotgun cleaning kit, as well as adapters and accessories that can be used with other rods. After you've cleaned the bore, use a lightly-oiled cloth to wipe away carbon that may have accumulated around the breech. Once this has been done, hit all the moving parts with a few drops of oil. This not only keeps the parts from wearing prematurely, but it also prevents rust and keeps the carbon soft the next time you fire your shotgun. If you own a pump or lever-action, you may want to clean the magazine tube. Frequently, you'll find the splintered remains of magazine plugs, not to mention loose pellets that have wandered away from their shells. Neither will help your gun's performance, so it never hurts to pop the top and take a look inside. The outside of your gun's metal should also be wiped down with a lightly-oiled cloth. Some people have more salt in their sweat than others, but all fingerprints will eventually rust if the firearm is allowed to sit long enough. Also, never, never, ever, put a shotgun, or any gun for that matter, in a zippered case and shove it under the bed. The bore or bores will almost invariably rust and pit because of moisture trapped in the case. If the truth were known, the zipped-up case under the bed is probably the number one killer of shotguns.

All and all, there is nothing really difficult or mysterious about keeping any type of shotgun in good working order. Most cleaning procedures are the same as those we use for our rifles and revolvers and amount to little more than the application of a little common sense and elbow grease. So, if your shotgun happens to be lying in a case in the dark somewhere, get it out! Whether it be a newly-manufactured reproduction or a vintage original, it will always give its best performance after it receives a little shotgun maintenance.

On side-lock guns it's necessary to remove the side plates and drift out the retaining pin of the trigger group before the stock can be removed. Be careful; side-lock stocks are generally pretty delicate because of their complicated inletting.

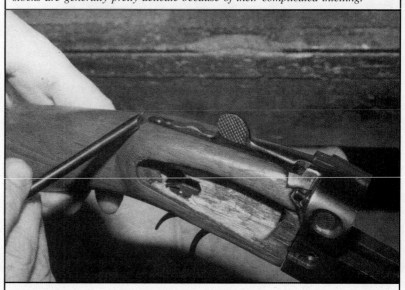

When reassembling a side-lock, don't over-tighten the tang screw. If you do, it may protrude from the top of the tang.

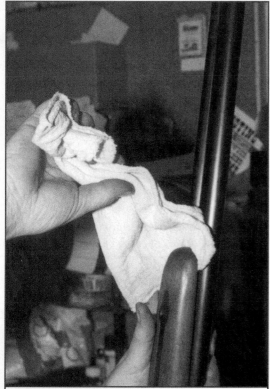

When reassembling your side-by-side, try placing a rag between the forearm and the barrels to buffer the forearm as it snaps into place. This will keep your forearm from cracking down the middle.

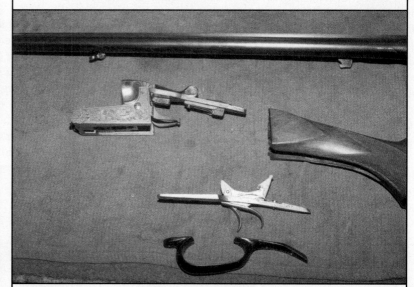

This is a box-lock action with the trigger assembly removed. Not all box locks have removable trigger assemblies like this one. This gun is further unique because it uses a tang to retain the buttstock. This gun was made by J.P. Sauer and is a good example of European workmanship.

Loading The .32 Winchester Special

Author's first rifle from Dad. A Model 1894 .32 Winchester Special, circa 1927.

with Black Powder

By: Kenny Durham,
aka KID Durham

What is so special about the .32 Winchester Special? For me, the answer is easy. It's the rifle that Dad bought for me when I was 14-years-old - my first rifle, and what a special rifle it was! On the wall of my bedroom hung a gun rack that held three guns. In the bottom slot was my 12-gauge shotgun Dad had bought from Montgomery Ward's the opening day of pheasant season in 1962. The middle slot cradled my Crossman pellet gun that had spelled doom to many sparrows, starlings, and ground squirrels whenever it was taken afield. But the top slot of the gun rack, the place of highest honor, was reserved for my Daisy Red Ryder BB Gun given to me as a Christmas present from my grandfather when I was seven-years-old. I still have it! One September day, I came home from school and flopped down on the bed in the room I shared with my brother. I glanced up at my rack of guns hanging on the wall. I stared at them for a few seconds before I noticed something different about the rifle in the top slot. Something about my Red Ryder was different! But what?

Then it began to sink in. The rifle was not my Red Ryder, but rather a very real lever-action Winchester that looked old, like the rifles in the Westerns on TV. I sprang to my feet and gently lifted the heavy rifle out of the rack. It was beautiful. In an instant, I knew Dad had bought the rifle for me. The neighbor next door had a .30-30 Winchester Carbine so I recognized it as a model 1894. But this rifle was not a carbine. It had a long octagon barrel and a crescent butt plate giving it that "old-fashioned" look that I had already come to appreciate in rifles. On the barrel was stamped .32 W.S., which meant nothing to me at the time. For the rest of the day the old Winchester never left my hands except during supper, and probably only then at Mother's insistence. As time passed, I became familiar

CAL. .32 WINCHESTER SPECIAL

For use in various Winchester, Marlin, and Remington rifles.

Two Winchester .32 Specials. The one in the foreground has the common semi-buckhorn sight, while the one in the background has the special "SMOKELESS" sight.

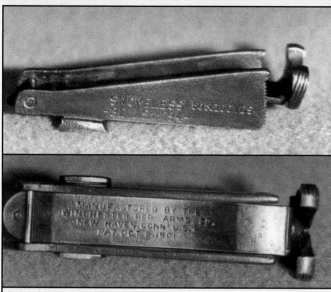

Special "SMOKELESS" sight common on many early .32 W.S. Model 1894s.

Bullets used in testing (left to right): RCBS .32-170 RNFP, Saeco 632 165-gr. RNFP, and Laser Cast 170 RNFP from Oregon Trail Bullet Co.

cartridges for their new lever-action, the .25-35 Winchester and the .30 Winchester Center Fire (.30-30). There are some who claim that the .32 Winchester Special was introduced in 1895 and as late as 1906. However, to me, it makes more sense that the .32 Winchester Special was introduced in 1902, the most often posted date. Let me explain why. Records show that the take-down Model 1894 rifle in .32 W.S., serial number 138XXX, was made in 1898. It is entirely possible that this rifle could have been rebarreled after 1902 or the receiver remained in inventory until 1902, at which time the rifle was completed. Without knowing the exact history of the rifle, we cannot conclude that the .32 Special cartridge was introduced before 1902. Another feature of many early model 1894 rifles chambered for the .32 W.S. was a special rear sight labeled "SMOKELESS -.32WS M94, 50 & 100YDS." The Model 1894 solid-frame, circa 1927, .32 W.S. bears the more common semi-buckhorn sight and the Model 1894 take-down, circa 1898, has the SMOKELESS sight.

Left & right: RCBS .32 W.S. Dies. Center die is a .32 caliber neck-expanding die from RCBS Cowboy Dies.

with the .32 W.S. as a sibling to the .30-30 Win. When it came to talking about deer rifles with friends at school, I would always have to explain to them that the .32 W.S. was just like the .30-30, only a little bigger. The .32 W.S. was the first cartridge I ever reloaded, and that was accomplished on the LEE loading kit that I saved up to buy. For me, my model 1894 Winchester Rifle .32 Winchester Special made in 1927, is just as special as it was that September afternoon so many years ago when I first held it in my hands.

Two good .32 caliber bullets, but only the one on the left is suitable for black powder.

.32 Winchester Special History

The model 1894 Winchester rifle is the most popular lever-action rifle ever built. Five chamberings were the mainstay of the model '94 for many years. First to appear with the introduction of the "94" were the .32-40 and the .38-55. Both of these cartridges had been around for years with a reputation for accuracy. Marlin had been chambering their lever-actions for these two calibers since 1881, but Winchester did not have a model suited to the .32-40 and .38-55 until John Browning designed what was to become the Winchester Model 1894.

In 1895, Winchester introduced two new smokeless powder

Why did Winchester bother with the .32 Winchester Special? It was one of the first cartridges to be introduced for which there was no practical need. Winchester already had a .32 caliber cartridge in the .32-40 and the new .30 WCF smokeless cartridge was state-of-the-art. So, why mess with another .32 cartridge? The answer is simple. To sell more guns! But, I think the reasoning goes deeper. Old habits die hard, especially among shooters. I suppose there was a certain amount of skepticism

Saeco # 632, 165- gr. round nose, flat point bullet mould. Bullet on sprue plate is lubed with SPG.

Powders used in testing: Pyrodex Select RS, Elephant FFg, Goex Cartridge Grade, and Swiss 1-½ FG.

By seating a bullet in an empty case then checking it in my rifle, I determined that I could seat the Saeco bullet with two lube grooves exposed and easily chamber the round.

surrounding this new .30 pipsqueak of a cartridge. Most big game rifles prior to 1894 had been chambered for .38, .40, .44, or .45 caliber bullets. The .32-20 W.C.F. and .32-40 Ballard had established the ".32" as an accurate caliber. So, to reassure the dedicated ".32" and larger caliber believers, Winchester simply opened up the new .30-30 case to accept a .32 caliber bullet and the .32 Winchester Special was born. Also, consider that designing and chambering the 1894 for the .32 W.S. required little additional effort for Winchester. They already possessed the tooling for .32 caliber, 1:16 twist barrels. The cartridge carrier is the same for all 1894s, and the .32-40 cartridge guide required no alterations for the .32 W.S. In reality, from a business viewpoint, it was a no-brainer that the .32 W.S. should exist.

The .32 W.S. is a smokeless powder cartridge and was never factory-loaded with black powder. However, Winchester touted the new .32 as being a better cartridge to reload than the .30-30. The reason being was that since smokeless powders were unavailable to the general public, the only option was to reload a cartridge with black powder. The 1-turn-in-16-inch twist of the .32 W.S. made it a better choice for black powder than did the 1-turn-in-12-inch twist of

Seating depth measured using a depth gauge.

the .30-30. But what about loading the .32 W.S. with black powder? The idea seems somewhat analogous to using the "bug sprayer" or "hair dryer" attachments that came with my wife's vacuum cleaner. Yeah, they sort of work, but why bother? I have to wonder how many (or how few) have actually loaded the

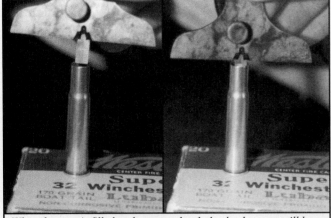

When the case is filled to the proper level, the depth gauge will be on or slightly above the case mouth.

A case charged with powder and a fiber wad seated ready to accept a bullet.

.32 W.S. with black powder.

Finding the Right Bullet

There are two prerequisites for a lever-action black powder bullet. First, it must have the flat point for use in tubular magazines. Second, it must have multiple grooves to carry the amount of bullet lube needed to handle the black powder fouling. Photo 5 shows two .32 caliber bullets suitable for the .32 W.S. and the .32-40. The bullet on the left is a Saeco #632, 165-grain flat nose. The bullet on the right is a Laser Cast Silver Bullet from Oregon Trail Bullet Company weighing 170 grains. Although both are good smokeless powder bullets, only the Saeco has the lube-carrying capacity required for black powder. Lyman also makes a bullet mould for casting a 165-grain RNFP (round nose flat point). RCBS produces a 170-grain RNFP gas check bullet intended for smokeless powder. It has only one large lube groove but combined with the small groove ahead of the seated gas check, it marginally carries enough lube to be used with black powder. NEI lists a 175-grain RNFP gas check bullet that appears

Bullet started into case, ready for final seating. Notice the slight belling of the case mouth. Only a little flaring is required.

.32 Winchester Special ammo loaded with black powder and ready for a trip to the range.

Three cartridge/bullet combinations used in testing (left to right): RCBS 32-170, Saeco 632, and Laser Cast 170 RNFP (used with Pyrodex) from Oregon Trail Bullet Co.

suitable for black powder. However, it may be too long to stabilize in the 1:16 twist of a .32 W.S.

Reloading Dies and Brass

Traditionally, only standard two-die rifle loading die sets have been available for .32 W.S., assuming the reloader was using either jacketed or gas check bullets. Such is the case with my RCBS dies made in 1968. Fortunately, three-die sets are now available, which include a neck-expanding die to slightly bell the case mouth to accept a lead bullet. One example is the RCBS

The Swiss powder produced the best five-shot group, measuring 4 inches wide by 2 inches high.

Cowboy series of dies. The RCBS Cowboy dies are available in .32-40 and .32 W.S. Since I already have a two-die .32 W.S. set, all I needed was a neck- expanding die. I needed a set of .32-40 dies for a rifle being built, so I purchased set of RCBS Cowboy dies. Since the .32-40 and .32 W.S. use the same diameter bullets, the neck-expanding die works for either caliber. Another option would be to purchase a custom expander die from Buffalo Arms Company or Redding.

Brass for the .32 W.S. is not nearly so plentiful as it was a mere ten years ago. In the past, most retail outlets selling reloading equipment and components seemed to always have a few boxes of Winchester Brand .32 W.S. brass on the shelf. Nowadays, it's rare to find new .32 W.S. unprimed brass in stock. Among a quick check of a few suppliers, only Midway listed having .32 W.S. brass in stock. Buffalo Arms can supply .32 W.S. brass, but their catalog indicates that it is formed from another caliber, such as .30-30, and therefore not head-stamped as .32 W.S. However, knowing Dave Gullo and the folks from Buffalo Arms, I'm confident that their .32 W.S. brass is of top quality and the proper length. Brass for the .32 W.S. can easily be formed from .30-30 case by simply running them through the .32 W.S. sizing die. The expansion from .30 to .32 presents no problem. However, cases formed from .30-30 brass will be a bit

short. Finally, the other obvious source of brass is factory-loaded ammunition produced by Winchester and Remington.

Loading the Cartridges

My first attempt at loading black powder in my .32 Special was in 1974. In our local fall Muzzle Loading Shoot, one of the matches was a black powder cartridge rifle match. Back then, I didn't know much about loading black powder cartridges. All I had were jacketed bullets so I filled the cases up with Dupont FFFg and Remington jacketed bullets. Believe it or not, I won the match! Back then, I was gratified that I won. Now, thinking back, I'm astonished that I won! Ignorance is bliss after all!

For testing, I used Swiss 1-½ FG, Goex Cartridge Grade, Goex FFFg, Elephant FFg, and Pyrodex Select. The primers chosen were Remington 9-½ large rifle with Swiss powder, Remington 2-½ large pistol with Elephant powder, and Federal 215 Magnum rifle primers with Goex Cartridge Grade, Goex FFFg, and Pyrodex. The first step in developing a load was to determine the maximum powder capacity by establishing the depth to which the bullets would be seated. By seating a bullet in an empty case then checking it in my rifle, I determined that I could seat the Saeco bullet with two lube grooves exposed and easily chamber the round. Next, I used a depth gauge to measure the length of bullet to be seated inside the case. A wood dowel works well, too. Finally, by filling the case with powder to the level measured on the depth gauge, we can determine the volume of powder to be used. A Lyman 55 Black Powder Measure was set to throw a charge of powder to fill the case to the determined level, plus a bit more to allow for a small amount of compression. The cases were charged by dropping the powder through a 30" brass drop tube, then a Walter's 0.030" fiber wad was seated atop the powder column. Next, using the neck expanding die, the powder charge with wad was compressed to the pre-determined bullet seating depth. The net result of the compression amounted to about 0.060." Now, to seat the bullets, we start by backing the seating die out of the press enough to ensure that the case mouth will not be crimped during the seating process. Seating and crimping the bullet in a single step is fine for jacketed bullets having a cannalure or hard lead bullets having a crimping groove. But, soft lead bullets used for black powder cartridges should be crimped in a separate operation. We begin the seating process by carefully centering a bullet into the case

The five-shot group with Elephant FFg produced the second best group measuring 4-½ inches x 2-¾ inches

mouth, then running the cartridge into the seating die. Finally, once we have all of our bullets seated, we can adjust the seating die to place the amount of crimp desired on the case mouth. One more pass through the seating die completes the loading process, giving us some excellent looking black powder cartridges for our .32 Winchester Special.

The bullets used for testing Pyrodex loads were the Saeco #632 and the Oregon Trail Bullet Co. Laser Cast 170 RNFP. The seating depth for the RCBS bullet is greater than for the Saeco bullet. However, I did not change the setting on the powder measure. Therefore, the Pyrodex loads were slightly more compressed with the RCBS bullet than with the Saeco bullet.

At the Range

Six different loads were tested: four black powder and two Pyrodex. All groups were fired at 100 yards from a bench rest using only the front blade and semi-buckhorn rear sights. Unfortunately, these sights are not the most conducive to shooting tight groups. The surprising result is that all of these loads shot about the same size groups. The Swiss powder produced the best five-shot group measuring 4 inches. wide by 2 inches high. If the wide shot to the left had gone into the group with the other four ...Murphy's law. The five-shot group with Elephant FFg produced the second best group measuring 4-½ inches x 2-¾ inches, but is only slightly smaller than the other black powder loads. The Pyrodex loads averaged about 5-inch by 4-inch groupings.

(After I received a Montana Vintage Arms Model 130 - Windgauge Sporting Tang sight to put on my .32 Winchester Special, further testing produced tighter groups.)

See ya at the range!

Loading information for the .32 Winchester Special

Powder	Weight (gr.)	Case
1- Swiss 1-½ FG	43.0	Win. Super X
2- Elephant FFg	42.0	Win. Super X
3- Goex Cartridge	42.6	New W-W
4- Goex FFF	41.5	Win. Super X
5- Pyrodex Select RS	N/A	Remington
6- Pyrodex Select RS	N/A	Remington

Primer	Bullet	Avg. Velocity
1- Remington 9-½	Saeco #632	1441 fps
2- Remington 2-½	Saeco #632	1341 fps
3- Fed. 215	Saeco #632	1399 fps
4- Fed. 215	RCBS 32-170	1322 fps
5- Fed. 215	OTBC 170 RNFP	1450 fps
6- Fed. 215	Saeco #632	1481 fps

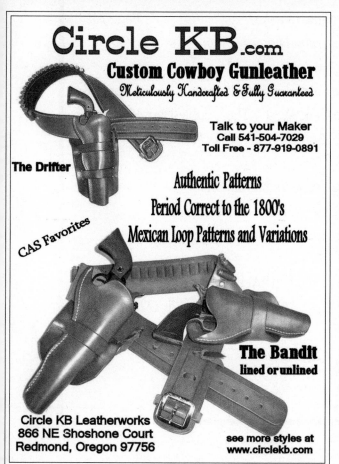

Black Powder and the Old West
Chapter 4

History, Hunting and Tall Tales

Code Duello

By: Michael W. Cuber, aka Kid Quick

The art, or practice, of pistol dueling evolved from sword fighting and the concept of "Trial by Combat." Just as David confronted Goliath on the field of battle to determine whose God was the greatest, so prevailed the notion that if one survived the field of honor, he was both justified and protected by God. As firearms began to replace swords in the early 1700's, it was realized that some etiquette would need to be established to ensure a fair contest for opponents. In 1777, the Code Duello was drafted in Ireland. This code consisted of 26 rules to govern pistol dueling and was quickly accepted throughout the British Isles and colonies. In America, the duel was considered a viable means for personal and political conflict resolution.

In the case of Aaron Burr and Alexander Hamilton, the duel offered the appealing possibility for one to eliminate his political opponent. Hamilton suspected Burr of being a British loyalist and conspirator. To Burr, Hamilton was a relentless watchdog who drew attention to every political deal that Burr tried to make. When Hamilton accepted Burr's challenge to a duel, it must have seemed like an attractive solution to both men. On July 11, 1804, both men turned and faced each other with flintlock dueling pistols. Hamilton's pistol failed to fire; Burr's pistol did not! Burr drove a fatal round ball into the midsection of his opponent. The death of Alexander Hamilton was a tragic event for the nation; however, it did manage to disrupt Mr. Burr's political career. Wanted for murder, Mr. Burr had to flee to Canada, and later Britain. After the War of 1812, he resurfaced in America, but his reputation was pretty well destroyed. Some claim that Hamilton accepted his dueling pistol from Burr's cased set, and that it was either not properly loaded, or that it may have been tampered with by Burr. The truth of this will probably never be known. Ultimately, Alexander proved that he was willing to give his life for his country when he met Mr. Burr on the hilltop in New Jersey.

Alexander Hamilton and Aaron Burr were neither the first, nor the last, public figures to settle their disputes with pistols. The 7th President of the United States, Andrew Jackson, faced off with one Charles Dickinson in 1806. Mr. Jackson felled Dickinson with a well-aimed shot and went on to become President in 1829. James Barron killed naval war hero Stephen Decatur in a duel in 1820. Mr. Decatur had earned his fame in 1804 by recapturing the U.S.S. Philadelphia from the Barbary pirates who had seized the ship off the coast of Tripoli. Mr. Decatur's death was another sad day for America, but it did not, by any means, impede the practice of pistol dueling. In 1859, Senator David Broderick was killed in a duel with Judge David Terry. Although pistol dueling was widely accepted by society, it was technically never legal in this country. Remember, Aaron Burr became a fugitive after his duel with Alexander Hamilton. By the 1870's, the practice of dueling to settle disputes had been outlawed in most civilized lands; however, it continued to be practiced in the more remote parts of the American West and in other remote regions of the world, such as Australia and Africa.

The last recorded duel in modern times occurred in Bakersfield, California in 1901. Noted gunman James McKinney challenged a man named Red Sears to a duel (in this duel they used six-guns and not percussion duelers). McKinney killed Sears, and then fled to Porterville, California, a small mining community about 60 miles northeast of Bakersfield. When local lawmen tried to apprehend McKinney, he turned violent and shot his way out of town. As stated earlier, the commonly held view regarding dueling was that a higher authority somehow vindicated the winner. This feeling, in the minds of many, transcended written law. In some regions, where laws and justice were either scarce or non-existent, many began to believe that the law was simply worn on the hip and dealt out as needed. This may explain why a number of notable gunmen spent time both serving and breaking the law.

Most gunmen had an appreciation for the spirit of Code Duello, but they also knew full well that its rules could get them killed before any duel actually took place. Dueling, for the most part, degraded into "getting the drop on your opponent" and killing him before he could return the favor. Still, the spirit of Code Duello was carried on well into the 20th century. During both World Wars there were incidents where ace fighter pilots went one-on-one with known enemies in the sky while their fellow pilots held off. These individuals eventually established their own code, with rules such as not firing on a man after he had ejected from his aircraft.

Perhaps the best example of the spirit of Code Duello occurred during General John "Black Jack" Pershing's expedition into Mexico in pursuit of Poncho Villa. After learning that a close associate of Villa, Colonel Julio Cardenas, was possibly at a ranch near the hamlet of San Miguelito, General Pershing dispatched a young lieutenant with some troops to stake out the ranch. This scouting party had no luck initially but later, while purchasing grain, the lieutenant noticed some rough-looking horsemen when he passed through the town of Rubio. On a hunch, the lieutenant had his men turned towards another Cardenas' ranch just outside of Rubio, near the hamlet of Saltillo. When the lieutenant and his men were convinced that Cardenas was, in fact, at the ranch, they attacked in open-topped touring cars. When they entered the ranch compound, the young lieutenant, who went by the name of George S. Patton, drew an ivory-stocked .45 Colt S.A.A. and jumped from his car. He could have been content to simply take cover and issue commands to his troops, but instead he chose to stand his ground with three mounted Villista's who were only too eager to accept his challenge. The first shot from the lieutenant's Colt took one of the riders off his horse. Lieutenant Patton then proceeded to shoot the second rider's horse out from under him, and with his last three shots, he assisted his troops in dispatching the third rider.

Later, after being wounded in World War I, Patton wrote a letter to his wife. In this letter, he confided that he'd been afraid at times and had felt like taking cover, but after thinking about his many uncles and relatives who had served in combat before him, he instead chose to, "Let God and fate decide." This was essentially the essence of Code Duello from its beginning. If he had been born 100 years earlier, it would have probably been a safe bet to say that General George S. Patton would have been a proponent of the Code Duello.

Black Powder n' Cactus

By: Michael W. Cuber, aka Kid Quick

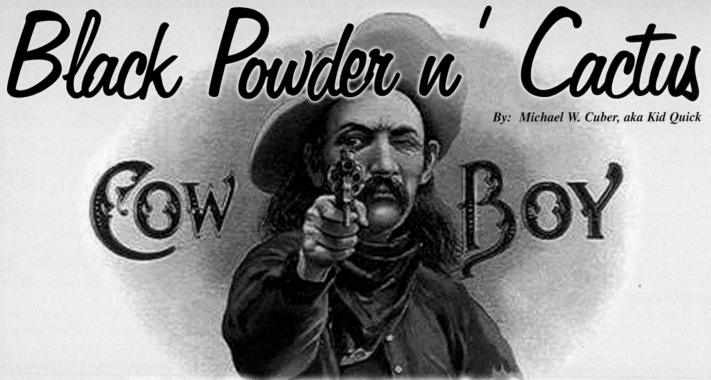

COW BOY

THE GUNFIGHTER'S LIFE

The sun finally rose over the bullet-riddled adobe walls of the pueblo. Already, there was a crowd gathering around the hole in the wall where the cactus and mesquite had been placed. Perhaps they had to look in order to dispel their own fears. He didn't look like much of a threat in the daylight. In fact, he looked quite old. He didn't even have a gun. His wrinkled red face still bore the agonized expression from the events of that night. His fists still tightly clutched the thorn brush that had ensnared him. Even as the flies began to swarm in on the drying rivulets of blood, his posture, along with the agonized expression, perfectly captured his last moment struggle for life. No one was certain when his struggle had actually ended. The trooper in the bunker in front of the hole in the wall had fired on him first. When he did not go down, the Gatling gun crew in the other position opened fire. The muzzle blast of the Gatling gun and the Trapdoor Springfields had briefly caused him to cast an enormous shadow during the shooting. A few groans had come out of the smoke-filled darkness afterwards, but no one dared to venture forth to investigate, not in the dark at least. During times of darkness, fear rules, although no one would admit it. They had to be content to wait until morning when the rays of light would wash away the fear. Then, and only then, did they venture forth and look at the pitiful Apache who had been caught in the cactus.

Few gunfights of the Old West actually occurred in the same manner that is portrayed in Hollywood movies. Make no mistake about this, there were many stand-up, to-the-death gunfights, but these events were not as glamorous as movie directors would like us to believe. Many times there were no ultimate winners, and many times good did not prevail over evil. Frequently, it was the very young and the very old that would be caught in the middle of the disputes that turned to bloodshed. Killing another human being has always been ugly business.

Clay Allison referred to himself as a "shootist," which may

have been a feeble attempt to cast an aura of respectability to his otherwise peculiar habit of killing people. It would be only logical for some people hearing the term shootist to make a mental association with the term duelist, the definition of which means "a person skilled in the art of pistol dueling," a once respectable practice. In dueling, two parties would meet on equal terms and allow "God and fate to decide," but this was rarely the case with those who considered themselves shootists or gunfighters. By modern standards, most of the men of the late 1800's who thought of themselves as gunfighters would be branded as homicidal sociopaths if they were alive today.

John Wesley Hardin's career started shortly after he stabbed and beat another boy who was heckling him. A year after this incident, Hardin shot and killed a black man who had challenged him to a fight. By 1868, 15-year-old John Wesley Hardin was a wanted man. When he was captured 10 years later, Hardin confessed, or perhaps boasted, that he had killed 44 men. Most of Hardin's victims were men that had tried either to apprehend him or to argue with him at the gambling halls and brothels that Hardin frequented. At one point, Hardin may have became acquainted with Wild Bill Hickok, and it is apparent from record that Hardin had great esteem for the older gunfighter, but the relationship dissolved when Hardin could not contain himself and killed a man for snoring in a hotel in Abilene, Kansas.

Another terror of the Western Frontier that perhaps could not contain himself was Jesse Woodson James. Born in 1847, Jesse served with Confederate guerrillas during the latter part of the Civil War. After the war, he maintained close contact with many of his confederates. In 1866, Jesse and his brother Frank, along with several other ex-guerrillas, robbed the Clay County Savings Association in Liberty, Missouri. This was the first daylight bank robbery of the American West, and the James brothers managed to ride out of town with the tremendous sum of $60,000. During their flight from the bank, a young college student was deliberately shot and killed, and later during another bank robbery, Jesse shot and killed a young bank teller for apparently no reason at all. The Clay County Savings robbery would characterize Jesse's career for the next 15 years.

Of the numerous figures of the Old West that lived and died by the gun, perhaps no other gunman's life has been more romanticized than the life of Henry McCarty, otherwise known as Billy the Kid. Born in 1859 in New York City, young Billy migrated west with his mother and eventually arrived in Silver City, New Mexico. Like Hardin, Billy turned man-killer at an early age. Some credit him with as many as 21 killings, but the real number probably lies between six and nine. While working at a couple of different ranches, Billy proved his ability with a rifle, but he was too slight of build for the hard work demanded of a cowboy. The Kid had already encountered some scrapes when he began his employment for an English gentleman by the name of John Tunstall. Tunstall must have seemed like an honest employer and those under him would

later prove "loyal to the brand," especially Billy the Kid. When Tunstall was assassinated by rival cattlemen, Billy's career as a gunman took off in earnest. Although he was legally sworn in on the posse that pursued Tunstall's killers, Billy's pursuit of justice would lead to his own eventual demise. After several killings and close calls, Billy's one-time friend, Pat Garrett, finally blasted him into a legend.

While many gunfighters, such as Harvey Logan, Jesse James, and the Younger brothers, seemed to be motivated by greed, others, like Billy the Kid and John Wesley Hardin, seemed to be able to kill for no apparent reason at all. The one trait that all gunfighters seemed to possess was the ability to kill instantly at the slightest suspicion of any personal danger. Many of these gunmen would have liked the public to view them as duelists, but few of them proved keen on the idea of letting "God and fate decide."

Some notable gunmen, such as Wyatt Earp, chose to ride on both sides of the law for a time. Wyatt was born on March 19, 1848 in Illinois, and like other young men who would eventually head west, he had older brothers who served with Union forces during the Civil War. Wyatt would stay close to his brothers for many years after the war. The Earps, like most people who settled in cow towns, were disposed to gambling and making a fast buck. This is not to say that Wyatt was a chance taker; he was most decidedly not. He was a businessman, who at times augmented his income from gambling and liquor sales by serving as a lawman. This arrangement allowed Wyatt to protect his gambling and saloon interests, while at the same time maintaining a clean image with the public. Although he proved to be a tough product of the Western Frontier, there is no record that Wyatt actually killed anyone prior to the infamous shootout near the O.K. Corral. He was involved in a shooting that took place outside a dance hall in Kansas, but was assisted by another

marshal and several citizens during the course of the shooting which left only one cowboy dead. When the story appeared in an eastern law enforcement journal, Wyatt had been credited with the taking of the young cowboy's life. Furthermore, Wyatt Earp did not think of himself as a gunman. In later years, Bat Masterson would recall that Wyatt preferred to settle arguments with his fists, and that Wyatt was a skilled fighter who frequently did not carry a gun while on duty as a lawman. Prior to Tombstone and the O.K. Corral incident, Wyatt supposedly marshaled in Ellsworth, Dodge City, and Wichita, Kansas, but actual records from Dodge City and Wichita show that he was frequently employed only part-time or as an assistant. There is no record of his employment in Ellsworth, and if he did marshal there, the job was short-lived. One trait that all who knew Wyatt agreed upon was that he was a man absolutely devoid of fear during confrontations. After the O.K. Corral, Wyatt would try to evade the gunfighter mystique for the rest of his life.

The more respectable of the breed, who at times placed themselves in great danger for the cause of justice, were the many peace officers, scouts, soldiers, and vigilant citizens who took it upon themselves to make the West safe for decent folks. Of these, none was more flamboyant than James Butler "Wild Bill" Hickok. Wild Bill was born in Illinois in 1837, the same year that Samuel Colt introduced his '36 Patterson. It is ironic that Wild Bill came into the world at the same time that Colt chose to introduce his revolvers, and it would be Colt's products that would accompany Wild Bill for most of his life. During the Civil War, Wild Bill served as a Union Scout. Later, he would serve again as a scout during the Indian Wars and, later still, as a marshal in Hayes City and Abilene, Kansas. Some accused Wild Bill of being something of a peacock, but his courage under fire could not be denied. He once broke through a line of Indians on horseback that had surrounded an Army element in Colorado. Before his law enforcement days were over, Wild Bill had killed four toughs in the line of duty. Unfortunately, his penchant for drinking and gambling, coupled with his failing eyesight, led to his destruction. After accidentally shooting a fellow deputy, Wild Bill drifted north to Deadwood, South Dakota where he was shot in the back by a cowpuncher by the name of Jack McCall. This occurred in 1876, and Deadwood, South Dakota proved to be the 'end of the trail' for Wild Bill.

History records the names of the many individuals who unwaveringly stood on the side of justice. Some of these include Bat Masterson, William 'Bill' Tilghman, and Perry Owens, but there were others, the names of which have mostly been forgotten. Occasionally, we can glimpse the name of one of these individuals on a headstone in a cemetery. They may have fought in a skirmish or feud, which has nearly been forgotten, but they distinguished themselves by being able to fight back and kill when the necessity arose, and whether they will be judged innocent or guilty, they will forever be remembered as Gunfighters!

A Buffalo Tale

By: Dave McDonald

"Wow! There's a sight you don't see every day." Not anymore at least. It's hard not to stare as about a dozen head of buffalo trot over the rise. You wonder what it must have been like in years past when the old timers talked about the buffalo covering the hills like the blades of the prairie grass. In the back of your mind, you know the herds were probably never that large in this area, but your heart tells you they should still be out there. But, you remember that right now you can't be thinking that way. You're not there by chance. You've been a peace officer for almost 20 years now, since `82. This area is now ruled by the plow and planter. The farmers have been complaining to the Sheriff about these buffalo destroying crops and eating up the hay they depend on to feed their livestock. So, there you are, and your job is to deal with it. But as you stand there with nothing more than a pistol on your hip, you wonder just what they expect you to do about it. Sure, there's a carbine on your mount, but the only effect that would have on a buffalo would be to tick it off, and start all of them chasing you. That's not really the solution you were looking for.

You keep a watch on the herd, and your eye is drawn to an old cow. As you watch, you remember what an old buffalo runner told you about this herd. "The herds ain't led by the biggest bull, like some people think. You find the oldest, rankest cow in the bunch, and she's the one the others will follow." And there she is, just like that old boy said. He also said it's about time for the cows to be dropping calves, and that old cow looks fat. When she turns her nose into the wind they all follow. When she starts to run, you know the others will eventually go the same way. If you can get them headed in the right direction, maybe you won't have to shoot any of them, at least not today.

By maneuvering around on the hillcrests and watching that old cow, you find you can get them moving. You're not really herding them like cattle, just getting that old cow to go the way you want. After a couple hours work, they've moved off far enough that they'll be someone else's problem for a while. But you know, deep down, that very soon the time will run out on these buffalo, as it already has on the vast herds before them. And you also know that, once again, it won't be the buffalos' fault. The animals are just doing what they have done for thousands of years. If this herd falls as well, once again, it will be man's fault. But today this herd lives to run again.

A few weeks go by and you get word of the buffalo now and then. The old cow has her calf on the ground now. Everybody talks about seeing them now and again. Everyone comments what it must have been like in the old days, but this is a new century. No one really understands the buffalo anymore, and no one wants to tolerate them. One way or another the herd has been cut down to almost nothing. One old bull and that old cow and her calf are the only ones left, still running free. That also means the Sheriff is still getting complaints, and you still work for him. The two of you talk it over and he tells you to watch the buffalo, and if they are endangering anyone, to shoot them. Knowing human nature, you realize that man will be unable to stay away from the buffalo and the animals will pay. So, with mixed feelings, you dig out the one rifle you can depend on when you are forced to take that step. It's an 1874 Sharps, .45-90 caliber, the one they call "the buffalo rifle." You've shot it many times, learning about its accuracy at targets on distant hillsides, but never at a real buffalo. You take out a box of cartridges, something else from days gone by; heavy 500-grain cast lead bullets over a large charge of black powder.

As you check the rifle and look at its lines, you once again wonder what it would have been like. What could it have felt like lying on a hilltop with a belt full of rounds, making your stand as the herd covers the land around you? You'd like to have a glimmer of that experience, but you also want to see those big animals stay out there, somewhere other than just in your imagination. But it's not to be. You hear a tale of the big bull falling in a county south of you. The story is that the bull was chased over six miles and shot nine times before going down. You hang your head a little, knowing it should have been different. Then you learn that, for some reason known only to God, a farmer has cut the buffalo calf out and taken it away from the old cow. Now the last member of that herd you saw lope over the hill is hanging around the farmer's place trying to get back to her calf. Small wonder that she's already attacked the farmer once. He's going to be all right and when no one's looking, the corners of your mouth turn up in a barely suppressed grin. But as you mount up and see the old Sharps, the grin rapidly fades. Maybe she'll be gone by the time you get there but you know there's really no way out now for either of you.

Cresting the hill you see the farm, and there's the old cow, running back and forth along the fence line. It looks like she's already taken down a couple of fences. The farmer won't even come out of the house. You grab the Sharps and a handful of cartridges and try to get into a position so you can get a clear shot but also have a little cover if you need it. The Sharps is loaded with one of those heavy black powder cartridges and more are tucked into your gun belt. You've hunted your entire life, and you know the chances of stopping this agitated buffalo with one round are almost zero. The old cow determines how the story will unfold, and you realize this isn't going to be like the tales of old. No lone hunter lying on a hill shooting 300-400 yards. Nope, this is going to be on a running animal at 50 yards or less.

The buffalo starts to run down the fence and out of reflex, you bring the heavy rifle up and start to swing it on target. Your right

hand has cocked the hammer and set the trigger, seemingly on its own. You've shot game on the run and on the wing before, but never with a gun that has double set triggers. Your elbow hits a fence post before the heavy rifle is in place, and the gun belches smoke, the slug going harmlessly into the dirt. Cussing yourself for such a greenhorn mistake, you reload the rifle and get back on target. The cow is running back down the fence line when you learn another lesson. Looking at a buffalo 45 yards away through the peep of a vernier sight, all you see is brown fur. The buffalo swaps ends and you do your best to line up on her rib cage as she runs. If you're really lucky, you can get a round through her lungs then, no matter what else happens, she'll go down eventually. Everything feels right about the shot, and you squeeze the trigger without thought. The Sharps roars and bucks, you hear a clang, and you see her stumble.

Even though you know you hit the buffalo, part of your mind wonders what that clang was all about. The other part of the mind has already caused you to reload the rifle and bring it back up to your shoulder. Damn good thing, too, because for one reason or another, she's coming down the hill right at you in one final run. The front sight crosses her head and she disappears in that cloud of black powder smoke as the Sharps roars one more time. The reloading process happens again, but as the smoke clears, you know it won't be needed. The old cow has piled up for the last time, just feet from where you last saw her running. Those mixed emotions kick in again. You know you've just done something not everyone can do, but your heart already misses the sight of those shaggy creatures running over the hills. Out of instinct you move to the animal and check to make sure it's done, just like your Grandpa taught you. You have to lay your hand on that shaggy hide just one time. The farmer sees you unload the old Sharps and he realizes it's over. He comes out of the house, wanting to express his gratitude, but you really don't feel like that right now. Why couldn't he have left well enough alone? You put the Sharps back in the case, mount up without a word, turn your back on the farm, and ride away.

Author's Note: The story is true and took place in May of 2001. The author is a full-time Deputy Sheriff in Northeast Iowa. He is also an NCOWS member and has participated in buffalo rifle events at the Prairie Fire Range near Ackley, Iowa. Having heard the metallic clang when shooting buffalo targets, he was naturally puzzled when the same sound came from the live buffalo as the event unfolded. A check revealed that the heavy slug had passed entirely through the animal's lungs and struck a steel tube gate behind it as the buffalo ran past. He used a Pedersoli 1874 Sharps reproduction that had been rechambered to .45-90 caliber.

As you may recall in the classic Walt Disney movie *Mary Poppins*, the Banks family has a neighbor named Admiral Boom who is a retired British Naval Admiral. Admiral Boom has configured the roof of his Victorian house to resemble the deck of a British Ship of the Line, complete with a naval cannon. From his helm atop his house, Admiral Boom keeps tab of the comings and goings about the neighborhood, and a sharp eye on the weather. He uses the cannon as a "time gun" to announce the hours of 8:00 a.m. and 6:00 p.m. It is said that, "The world gets the time from Greenwich, but Greenwich gets its time from Admiral Boom." The Admiral's self-appointed call to duty is tolerated by the neighbors, but not always appreciated.

When the clock approaches 6:00 p.m. at the Banks household, the call, "Posts everyone!" goes out. This "alarm" means that Admiral Boom is about to fire the time **By: Kenny Durham,** cannon. Suddenly, everyone stops what they're doing ***aka KID Durham*** and heads for predestined stations throughout the house to prevent prized vases, statues, and paintings from falling off the wall or toppling off their perch. Moments later, as the clock strikes 6:00 p.m., a thunderous roar shakes the house as the Admiral fires his cannon. The Banks household manages to catch or steady any breakable treasure that is shaken from its foundation with a routine matter-of-fact attitude. After a few moments, the reverberation from the Admiral's time cannon fades away, and all the valuables are secured back in place. The Banks' home then returns to business as usual. This was NOT the case in the household of my good friend Jack Duncan, however.

Jack was a gunsmith, not by trade but by his choice avocation. I'm sure that his gunsmithing supplemented his income but, more importantly, it provided him with a well-needed diversion from the toils of life. Jack grew up in the 1930's and 1940's when there was little interest in black powder shooting. He was interested in building custom high-powered rifles. Jack also appreciated fine shotguns. He once told me that he would pay a considerable sum for a shotgun because shotguns were hard to build. He could, however, make all the rifles he wanted for only a few dollars. Handguns, on the other hand, were another matter. When it came to pistols, Jack had the same attitude as Matthew Quigley, "Never had much use for a shooter." Jack liked to shoot handguns; he just hated and refused to work on them. As a necessary item to Jack's gunsmithing activities, he built a special test-firing pit in his furnace room in the basement of his house. Jack usually tried to conduct his basement test firing when no one else was home, but there were times when it was just not possible. Since most of his spare time was spent doing gunsmith work, it was not unusual for him to touch off a 30-06 in the furnace room test pit, provided he gave the inhabitants upstairs the proper warning. Much like the "Posts everyone!" alarm sound in the Banks' home, there was a specific protocol for Jack to follow in order to alert the upstairs inhabitants when he was about to test-fire a gun.

Jack's son-in-law is one of my best friends, and together we managed to get Ol' Jack interested in muzzleloaders. I had just finished building a muzzleloader, and Jack had watched me build my gun with great curiosity. Given Jack's love of high-power rifles and disdain of working on handguns, we were surprised by his announcement that HE was going to build this muzzleloading pistol. When Jack took on a new project, he was consumed by it until finished. It was on a Wednesday evening that he told us that he was going to build a muzzleloading pistol. A section of a .45-70 barrel, an old shotgun lock, a chunk of scrap Maple, and several other junk parts from an old scattergun were hastily assembled into a single-shot percussion pistol. By Saturday afternoon he was putting on the finishing touches. Now, the moment of truth was at hand: the test firing. Jack couldn't wait to test-fire his new creation. We were soon headed to the test-firing pit in the basement furnace room with black powder, lead balls, percussion caps, and the new pistol in hand. Admiral Boom would have been proud.

Jack's tolerant wife had always understood her husband's need to test-fire guns without having to drive to the firing range. With all the high-powered "Blue Pill" proof test loads he torched off in the basement, there was never a problem. The muzzleloading pistol was about to change all that! To fully appreciate the dynamics of what was about to happen, I must set the stage a little for you. I don't remember what season it was, but I do remember that it was the cold time of the year. Jack's elderly mother had recently arrived and just settled in for an extended visit. Although she had raised Jack and knew about his mischievous nature, she was not accustomed to living in a house where rather large explosions emanated from the basement. Furthermore, on THIS particular Saturday, Mrs. Duncan was entertaining a couple of other ladies who had stopped by for a cup of tea. Jack's youngest daughter was still living at home and was taking a nap. One other thing you should know, the sheet metal access door to the furnace fan was open and the squirrel cage fan was running.

Now in the basement, Jack asked me what the appropriate powder charge for a .45 caliber pistol should be. I told him that 30 grains would be a good average charge for target shooting. Jack's reply was, "Yeah, but this is for test-firing, so we should use more powder." I said, "Okay. How much do you want to use?" Jack decided that we should use at least a double charge as a sort-of proof load. Neither one of us had any reason to doubt that the gun would not hold together. So, we settled on a 60-grain charge of FFFg and a patched round ball. Soon the pistol was loaded and we were ready at last to fire the gun. Jack stepped up to the firing pit, eased the hammer to full cock, and placed a percussion cap on the nipple. All was ready.

Oh, did I mention that in our haste to test-fire the new gun, protocol had flown out the window? Jack COMPLETELY forgot to inform the inhabitants upstairs of what we were up to. Jack was grinning from ear-to-ear like a child on Christmas morning as he pulled the trigger. The gun roared and bucked in Jack's hand. The big grin on Jack's faced turned to anguish as the "BOOM" was immediately followed by a rather large "CRASH" from directly above us upstairs. Suddenly, it was strangely silent except for the whirring of the furnace fan. The black powder smoke floated from the low ceiling through the open door of the fan, which whisked the smoke away and distributed it throughout the rooms upstairs.

Jack looked at me and said something that is best not repeated about having forgotten to warn his wife. He hurriedly stuck the pistol in his belt and threw on his coat. We could hear the dining room chairs sliding on the hardwood floor as the ladies stood up from the table. Then we heard coughing from the acrid, pungent odor of the black powder smoke. Next, loud clomping footsteps headed our way. Mrs. Duncan, not knowing we were in the basement, thought the furnace had blown up and something was on fire. Jack's daughter was abruptly awakened from her nap, and Jack's poor mother was frightened out of another year of life, which she could ill afford. Down the stairs the entourage came. We were trapped. Trapped like a couple of kids with berry pie all over their faces. Jack's daughter passed everyone and hit the bottom of the stairs first. To our astonishment, THEY didn't realize WHAT had happened! They thought something was wrong with the furnace. They thought WE had come to the rescue and had just gotten to the basement ahead of them! "What happened, Dad?" "Uh, well uh, not sure, uh, let me see, uh, I think the furnace just backfired or something like that. It seems to be okay now, though. Let's all go back upstairs." I kept my yap shut and stared at the floor.

Jack had just about pulled off the charade when Mrs. Duncan saw the pistol in Jack's belt peeking out from under his coat. "And what's this?" she asked, pointing to the pistol. Knowing he had been caught, Jack muttered, "Oh, I think that's what made the furnace backfire." In an instant, Mrs. Duncan discerned the truth. She looked at me as if I might be the source of Jack's having gone astray. Once again, it was silent except for the whirring of that miserable fan. I imagine we looked pretty stupid. I was about 26 years old at the time, but Jack was in his 50's and stood 6'-6" tall and weighed about 280 pounds. The ladies' scornful looks spoke volumes as they turned and headed back up the stairs without saying a word. When they reached the top of the stairs, Mrs. Duncan turned and said, "You've got a mess to clean up here!" referring to a broken ceramic teapot lying in pieces on the kitchen floor. I made my way back out to the shop while Jack attended to his domestic duties. Soon he came back out to the shop where he grinned and said, "Wish I coulda seen the look on their faces when that gun went off!" We both laughed until our sides hurt.

Later, Jack pretty much regained his credibility by taking everyone out to dinner that evening. But it wasn't over yet. When they arrived back home from dinner, the house was cold. So, Jack turned up the thermostat a little more. A half-hour or so later the house was not any warmer. In fact, it was even colder than before. The women of the house were complaining, but Jack insisted that everything was okay. "It's just a cold night and it will take a while for the house to warm up!" More time passed and still no warmth. Finally, after more persuasion, Jack went down to the furnace room to check it out. A short search revealed the problem. In all the hundreds of high-powdered rounds he had fired in the basement, none had ever caused a problem with the furnace. This time, however, the concussion from the black powder had blown out the pilot light in the furnace! No muzzleloaders were ever test-fired in the basement test pit again!

Teddy Roosevelt Moves West

By: Jocko Jackson

I was a restin' in front of the blacksmith shop, as it allowed the most shade of any building in town. Not much of a town here in the Dakota's, with only a stable, two saloons, and a run-down hotel that doubles as a eatin' place and stage stop. While I was watchin' the dust devils dance in the street, a stranger came out of the hotel and headed my way. I noticed he was dressed as a working cowhand, yet he had just a mite better outfit than your average cowpuncher. He was wearing new chaps, boots, and a shirt, as well as a brand-new Stetson hat. He was a packin' an ivory-gripped revolver in a new gun belt, and I could see the brass cartridges a shinin' in the sun. In the crook of his arm he was a carryin' an 1876 short-magazine Winchester. I also noticed he traveled straight-legged, unlike the bow-legged stance of a seasoned rider, and the word "dude" came to mind.

As I sat outside the shop, I saw that the big blacksmith had been a turnin' out a fine set of horseshoes that he had heated, shaped, punched, and then dipped into a bucket of water. They were then thrown into a small pile on the dirt floor. The stranger strolled through the big doors of the blacksmith shop, nodded my direction, and went in. He then inquired about purchasing a horse and rig since he was now going to be a rancher. As he was a talkin', he reached down and picked up the top shoe off that pile on the floor, and let me tell ya, them shoes were a long way from bein' cool. As a wisp of smoke came from the stranger's hand, I could tell he sure got shuck of that shoe! The blacksmith, with a smile tuggin' at his lips, asked, "Hot?" The stranger, gingerly rubbing his hand, replied, "Nah, just don't take me long to look at a shoe!" Later I learned the stranger went by the moniker Roosevelt, Theodore Roosevelt. I gave him a month!

By: Kenny Durham,
aka KID Durham

More Gun Than He Bargained For

A friend of mine decided that a .62-caliber, Hawkin-style, muzzle-loading rifle would be just the ticket for rendezvous trail walks where a large diameter ball would be a distinct advantage over smaller-diameter round balls when it came to split the ball/axe shoots, cut the crossed strings, tack drives, card-edge shoots, etc., at least theoretically. He purchased a .62-caliber barrel and proceeded to build a nice rifle. Upon completion, we took the rifle to the range and worked up a load of 70-gr. FFg black powder and a 0.615 round ball. We had feared that the recoil would be substantial, maybe even too brutal to be practical for repeated use. We found that the 70-gr. powder charge was manageable and the rifle's bark was worse than its bite. However, one day during a trail walk, we learned what kind of "bite" it could have. Jack got to talking and instead of paying attention to what he was doing, he triple-charged the piece with 210 grains of FFg black powder.

In his usual nonchalant, relaxed state, totally unaware of what he had done, Jack prepared for the shot. Aiming uphill at a "swinger" that was an old farm disk standing on a slope, Jack, covered with pine needles and wearing loose-fitting slick moccasins, unleashed the fury within. What happened next is one of those chains of events that no one could plan and that seemed to unfold in slow motion. The blast of the rifle was awesome. The flame from the muzzle was visible in broad daylight. The recoil tipped Ol' Jack over backwards. His feet flew up into the air as though invisible rockets were tied to them. He landed on his back, then proceeded downhill head first on a bed of slick pine needles. One moccasin went straight in the air ...along with the rifle. The rifle hung in mid-air for a second, then landed flat on the bed of pine needles and proceeded to follow its owner downhill. Jack managed to get stopped by a big clump of huckleberry bushes. The rifle got stopped by Jack's behind ...crescent butt plate first.

While all this was going on, the work done by the big .62-caliber bullet was causing pandemonium, too. Seems that due to the increased powder charge, the shot went high and the bullet hit the chain from which the disk was hanging. I don't remember whether the bullet broke the chain or hit it with such force that it knocked the chain from the tree branch. However it happened, the disk hit the ground edgeways and reverted back to its intended purpose in life of disking up "Mother Earth" AND headed in OUR direction. We all scattered to get out of the way - except for poor Ol' Jack who was struggling to get the forked-end down. He heard the commotion and looked back uphill to see the revengeful disk coming straight towards him, the chain clanking against the disk and flailing the dirt with every revolution. Jack scrambled as best as he could to get out of the way, but with one bare foot and a slick moccasin on the other, he could go nowhere. Turns out that he was perfectly safe as the disk passed by him several feet away as though it was totally ignoring the author of all this drama and was on a higher mission - the camp below.

At the base of the hill, Bearpaw and his wife, Two Moons, (how she got that name is a whole other story) had setup their tepee lodge. Two Moons was standing by an outside fire stirring a Dutch oven full of stew for the upcoming potluck that evening. The Dutch oven hung on a horizontal rod supported by a "Y" stake in the ground at each end. Two Moons heard the commotion and looked up the hill to see what was happening. She saw the rolling disk coming toward her and got out of the way, but the disk hit one of the "Y" supports, dislodged the crossbar, and spilled the whole pot of stew into the fire. The disk, having dissipated its energy, came to a rest on the other side of the fire pit. Two Moons fright of the whole situation now turned to rage as she saw her prize-winning stew quenching the fire and creating a plume of dirty ashes billowing skyward. She let out a shriek and covered the 50 yards uphill to where the rest of us were in only a matter of seconds. The expression "madder than a wet hen" suddenly took on new meaning. It was obvious to Two Moons that Ol' Jack had contrived this whole mess just to ruin her day and, furthermore, if he couldn't shoot any better than that, he ought to stay home!

Jack shook his head and wandered back to camp without finishing the trail walk. The rifle was retired immediately and never fired again as long as Jack owned it. This was in about 1983, if I remember right. Jack died in July of 1999. Someone else bought the rifle from his wife not ever knowing what had occured.

By: Katha Higginbotham

Hunting Tatanka

In November 2001, my husband Dave and I left south Texas and drove (in an air-conditioned truck, as opposed to a bumpy wagon) all day to reach Dodge City, Kansas. We were provisioned with a wall tent, tent poles, camping supplies, saddles, rifles, cartridges, boots, hats, and 1870's-period clothing. We had been invited by Lee and Tamie Hawes of Hawes Ranch to come hunt buffalo, or Tatanka (pronounced Ta-tahng'-ka) as the Sioux Indians called them, the way hide hunters had in southwest Kansas in the 1870's. Like a kid at Christmas, I began to conjure up visions of myself riding at full gallop across the open prairie alongside a heard of stampeding buffalo. You know, the way Kevin Costner did in *Dances with Wolves*. I would pull my rolling block rifle from its scabbard and fire point-blank at a huge bull. He would drop and slide to a stop, dead on arrival! Well, that's the way it is in the movies, but not in real life. I soon learned that the reason you would be riding at full gallop is because the buffalo are so fractious that, at the mere glimpse or smell of a horse or human, they would take off for parts unknown. And, if you were lucky enough to get that close, it would be extremely dangerous. The bulls will protect each other if one goes down, and the cows are very defensive of their babies.

When we arrived in Dodge City, we soon learned that Main Street is almost as it was a century ago. Settled by buffalo hunters, and later flavored by the arrival of the railroad and cowboys bringing herds up from Texas, Dodge was simply a long street of bordellos, saloons, outfitters, a trading post, and more saloons. We rambled around Dodge, taking in Boot Hill Cemetery. Later, we "bellied up to the bar" at the Long Branch Saloon to sip *sasparillie'*.

Today, Dodge City offers a variety of shops and historical sights to see. I enjoyed seeing the pictures of the pioneer women and ladies of the evening, as well as the women who came after the frontier was settled. I searched their faces for some sign of who they were and how they must have felt coming to this harsh land. Many of them had died at a young age due to consumption, childbirth, or diseases. Still, it would have been an exciting time to have lived.

I took special interest in their clothes. I was trying to find just one picture of a lady in a split skirt. I hate to tell you girls, but it wasn't there, at least not in the 1870's. I must admit that I cheated on my own clothing, however. When Lee said everything

The author holding a real prairie bouquet.

had to be period-style (no jeans), I told him I couldn't ride sidesaddle. So, he agreed I could wear split skirts, but they had to look like a full skirt when I was off the horse.

Tailoring clothes for the trip was an experience within itself. We scanned hundreds of pictures from library books and from our own collection trying to find information for ladies' clothing in that time period. Lee had said to be prepared for weather ranging from the 20's to the 80's, so I decided on a coat made of heavy wool, flannel-lined, with acetate undersheeting. As I chose a material for the coat, I savored the feel of the different wools, and wondered if this must have been what women of the Old West had done. Finding patterns for exactly what I had in mind was difficult. It took a number of alterations to make the patterns

The team gathered together to make a plan of attack.

work. All in all, I came away with one store-bought riding outfit, two split skirts (one a little dressier than the other), two blouses (one store-bought and one homemade), and a full-length, homemade, heavy winter coat, which was split for riding.

We drove from Dodge to a place called Mount Jesus. Legend has it that General George Armstrong Custer gave the point its name as he passed by on the trail from Camp Dodge to Camp Supply. Today, there is a cross and pulpit marking the spot and Easter sunrise services are held there each year. They told us that you could see four counties from atop the mount, the highest point in Clark County. At Mount Jesus, we met our scout, Joey Moore, wrangler Cody Hawes, and skinner Aaron Goodman. All the gear was loaded onto a wagon pulled by a beautiful pair

of famous white Percherons named Bob and Stormy. They were in the TV movie *Sarah, Plain and Tall.*

We proceeded to camp via horseback and wagon, leaving all resemblance of civilization behind. It was like being born again into a different era. The Kansas wind, which blows all the time, seemed to blow away the present and carry us into the past. I've heard stories of women who were driven insane by the constant blowing of the wind. It's said that women are like butterflies and the wind can blow them away, but men are like buffalo, they don't pay any attention to it.

It was late evening and getting cold when we arrived in camp. Our camp was near a watering hole, and consisted of three 18-foot tipis, rope corral, a chuck table, the cook's fire irons, and a bath tent, which would not have been a part of an early buffalo camp as the men wore the same cloths for weeks on end and

Taking the horses to water after a hard day's work.

became infested with bugs of every kind. Indian women used to place their infested buffalo hides on anthills allowing the ants to debug them.

Moose and Jeff Keller, the camp cooks, made us a supper of elk, buffalo, and biscuits and gravy, ready to eat. We pitched our tent, while everyone else moved into their tipi homes for the next four days. Let me say right here that living for an extended period of time in a wall tent is NOT my idea of exciting. I soon understood why pioneer women never had on corsets, as was the style of the day. Try pitching a tent, watering horses, or cooking over an open fire three times a day with a corset on!

The next morning, we rose before dawn to find a breakfast of sausage, ham, and flapjacks. Then we saddled up, adjusted our stirrups, checked the cinches, and headed out to hunt *"buffler."*

All saddled up and ready to go hunting.

Dave was carrying a rolling block he had built, which is a copy of an original 16-pound buffalo rifle chambered in .50-90. I, on the other hand, carried his rolling block sporting rifle in .50-70. We rode several hours before Joey brought word that he had spotted the herd off to the east. We had to ride along a sharp rim and through deep draws to get into a position where we would be down wind of the herd. We then dismounted and walked, bent low, carrying rifles, cross-sticks, and gear to a spot where we could see the buffalo. When we had to move out from behind the ridge back into clear view of them, the lead cow's head shot up to watch us moving through the tall grass. Lee explained that in a crouched position the buffalo took us for coyotes.

The herd became uneasy and began to move a little to the south. Dave quickly set up the cross-sticks and got into position to shoot. The men talked it over and decided on a prize bull about 220 yards away. Dave took aim with the .50-90, but a cow stepped in front of the bull so Dave had to wait as she slowly grazed ahead. The herd was becoming more nervous and started moving away a little faster. The cow stepped up a little, but this still left Dave with a difficult site picture, since her rump was flush with the bull's shoulder. Dave figured the wind to be blowing south to north about 30 miles per hour. He wanted to make a clean kill with one shot, but with the cow's rump in the way, it left him little room for error.

Heading out on horseback to do some hunting for Tatanka.

Considering the wind drift on the bullet, he pulled just off the cow's rump and touched off the big 50. The 720-grain, NEI Higginbotham Lone Star #378 B bullet, pushed by 105 grains of FFg Goex powder, held true to course. It was a good solid hit and the bull humped up.

At this point, I was a little surprised. In the movies, the buffalo drop immediately. Lee explained that it's seldom that a bull can be knocked off his feet unless it happens to be a spine shot. So, our buffalo went about 20 to 30 yards before dropping straight down on his feet. Joey approached the downed animal very cautiously while keeping an eye on the other bulls, which had stopped about 800 yards away, and then hailed us to join him. I was amazed at the size of the bull. He was beautiful! The fur on his head was about 10 inches long and soft to the touch, and the horns were strong and in good condition. Lee gauged that this bull was approximately six years old, because older bulls usually have stub horns due to wear. The shot was a clean one. It had entered the lungs and exited the other side, not hitting any bone. It was shot through the "lights" as the old runners would say.

The men shook hands and congratulated each other on a good hunt while I took pictures. Then it was over. It had all happened so fast that I was suddenly disappointed. All the plans I had made of riding ahead of the hunters to get snapshots and taking zoom shots of the buffalo were gone. What had happened? I had gotten so caught up in the hunt that I had missed the prize photo. I learned that when it's time to pull the trigger, you can't wait to take pictures. You may have heard the old saying "either fish or cut bait," because you can't do both. Well, I learned to either take pictures or hunt. A good photographer must not do anything to impede the hunt, but should still manage to get good pictures.

As for me, I would rather hunt. It was great! Would I ever shoot a buffalo? Yes, if I needed the meat, which is excellent. It would be very exciting to sight-in on a live buffalo and then squeeze the trigger. A person must be very concentrated and disciplined not to let the excitement of the hunt interfere with the shot.

After we rode back to camp, the skinners went out to do their work. On hindsight, I would have liked to have been in on the skinning because it was a big part of buffalo hunting in the 1870's, even though the hunter very seldom skinned his own buffalo because he/she thought that was below his station. I'm sure if we had asked Lee, he would have allowed us to watch. The skinners brought the heart back to camp, which was the size of a football. Moose cooked it up for supper the next night.

That night, as I lay in our tent, warm under blankets and a buffalo robe (no, not a fresh one, but one that Dave already had), I listened as the folks around the dying campfire spoke softly while sharing stories of hunts and past experiences. Dave recalled the story that Wayne Gard wrote about in his book *The Great Buffalo Hunt*. It's the story of Henry Inman who was caught out in a terrific blizzard.

"*... Fearing he would freeze to death, he quickly killed an old bull, slashed open his belly, and pulled out the viscera. Then he crawled into the cavity, which protected him from the wind and snow, and was warm enough to keep him comfortable until morning. At daybreak the storm ceased, but the ribs of the buffalo had frozen together and locked him inside. Fortunately, his companions came near enough to hear him yelling and rescued him.*" I felt I had truly been allowed to go back in time.

We would like to express sincere appreciation to Brain Fitzgibbons of New Mexico for the fine canvas cartridge belt that he made for Dave. Thanks to David Barnes for going over our saddles and saddlebags to make sure they held together, and for loaning us his leather-covered canteen. David also made Dave a rifle boot that attaches to the saddle horn, which especially came in handy for carrying a 16-pound rifle comfortably. Special thanks to all the ladies who gave me help and ideas about my wardrobe. Most of all, I would like to thank my husband for encouraging me to go along and share in the hunt.

A friend called to tell us that the *Outdoor* channel had aired the hunt on a program called *One Shot Challenge*. We didn't see it, but the memories are forever etched in my mind.

The Gun That May Have Won The West

By: Andy Fink, aka Chucky

I was 14 in 1886 when Ma and Pa were killed by a no-account drifter. I had been pulling my own weight around the farm for some time, so I got plenty of exercise doing the chores. Ma always fed us young'ns well, so I wasn't scrawny, but fairly good size for my age. We weren't rich and we weren't poor. In fact, Pa always said we were richer than the folks in town because we were close to the land. On a cool fall morning, as the sun came over the hills; glistening off the Snake River, and the geese dropping in. I could be found hunkered down on a stump behind the aspens, listening to the sounds of the wind on the water, the rustle of the leaves, and the chirp of the squirrels. It was times like those when I knew Pa was right – God was all around us and we were rich because we had this bounty. I loved the woods, the river, and the marsh areas, and would spend every free moment I had amongst them. It was not far from us that Lewis and Clark came through on their expedition in 1803 to map out the Northwest.

Pa had bought an 1883 Colt double-barrel 12-gauge with an extra set of matched barrels for himself when we left Pennsylvania three years ago. He used it for everything from turkeys, geese, and ducks, to hunting deer and elk, for which he would load it with great big slugs. It was then that Pa had turned over to me one of his prize possessions, which was one of the two guns that we owned. I couldn't really believe it when he handed it to me, as it had been given to him by his brother only eight years before and had come all the way from England. It was a thing of beauty, finely-engraved, with a side lock mechanism versus the thumb lock on the top behind the action. It had 30-inch barrels, with one being inscribed with "J B CLAYBROUGH & BROS LONDON LAMINATED STEEL" on the barrel. It had two big hammers, sometimes referred to as mule ears, which took both of my hands to pull back the first time I tried.

The gun was huge, taller than me at the time, and was a 10-gauge to boot. I could barely lift and aim it, much less shoot it. Pa helped fix up a sling so I could carry it, and also loaded some lighter loads with more wadding than powder so it didn't kick my shoulder off.

He always impressed upon me that when handling any firearm there were three things to remember: always treat it as if it were loaded, never point it at anything you didn't want to shoot, and when you did shoot, make sure you hit what you were aiming at.

Three years was plenty of time to get used to the weight and feel of that shotgun. The action was smooth as silk. I could shoot two geese coming in to land as they skimmed

THE DOUBLE-BARREL SHOTGUN

Kenny Durham, aka KID Durham, shooting his original Meredan Arms double-barrel.

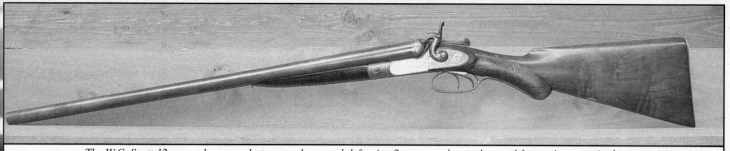

The W.C. Scott 12-gauge hammer shotgun made a good defensive firearm, and was also used for putting meat in the pot.

across the water, open the action, kick out the shells over my shoulder, reload, thumb back the hammers, and pick off another two as they were flying away. I still used the make-shift sling though, as it was heavy carrying it for hours at a time, and I had practiced using it so I could swing the gun up to my shoulder fairly quickly.

One night, a drifter had come by riding a pinto with a splayed right rear hoof. Pa told the drifter that he could sleep in the barn. I got up early that morning and was hunkered down by the river by sun-up. I had three geese by eight o'clock, so I headed back to the house, which was a five-mile walk. I could smell smoke before I reached the last hill and began to run. Looking up, a cloud of black and gray billowed above the hill. Reaching the crest, I could see that the house and barn had burned to the ground and there were bodies lying in the yard. My heart jumped in my throat and I stopped, staring at something that I had no concept could ever happen. I made my way slowly down

The J B Claybrough & Bros. 12-gauge hammer gun had a side-latch versus the standard thumb-latch on the top.

the hill, stumbling in a daze, hoping beyond hope that someone was still alive. Finally, I stood over them. Ma and Pa were dead – shot. Little Eric had his head bashed in and Sara... I didn't want to think about what had been done to Sara.

It took me most of the day to bury my family and run out of tears. I finally got up and shifted through the ashes, but found nothing, and then looked at the signs in the yard. The tracks were clear – the drifter had headed East toward town.

The first thing I decided to do was to eat. Not because I was hungry, but because I knew I would need strength to do what had to be done. Pulling the feathers out of the goose I caught seemed to take ages, but I finally got most of them. I roasted the goose over the burning coals of my home and then ate every bite. My bag had four shells left in it. I got up and started walking the ten miles to town.

It was late when I walked down Main Street. There was a full moon, and the lanterns were lit so it was easy to spot the pinto at the hitching rail of the saloon. I walked in pushing the saloon doors open. Before going in, I did something I had never done before. I pulled the hammers back cocking my shotgun after checking the chambers. I didn't want to waste any time getting my revenge. The muzzles were pointed down at the sawdust floor and the sling was over my shoulder.

No one really noticed me at first. The drifter was sitting over at the back of the saloon playing poker. I could see the gauntness of his face and the meanness in his eyes.

"Drifter," I yelled in my high voice that cracked. "You murdered my family!"

It became silent as everyone turned towards me, and the men in the saloon backed away and to the sides of the table. The drifter stood up. He was lean, had stubble on his face, and was bleary-eyed.

"You must be a fool, kid. I don't even know you." His voice

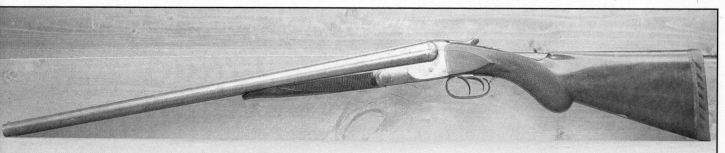

The Colt Model 1883 double-barrel, hammerless shotgun was manufactured from 1883-1895, and was commonly seen in the Old West.

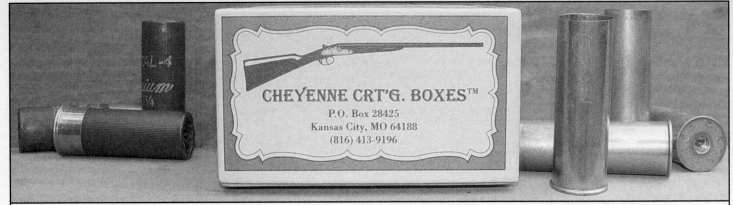

Both paper and brass shotgun shells were found in the Old West, (left) 10-gauge pager shells (right) 12-gauge brass shells.

slurred as his right hand moved closer to his holstered sixgun. My right hand was on the straight grip portion of the gun. As I pushed down, the muzzles swung up as the sling moved on my shoulder.

"That's my father's Colt shotgun you got tied to your saddle," I exclaimed as the barrels came up even with my waist and I pulled the trigger. The two rounds of 10-gauge birdshot plastered him against the wall, and I stood there surrounded in black smoke as the tears began rolling down my cheeks.

Just as the double-barreled shotgun, or scatter-gun as some referred to it, played an integral part in helping the young man in this story bring his parents' killer to justice, it also played a major role in settling the West. It was used everyday by homesteaders, ranchers, hunters, shotgun guards, marshals, and sheriffs. It was the gun that the wives of farmers and ranchers kept loaded behind the door for protection, or for shooting at a fox that was trying to get into the hen house. The shotgun probably saw the demise of many Westerners, both good and bad, as well as providing a meal for a family on a regular basis. It was a firearm that was probably seen in more households than any other gun.

Shotguns were both plain and exquisitely-engraved, short-barreled and long-barreled, in gauges from 20-gauge to 8-gauge, with pistol grips or straight grips, and with or without hammers. Many of them came from England, France, Belgium, Germany, and Spain, as well as those made in the United States.

With the exception of using the Winchester 1887 lever-action shotgun, when shooting in the Frontier Cartridge category, today's cowboy action shooter must use a double-barrel when shooting black powder. I have seen many black powder enthusiasts use original antique firearms, and I have used my father's Colt 12-gauge when shooting Frontier. Others will use a Fox, Scott, Stevens, European American Arms, Baikal, or Stoger shotgun. SASS has its own special double-barreled Baikal hammer gun imported by European American Arms, and there are a number of other companies that at the time of this printing are planning on importing double-barrels in both the hammerless and hammer versions for cowboy action shooting. All of them work well.

Every time I shoot in a black powder category and use a double-barrel, I am reminded of what it must have been like back in the 1800's, whether it was a young man out shooting ducks for his family's meal, a homesteader defending his property from the cattleman, or a stagecoach guard shooting back at Indians or thieves. Even today, a good double-barrel shotgun can be a decent defense gun, and the old originals are still viable hunting firearms. If you haven't ever shot black powder in a double-barrel give it a try. You might just decide to join the numerous shooters that enjoy the nostalgia of yesteryear by shooting black powder.

Though shotguns were used on an everyday basis, many of them were not only exquisitely engraved, but also had fine carvings on the stock such as this Le Page 12-gauge hammer gun.

The Frontiersman and the Muzzleloader

By: Andy Fink, aka Chucky

The Blackfoot had trailed him for the last eight days. He was tired, but enjoyed the warmth of the morning sun after riding through the cold night. The grass on the seemingly endless prairie slowly wove back and forth with the light breeze.

He was riding a piebald mare and holding a lead rope to the pack mule with one hand on his saddle horn, while the other held a rifle across the saddle. His eyes ranged back and forth in front of him, but occasionally he would glance behind him hoping he wouldn't see the dust cloud he knew was there.

It was 1851 and he had been trapping along the Dakota rivers. The Blackfoot hadn't taken kindly to him trapping their beaver and mink. He'd made friends with the Sioux, the Cheyenne, the Arapaho, and the Cherokee, but the Blackfoot just didn't seem to like the white man. Maybe they instinctively knew there would be more pale faces heading west in the next few years encroaching on Blackfoot hunting grounds.

He wore buckskins, had a floppy felt hat on his head, shoulder-length yellow hair, and moccasins on his feet. His rifle was carried in a soft elkskin sheath decorated with Indian beadwork and fringe. Although he carried an 1848 Colt Walker .44 in his belt, it was the .54 caliber Hawken that was ever ready to his hand.

A small group of trees appeared ahead in the distance indicating there was water and temporary cover. He nudged his horse with the heels of his moccasins and it broke into a canter.

As they rode up through the grove of aspens where a little creek ran through, he scanned the area to make sure they were alone before he tied the piebald and mule to a couple of trees close to the bank so they could drink. After filling the canteens and quenching his thirst, he grabbed some jerky out of his possibles bag, and taking his Hawken, he moved over to a fallen log at the edge of the trees to look out over the prairie. There was a slight hint of dust in the air at the horizon, and he hoped it wasn't what he thought it was, but he knew better.

Going back to the animals, he pulled off the mule's pack and rummaged through it, pulling out the minimum of necessities, and then packed them in his buffalo coat behind the cantle of the piebald's saddle. He really didn't want to leave the beaver and mink pelts, but he knew he couldn't continue making a run for it pulling the mule behind him. Taking another drink while munching on his jerky, he slid his Hawken out of the smooth elk-skin sheath. It was loaded with a percussion cap on the nipple. There was a small piece of leather between the cap and the hammer to lessen the risk of it going off if dropped or if the hammer was hit hard on accident.

He knelt down by the tree, rested the Hawken against the log, and then pulled out two .54 caliber balls and placed them on top of the log. Each had a lubricated patch wrapped around it. He knelt behind the log, laid the Hawken over it, and waited. The maximum distance he wanted to shoot at men on horseback was 150 yards. He had marked his spots of distance riding in, so he was pretty sure of what his sight picture would have to be. He figured he could get two, maybe three, before he might have to pull out his Colt Walker, but hopefully putting a few down would give him time to put some

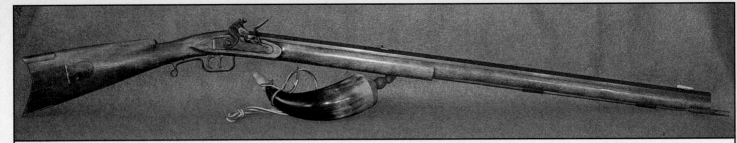

A modern-day Hawken Flintlock with a period-correct powder horn. Note the double-set triggers and the large blade front sight.

distance between them. Besides, if they kept coming, maybe their curiosity with his pack and their fancy for mule meat would hold them up some.

He knew from his own experience, as well as from the exploits of other marksmen of that time, that the large-bore Hawken, or plains rifle, was a formidable weapon clearly capable of death-dealing accuracy. On a good day, when a man's luck was with him, a kill shot beyond 200 yards was not impossible.

He could see them now. They rode in a bunch, not single-file like you usually see. Picking up the Hawken, he took a breath, let half of it out, placed the bottom of his front sight in the notch of the rear sight, and aimed at the face of the first rider. He pulled the rear set trigger, and then slowly squeezed the front trigger. "BOOM!" He

then the slid quickly back to the creek and his waiting horse. Jumping into the saddle, he broke into a gallop and headed away from the little oasis in the plains.

Those that dared to open up the West in the mid-1800's and earlier usually didn't have the luxury of having repeating rifles. Although there were a few, such as the Patterson revolving rifle or carbine, most frontiersman, or plainsman as they were called then, used the plains rifle.

First the flintlock, and then the percussion rifle, were the firearms of the day. There were a few double rifles, but most were single-shots. Many of those used came from Europe, while others were made in Pennsylvania, Kentucky, Tennessee, Connecticut, and the Carolinas. They came in all calibers, from as small as .32, normally

A Hawken Flintlock with a possibles bag and a typical Frontiersman's knife. Note the patch box and double-set triggers.

didn't wait to see what damage he had done, but instead grabbed his powder measure and poured about 80 grains of black powder down the barrel, placed the bullet and patch on the muzzle, tapped it down with the starter rod hanging around his neck, and then taking the ramrod, rammed the bullet down until it stopped. Bringing the rifle to his shoulder, he was ready. The men had split apart and were coming at a gallop, and there was a riderless horse, so he knew he had hit his target. He fired twice more and brought two more down before they finally dismounted and brought their horses to the ground. He quickly reloaded his Hawken, and then pulled out his revolver and fired two quick shots to let them know he was well-armed. He

referred to as a squirrel rifle, to as large as .72 caliber. The plains rifle was usually shorter than the Kentucky rifle. It was rugged, utilitarian, usually of a larger caliber, such as .50 or .54, and designed to be carried on horseback over the saddle during a long day's ride. Although there were many such rifles used on the plains going west, the Hawken just happened to be one of the most famous. You could see all sorts of single-shot muzzleloaders on the frontier, from the 1803 Harper's Ferry rifle, which was the first rifled firearm issued by the U.S. Army, to the more modern Hawken that first appeared in the early 1830's as a flintlock before being built as a percussion rifle. Not only were rifles used on the Western frontier, but there were also

The Browning Hawken rifle in .50 caliber shown with Navy Arms' caps.

Traditions' "Shenadoah" .50 caliber shoots well, and has the typical patch lock and high-blade front sight seen on many Hawkens.

many smooth bores. Indians had them, and many families used them for squirrel and bird hunting. These muzzleloaders, at the time, especially the percussion ones, were what kept families from starving and trappers from being wiped out by the Indians. A muzzleloading rifle in the right hands could put a bear down or pop a squirrel off a tree limb depending upon what you wanted in the pot.

Jacob Hawken and his brother Samuel established themselves in St. Louis in 1820 and began manufacturing rifles shortly thereafter. By the time the plains rifle appeared in the early 1830's, their rifle was quickly becoming famous throughout the West. Kit Carson owned

Shenandoah, the Crockett imported by Traditions, or the Thompson Center Hawken, which you can get as a kit rifle, make excellent plains rifles. Lyman makes an excellent .54 Hawken plains rifle that is authentic and also accurate right out of the box, and the Browning Mountain Rifle is a sight to behold. Original smooth bores, such as the Rabone Brothers & Co. 16-gauge are a little harder to come by, but they are available, and you can usually find them for a reasonable price at a local gun show.

We must remember that metallic cartridge firearms did not appear on the frontier until the 1860 Henry .44 Rimfire appeared, and that

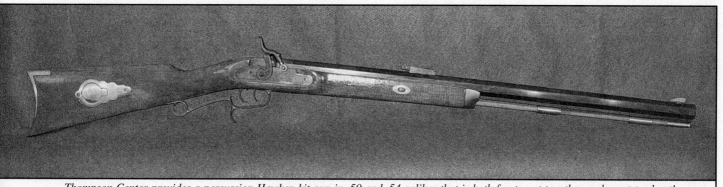

Thompson Center provides a percussion Hawken kit gun in .50 and .54 caliber that is both fun to put together and great to shoot!

one, as did Jim Bridger, James Clyman, William H. Ashley, and Edwin T. Denig of the American Fur Company, as well as many others of the later era of the fur trade and the era of the frontiersman, plainsman, and early Indian scout. Most of these rifles were in .45, .50, and .54 caliber.

A variety of muzzleloaders are available today. Some, such as the modern flintlock Hawken, are custom-made. Others, such as the

didn't really get out West in any significant numbers until the end of the Civil War. So, if you really want to feel what it was like in the 1840's or 1850's, strap on a Patterson Colt .36, a big Walker .44, or grab up a Hawken .50 or .54 and head out to the range for a day of fun.

The side lock of the Hawken Flintlock shown has a pin through the flash hole to ensure that the hole is clean of powder and will ignite when the flint hits the flash pan.

The typical patch box normally seen on the Hawken contains a space for lubricated patches.

Medicine Bill............

"Ace of Scouts"

By: Corby Christensen, aka Rex O'Hurlihan

In 1867, George A. Custer said of Will Comstock, "No Indian knew the country more thoroughly, he was perfectly familiar with every divide, watercourse, and strip of timber for hundreds of miles in either direction. He knew the dress and peculiarities of every Indian tribe and spoke the languages of many of them. Perfect in horsemanship, fearless in manner, a splendid hunter, and a gentleman by instinct, as modest and unassuming as he was brave."

However, Wyatt Earp held a different opinion. Earp said he felt the prevailing ideas of what went on during extermination of the buffalo herds may have been drawn from Buffalo Bill Cody's widely advertised shooting match against Buffalo Bill Comstock for a "doubtful title" and an entirely "mythical championship." According to Wyatt Earp, the contest demonstrated nothing more than the ability to shoot from the back of a running horse and was meaningless to a real buffalo hunter. Of course, Wyatt Earp was a bit innovative in his buffalo hunting techniques as well.

Theodore R. Davis, a reporter and sketch artist for *Harper's Weekly* wrote, "William Comstock, or Medicine Bill as the Indians called him, has lived on the plains for 20 years. He is quiet and unassuming in manner, small in size, and compact in proportion. He is one of the best riders on the plains, with which he is probably more familiar than any other white man who roams over them."

Will, whose full name was William Averill Comstock, was born in 1842 at Comstock, Michigan, a town named for his father. He came from a good and highly-respected family. His father was "General" Horace Hawkins Comstock, and his mother was Sarah Sabrina Cooper, a niece of the famous novelist James Fenimore Cooper. Will was the youngest of four children. His father was the first senator to be elected from Kalamazoo County, Michigan.

Sarah Cooper Comstock, the "General's" first wife, was a distinguished gentlewoman. The Township of Cooper in Kalamazoo County, Michigan, was named for her. After her death in 1846, when Will was four-years-old, the "General" moved to Ostego, and married again.

When the "General's" estate failed, Will went to live with his oldest sister, Sarah Comstock Wakeley, in Wisconsin during 1854-1857. Will apparently had little formal education. He mostly spent his early boyhood with his father, but later was under the guidance of Sarah, his older sister, who was a graduate of Eames School of Kalamazoo, where he received the basis of his book learning.

Most likely, Will's love of adventure, Indian lore, and woodcraft was inspired by the writings of his celebrated great uncle, James Fenimore Cooper. It is at least certain that Will left for the Western plains at an early age. By the time he reached 20 years of age, he had acquired an enviable reputation as a hunter and guide. He served as a Pony Express rider at the same time as Wild Bill Hickok and Bill Cody. He learned several Indian dialects and could follow trail signs with the best of the Indians. Will's prowess with a rifle earned him the title of "Buffalo Bill" while he was a scout at Fort Wallace where he regularly supplied the soldiers with fresh buffalo meat. The title of "Buffalo Bill," which the officers of Fort Wallace had bestowed on Will, had also been used by the officials and workers on the Western extension of the Kansas Pacific Railroad along the Smoky Hill River to designate their hunter, William F. Cody. The Goddard Brothers had contracted to feed the railroad laborers and had hired Cody to hunt buffalo for them. Somehow discussion arose as to who was the original "Buffalo Bill." It was finally decided that a purse of $500 should be raised and a hunting contest staged between Comstock and Cody to settle the dispute. And so it was that one of the most spectacular contests ever staged on this continent took place.

Cody, who had been hunting buffalo steadily for months, had his horse trained to a hair, and the animal had been kept in daily practice. Will's mount was a good buffalo horse, but one not used so systematically. Both men were excellent shots. Cody used his favorite .50 caliber Sharps for the hunt, and Comstock used a Henry's rifle. The hunt was to run for the period of one day from sunrise to sunset. The start saw both men galloping into a herd of buffalo blazing away with their rifles. The final tally at the end of the kill was Comstock, 48; Cody, 69. Cody won the purse and became officially the only "Buffalo Bill." Afterward, Cody remarked that Comstock's choice of the Henry's rifle caused him to lose the day. Cody was convinced the heavier .50 caliber slugs of his Sharps gave him the advantage.

Despite his defeat, many of the plainsmen considered Will Comstock the better man. Charles E. Chase's published comment attests to that feeling: "Bill Comstock could take Buffalo Bill out at night and lose him. Cody was a good man, but Comstock — and I am not alone in this — was a better man." Chase knew both men intimately and was well qualified to judge.

His knowledge of the Indian languages made him invaluable as an interpreter in the numerous councils and conferences held by the army officers and Indian chiefs. In one conference between Colonel G.A. Custer and Pawnee Killer, he interpreted the attempt by Custer to cajole the Indians back to the vicinity of Fort Wallace. Gifts of coffee and sugar were made, but Pawnee Killer wanted ammunition, which Custer denied. The parley ended on a congenial note with Pawnee Killer's promise to be good. This was just prior to Pawnee Killer's attack on a military supply train.

By the time Will was 26-years-old, he was Chief of Scouts and Interpreter at Fort Wallace. He was a favorite scout of General Custer, and was nationally known as the "Ace of Scouts."

In 1867 while scouting for Custer, Will found himself guiding a military wagon train to and from Fort Wallace. The train was under the command of Colonel Cook and Lieutenant Robbins. The initial march was made from Beaver Creek, and the only incident worthy of remark was an observation of Will's that proved how thoroughly familiar he was with Indian strategies. Will said the red men would not waste time by attacking an empty wagon train, but rather would wait for it to take on supplies, then hit it on the return trip. He said, "If the Injuns strike us at all, it will be about the time we are comin' along back over this very spot. Now mind what I tell ye all."

The train and escort were moving over a level plateau, which to the unpracticed eye seemed to not recess or obstruct the visibility or concealment of an enemy. Everything appeared to be in open view. Yet such was not the case. Ravines ran along the open ridges and, though not perceptible at a glance, were visible if looked for. Comstock's keen eyes took in all at a glance, and he recognized the threat these timberless

Corby Christensen

ravines posed as a point of ambush for marauding Indians.

On the return trip, Will, who was always on the alert, spotted the heads of Indians peeking out of the ravines. He brought their presence to the attention of the officers. When the Indians realized their cover had been blown, they rode down on the wagon train. Approximately 600 warriors mounted on ponies and armed with carbines defiled down the slope towards the soldiers. Comstock and the officers were able to estimate roughly the full strength of the party and were able to set up a line of defense against what seemed to be a hopeless situation. The terrain was ideal for the Indian mode of warfare, and the best defense the soldiers could mount

was on foot. Colonel Cook took one flank and Lieutenant Robbins the other. Comstock, who remained mounted, galloped from point to point wherever his presence was most needed.

On came the Indians, filling the air with war cries. They attempted to stampede the horses and draught animals of the train, and then in the excitement that followed, they planned to massacre the escort and drivers. The wagonmaster was ordered to keep the train moving in a column of twos and up close to the defenders. The last injunction was hardly necessary, as the frightened teamsters, glancing at the approaching warriors and hearing their savage shouts, were sufficiently anxious to keep closed up.

The Indians made several rushes at the moving wagon train. Each attack was met with a well-delivered volley of rifle fire from the soldiers. At one point, the Indians withdrew being unable to scatter the train's animals. The soldiers cheered, and Comstock taunted the retreating Indians in their own language. The Indians withdrew to a point just beyond the soldier's rifle range and parleyed. Comstock was overheard saying, "There's no such good luck for us to think them Injuns mean to give it up. Six hundred red devils ain't agoin' to let 50 men stop them from gettin' at the coffee and sugar that is in these wagons. And they ain't agoin' to be satisfied until they get some of our scalps to pay for the bucks we popped out of their saddles a bit ago."

Comstock was correct. The Indians were not about to give up their attack on the train. They did, however, change the style of their attack from one of mass frontal assault to what has to become a standard of Western Indian raids on wagon trains. The warriors, mounted on ponies, began circling the moving wagon train, and individual warriors made closer circles and delivered rifle fire into the train and its defenders. This mode of attack continued relentlessly for three hours. Just as the soldier's ammunition reserves were beginning to wane, the column was relieved by Colonel West and a detachment of cavalry. The Indians made a hasty retreat, and Colonel Cook, along with Comstock, rode out to meet their comrades. Later, Comstock

commented that it was a "near run thing."

Being a man of few words with an even disposition, Will was safeguarded against the sort of shooting affairs so common on the frontier in his day. Even more of a protection was his reputation for being lightning quick on the draw and deadly accurate with a revolver. Certainly, on one occasion, this reputation was proven to be well-founded.

A contractor by the name of Weightman agreed to pay Will a certain sum of money if he were shown the locations where sufficient wood could be cut to fulfill a contract. Will led him to the locations, one of which was Big Timbers, about 40 miles from the Post. Several hundred cords of wood were cut and delivered, but the contractor failed to make good on his promise to Will. Weightman had frequently boasted that he was a member of the Quadrille Guerillas, which sacked Lawrence, Kansas on August 21, 1863, and he posed generally as a "bad man." Such actions had aroused strong feelings against Weightman, and apparently Will decided that the time had come for him to call Weightman out.

The Post trader received word from his friend, Will, that on the following morning he would bring a "black-tail" for his dinner. Will frequently brought in game, so the trader supposed that he would be given a black-tail deer the next day. It seems, however, that Will intended to warn him in this cryptic way that trouble was brewing.

Will timed it the next morning so that he and the "bad man" met on the porch of the trader's store. Charles Chase claimed to be an eyewitness and later reported, "Comstock got Weightman in the store and both started to draw at the same time... Comstock fired four shots before Weightman ever pulled the trigger. When they turned Weightman over, every one of Comstock's shots had hit in his heart and the four holes could have been covered with a silver dollar."

The Commander of the Post had Will arrested and turned over to the civil authorities at Fort Hays, Kansas, for trial. When arraigned before the court, and asked by Judge M.S. Joyce how he would plead, Will answered, "Guiltily, sir." The Judge asked him if he did not wish to alter his plea. The scout replied, "No, sir." The Judge immediately exclaimed, "Ye are a damned fool for tellin' it. I discharge ye for want of evidence."

In August of 1868, while encamped not far from Big Spring Station in Kansas, Comstock and Abner T. "Sharp" Grover paid a visit to the nearby Indian village of Turkey Leg. Part of Comstock's visit was to inquire if any of the Cheyennes had taken part in the murderous raid in the Saline Valley.

Comstock and Grover spent a couple of hours in friendly conversation with Turkey Leg and several of his warriors. Will always carried in his belt a beautiful ivory-handled Colt's revolver. During his visit with the Indians, several of the young braves endeavored to barter with Will for possession of the pistol. Some excitement and consternation came of Will's desire not to part with his revolver.

Some months before, when riding together at the head of a column in pursuit of Indians, Comstock, who had observed that he and Custer carried similar revolvers, remarked that the General ought to have the pair and laughingly added that he would carry his until they found the Indians, and after giving them a sound whipping, he would present the Colt's to Custer. After hunting Indians all summer, but never finding them, Comstock frequently joked that if he had to wait until the Indians were found and whipped before making his gift to the General, he might be forced to go armed for a long time. Custer later recounted, "None of us imagined that the revolver, which was so often the subject of jest and of which Comstock was so proud, would be the pretext of his massacre."

Comstock and Grover made their departure from Turkey Leg's camp under escort of the chief's son and several other warriors who professed the deepest friendship for them. As recounted by "Sharp" Grover, when they were a short distance on their way, several other Indians joined with the scout's party. The escort left, but the new arrivals continued to ride on with the scouts. Two of the braves dropped back and began firing their rifles. Comstock was instantly killed, and Grover was shot through the back and left lung. The attack seemed centered on Comstock, and Grover, though seriously wounded, was able to make good his escape.

General Bankhead sent out a detachment to bring the body of Will Comstock into the Post. Comstock was buried at Fort Wallace in the northeast corner of the Post Cemetery. Will's prized Colt revolver was not found. Will Comstock's body still lies there, so far as we know, in a grave unmarked and unhonored. He met his death on August 27, 1868, in his 26th year. For the winning of the West, in such a short span of time, few men did more.

The author of this article is a descendant of Will Comstock. Recommended reading and resource material used in preparing this article comes from *The Comstock Family History*, *My Life on the Plains* by G.A. Custer, *Wyatt Earp Frontier Marshal* by Stuart Lake, *Custer and Crazy Horse* by Stephen E. Ambrose, *The Custer Album* by Lawrence A. Frost, *Buffalo Days* by Col. Homer W. Wheeler, and *Buffalo Bill's Wild West* by R. Wilson.

Black Powder and the Old West
Chapter 5

Shoots and Tips

Black Powder Cartridge

By: Kenny Durham,
aka KID Durham

Author Kenny Durham shooting his custom Stevens 44-1/2 in .40-65 caliber.

Rifle Silhouette Shooting

The sport of "Siluetas Metalicas," or Metallic Silhouette, shooting has been around for many years now. Originating in Mexico, the game of shooting metal cut-outs of animals in the shape of gallinas (chickens), javelinas (pigs), guajalotes (turkeys), and borregos (rams) with high-powered hunting rifles was brought to the southwest regions of the United States. The sport caught on rapidly in the 1970's, and has since spawned many variations of the game to include 15 different categories for rifles and several categories for handguns. Rifle silhouettes include everything from air rifles to military semi-automatic. But the fastest growing of all the rifle silhouette shooting, and the most fun, is the Black Powder Cartridge Rifle category. Black powder cartridge rifle silhouette is shot at the same range distances and targets as high-power rifle silhouettes, but that is where the similarities end.

This sport is to single-shot black powder cartridge rifle shooters what cowboy action shooting is to sixgun and lever-

Participants in the 2002 Montana BPCRS Championships firing at turkeys and rams. Shooters in the foreground (front to back) are Ron Long of Ballard Rifle Co., writer Mike Venturino, and Jim Gier of Montana Vintage Arms.

action rifle shooters. Black Powder Cartridge Rifle Silhouette, or BPCRS, became a bona fide NRA silhouette competition in 1985 when the first BPCRS National Championships were held at the NRA Whittington Center near Raton, New Mexico. The rifles used in BPCRS are the big single-shot cartridge rifles of the buffalo hunting and long-range target shooting eras of the late 1800's. With this sport, single-shot rifles, including Sharps, Remington, Ballard, Winchester, Springfield, Stevens, and a few others, have been brought back to life in such a manner to ensure that they will be in use for decades to come.

A Life-Size Shooting Gallery

As a kid growing up, do you ever remember going to the county fair and shooting at targets, moving and stationary, in a .22 shooting gallery? To me, that is exactly what BPCRS is like, only on a life-size scale and shot with big rifles having a big "BOOM." The targets are life-size steel cut-outs of chickens, pigs, turkeys, and rams, and

Chickens, shot off-hand at 200 meters, are the most difficult targets to hit.

the distances at which the targets are fired are 200 meters, 300 meters, 385 meters, and 500 meters respectively. To score in this sport, the target must not only be hit, but must topple off its feet, too. Consider that when shooting at the 500-meter rams, it takes the bullet about 1-1/2 seconds to get to the target. The shooter has time to make a clean shot, eject the spent case, and watch the target fall over. By the time the resounding "CLANK" is heard, three seconds have elapsed. That is what makes this game so much fun.

While the 500-meter rams make for carefully-aimed, long-range shots, the 200-meter chickens are a stark contrast in shooting, requiring the steady hold and trigger squeeze of a Schuetzen shooter. A life-size chicken over two football fields away is a small target at which to shoot off-hand. However, it is every bit as satisfying, and more so, to send a chicken spinning into the dirt as it is watching a ram tip over slowly from a dead-center hit. The pigs at 300 meters are the easiest targets to

Typical BPCRS rifles commonly used: (top to bottom) Stevens 44-1/2, 1874 Sharps, Ballard, 1875 Sharps, and 1885 Winchester/Browning.

hit, and the easiest to take for granted, too! They are not hard to hit, but they sure are easy to miss! Turkeys (385 meters), in degree of difficulty, are second to the chickens. The shape of the turkey body presents the most circular form of the animal targets, but leaves little room for error in windage. Pigs and rams are a study in elevation, having a lot more area for errors in adjusting the windage, but it is not so with turkeys. Errors in calculating the wind with turkeys result in shots to the right and left of the target. And, with turkeys, there's not a whole lot of room for mistakes shooting high or low either. Many are the times that I have lucked out by getting a hit in the leg or neck of a turkey

when the shot was, in reality, too low or too high.

Just to throw in another item with which to contend, BPCRS is a timed event. The relay starts by the shooters being called to the line, and when in place, given a 30-second "READY" command to load their rifles and prepare to shoot. When the 30 seconds have expired, the "FIRE" command is given and the relay has seven minutes in which to fire sighting shots on stationary targets and five record shots for score. Once the shooter is finished sighting in and begins shooting for record, they cannot return to the sighting target. The record targets are shot left-to-right in sequence, hit or miss. Out-of-order hits count as misses.

When time has expired, a "CEASE FIRE" command is given. The line is made safe and the targets reset. The relay is returned to the firing line with another 30-second "READY," followed by five minutes for five record shots. Sighting shots are allowed only on the first bank of targets, and relays may be 10-shot or 15-shot, depending on whether the match is a 40-shot or 60-shot event.

Single-Shot Black Powder Cartridge Rifles for Silhouette

The rifles approved for use in BPCRS are single-shot hunting or military-style rifles originally made for black powder cartridges. The design has to have been one manufactured in the United States prior to 1896, typical of the era, and must have an exposed hammer. Rifles may be originals or reproductions, with a maximum weight limit of 12 lb. 2 oz. The NRA rules specify 20 different designs that were manufactured in the late 1800's, plus an additional six models that either came along

Pigs at 300 meters are the easiest targets to hit, as seen by the five-in-a-row hits scored on these.

after the turn of the century, such as the Stevens 44-1/2 , or those developed in recent years but having roots that reach back into the 1800's, such as the Browning models B78 and 1885, and the Sharps Model 1875, which was built only as a prototype.

Of the original designs, the Model 1874 Sharps and the Winchester 1885 "Highwall" are the most popular. Following these two are the Remington Rolling Block and the Ballard rifles. In smaller numbers, the Sharps 1875 and 1877 models, Remington Hepburn, Stevens 44-1/2, and the Springfield "Trapdoor" pretty much fill out the list. The Browning "Highwall" version of the late 1900's, when combined with the number of original Winchester Highwalls and other Highwall reproductions in use, comprise the biggest percentage of action type in use. Most of the 1874 Sharps models are of new manufacture. Interestingly, the original rifle actions that are in use, are mostly Winchester Highwall, Remington Rolling Block, Remington Hepburn, and Springfield Trapdoor. When referring to original rifles, I used the term "original action" because very few complete original rifles, other than military, are used in BPCRS. The reasons are that, in many cases, the more than 100-year-old barrels, through use or neglect, are no longer capable of the accuracy that silhouette shooting

Four of the most popular silhouette cartridges (left to right): .38-55, .40-65, .45-70, and .45-90.

requires. Also, the rates of twists in some of the calibers being used are too slow to stabilize the long heavy bullets needed for accurate shooting out to 500 meters. Therefore, most BPCRS rifles are of entirely new manufacture or built using an original action as the foundation.

The list of U.S. companies building rifle models of the late 1800's are: Shiloh Rifle Manufacturing Co., makers of 1874 Sharps pattern rifles; Axtell Rifle Company, maker of 1877 Sharps pattern rifles; Ballard Rifle Company, makers of Ballard and 1885 Winchester pattern rifles; CPA Corporation, makers of Stevens 44-1/2 rifles; C. Sharps Arms Co., makers of 1874

and 1875 Sharps and 1885 Winchester pattern rifles; Lone Star Rifle Co., maker of Remington Rolling Block pattern rifles; D Z Arms, makers of Remington Hepburn pattern rifles; and Meacham Tool & Hardware Co., makers of 1885 Winchester pattern rifles.

In addition, U.S. Companies such as Navy Arms, Dixie Gun Works, and Cimarron Arms import 1874 Sharps, Remington Rolling Block, and Winchester Highwall pattern rifles manufactured by Davide Pedersoli & Co. and Aldo Uberti Co. If these sources aren't enough, there are gunsmiths and custom rifle builders operating small gun shops scattered throughout the country who build complete rifles from scratch or on original actions. What this all means, and this is where I get excited, is that you can purchase, or have built, virtually ANY design or model of rifle from the late 1800's!

Rifle Configurations and Calibers for Silhouette Shooting

The "standard" rifle configured for BPCRS shooting has a 30" heavy barrel and a butt stock with little or no drop in the comb to minimize recoil. The buttplate may be of the crescent-style, but the shotgun-style butt is preferred, especially with the heavy recoil of the big ".45s." The stock may also have a cheek piece as long as it is not a roll-over style. There are also limitations on the dimensions of the stocks to maintain a "hunting" or "target" style of rifle. Special "off-hand" and Schuetzen-style rifles are not permitted. Barrel lengths vary from 28 to 32 inches; but barrels shorter or longer than this are either too lightweight for good off-hand "chicken" shooting (short barrel) or exceed the weight limit (long barrel). Another feature that we find on the majority of BPCRS rifles is a "set" trigger that allows the trigger to be adjusted to only a few ounces.

When it comes to choices of calibers for BPCRS, the variety

At 500 meters, rams are the long-range aspect of BPCRS.

Alex Huston of Boring, Oregon shooting silhouettes from the classic prone cross-stick position.

available should please anyone. From the light recoil of the .38-55 Ballard/Winchester cartridge to the thunder of the .50-90 "Big 50" Sharps, we have an excess of 25 or more cartridges to choose from that meet the requirements of being a U.S. black powder cartridge. Some of these were "hunting" cartridges, while others were developed as "target" cartridges. The most popular cartridge is the .45-70 Government, which is the standard by which all black powder cartridges are compared. The .45 x 2.4" (.45-90) and the .45 x 2.6" (.45-100) are fairly common, too, but produce more recoil. However, the National Championship has been won with both of these cartridges. The .45-70 is also, without a doubt, the easiest black powder cartridge to load, especially for someone just getting started, and brass and dies are stock items at any store selling reloading equipment.

The second most-used cartridge is the .40-65 Winchester, which is a .45-70 case necked down to .40 caliber. This cartridge was originally chambered for the 1886 Winchester lever-action rifle and loaded with a 250-gr. bullet. With the passing of the black powder era, the .40-65 became obsolete and little known among shooters. However, the sport of BPCRS and the desire for a .40 caliber cartridge that provided sufficient "knock-down" energy, but having milder recoil than the .45-70, brought the

Shooter Steve Morris of Glenoma, Washington is shooting off-hand at a chicken. His stance and hold are excellent examples to follow.

.40-65 back to life. Add to these features that the .40-65 is easily formed from .45-70 brass, and we have a cartridge that is ideally suited to this game. In fact, so much so that new correctly head-stamped .40-65 brass is being produced by Starline, thereby making case forming optional rather than a necessity. The one change to the .40-65 from the old days is for silhouette shooting; the 250-grain lever-action bullet has been replaced with bullets weighing up to 420 grains.

Another less popular, but very accurate, .40 caliber cartridge is the .40-70 Sharps Straight (.40-70 SS). Unfortunately, this cartridge suffers from the limited availability of brass and, to a certain extent, dimension variations of chambers and loading dies between manufacturers, which can give a beginner fits. The .40-70 SS is an excellent cartridge, but I would advise beginners to get some experience under their belts with loading and shooting the .40-65 or .45-70 before tackling the .40-70 SS. There are other historical .40 caliber cartridges, too, both more and less powerful than the .40-70 SS, but none of them are as easily mastered as the .40-65 Winchester.

The .38-55 has gained a considerable following in the last

A typical Black Powder Cartridge Rifle Silhouette range is like a life-size shooting gallery.

two years as a capable BPCRS cartridge. The advent of Swiss black powder and bullets designed for long-range shooting in the .38-55 has many shooters taking a hard look at this cartridge. In the early days of BPCRS, the .38-55 was considered to lack the "knock-down" power required to topple the 500-meter rams. Not anymore! Of course, there have been instances where a ram did not go down, but my wife shooting her CPA Stevens 44-1/2 in .38-55 has yet to leave a "hit" ram standing in two years of shooting. The Lyman 330-grain bullet doesn't slam the rams into the dirt, but they slowly crash to the ground, dead just the same. When spotting for her, I have learned to watch the rams VERY carefully before lamenting, "I didn't see any hit, you missed," only to look back through the scope and find the ram lying on the ground. While spotting for her during her second BPCRS match, I saw the bullet strike the dirt just under the throat area of a ram and immediately stuck a pin in the spotting board to show where she missed. "But it fell down," she lamented, "Doesn't that count?" In amazement, I looked again, and, sure enough, the ram was gone. When the target was reset, I could see where the bullet had struck in the "V" of the throat.

Due to the light recoil, the .38-55 is an ideal cartridge for junior shooters and women. Lighter bullets producing little recoil can be used for all distances to start with. Then, when the lady or youngster is ready, heavier bullets and powder charges can be

Montana shooter Bruce Garbe competing in the scope class in the National Championships at Raton, NM.

used. Who cares if an occasional target remains standing from lack of energy with a light bullet. It is far more important for beginners to learn the fundamentals and enjoy the process than to immediately begin to develop a fear that they are going to get slammed from the recoil of the rifle.

Earlier, I mentioned the .45-90 and .45-100 as cartridges for BPCRS. A few of the top shooters in the country use these cartridges, and do very well with them. Some consider the .45-90 to be inherently more accurate than the .45-70. I have rifles in both calibers and they all shoot equally well. Incidentally, I have shot my two highest scores (both the same) using a .40-65 and a .45-90, so take your pick. The .45 cartridges, longer than the 2.4-inch .45-90, are more powerful than needed for BPCRS and better suited for long-range target shooting or hunting.

Black Powder Cartridge Rifle Silhouette Ammunition

The BPCRS rules require that ammunition must be loaded with black powder or Pyrodex using lead bullets without metal gas checks. As of this writing, no black powder substitutes other than Pyrodex are allowed. Therefore, ammunition for BPCRS is pretty much a hand-loading proposition. There are a few sources for commercial or custom-loaded black powder cartridges, but the price is not cheap. The one component that is becoming much more available is cast or swaged bullets from commercial sources. However, the vast majority of BPCRS shooters still cast their own bullets. Another attribute of BPCRS ammunition requires that it be "target" or "match" quality, and that it must be capable of producing 1-1/2 minute-of-angle (MOA) 10-shot groups, which is 3 inches at 200 yards. For

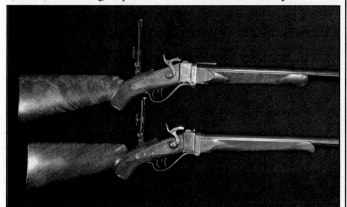

Two fine 1877 Sharps pattern rifles from the Classic Rifle Company in Bend, Oregon.

example, the mid-section of the 500-meter ram measures a mere two MOA from the belly line to the top of the back, leaving little room for error. This degree of accuracy requires that ammo must be tailored for the rifle in which it will be fired. Ammo such as this can seldom be produced in a factory. The loading procedures involve more details than this overview of the sport covers and have been detailed elsewhere in this book. (Check out *Loading Black Powder Cartridges for Single-Shot Rifles* in the *Ammunition, Reloading, & Cleaning* chapter.)

A Comfortable Mat, Cross-Sticks, Blow Tube, and a Good Spotter

The 200-meter chickens are the only targets required to be shot off-hand in BPCRS. The other three distances are shot from a resting position using wooden cross-sticks to support the rifle. Cross-sticks aren't a requirement, but all shooters use them since most shoot from a prone position. But, I have seen some sitting on the ground, or sitting on a stool, using cross-sticks, too. When shooting prone, it is nice to lay down on a comfortable pad or shooting mat. Shooting mats consist of everything imaginable, including store-bought mats, scraps of carpet, canvas-covered foam pads, Indian blankets, and buffalo robes.

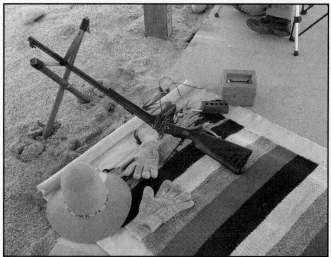

Notice that the cross-sticks are equipped with a leather strap on which to cradle the rifle versus resting the rifle in the "V" of the sticks.

Cross-sticks are another source of self-expression for the shooter, too. They must be made of wood and either be tied or bolted together so that they hinge and pivot. Metal spikes are allowed to facilitate sticking the cross-sticks into the ground. The NRA rule book lists the specifications and allowable dimensions for cross-sticks. As long as the rules are adhered to, cross-sticks may range all the way from long, slender, leather-wrapped sticks tipped with antler tines for decoration, to utilitarian 1" x 2" hardwood boards with a piece of felt lining the "V" on which to rest the rifle. Some designs utilize a leather strap that spans the upper ends of the cross-sticks, which provides a cradle on which to support the rifle without it actually contacting the sticks. Supposedly, this method helps to dampen the effects of barrel vibration.

Another item required is a blow tube, or blow pipe as some call it. The purpose of the blow tube is to facilitate getting some moisture from one's breath into the bore between shots to soften the black powder fouling. Fouling that becomes hard and dry will degrade accuracy very quickly. Blowing between shots also

A life-size chicken at 200 meters presents a small target and often escapes without "bullet splash" anywhere on its body.

A good "center hit." Pigs have a bit of room for error left and right, but little room for error in elevation.

helps to cool the bore slightly, which can be critical in hot, dry conditions. Anywhere from three to ten or more breaths of air blown gently through the bore are required depending upon conditions. Most blow tubes are constructed from a cartridge case fitted with copper or plastic tubing. Traditional ones are copper, but plastic is cheaper and easier to manipulate. By using a blow tube constructed from a cartridge case and inserted into the chamber when blowing, we can keep the chamber dry while moistening the bore.

BPCRS is also unique in that it is a team effort between the shooter and a spotter. The spotter, or coach, usually takes on the responsibility of monitoring the shooting conditions, giving sight adjustments to the shooter, and reporting where the bullet strikes, be it a hit or a miss. Without a spotter peering through a telescope, it is very difficult for the shooter to see where the bullets are striking. Add to this changing light conditions, heat waves (mirage), and changing winds that can move a bullet four or five feet one way or the other, and the importance of the spotter becomes readily apparent. Most of the time, shooters switch off spotting for each other and develop a close-knit team that knows that shooting habits and capabilities of each other. Just as the saying goes, "behind every good man is a good woman," one can say that "behind every good BPCRS shooter is a good spotter." In my case, it is often one-in-the same, because my wife, Sherri, spots for me much of the time. As a matter of fact, the individual spotting for the winner of any BPCRS match usually deserves as much credit as the shooter for anchoring the win.

Other Variations of BPCRS

In addition to the standard BPCRS format, there is a "scope" class that allows period scopes of the late 1800's to be used on black powder cartridge rifles. Several companies are producing scopes and mounts that are reproductions of, or patterned after, original scopes. One of the drawbacks of the original scope mounts is that they are not designed to be quickly adjusted for changing conditions. However, the NRA Silhouette committee recognized that strict adherence to traditional mounts was limiting participation in the scope class and served no useful purpose. In 2001, the rules concerning scope mounts were modified by approving scope-mount designs that allow for easier and more precise adjustment, but maintain a definite late 1800's-style and appearance.

Another variation of BPCRS deals with the military rifles of the black powder cartridge era. Probably the most widely-used rifles are the Springfield Trapdoor and the Remington Rolling Block. The rifles must be as originally equipped, and the service sights must be used. One might think that with using a military rifle, the scores would be way down, but that is not the case. In the hands of a good marksman, an 1884 Springfield equipped with a Buffington sight and carefully-crafted ammunition makes for formidable competition.

For more information on rules and to get a listing of matches in your area, contact the NRA Silhouette Division.

BPCRS is a shooting game unlike any other. If you enjoy the single-shot rifles of the late 1800's, long-range shooting, and black powder, then Black Powder Cartridge Rifle Silhouette shooting is a game for you! See ya at the range!

One more "half-minute" right and this hit would have missed, but ANY hit on a turkey is a good one.

This shot is about as good as it gets. Notice how easy one could slip a bullet under the belly or over the back. It is a truly unlucky shooter that puts a bullet through the hole in the horn, but I've seen it happen.

The black powder sixgunner, be it with percussion or cartridge-firing sixguns, has a myriad of choices when it comes to choosing the leather that will be used. Whether that choice be truly authentic period leather, or "B" Western movie-style, there are many skilled craftsmen waiting to serve the needs of black powder shooters, history enthusiasts, or western movie buffs.

Holsters arrived much later than firearms. Single-shot pistols were most often stuck in the waistband or belt, as were the first Colt revolvers on the Paterson platform. Early Walker and Dragoon sixguns were normally carried by the horse with the use of a pommel holster placed over the saddle horn with the pistols hanging on each side of the saddle in front of the rider. With the coming of the very portable 1851 Navy, it soon became

draw holster of the 1850's.

In the 1870's, a new holster design appeared - the Mexican Loop. This is basically the Slim Jim fitted with a full backflap or skirt that was then slotted to accept the pouch that formed the holster body. The entire holster and backflap were made of one piece of heavy leather, with the folding over of the backflap and the insertion of the holster into the loops forming a natural belt loop. This style of holster was carried on a wide cartridge belt holding sixgun cartridges, lever gun cartridges, or both.

The Mexican Loop was extremely popular, as pictures from the last quarter of the 19th century show. Crafted by many artisans in leather, such a E. L. Gallatin and F.A. Meanea of the Wyoming Territory, the Moran Brothers of Montana, and S.D.

Original Gun Leather of the Old West

By: John Taffin, aka Sixgunner

Available Today

apparent that a sixgun could very easily be carried on the person in the proper leather. Early on, the U.S. Army went to the protection and security offered by the full flap holster, with both Artillery and Cavalry units wearing their military-issue revolvers butt to the front and high about the waist. When returning to civilian life, many soldiers cut away all the excess leather giving quicker access to their sixguns.

By the 1850's, saddle makers across the country were offering custom leather to sixgunners. The first leather to allow a relatively quick draw was the California Pattern or Slim Jim style of holster. This type of sheath featured an open top, and was provided either with full coverage of the trigger guard or cut away in the trigger-guard area. The Slim Jim was the fast-

Myres of El Paso, Texas, the Mexican Loop provided security with relatively fast and easy access to the sixgun. As more and more men began to live in towns, gunleather changed from that worn on a wide cartridge belt to concealment style, with the shoulder holster being very popular whether offered as a pouch style that hung straight down under the armpit of the off side or the Skeleton Pattern that was a simple design with full backflap utilizing a leather-covered spring clip around the cylinder, mated with a small leather toe to accept the end of the barrel.

Early Western movies used truly authentic leather - the Mexican Loop and the Slim Jim. However, that soon began to change as the Drop Loop holsters began to appear on such stars as Tim McCoy, Tom Mix, Roy Rogers, and Hoppy. This type,

Black Hills Leather double rig for S&W Model #3 Russians - one S&W is an original, circa 1874, while the other is a Navy Arms replica.

A shoulder rig for a 4-3/4" Colt SAA by Cheyenne Custom Cowboy.

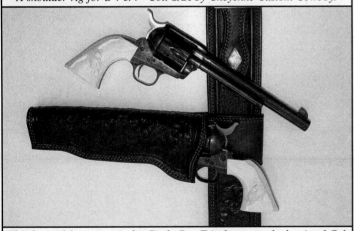

This beautiful custom rig by Circle Bar T is for a matched pair of Colt Single Actions with ivory grips.

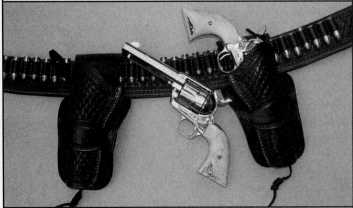

A double rig custom-crafted by Walt Ostin of Custom Gun Leather.

also known as The Buscadero, is made by threading the backflap of the Mexican Loop holster through a slot in the belt before the holster body is placed in the loops cut into the backflap, or through a separate loop riveted to the holster skirt. Hollywood may have gotten away from true traditional sixgun leather in the 1920's and 1930's, but movies, such as *Tombstone*, *Last Stand at Sabre River*, *The Rough Riders*, and *Crossfire Trail*, have started the trend back to truly authentic holsters and sixguns on the screen, as did the cable TV series *Bordertown*.

A whole book could be written just on leather. In fact, one excellent book, *Packing Iron* by Richard Rattenbury, has been written. The best we can do in these few short pages is to highlight several makers with a few sentences and some pictures, knowing full well that a picture is truly worth a thousand words.

BLACK HILLS LEATHER: Rudy Lozano of Black Hills Leather is well-known for producing quality 19th century style leather. When Navy Arms introduced the S&W New Model .44 Russian, around the same time that Smith & Wesson came forth with the .45 Schofield Model 2000, Rudy turned out a most beautiful outfit with a fully-lined cartridge belt and twin holsters, one right-hand and one left-hand, both made to hang straight. The holsters are of the Mexican-style with two loops around the holster body, a full backflap, and are also fully-lined. Both holsters and the cartridge belt are finished with a double-border stamp and then dyed black - a beautiful outfit. Black Hills Leather has a full line of traditional leather to fit all single-action sixguns.

CIRCLE BAR T LEATHER WORKS: Bart Ballew turns out quality sixgun leather from the hills of Missouri. Circle Bar T individually custom crafts each rig for every customer. I recently had Bart build a combination traditional/Western movie style rig pattern after that worn by Gary Cooper in *The Plainsmen*. As Wild Bill Hickok, Cooper carried a pair of sixguns in Slim Jim style holsters with long shanks to hang low with the butt to the front. Cooper's were sharply angled with the muzzle to the rear. However, I had mine made to hang low, but straight, so they can easily be worn with the butt to the front, or the butt to the rear. Ballew did his best work on this rig, with special carving and a custom belt buckle. Bart makes beautiful, traditional-styled leather and can probably fulfill whatever you may desire.

CUSTOM GUN LEATHER: Rawhide Walt Ostin of Custom Gun Leather not only offers top quality leather, but also a very large variation of traditional holsters and belts patterned after those from the 19th century. Walt's leather is of three types: Old West, B Western, or TV Cowboy. For the black powder shooter who wishes to stay with the old tried-and-true designs, Custom Gun Leather provides the Frontier shoulder holster, a Skeleton pattern; and the California Pattern or Slim Jim holster, including a lower-riding, straight-drop version known as the Gunfighter Slim Jim. Variations of the Mexican Loop style of holster include the Cheyenne, the Russell, the Montana, the Kansas, the Utah, the Colorado, the Texas, and Ostin also offers his version of the John Wayne rig complete with a folded-over cartridge/money belt.

EL PASO SADDLERY: Bobby McNellis of El Paso Saddlery heads up a leather crafting tradition of more than 100 years, going back to designs originally brought forth by Tio Sam Myres. A look at the old S.D. Myres catalog will reveal that El Paso holds many leather patterns from the shop that often hosted some of the best of the Old West gunmen. In the authentic 19th century style, El Paso offers a wide range of leather goods, including saddlebags and pommel bags with one or two holsters incorporated under the flap.

Cartridge belts can be single-weight leather, fully-lined, or of the folded-over cartridge and money belt style. Rifle scabbards and Sharp's cartridge boxes also add authenticity to cowboy action shooting costuming.

El Paso's shoulder holsters include the Tombstone Speed Rig, a spring clip skeleton style; the 1879 Texas, with a straight hanging pouch under the armpit; and the 1895 Hardin, copied from the shoulder rig worn by John Wesley Hardin and made in the El Paso leather shop in 1895. For belt wear, there is the 1849 Californian, originally made for percussion sixguns; the 1870 Slim Jim; the 1880 Mexican Loop; and the 1880-S, with more leather cut away from the trigger guard and hammer for a smoother draw. The 1890 and 1890-S are also of the Mexican Loop style with one loop riveted to the backflap and a slight forward cant to the muzzle, while the 1897 Sweetwater is a Mexican style holster with a single loop both around the holster body and also under the toe of the holster. For those that combine military history with black powder shooting, El Paso offers the full-flap 1860 holster and the half-flap 1880 U.S. Cavalry holster, plus matching military belts of leather with a wide range of buckle designs, or the canvas-style made to take rifle or sixgun cartridges.

WILL GHORMLEY: Will Ghormley specializes in authentic designs. His Pistolero rig, which covers the trigger guard and hammer, is carved in the old-time incised style that was found on frontier leather of the mid-19th century; the West Texas features a half backflap and the hammer and trigger guard are slightly exposed; and the Adobe has a backflap, a holster loop, a fully-enclosed trigger guard, and an almost fully-covered hammer. His custom Cheyenne rig is lined with red leather, and the holster itself is of the Mexican style with two holster loops, and fully-carved with a darkly-dyed background. The matching cartridge belt also features leather rosettes with a red background and nickel spots, making it a great rig for a special single-action sixgun. Ghormley also offers saddlebags and pommel bags complete with built-in holsters, saddle scabbards, and all manners of cartridge belts, cartridge pouches, spur straps, and wrist cuffs. Ghormley is more than an artist in sixgun and levergun leather, he also crafts authentic old-time saddles and carved leather paintings of Old West characters and scenes.

GREASEWOOD: Dudley Lewis turns out classic old-style sixgun holsters and matching belts, either of heavy-weight single leather or lined, for all models of single-action sixguns. One of my favorite rigs is from Greasewood and consists of a matched pair of straight-drop Mexican Loop holsters for 7-1/2" Colt Single Actions. The holsters of single-weight leather are fully-carved with a large rose, and then filled out with rose petals and vines, all with a stippled background. The holster skirt is plain, except for two border lines around the edge and one line around each loop. The belt itself is of the cartridge and money belt style made from Wickett and Craig heavy-chap leather, making it very strong but pliable enough to be comfortable as it conforms to the body. With a full row of cartridges and two heavy sixguns, the rig rides high and comfortable. This particular rig is finished in an antique-looking, dark-brown finish that adds to the mellowness of the leather itself. Greasewood can supply belts and holsters for all single-action sixguns.

KIRKPATRICK LEATHER: The Kirkpatrick boys offer some of the finest traditional leather to be had whether for cap-n-ball sixguns, cartridge conversions, or standard single-actions.

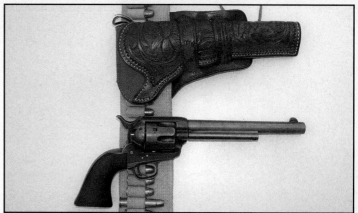

Cheyenne holster and web belt by El Paso Saddlery. This sixgun is an original U.S. Cavalry Colt .45.

Authentic 1850's-style leather by Will Ghormley.

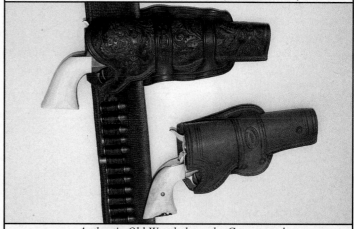

Authentic Old West holsters by Greasewood.

Colt 1860 Armys ride in 1850's-style Prospector leather by Kirkpatrick Leather.

The modified Old West design, complete with a cartridge slide for packin' in town, is by Legends in Leather.

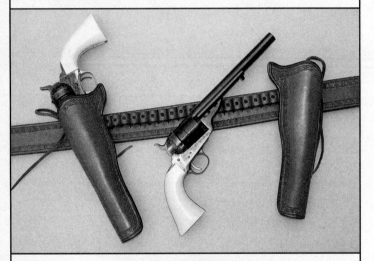

Double Slim Jim set by Bob Mernickle for Colt cartridge conversions.

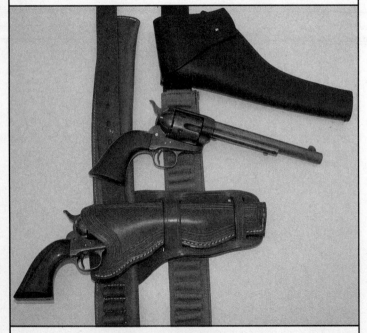

Navy Arms not only supplies replica single-actions, but both Cheyenne and Military flap-style holsters as well.

When I came up with a pair of cartridge conversions in .44 Colt, the choice of leather was easy. Kirkpatrick Leather had built me a double Prospector rig earlier for a pair of 1860 Armys that consisted of fully-lined Slim Jim style holsters that hang straight on the belt making it easy to wear them butts to the front or to the rear. The matching belt is also lined, with everything basket-stamped and a light tan color. Even though it was made for the 1860 Armys, the fact that they have square and open bottoms also leaves enough room for the ejector housings of either the Richards or Richards-Mason Conversions in .44 Colt. For shooting black powder with 7-1/2" Rugers stainless-steel Vaqueros, I use a floral-carved black Prospector double rig, and I recently added another Kirkpatrick Prospector in plain black to carry two 4-3/4" Colt Single Actions. This style carries the 4-3/4" Colts high and out of the way making it very comfortable to wear.

LEGENDS IN LEATHER: Jim Lockwood of Legends in Leather provides authentic leather of a different style - authentic "B" Western. Not historically-accurate leather, as far as coming from the 19th century, but rather "B" Western and TV Western leather as worn by our boyhood heroes. By carefully researching old movies and books about movies, exploring the many Western museums and taking pictures, and by visiting with the stars of the era, Lockwood has developed a library of patterns that duplicate the personal rigs of most of the popular Western heroes that are fully-lined, carefully hand-crafted replicas in the appropriate colors that are either plain, carved and sewn, or laced just like the originals.

Some of the rigs that Legends in Leather offers include the Buck Jones; the Red Ryder, patterned after the rig worn by Wild Bill Elliott as Ryder; the Hondo, John Wayne's rig; the Bar 20, Hoppy's rig; the Durango Kid, Charles Starrett's belt and holster; King of the Cowboys, patterned after Roy Roger's rig; and the Masked Rider, named for the Lone Ranger.

NAVY ARMS: In addition to offering virtually every black powder sixgun, levergun, and single-shot rifle imaginable, Navy Arms also offers a line of excellent leather to fit the sixguns they offer. Available in a brown Mexican-style or black military flap holster, this quality leather complements the replica sixguns from Navy Arms very well.

OLD WEST REPRODUCTIONS: Rick Bachman is one of the first, perhaps the first, to hand-craft period leather using his extensive collection of original leather, guns, photos, and artifacts, all of which help him to understand the Old West. Rick Bachman says he started Old West Reproductions with one purpose in mind - historical accuracy. Bachman uses only Hermann Oak Leather, which even makes his leather authentic since it comes from the same shop that has been tanning it for over 100 years.

Old West Reproductions offers holsters and belts that are modeled after well-known designs of a century ago, bearing such names as The Helena, originally made in Helena, Montana by E. Goettlich; The Cheyenne, patterned after that made by F.A. Meanea of Cheyenne, Wyoming; The Gallatin, from E.L. Gallatin, also from Wyoming; and The Miles City from the Moran Brothers of Montana. Bachman offers more than a dozen designs of authentic period holsters, as well as several belts, including the popular folded-over money belts, and shoulder holsters, rifle scabbards, saddle and pommel bags, wrist cuffs, spur straps, and even the spurs themselves. In the 1880's, J.S. Collins of Cheyenne made a specially-tooled holster for a man that would ultimately become one of the greatest of all our presidents. Of all of Bachman's work, my favorite has to be that holster modeled after the one worn by my ultimate hero, Theodore Roosevelt. In the 1880's, Roosevelt carried his engraved and ivory-stocked 7-1/2" Colt Single Action Army in a flower-carved holster worn with the butt to the front and on his left side. Bachman offers a special version of his Cheyenne holster that is a replica of Roosevelt's holster complete with floral carving and buckskin lining.

Two old-time designs by K.C. Miles.

RED RIVER FRONTIER OUTFITTERS: Red River is one of the very early suppliers of authentic leather, and Phil Spangenberger of Red River is one of the premier promoters of 19th century styles in leather, guns, and clothes. All of his rigs are special-order only for all 19th century single-action sixguns and replicas, including cap-n-ball revolvers and the largest of all the percussion sixguns, the 1847 Walker. He even makes a Paterson holster made to accept the profile of the Colt Paterson with its folding trigger.

Slim Jims are available for all Colt, Smith & Wesson, and Remington single-action sixguns, real or replica, as is the 1870's Mexican Loop holster. The Wes Hardin accepts most of the guns, completely covering the hammer, and is fitted with three rows of two cartridges each on the holster body. Cartridge belts, such as the Buffalo Hunters Cartridge Belt that is 3-1/2" wide with loops for the Old West single-shot rifle cartridges (.45-70, .45-110, and .50-70) and two styles of sixgun cartridge belts, are offered with built-in or sewn-on billets. All outfits are available plain or border-stamped in several styles and finished in a russet color.

An Old West Reproductions version of the holster worn by Theodore Roosevelt and the Dakotas in the 1880's.

SAN PEDRO SADDLERY: Ed Douglas of San Pedro Saddlery offers pigskin-lined outfits, such as a double rig consisting of a pair of Slim Jim holsters and matching belt, for 7-1/2" Colt Single Action Army sixguns in .45 Colt. All of San Pedro's leather is based on authentic old-time designs, or Hollywood's rendition of the same, such as the shoulder holster worn by Val Kilmer as Doc Holliday, known as The Huckleberry.

San Pedro offers a floral-carved Huckleberry made for the 4-3/4" Colt Single Action, as well as The Montana Skeleton, patterned after an old-time design featuring a spring clip around the cylinder and a toe piece to accept the muzzle end of the barrel, with the rest of the gun being exposed. San Pedro's Mexican Loop design is known as The Two Loop, and The Rio Bravo is patterned after the Duke's rig. They also offer shotgun shell slides, cartridge belts both of leather or canvas, sixgun or rifle cartridges, and shotgun shells.

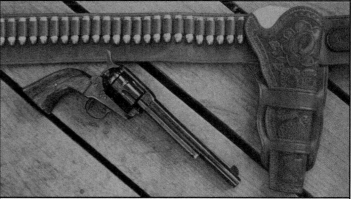

Holster by Red River and Bowie knife by Camillus Cutlery Co.

TEXAS JACKS: Texas Jacks, the leather division of Cimarron Firearms, offers authentically-styled Old West leather to complement the single-action sixguns offered by Cimarron. The Texas Jack Slim Jim Crossdraw is a very neat, trim version without any pieces of excess leather. Both the plain finished Uvalde Double Loop and the heavily border-stamped Cheyenne Double Loop are, as their names imply, replicas of Mexican Loop holsters from the 1880's, with matching cartridge belts available for both.

Texas Jacks also offers a particular favorite of mine, The Teddy Roosevelt, a hand-carved Cheyenne holster made to fit a 7-1/2" Colt, just as Roosevelt's did, or for 4-3/4" and 5-1/2" barrels also. This holster and belt are also available in a carved Texas floral pattern. The South Texas features a Mexican Loop

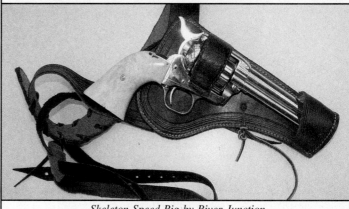

Skeleton Speed Rig by River Junction.

Various authentic holsters available from Old West Reproductions.

Single-loop and double-loop 1880's leather by Trailrider.

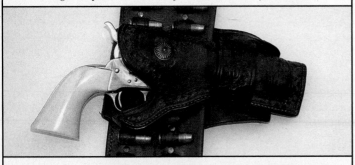

Antiqued double-cartridge belt and holster by Wild Rose Trading Co.

An 1880's-style Mexican holster is still practical today.

holster with one wide loop around the body that is fastened to the skirt or backflap rather than being cut from it, and it is also finished in a distinctive geometric-stamping pattern.

TOMBSTONE LEATHER: When I restored a 7-1/2" 1st Generation Colt Single Action Army, I turned to Tombstone Leather for a traditional rig for this special sixgun. The answer was their Cheyenne consisting of a lined belt with full cartridge loops, matched up with a 19th century style Mexican double-loop holster of single-weight leather that covers the bottom of the trigger guard. It looks exactly like the kind of leather that was offered by the great saddle makers, such as F.A. Meanea and S. D. Myres 100 years ago.

Tombstone offers a full line of leather goods for traditional shooters, including cartridge slides, special shotgun belt slides, boots for shotguns, and saddle scabbards for lever-actions, as well as both single and double weight holster rigs, including shoulder rigs.

TRAILRIDER PRODUCTS: Jim Barnard of Trailrider is such a traditionalist that he shoots an original Spencer Carbine. Many of the holster designs reflect Barnard's authentic Western interest and cannot be found anywhere else, such as The Utah Scout, patterned after a holster worn by one Lewis Grant who was a peace officer in the Utah Territory. The Trailrider Slim Jim rendition is the Alder Gulch, available to be worn straight or with slight cant, and with the butt to the front or to the rear, while The Fort Worth has a real period look since it has a wide backflap, but one that only extends down half of the holster. Two of my favorite Trailrider holsters carry 1st Generation 4-3/4" .44-40 Colt Frontier Six-Shooters, one on the strong side and the other with the butt to the front. The Wolf Creek is Mexican Loop style with two loops cut in the backflap, while the Gila Bend has one concho-decorated wide loop that is riveted to the holster skirt. Mated up with a folded-over money belt with cartridge loops on the center, the entire outfit makes a most comfortable and lightweight rig. For the traditionalist, Barnard offers flap holsters, cap boxes, cartridge boxes, cartridge slides, and officer and enlisted men waist belts with a wide choice of military buckles, saber belts, and Prairie cartridge belts.

WILD ROSE TRADING CO: Chuck Burrows of Wild Rose Trading Co. offers a unique service - traditional leather with a modern antique finish. My Wild Rose "antique" outfit consists of a 4" wide cartridge money belt with two rows of sixgun cartridge loops, 38 in all, as well as eight loops for shotgun shells. It is of a reddish color, complete with stains that duplicate years of wear. The holsters are Mexican Loop style, both of which fit 5-1/2" Colt Single Actions perfectly. One holster is of the single-loop design with a sewn-in plug at the muzzle end, while the other has two loops and a closed bottom without the plug.

Wild Rose offers a full line of Slim Jim and Mexican Loop holsters, as well as cartridge belts, both single and double weight leather; chaps in Batwing and Shotgun style; wrist cuffs; and knife sheaths. Most items are available plain, border-stamped, basket-stamped, or fully-carved.

Shooting black powder is an almost spiritual connection to our country's past history, and traditional leather adds greatly to the feelin'.

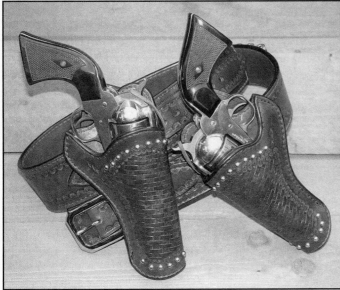

This rig by Rocking A Brand Custom Leather is a double shoulder holster that is easily converted to a two-gun belt rig as shown.

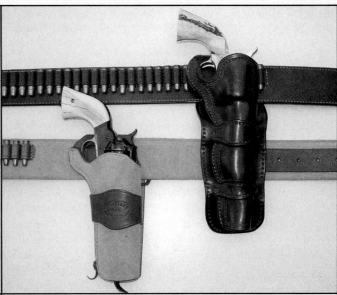

Two great rigs by Tombstone Saddlery - a Mexican style for a 7-1/2" single-action, and the John Wayne style for an 1890 Remington.

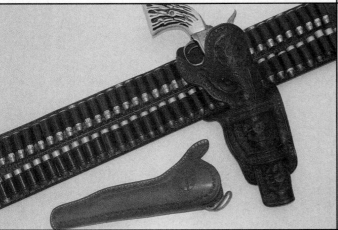

Whether you are carrying heavy or carrying light, these two rigs by Texas Jacks work great.

A close-up of a holster, belt, and knife scabbard by Wild Rose.

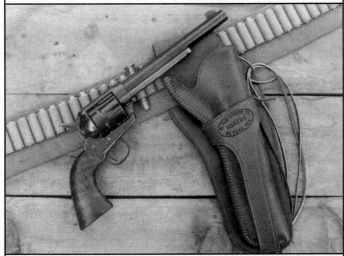

This rebuilt 1st Generation Colt Single Action Army carries authentically in the 1897 Sweetwater by El Paso Saddlery. Do you know the significance of the .45-70 round in the middle of the web belt?

If only it could talk! This original, Mexican, two-loop holster, maker unknown, carries a 1902 Colt.

By: Captain George Baylor

The Frontiersman Category in SASS is the category that everyone watches, but few people shoot. They watch it because it's exciting, noisy, and realistic. The category requires the use of black powder or black powder substitutes in all of the guns; percussion pistols, pistol-caliber lever-action rifles (just like the other categories), and either a side-by-side shotgun or a lever-action shotgun, but no pump models. The pistols must be fired one-handed. It's one of the smaller categories in SASS because of the *perceived* difficulty.

I had watched the Frontiersman Category shooters for some time, and finally decided it looked too difficult for me. I knew that dealing with percussion pistols is time consuming and frustrating, the pistols were uniformly unreliable, and that getting five good bangs from a pistol on a stage seemed to be a rarity. Colts (clones, of course) dropped their loading levers in mid-string, had poor sights that usually shot high, and became hopelessly jammed with spent caps, however Remingtons also had their own problems. We are dealing with pre-Civil War technology levels, after all, which gives me more and more respect for people who actually fought with these weapons. Additionally, real black powder is dirty, smelly, and hard to clean up. If you arrive home or to the hotel after shooting black powder, your lovely significant other will consign you to the shower and your period-correct cowboy clothes to the burn bag. Don't even think of cleaning your weapons at the hotel room when attending an out-of-town match unless she has a fetish for a smell like the fires of hell.

A Savior

However, there is a pistol that is built to modern standards and is, for a percussion pistol, reliable and easy to shoot - the Ruger Old Army (fixed-sight version designed specifically for cowboy action shooting). It comes in

a stainless version, a plus in a percussion pistol, and has good sights and action out of the box. Its only downside is that it's one of the most expensive pistols in the class. On the other hand, if you have a gunsmith make an 1860 Army replica actually work, it'll cost you more. For right now, let's just deal with making the Ruger work for the Frontiersman Category.

First of all, don't get an action job done unless the gun really needs it, and don't change the hammer spring because the heavy stock spring is necessary to bust caps. Generally, Ruger Old Armys have good actions out of the box, and they generally shoot to point-of-aim. The cure for the former is a gunsmith. The Ruger three-screw action tunes easily, and if you like lighter-than-stock trigger pulls, talk to Rowdy Yates at Lee's Gunsmithing. The cure for the latter is to send the gun back to Ruger with a test target showing you can shoot tight groups, but not where it's pointed.

Shooting Percussion Pistols

The following constitutes the easiest, least time-consuming method of shooting percussion pistols I've found:

We're not looking for the cheapest method or even the most authentic method, but instead trying to find a way to load ten chambers per stage and get ten bangs with the least amount of effort in order to attract the largest number of people to the Frontiersman Category.

First, buy two brass powder flasks, the kind with the screw-on cap and screw-on spout. For competing with the Ruger Old Army, you want nominally 25 or 30-grain spouts. You can go higher if you like more recoil, more smoke, and more velocity, but they aren't necessary or desirable qualities in CAS competition. Fill both spouts with Clean Shot; FFFg gives the most realistic loads, while FFg will give a little bit less recoil and velocity. Make up two powder flasks because you'll use one in the course of a day, and you can use the other one so you don't have to bring bulk powder to reload the measure at the range. We're using Clean Shot instead of the "holy" black powder simply because it's easier to use than real black powder. It makes its own lube, so bullet lubes aren't necessary, it normally doesn't foul the barrel or the base pin, and it cleans up

To prepare the pistol for loading, lock the cylinder in place with the ram.

easily. Accuracy and velocity are also on par with black powder. It is not classed as an explosive, and is available where black powder is restricted.

Percussion Caps

The instructions call for #10 caps, but #10 and #11 Remingtons, #11 CCI, and RWS #1075+ fit as well. However, I find #10 Remingtons work best for me. You might start there and save a lot of trouble because I operate on the "if it ain't broke, don't fix it" principle.

Nipples

The stock nipples work fine with Remington #10 caps. Put "Never Seize" on the threads, and keep them clean and replace as necessary.

Loading

There should be no lube in the chambers, but wipe each chamber with a patch if in doubt. (You're using a stainless gun, so you could have left the cylinder dry when you cleaned it.) Before loading, cap each chamber and fire the caps to clear out any lube in case you've gotten any near it, but this isn't necessary with a dry cylinder.

At a match, unless instructed otherwise by match officials, insert the powder and ball at the unloading table, and then cap at the loading table. A percussion pistol is not considered loaded until it is capped.

Then put the weapon on half-cock so the cylinder can be rotated. To start

with, push the rammer down to lock the cylinder in place. Next, put your index fingertip over the powder spout, turn the powder flask upside down, and then push the powder release with your thumb. Shake the powder a couple of times, release the powder release button, and turn the powder flask right side up. Now look at the spout. You should see powder to the end. Next, carefully insert the spout into the chamber, and then look in the chamber for a consistent level of powder.

For Light Loads

The Ruger rammer does not extend far enough to compress less than 35-grain charges. The pistol was originally designed for hunting, and stronger charges are used for that sport. However, if you want to shoot hotter loads, go ahead. But if you would like to shoot 20-30 grains, the use of a filler

Preparing to insert a measured amount of powder.

is required. After you have put in a measured charge of powder, fill the chamber with cornmeal or cream of wheat before the next step.

Seating the Ball

Insert a .457 round ball (Bonus Bullets cast round balls work as well as the more expensive Hornady and Speer swaged ones for what we're doing), and then release the rammer. Next, rotate the cylinder one chamber so the ball is centered under the rammer, and then firmly seat the ball. You may have a ring of lead shaved by this action which must be removed so it does not bind the cylinder.

Wait, didn't you forget the Wonder Wad or lube?

No. You may use a Wonder Wad if you

wish since it won't hurt anything, but the .457 round ball will seal adequately to prevent chain fire. Chain fire is really caused by loose caps, and the cylinder design of the Ruger makes that unlikely to happen. You're going to clean off any loose powder off the front of the cylinder, aren't you? Clean Shot makes its own lube, so it doesn't need a Wonder Wad, yak butter, chocolate chip cookies, or whatever shooters of the "holy" black powder use to seal and lubricate their pistols.

Now, cap the pistol (at the loading table, of course, when at a match). Use a short dowel to push the caps on to seat them. Additionally, before using the caps, look at them to make sure they still have their colored chemicals in them because they fall out sometimes, and therefore that cap won't fire.

Keep your hands behind the cylinder gap, because if you have an accidental discharge, at least you won't burn your hands. (Of course, when capping, you're at the loading table pointing the weapon downrange.) When finished, you should have the hammer down on an empty chamber. Do not push them on with your finger unless you like emergency and reconstructive surgery. Do not use the hammer to push them on either; you may slip and the gun will go "bang." If you're practicing at a range, no one will notice, but at a match you will at least get a stage DQ.

To carefully load the chamber, fully insert the powder measure.

Insert a .457 soft lead round ball.

Release the lever and rotate the cylinder until the ball is under the ram.

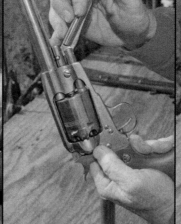

Make sure the ram is centered over the ball.

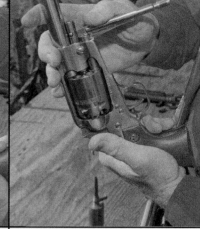

Fully rotate the loading lever. Note the lead ring around the ram, which guarantees a good seal. If there's no lead ring, the ball is too small.

While you can use caps straight from the tin, it is much faster using a capper. Remember to be simple and not cheap. So, you should buy at least two Cash Cappers, the kind that are all brass, hold 100 caps, and are snail-shaped.

Lower the hammer over the empty chamber or safety notch of the empty chamber.

Shoot the stage, don't miss, and shoot fast.

At the Unloading Table

Point the pistol up at 45 degrees, half-cock the hammer, and check for spent caps. If necessary, pull them off with your 1870 period-correct Leatherman tool (or small needle-nosed pliers). When everything's unloaded, repeat the powder and ball steps at the unloading table.

After three to four stages (okay, six or seven on a busy day), I take the cylinder off and clean the nipples with a patch, pre-soaked in 91% isopropyl alcohol, and brush them with a stainless-steel toothbrush as well. I then wipe the base pin and the front of the cylinder clean. However, make sure you keep the cylinder dry. Spray a little lubricant of your choice on the base pin because unlike "real" black powder, Clean Shot is not lube finicky.

Survival Kit

Someday, you'll need to remove a ball from a cylinder because you might have accidentally tried to load two (it happens), or may need to unload a chamber. For this you need a nipple wrench, either the stock one that comes with the gun or an appropriate-

sized socket driver, a 1/8" x 3" dowel, and a brass hammer.

To remove a ball, remove the cylinder from the pistol and unscrew the nipple. Pour the powder out the nipple hole, and then insert the dowel and pound out the ball(s).

Cleaning

At the end of the day, take the cylinder out to clean. Spray it with Windex with ammonia. (If you're really cheap, you can get the cheapest window cleaner without ammonia and add a little white vinegar. Black Powder shooters often brag about how cheap they are, so feel free to brag on this, too.) Clean the nipple area with the stainless steel toothbrush, remove the nipples, and brush clean as needed. Don't lube the cylinder because it's stainless-steel, just dry it. Clean and lube the base pin with your lubricant of choice, and toothbrush the fouling off the frame after dousing with Windex/vinegar. Run a bore snake through the bore, lube with your lubricant of choice, and then reassemble.

That's about it for cap-n-ball the easy way. Your rifle and shotgun have to be black powder or a black powder substitute in Frontiersman, but that's a whole different article. However, it is not difficult in either case. The Frontiersman Category might require a bit more effort than Traditional or Duelist, but it's more fun firing that big smoke wagon one-handed and making all that noise and smoke.

Now cap it, pressing the cap on the nipple with firm but gentle pressure using a dowel.

Now you get to make smoke!

Members of the Rocky Mountain Rifle Club of Butte, Montana posing in front of the Schuetzen House in 1919.

BLACK POWDER SCHUETZEN MATCHES AND RIFLES

By: Kenny Durham,
aka KID Durham

In our modern age, with so many diverse recreational activities on which we can spend every spare minute we have, it is hard to visualize just how significant a place target shooting occupied as the primary recreational activity for early Americans. Every town had a rifle or shooting range of some sort, and it was common for rivalries to develop between communities. When one settlement challenged a neighboring town to a rifle match, it often meant that work was set aside for a day or more for such a festive occasion. Often times, large crowds gathered for the sociability, watching the day's shooting events. The types and kinds of shooting varied greatly, too. German and other European immigrants brought to America a new style of target shooting that became known as "Schuetzen" shooting.

Germanic influence has been present in American firearms and shooting beginning when the first German immigrant came to America with a rifle. The Kentucky rifle, the first truly American rifle, is a direct descendant of the German Jager rifle. Surely, no one can deny the influence of German Mauser rifles on our modern bolt-action rifles. Even the round bull's-eye targets we use originated in Germany.

After the Civil War, Schuetzen matches became extremely popular. The first national Schuetzenfest was held in New York City in 1866. In these matches, the shooter did not rest the rifle over a log, use cross-sticks, or lay on the ground prone to support the rifle. Schuetzen matches were fired from the standing or off-hand position, taking no artificial support. The rifles used in Schuetzen matches had evolved from hunting rifles into target rifles expressly suited for off-hand shooting. The most distinctive feature of a Schuetzen rifle is the buttstock, with its perch-belly shape and Swiss buttplate with prongs on the heel and toe that slip comfortably over the shooter's arm just above the biceps. The buttstock of some Schuetzen rifles had so much drop and such a pronounced cheek rest that they appeared misshapen and almost grotesque. However, when one picks up a good Schuetzen rifle and mounts it properly, the questions with regard

Steve Brooks shooting his Ballard Schuetzen rifle. Notice the straight upright position, rather than leaning the head over or down on the stock.

to the weird shape disappear. This distinctive style of stock allows the shooter to assume a very straight, head-up posture, the result of which means that the rifle can be held steady for a much longer interval of time in which to fire the shot before fatigue sets in. The targets were "25 Ring German Targets" and usually fired at 200 yards. The highest score value of a shot was worth 25 points and the lowest was 10 points, making a possible total of 250 points in a 10-shot match.

Although America had adopted and embraced Schuetzen shooting, the sport remained inextricably linked with German culture. Schuetzen rifles were identified with German culture just as lever-action rifles were a part of the American Old West. Schuetzen matches remained very German, often being referred to as "German Matches" since Schuetzen is the German word for shooting. That changed in 1915 when a German U-Boat sank the British luxury liner *Lusitania*, killing 124 American passengers. The Great War with Germany brought about an almost overnight cessation of anything "German." Even American breweries that aligned themselves with the German heritage of Lager beer, and touted it as "German Beer," removed any references to Germany from their labels and advertising. The Schuetzen rifles fell silent, even among the American-German communities. I'm certain that some Schuetzen shooting continued, but under a much subdued atmosphere. After World War I, Schuetzen shooting enjoyed a revival, but the inextricable ties and post-war attitude towards Germany in the U.S. kept matches pretty low-key. World War II ended whatever revival Schuetzen shooting had enjoyed between wars. In the 1960's, the modern era of Schuetzen shooting was born and continues today across America.

Black Powder Cartridge Schuetzen Today

As with other late-1800's styles of shooting, Schuetzen matches of the black powder cartridge and early smokeless powder cartridge

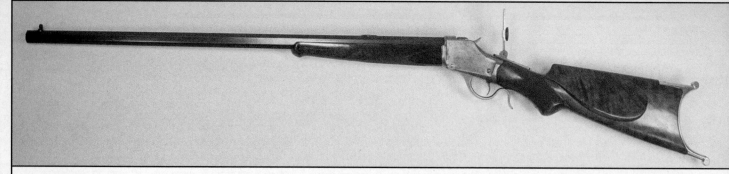

Beautiful, 100% original, .38-55 Winchester "Highwall" off-hand target rifle.

era are making a comeback and are referred to as Traditional Schuetzen and Black Powder Schuetzen matches. The International Single Shot Rifle Association sanctioned a special class termed Traditional Schuetzen in 1999. The Traditional Schuetzen is based on a technology cut-off of 1917, which allows for the use of smokeless powder and any externally-adjusted telescopic sight. Although there are no sanctioned rules that I am aware of, Black Powder Schuetzen matches are loosely based on a technology cut-off of 1896, and usually follow the similar rifle and ammunition requirements of Black Powder Cartridge Rifle Silhouette shooting. But, since there are no formal "Black Powder" Schuetzen rules, match programs vary as to what is allowed. Exceptions are made to expressly allow Schuetzen-style rifles, including those with palm rests and sometimes including a scope class when enough shooters have scope-mounted rifles. Small bore .22 caliber Schuetzen matches fired at 50 yards on a reduced-size target are popular, too.

One place where Black Powder Schuetzen shooting is making a big comeback is in Butte, Montana. For the past ten years, the Butte Gun Club, formerly the Rocky Mountain Rifle Club, has been holding Schuetzen matches organized by A. P. "Butch" Ulsher and Fred Earl. Monthly matches are held in the historic Schuetzen House from December through April. Just as in the 1800's, today's black powder Schuetzen matches are festive occasions.

See ya at the range!

Engraved Ballard Schuetzen rifle in .22 caliber rimfire.

A 2nd Generation Ballard Schuetzen Rifle complete with palm rest.

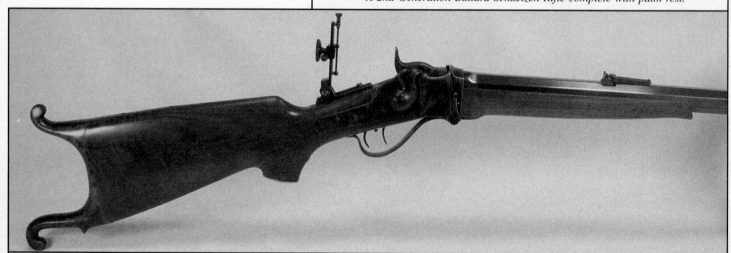

Reproduction of the 1874 Sharps Schuetzen Rifle by Pedersoli.

Loading and Shooting Tips for Frontier Cartridge Guns

By: Ray Walters, aka Smith n' Jones

Black Powder Cartridge or, more correctly, Frontier Cartridge, is now one of the fastest-growing categories in cowboy action shooting. The reasons for this increased popularity are many and varied, but what it comes down to, for must of us, is that it is just plain ol' fun. When you get in a posse with a bunch of these crazies, you can't help but have as much fun watching them as they are having making "the smoke." The "dark-siders," as many of them like to be known, are a special breed who don't mind a little muss and fuss when compared to the deep satisfaction of knowing that they are shooting about as close as possible to what it must have been like back when most of these "cowboy" guns were first developed. Another very satisfying aspect of shooting black powder is hearing the uninitiated and/or unlearned cough, wheeze, and whine about the haze and smell that permeates a stage where Frontiersmen are doing their thing.

Thanks to technical improvements in the base components, the world of black powder cartridge shooting has gotten a lot simpler in recent years, and the new replacement powders, lubes, and bullets available to shooters keeps growing every year. For a number of years, the choice was pretty much between "real" black powder or Pyrodex, marketed originally by Hodgdon Powder Company more than three decades ago. Now, there are a number of new or newer propellants on the market, most of which are cleaner, safer, and more user-friendly than good ol' black. The first, and to my way of thinking the most important reason for using black powder replacements, is that they do not contain sulfur in their chemical make-up, and therefore do not create the steel damaging by-products that can ruin a gun bore in no time at all. While it is always a good idea to clean your black powder (or any other) firearms as soon after shooting as possible, you are less likely to ruin a good gun if you do forget the cleaning process for a few days when using substitutes. In fact, while going through some of my "cowboy" guns one evening to see which ones might need a little routine cleaning and maintenance, I discovered that I had not cleaned my Marlin 336-Cowboy .38-55 WCF, which I had taken to the Shootists Holiday and had inadvertently shot a few rounds of Hodgdon Triple 7 through. The discovery was made more than a month after the fact, and I just knew that I was going to be replacing a barrel. The "crud" was very hard and took some softening with Windex and Black Dawge's Dawge Whizz, but it finally broke loose, and after a lot of scrubbing with a bronze brush and WD-40, the bore was as clean and shiny as new. Boy, was I relieved. If I had been shooting real black powder there would, no doubt, have been some serious damage to the bore. The non-sulfur Triple 7 had given me a second chance, one that I won't soon be forgetting.

In addition to being easier on the bore, the replacement powders are addressed by the BATF as being in the same category as smokeless powders and, therefore, are not subject to the same shipping and storage requirements as black powder. On the negative side, as the die-hard charcoal-burners will tell you, it just doesn't smell or sound right. And they are right. There is something about that hollow "ka-thump" of a shotgun or big-bore rifle shooting the real stuff that just can't be mistaken for anything else.

Black powder cartridge reloading is, in its purest form, a whole lot different than loading smokeless rounds. But the good news is that, for most of us who pretty much limit our black powder shooting to cowboy action shooting (CAS), the process of putting together a good, functional pistol or rifle load is not all that difficult. In fact, with the introduction of the aforementioned replacement powders and, for that matter, real black powder, it is quite easy to develop a bullet and powder combination that will work quite well in just about any of the CAS qualifying firearms on the market today. By following a few simple safety rules and doing a little experimenting, anyone with some degree of reloading experience can successfully, even if somewhat slowly, make their own Frontiersman ammo.

The first concern is for safety. The big difference between smokeless powders and black powder, or any of the replacements, is that when loading any Frontiersman cartridge, the case must be filled with the powder and bullet leaving no air space between the two as is common with smokeless. Black powder has a much faster burning rate than even the fastest smokeless, and while it is a true burn, not an explosion, the rate is so rapid allowing air to mix with the burning powder can, and often does, create a detonation effect that can cause a very rapid disassembly of your firearm with potentially devastating results.

The next big difference is that these powders tend to leave a great deal of residue in the barrel after each shot. While many of the new replacements, like Clean Shot (now American Pioneer Powder), Clear Shot, and Hodgdon's Triple 7, significantly reduce this fouling material, there is still a significant amount left in most applications, and to remove it between shots necessitates the use of a good bullet lube with either a "cookie" or forced into the lube grooves of the bullet. I have found that any of the commercial lubes, such as SPG, Lyman Black Gold, Buffalo Creek Reliable #12, or Chey-Cast bullet lube, will work well, especially when used with a relatively soft alloy bullet. What has been most interesting for me is seeing how well the harder bullet lubes like Reliable #12 and Chey-Cast, when used under conventional hard-cast bullets in the form of a 1/16 to 1/8 inch "cookie," keep the burned powder residue soft, allowing the following bullets to clean the bore with each shot. Both of these lubes have a melting point of about 150 to 170 degrees and, by being harder, allow for easier storage as the harder lube has less of a tendency to pull out of a lube groove when making contact with another bullet and lube.

The ability of a good lube to keep fouling soft and on the

move is of extreme importance to any shooter, especially to a cowboy shooter who doesn't want to clean his guns after a couple of stages. In fact, that is how I first came to try one of the harder lubes in my own guns.

When I started competing in the Frontier Cartridge Category, I, like many others, simply filled a case with the appropriate amount of Pyrodex or Goex cartridge powder and seated a hard-cast bullet with a slight amount of compression of the powder. The results were a round that was accurate enough for CAS competition, but I ended up with sixguns that required that I clean the cylinder face and forcing cone every other stage or the guns started to bind as the fouling built up between the two. Even though I was getting quite a bit of fouling build-up in the bore, it didn't seem to affect the accuracy a great deal, and I noted only minimal leading in the bore. The big problem was cylinder to forcing cone fouling, and another problem was that if I only cleaned the face of the cylinder and shot a full 10 or 12-stage match, it was nearly impossible to remove the cylinder base pin.

Well, I put up with these minimal distractions for some time. One day, however, I was talking with Bruce Everhart who owns Buffalo Creek Supply and he asked me to try his new Reliable #12 bullet lube. His stories of dealing with some of the problems that I was having and how this new lube had been the answer to most of them was very intriguing to me, and I asked him to send me some to test. He suggested that the easiest way to load rounds with the bullets that I had on hand was to seat the bullet over a 1/16 to 1/8-inch lube "cookie," being sure to leave enough space for the cookie so as to not force it into the powder, thereby contaminating it. As soon as the lube arrived, I proceeded to melt a package of the stuff down in one of my wife's square, glass cake pans and place it out in the cold January wind for a few minutes. Next, I cut the rim end off a .44/40 case and proceeded to cut out little .44 caliber cookies. I charged 50 new Starline .44 WCF cases (primed with Winchester WLP primers) with 20 grains of Hodgdon's new Triple 7, pushed a #12 cookie over that, and seated an Oregon Trail, 200-grain, hard-cast bullet in the case. After all 50 were loaded, I went back and crimped them with my Redding seat/crimp die, and I was set to test my first batch of Triple 7 and Reliable #12 cookie loads.

At this point, I need to address the other main problem that I mentioned earlier, that being the cylinder base pin sticking in the cylinder, often so hard that it took pliers or a flat-blade screwdriver to free it. When I had mentioned this problem to Bruce, he suggested that I simply coat the base pin with #12 lube after cleaning the gun and the problem would go away. Needless to say, I did as instructed, and the next day I was off to the range on a cold and blustery January day to see what would happen. I fired all 50 rounds through a Cimarron 7-1/2" 'P' Model, and as Bruce had predicted, the cylinder showed no signs of binding, even after 50 rounds, and when I cleaned the gun that evening, the base pin pulled out with ease. As this was a function test and it was colder than the proverbial well-digger's drawers, I made little attempt to test the accuracy or the velocity of the load. As Bruce had told me, using the lube in cookie form would keep things soft and clean and, to some degree, rather greasy around the front of the cylinder. This is a small price to pay for keeping the gun functioning long-term without frequent cleaning.

When I ran the first Windex-soaked patch through the bore that evening, it came out incredibly clean. In fact, it was cleaner than the first patch that was run through the same gun after a similar number of rounds using 5.5 grains of Hodgdon TiteGroup. There was virtually no lead in the barrel, and a simple wipe-down of the face of the cylinder with a Windex-soaked rag removed all powder and lube residue. As is my habit, I swabbed out the barrel with a solvent/lube and sprayed the entire gun with WD-40, blew out all parts with 100 pounds per square inch of compressed air, wiped off the exposed surfaces, and was finished with the cleaning process.

The next test of any magnitude that involved the new lube and black replacement powder was at Trailhead 2002 held in Columbus, Texas in March. At that event, I shot the entire match, 12 stages, without cleaning the pistols or rifle, and all three worked flawlessly. The rifle was a Cimarron '92 in .44 WCF, and I used the same hard-cast bullet and cookie load in it. The first patch through each gun came out incredibly clean and leading was nonexistent.

As a follow-up test of the new lube, I performed the same test described above with one of Smith and Wesson's new #3 Schofield sixguns chambered in .45 S&W Schofield. The details of that experience are documented elsewhere in this book. (See *Black Powder and 1875 S&W Schofields* in the *Old West Firearms* chapter.)

In addition, I have had similar experiences using Chey-Cast's black powder lube in cookie form and came away similarly impressed. The main point of relaying the above information is to let the reader know that, while there is a lot to loading precision, long-range accuracy loads, it is a lot simpler to load for CAS events or for casual plinking than one might be led to believe. The emphasis on the harder lubes is done only to let you know how to easily load black powder loads for CAS using most of the components that you have on hand right now. The harder Chey-Cast and Buffalo Creek lubes work best for cookie-type lubing.

Shooting Tips

Competing in Frontiersman and Frontier Cartridge Category brings with it a whole new set of challenges. Notice that I said "challenges" and not "problems." Problems are for the uninitiated and non-creative among us. When you watch your first black powder competitor start making smoke, what invariably strikes you first is that they are usually shooting through a fog or heavy haze, especially on a calm, windless day. And if you think it looks difficult from the side or from behind the shooter, you should see it through the eyes of the shooter. Frontier shooters always hope for a breezy, if not windy, day to shoot. The worst-case scenario is shooting the first stage of the day when it is quiet and calm, the temperature is cool, and the

humidity is high. That first shot throws out an impenetrable blanket of white-gray smoke that just seems to hang there. From that point on you are at the mercy of the elements, but there are a few things that you can do to help yourself. First thing to remember is that, usually within the guidelines set out by SASS, a shooter is allowed to move more or less under the traveling rule observed in the game of basketball. You are pretty well free to move one foot while keeping the other one planted in one place. This can allow you to move two or three feet laterally to try to see around the haze. Additionally, a Frontier Cartridge shooter can often find an opening in the smoke by crouching down for a shot and then standing up. With the combination of lateral movement and moving up and down, you can usually help yourself considerably and get a shot off quicker than by just standing still and waiting for things to clear out.

Another trick that worked well for me at the Northwest Regional in Portland, Oregon this year was to take advantage of any geometric angles that relate to your target. In other words, use what you can see to find your target. In the case of the Portland shoot, the entire range is located in an old gravel pit that is easily 75 yards across and over 300 yards long. It is the perfect venue for a shooting range that is surrounded by subdivisions and businesses. This scene works very well for safety reasons, but because it is from 30 to 60-feet deep, there is very little air movement and it is not exactly conducive to shooting black powder. On one stage, the rifle targets were set squarely in the windows of a "building" about 35 yards from the firing line. After the first shot from my .44/40, the entire stage was shrouded in smoke. Because of the fact that the targets were in the center of the four windows and they were large enough that I could see most of the corners of the windows, I simply held the front sight approximately in the center of the four corners and let it fly. I only missed one shot using that technique. I never actually saw a target after the first shot, but I kept hearing the steel "ding" so figured the system was working quite well.

Another trick that I learned from an article by our friend Doc Shapiro is that when afforded the discretion of which direction to shoot a sweep, always move against the breeze. In other words, if the there is a very light breeze blowing from the right that doesn't blow the smoke away quickly enough, start your string on the left target and move towards the right or into the breeze. This way, what wind there is will help clear the smoke away from the direction you are going.

Target memorization is another way to deal with smoke when shooting large close targets. If it is a "dump" target (usually one target you place all five rounds on), maintaining a focus on where the target "was" will allow you to maintain the sight picture that you had before the first shot was fired, and then you just keep shooting and listening for the "ding." If you don't hear it, you best stop and try to get another visual before you shoot again.

Remember, the point of cowboy shooting is to have fun, especially for the Frontier shooters.

By: Kenny Durham,
aka KID Durham

Long Shots - Buffalo Rifle Matches

The hunters had crept as close as possible to the solitary bull buffalo standing at the foot of a small rise in the distance. The knee-high prairie grass obscured the bull's legs, but his head was up and facing straight ahead presenting the hunters with a perfect broadside shot. As the hunters got into position to make the shot, the shooter spread open a pair of cross-sticks in front of him, poking them into the ground. Sitting behind them, he cradled the barrel of his rifle in the "V" of the sticks, opened the breech, and slid a cartridge into the chamber. His partner, peering through a small telescope, remarked, "I think he is a little farther than we thought. Must be purt' near 800 yards, and he ain't quite as big as he looks." The shooter checked his sight setting and muttered, "I got 'er set for a bit over eight hunnerd. If'n I hold low at his heart, I should at least put one into the boiler, maybe even break his back."

"Watch the breeze from the left," cautioned the spotter as he saw the prairie grass ripple like a wave dancing across the water. "I see it," said the shooter, as he closed the breech of his Sharps in a single fluid motion, so smoothly that it made no sound. He eared the hammer to full-cock, lined up the sights, and squeezed the trigger. The rifle's roar shattered the silence and sent a cloud of smoke across the top of the waving grass. Just as quickly, it was silent again. "You got

Wyoming Creedmoor Buffalo Match has 800, 900, and 1000-yard targets.

'em," exclaimed the spotter. "I saw the bullet hit!" And then, the unmistakable "CLANK" of a bullet striking steel reached their ears. "It's a hit," said the scorekeeper. "Next shooter!"

No, this is not a buffalo hunt, but rather a modern-day buffalo match. The reason our two intrepid hunters could get no closer than 800 yards is because they were on a firing line with a dozen or more other shooters. Buffalo matches, or gong matches as they are sometime called, have become another very popular sport for shooting rifles from the black powder cartridge era. Without question, the granddaddy of all Buffalo matches is the Annual Matthew Quigley Buffalo Rifle Match, or the "Q" as it has become known, held each spring in Forsyth, Montana. There, several hundred shooters gather to shoot single-shot rifles at targets scattered across the prairie ranging from 225 to 800 yards. For example, 416 shooters attended the "Q" in 2002, and the match was won by Joan Jilka, who shot a Sharps in .40-65 caliber.

Another great match is the Wyoming Territory Creedmoor and Buffalo Match held on the Wasserburger Ranch north of Lusk, Wyoming in April or May each year. Kenny and Karen Wasserburger have been putting on this fine match for many years now, which consists of two days of shooting. On the first day you shoot 1876-

style Creedmoor circular steel targets at 800, 900, and 1000 yards, and on the second day, you shoot at various shapes at 200, 300, 600 and 1200 yards. Another such event is the monthly matches put on by the Great Basin Black Powder Cartridge Rifle Shooters of Bend, Oregon. At their range they have a variety of animal targets at distances from 200 to 1000 yards, and can move them to unknown distances on the mountainside, too. What was a 500-yard shot last month may only be a 460-yard shot this month. Yet another group is the North County Shootist Association at the Pala Range north of San Diego, California. Harold "Graybeard" Itchkawich sponsors the Long Range Buffalo Championship in early December of each year. The skinny on this match is using falling-block, single-shot rifles, sitting or with prone cross-sticks, black powder or duplex loads, and with steel targets ranging from 350 to 905 yards. It's that simple.

Buffalo matches are similar to a rendezvous in some ways. You might say that a buffalo match is a late 1800's version of a rendezvous, but not all are that way. Period dress is always encouraged, but seldom required. Many shooters misinterpret "period dress" to mean only "cowboy" duds, but that's not the case. Rules are different for each one since these matches are not sponsored by any governing organization. It would, no doubt, be detrimental to the sport if there were such an association. The uniqueness of each match is what makes

Buffalo targets are used at a variety of distances. This is the 1220-yard buffalo target used at the Wyoming Creedmoor Buffalo Match.

them so enjoyable. With this in mind, here are a few things we should be prepared for when planning on attending a buffalo or gong match.

If you received a flyer or program in the mail, read it carefully! Find out what types of rifles and ammunition

Period-era duds at buffalo matches are not restricted to cowboy or frontiersman-style clothing.

are allowed. If you are not sure about certain items, call the sponsor for answers. Some groups allow ONLY rifles from the buffalo hunting period of, say, 1865 to 1880. The Stevens 44-1/2 that arrived on the scene years after the "Buff Runn'n" days might not be allowed on the firing line. Also, if the program specifies "BPCRS-legal" rifles only, then you are limited to rifles having an exposed hammer and a 12 lb.-2 oz. weight limit. These kinds of limitations are unusual, but I have seen them on some programs. On the other hand, many matches allow any falling block action to be used, including a Ruger No. 1, as long as it is chambered for a black powder cartridge. At the Wyoming Creedmoor match one year, a shooter did very well with a .40-65 built on a Ruger No. 1 and shooting smokeless powder loads, too. This brings up the next issue, which is the type of ammunition allowed. Some matches limit ammunition to 100% black powder loads using lead bullets without gas checks. Others allow the use of smokeless powder and lead bullets of any kind. Copper jacketed bullets are almost never allowed because of the potential damage to targets that they can cause. I have not seen much regarding the use of scope-mounted rifles, but with the greater availability of period-style scopes and the addition of a Scope category to the Black Powder Cartridge Rifle Silhouette program, I'm sure they will have an impact on the buffalo events. The choice of caliber is entirely up to the shooter at any match I have attended. Cartridges are limited to the black powder cartridge era, but that leaves a lot of room for individuality. Probably the most popular

is the .45-70 and the longer .45 cartridges, but one will find almost any cartridge from .38-55 to .50-100 being used.

Prior to the beginning of the match, there is usually a sight-in period. Depending on range conditions, this may be the day before the event starts, and it's possible that no practicing on event days will be allowed. The distances to the targets may or may not be posted, or those in charge of the match may move the targets each day to make the match more challenging. The typical format for a buffalo match is for shooters to be divided into groups, each shooting a different target in rotation if range conditions permit. Shooters usually line up on the firing line in a "batting order," so-to-speak, as directed by the scorekeeper. There may or may not be any sighting shots taken. It is not uncommon for sighting shots not to be allowed at all, not even a fouling shot. So, be prepared for any shooting scenario. A typical match might consist of five shots at each target. Each shot may be scored as a simple "hit" or "miss" worth one point, or hits in a certain portion of the target may score a higher value than other locations.

Anything goes when it comes to putting on a buffalo match. However the match is scored, the shooting begins with the first shooter in the order firing at the designated target. In turn, the next shooter fires, and so on down the line until all have fired. The process is repeated until all shooters have completed the relay. Then, the scores are tallied up and the group moves on to the next target. Most matches allow the shooter to have a spotter to assist them in knowing where their shot struck. In some cases, the spotter may serve as coach, giving the shooter condition changes and sight adjustments. But, in some matches, the shooters are on their own and the spotter serves only as a scorekeeper.

Buffalo matches, due to their nature, may involve a lot of sitting around and not much actual time spent shooting. Some might consider this a drawback, but for most it's a chance to do a lot of visiting with friends, looking at fine rifles, and checking out what vendors may have to offer. See ya at the range!

Bear targets are a popular choice, such as this 600-yard target.

Some Western-action shooters that participate in cowboy action in the various smokeless powder categories may have thought about eventually shooting black powder. If you are one of them, you may want to try The Plainsman Event first. This is a side match that takes place at most of the major annual Single Action Shooting Society (SASS) events. It normally encompasses three scenarios that are both scored and set up the same way as the regular stages. There is, however, a large difference in the firearms and ammunition that are shot. First, you must use black powder or a black powder substitute in all of your firearms. The firearms used consist of a double-barrel shotgun (the purists use one with hammers, although this isn't required), a single-shot rifle, and two cap-n-ball revolvers. You are also normally required to shoot your revolvers in the duelist (one-handed) style.

There are a number of factors that you need to consider before shooting this event. For those of you wishing to load your own cartridges, I recommend that you read the appropriate articles and review the reloading information in this book. You may not wish to reload black powder cartridges, which is fine as there a number of companies that produce black powder cartridge ammunition, such as Ten-X, Dakota Ammunition, Inc. (previously known as Cor-Bon), and Black Dawge. You will, however, have to load your cap-n-ball revolvers yourself. FFFg powder or its equivalent is recommended. I have seen powder charges vary from a low of 15 grains up to a full 30-grain charge. You may want to experiment with your particular cap-n-ball revolvers to determine what charge provides the best accuracy. Your sixgun may take either #10 or #11 percussion caps on the nipples, so you should verify this before your first trip out to the range. By the way, make sure you take a tiny pick or, even

better, a thin knife with you since the caps will sometimes stick and cause the cylinder to bind. I occasionally carry a small Damascus blade around my neck so it is easy to retrieve. (This has also come in handy when prying out an empty, sticky case held in the chamber of a Henry, '66, or '73.) It is also wise to cap off your revolver before the match by going to a designated safe area and putting caps on all of your nipples, making sure your cylinder is empty, and firing them off. This should ensure that there will be a positive ignition when you bring your sixguns to bear at your first stage.

The Revolvers

Any cap-n-ball, six-shot revolver meets the requirement of the Plainsman Event (a six-shot revolver is recommended so that the hammer can rest on an empty chamber that has no cap on it). The most commonly used are replicas: the Remington 1858, the 1851 Colt Navy, or the 1860 Colt Army. These are available from a number of companies, such as Navy Arms, Cimarron, Taylor's & Co., Traditions, Dixie, and Cabela's. They are very reasonable, with new ones running from $130 to $200, or you can usually find a used revolver at your local gun store. The other cap-n-ball revolver that has a growing following is the Old Model Army Ruger cap-n-ball. This sixgun is rugged, well-built, and shoots well. Any of these sixguns will do the job, although you may have to check the timing or have your's tuned by a gunsmith. If you do, also have them check the hammer, sear, and bolt to make sure they are working correctly, engaging the moving surfaces with an adequate amount of steel,

The Plainsman Event

By: Andy Fink, aka Chucky

A pair of 1851 Navy Arms .36 caliber revolvers are a popular choice for the Plainsman Event.

Irving 142 firing his 1858 Remington .44.

and that the soft steel on many of the Italian imports hasn't worn down.

The revolvers that you use in this event are probably the most important of any of the firearms, as each of the three stages usually requires ten revolver shots, while the single-shot rifle is usually only shot one to three times, and the shotgun has only two to four rounds.

The Rifles

Any single-shot rifle of the period will work. If you are a Black Powder Cartridge Rifle Silhouette shooter and want to use your Sharps or Remington-Hepburn, that's fine. I have used my Pedersoli .45/70 and it worked fine, though loading it is a little slow. An original Remington Rolling Block in .43 Spanish also shot well and was a little easier to load quickly. The best rifle for me turned out to be a replica .45/70 Trapdoor Springfield. It has a shorter barrel, is easy to swing, and most importantly, it is the only period rifle that has ejectors. When you flip open the breech block on the receiver, it ejects the empty shell casing reducing your reloading time. The distances you usually shoot the rifle at run from 50 to 150 yards and the targets are fairly large. Sight your rifle in for 100 yards and you should be fine.

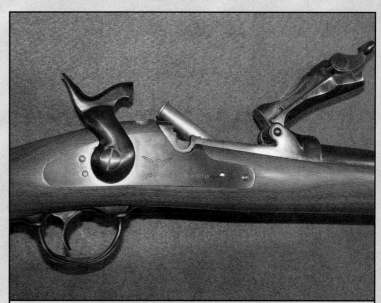

The Springfield Trapdoor .45-70 is the only rifle allowed in the Plainsman Event that ejects the fired cartridge.

(Continued on next page)

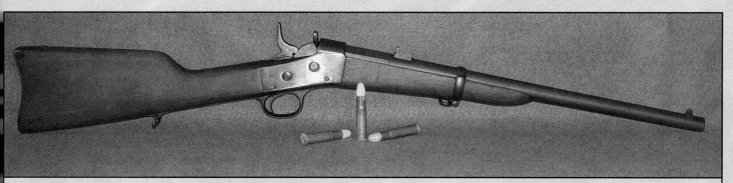

An original Remington Rolling Block carbine in .43 Spanish makes an excellent single shot-rifle, shown here with original cartridges from the late-1800's.

(Continued from previous page)

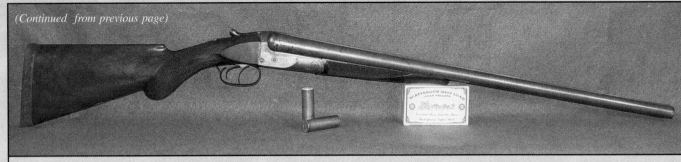

An original Colt 1883 12-gauge shotgun is not only fun to shoot, but also provides real authenticity to the event.

The Shotguns

There are two types of double-barrel shotguns that can be used, those with hammers and those without. Regardless of which type you choose, the shotgun cannot have ejectors, although extractors are fine. You can use an original or replica. Some of the best originals are European shotguns from London, Beligum, France, and Germany. Others include the Fox and Stevens, and I have used an original Colt 12-gauge myself. There are excellent replicas available from Stoeger, as well as the Baikal imported from Russia by European American Arms, and a number of other companies are in the process of bringing out a variety of new double-barrels for cowboy action shooting.

The black powder, old vintage firearms, and realistic stages of the Plainsman Event are a lot of fun and really bring you back to the Old West. Give it a try sometime -you just might find out you enjoy it!

The double-barrel shotgun is a major part of each stage.

European American Arms' hammer 12-gauge from Biakal is SASS approved and is an excellent choice for the Plainsman Event.

SHOOTING CAP-N-BALL SIXGUNS

in Cowboy Competition

By: Kenny Durham, aka KID Durham

In the 1800's, the saying went, "God created man, but Sam Colt made 'em equal." Today, with cowboy shooting so popular, we could say, "God created man, but Sam Colt made us grin from ear to ear." I've never seen a shooter who didn't have a big grin on their face after emptying a fully-loaded percussion revolver for the first time. If you throw in the fun of cowboy shooting, the fun of cap-n-ball shooting is ratcheted up a notch. That is, if everything works properly. Unlike cartridge sixguns, percussion revolvers can be finicky on what they like for loads and how they are tuned to operate. Solid-frame models, like the Remington, Starr, or Rodgers & Spencer, are more forgiving than the Colt-style "open-top" revolvers. Still, all cap-n-balls require attention to a few details, which, if attended to, will make them shoot as reliably as their cartridge-firing descendents.

Use a screw driver of the right size to loosen the screw holding the wedge that holds the barrel in place. After knocking the wedge out with a wooden dowel, remove the barrel.

Tuning for Smoothness, Speed, and Function

Cap-n-balls, as with cartridge guns, can benefit greatly from an action tuning, but the action tuning for a percussion revolver is different than for a cartridge revolver. The timing aspects are the same for both, but the big difference lies in the mainspring. In a cartridge revolver, the mainspring on a tuned action is deliberately lightened, with the spring being only heavy enough to fire the primer. Why this works so well is that the force of the spring is concentrated into the firing pin so it takes up a very small area, which is similar to a 110-pound lady stepping on your big toe with a spiked heel. Her total weight may be slight, but the pounds-per-square-inch (psi) is several times her body weight. Get the point? (Pun intended.) However, take that same lightened mainspring, put it in a percussion revolver, and it will not set off a cap. The reason is that the flat face of the hammer spreads the force out over a much larger area. Therefore, mainsprings on cap-n-ball revolvers are noticeably stronger, and for good reason. Not only does the spring need to be heavy enough to fire the cap, but also to hold the hammer in place against the force of the gas coming back through the nipple. I have seen occurrences where, due to a light mainspring and eroded nipples, the hammer was blown back to half-cock. And, when this happens, the spent cap is invariably blown back and falls into the action, causing the revolver to bind or lock up. So, before you send your percussion revolvers off for an action job, make sure the gunsmith is cap-n-ball savvy.

Place a little grease or bore butter on the ratchet end of the cylinder. This will make it turn easier.

Keep It Clean and Tight

Cap-n-ball revolvers remind me of steam locomotives in that they require diligent maintenance to keep them running their best. The fouling from black powder coming from the nipples gets into the action much more so than on cartridge revolvers. The only way to gain access for cleaning out the build-up is to completely disassemble the gun. After dismantling the gun, scrub the inside of the frame and the parts using your favorite methods, and then dry everything. I use an air compressor to blow any moisture or solvent from the frame. After drying, I spray Break Free into the frame and onto all the disassembled parts, allowing the oil to penetrate while I take care of other tasks. When ready to reassemble the gun, simply wipe the parts and the frame dry so that no oil or grease gets inside the action. The thin coating of oil remaining is sufficient. Such a thorough cleaning is not required after every shooting session, but often enough so we know that all is well on the inside.

With Colt-style open-top revolvers, we need to ensure that the barrel wedge is tightened properly. The barrel should be tight on the frame, but should allow the cylinder to rotate freely without binding, even when the gun is dirty. Finally, we need to ensure that our cap-n-balls have nipples that are in good condition. As the guns are fired, the flash holes will enlarge

The lubed threads on the cylinder rod should now allow the cylinder and barrel to be reinstalled easily, as well as being removed without difficulty after firing.

slightly due to erosion from the hot gasses. This erosion is normal, but it means that the nipples will need to be replaced at some point. Also, nipples can eventually become flattened from the hammer blows so the percussion caps will not fit properly, which will result in poor ignition or misfires. When replacing the nipples, be willing to pony-up the money for the best. It will pay off in the long run. While you're at it, buy a spare set, too!

Loading and Shooting

Before loading the revolver, there is some preparation that needs to be done to ensure that it will operate flawlessly. The place to start is on the inside. The grooves on the cylinder pin are designed to be filled with grease in order to accommodate and keep the fouling build-up soft. Without the grease lubrication, the cylinder will begin to bind after only a few firings. Even if we are using a black powder substitute, the cylinder pin needs to be coated. Thompson Center's Bore Butter works well for this, as well as for coating the nipple threads.

The final step in preparation for loading the revolver is to ensure that the bottom of the cylinders at the base of the nipple are free from oil, which will cause a misfire. We have always been told that popping a couple of caps on each chamber is

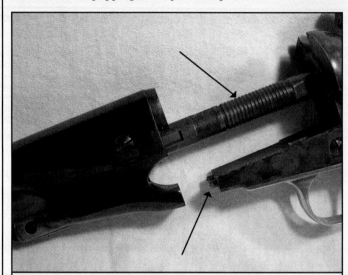

Apply bore butter thoroughly on the cylinder rod, as well as a dab on each of the two connecting pins shown by the two arrows.

sufficient to clear the nipples. But, remember, we are loading for competition and more diligence is called for. Starting with the empty cylinder, we cap all the nipples, and then run a cleaning rod with a patch from the muzzle stopping short of entering the cylinder. Next, we cock the hammer and push the cleaning rod into the cylinder and then "snap" the cap. Withdraw the cleaning rod enough to allow the cylinder to rotate and repeat the process on all the chambers. This method not only clears the nipple, but blows any remaining oil into the cleaning patch. Cap the nipples again and fire the second set of caps (without the cleaning rod) by pointing the muzzle at the ground and observing that the blast from each cap is apparent. Now we are ready to load 'er up.

The great thing about cap-n-ball revolvers is that we can customize our loads on the spot. Either with minimum loads, maximum loads, or somewhere in between, we can choose our performance based upon the situation. If you know that you need to knock a target over, then load heavy. If "hits" are all that is required, then you can load light, using a minimum charge of powder. I still shoot black powder in my revolvers because that's what I want to do. The black powder substitutes work well and allow the same degree of flexibility, but make sure you follow the manufacturer's instructions.

In my .36 caliber Navy Colts, I use 20 grains of FFFg black powder. This is not the minimum charge, but considerably less than maximum. The 20-grain charge fills the chamber enough so that I can seat the ball and slightly compress the charge before the loading lever reaches the limit of its stroke. A compressed powder charge burns better, cleaner, and more accurately. Also, I load each chamber individually. I used to pour in all of the powder charges and then seat the bullets. This all changed one day when, after I had all the cylinders charged, I sneezed. You can guess what happened. Powder went everywhere and I had to start over. The use of a loading stand would have been a good choice, too.

For cowboy shooting, the felt-impregnated wads are the only way to go for sealing the chambers and lubing the bore. The traditional method of topping off the cylinder with grease works fine for target shooting, but is unhandy for cowboy shooting. Ox-Yoke or similar wads are so easy to use and virtually eliminate the mess from cap-n-ball shooting. My loading procedure is this: pour a measured charge of powder into a chamber, insert a felt wad and place a ball atop the mouth, rotate the cylinder under the ram, and seat the ball into the chamber with just enough pressure to come to rest on the powder charge. With the loading ram still in the cylinder, I load the next chamber and then raise the ram and rotate the next chamber into the seating position. Leaving the ram lowered prevents the cylinder from inadvertently being rotated past the cylinder hand. When all five chambers are loaded, I finish seating the balls to the same depth and with the same seating pressure, because doing so ensures that the compression is the same for all chambers.

The final step is capping the revolver when it's our time to shoot. What we want is for our cap-n-ball to fire every time, without fail. For this to happen, we must first use the correct size of caps and then make sure they are firmly seated on the nipples. The seated caps do more than ignite the powder. They also serve to seal off the chamber and prevent fire from entering the nipple, thereby igniting an adjacent chamber. Having a cap-n-ball "chain fire" on you is a bit more excitement than most of us want. I've had it happen twice over the years. The first time was pure stupidity; the second time, an adjacent cap had apparently fallen off. It made a lot of noise and smoke!

The correct size of a percussion cap is the size that slides on firmly all the way without splitting or collapsing under stiff pressure, be it size 10, 11, or 12. We should not have to pinch the cap in order to make it fit tight. When the cylinder is capped, I rotate each chamber back into the capping position, and using a short wood or nylon dowel, press the caps onto the nipples to ensure that they are properly seated. Now comes the fun part; firing all five chambers reliably and accurately as fast as you can work the action. When the hammer slams down on the cap and the gun fires, the sidewalls of the cap will spilt, but they will still be held in place by the hammer. When the hammer is cocked for the next shot, the spent cap will be rotated through the recess in the recoil shield, and most often will be thrown clear or dislodged by the recoil of the succeeding shot.

When practicing with your cap-n-ball, fire a shot, and before cocking the piece, recheck the remaining caps. Are they all still tight? Is the exploded cap still held in place by the hammer? Is it split so that it will easily fall off? Next, cock the hammer, bringing the next chamber into battery. Does the spent cap fall off properly? In competition, it is wise to go slow enough to observe that the spent cap has not or will not fall into the action. By now we should have a good idea of how our revolvers are working and what areas may need attention. Properly loaded and operated, cap-n-ball sixguns are fast and reliably deadly. No gunfighter ever took Wild Bill Hickock and his pair of Navy Colts for granted!

See ya at the range!

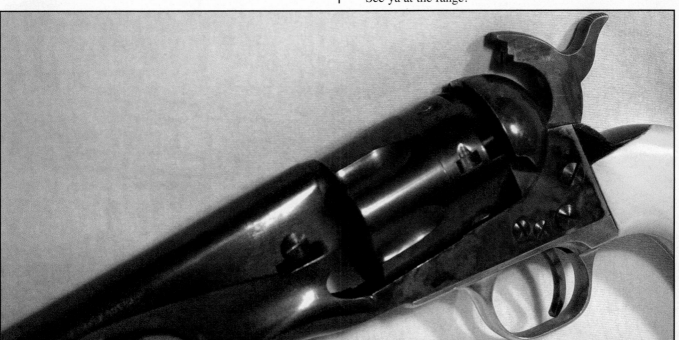

A finely-tuned cap-n-ball (with adequate lube and all the parts having been honed with emery paper, including the wedge) should allow all parts to be taken apart and put back together easily.

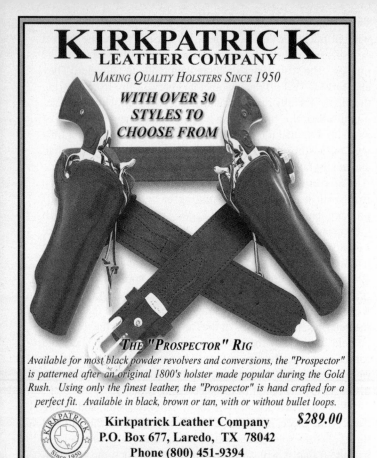

Contacts Directory

Accurate Arms Co., (931) 729-4207, www.accuratepowder.com

Ajax Custom Grips, (800) 527-7537, www.ajaxgrips.com

American Pioneer Powder, (888) 756-7693

American Western Arms, (877) 292-4867, www.awaguns.com

Axtell Rifle Co., (406) 842-5814, www.riflesmith.com

Badger Barrels, Inc., (262) 857-6950, www.badgerbarrelsinc.com

Ballard Rifle Co., (307) 587-4914, www.ballardrifles.com

Ballistic Products, (763) 494-9237, www.ballisticproducts.com

Bear Creek Supply, (913) 236-5380, www.buffaloc.com

Birchwood Casey, (952) 937-7900, www.birchwoodcasey.com

Black Dawge Cartridge Company, (972) 424-0326, www.blackdawgecartridge.com

Black Hills Ammunition, (605) 348-5150, www.black-hills.com

Black Hills Leather, (877) 712-9434, www.blackhillsleather.com

BlackPowderShooters.com

Blount, (763) 323-2300, www.federalcartridge.com

Bond Arms, (817) 573-4445, www.bondarms.com

Brooks Tru-Bore Bullet Moulds, (406) 932-5114

Browning, (801) 876-2711, www.browning.com

Buckaroo Bobbins, (928) 636-1885, www.buckaroobobbins.com

Buffalo Arms Company, (208) 263-6953, www.buffaloarms.com

Buffalo Brothers, (480) 986-7858, www.buffalobrothers.net

Buffalo Bullet Company, (562) 944-0322

Butler Bags, (800) 922-2247, www.butlerbags.com

Cabela's, (800) 237-4444, www.cabelas.com

CalGraf Design, (800) 367-5203, www.cal-graf.com

Camillus Cutlery Co., (800) 344-0456, www.camillusknives.com

Carrico's Leatherworks, (620) 922-7222, www.carricoleather.com

Cast Performance Bullet Co., (307) 857-2940, www.castperformance.com

Cheyenne Custom Cowboy, (866) 244-9269, www.cowboyleather.com

Cheyenne Pioneer Products, (816) 413-9196, www.cartridgeboxes.com

Chey-Cast Bullet Co., (307) 778-6636, www.chey-cast.com

Cimarron Firearms Co., (877) 749-4861, www.cimarron-firearms.com

Circle Bar-T Leatherworks, (877) 913-2047, www.circlebar-t.com

Circle Fly, (859) 689-5100, www.circlefly.com

Circle KB Leatherworks, (877) 919-0891, www.circlekb.com

Classic Rifle Co., (541) 385-9139

Clean Shot (see American Pioneer Powder)

Colonel Carter's Mercantile, (847) 548-9315

Competitive Edge Gunworks, (660) 731-5124, www.competitiveedgegunworks.com

Coonie's Explosives, Inc., (800) 713-6321

Connecticut Valley Arms, (770) 449-4687, www.cva.com

Coon River Mercantile, (515) 287-8315, www.coonriver.com

Cowboy Antiques, (309) 699-7499

Cowboy Corral, (800)-457-2279, www.cowboycorral.com

Crazy Crow Trading Post, (903) 786-2287

Custom Gun Leather (Walt Ostin), (250) 743-9015

Cylinder Stoves, (800) 586-6533, www.cylinderstoves.com

C Sharps Arms, (406) 932-4353, www.csharpsarms.com

Dakota Ammo/Cor-Bon, (800) 626-7266, www.corbon.com

Davidson's, (928) 776-8055, www.galleryofguns.com

Dennis A. Yoder Custom Leather, (610) 562-8161, www.yodercustomleather.com

Dillon Precision, (480) 948-9909, www.dillonprecision.com

Dixie Gunworks, Inc., (731) 885-0700, www.dixiegunworks.com

DS Welding, (818) 727-9353, www.dswelding.com

Dynamit Nobel, (201) 767-1995, www.dnrws.com

DZ Arms, (405) 691-1215, www.hepman.com

Eagle Grips, (630) 260-0400, www.eaglegrips.com

Elephant Black Powder (see Schuetzen Powder Co.)

El Paso Saddlery, (915) 554-2233, www.epsaddlery.com

EMF Company, (949) 261-6611, www.emf-company.com

European American Arms, (321) 639-4842, www.eaacorp.com

GALCO International, (800) 874-2526, www.usgalco.com

G&J Leather, (814) 535-1999, www.gandjleather.com

Get A Grip Pistol Grips, (208) 765-6565, www.pistolgrips.com

Gripmaker, (417) 461-1123, www.gripmaker.com

Gibbs Rifle Company, (304) 262-1651, www.gibbsrifle.com

GOEX Inc., (318) 382-9300, www.goexpowder.com

Greasewood, (602) 983-3770

Green Mountain Rifle & Barrel Co., (603) 447-1095, www.gmriflebarrel.com

Gunbroker.com, (972) 580-8018, www.gunbroker.com

Hawes Ranch, (620) 369-2204

High Noon Watches, (814) 720-3792

Heirlooms In Wood, (623) 878-6145

Henry Repeating Arms, (718) 499-5600, www.henryrepeating.com

Hide Crafter Leathercraft, (888) 263-5277, www.hidecrafter.com

Hodgdon Powder Co., Inc., (913) 362-9455, www.hodgdon.com

Hogue Grips, (800) 438-4747, www.getgrip.com

Hoppe's, (800) 962-5757, www.hoppes.com

Hornady, (308) 382-1390, www.hornady.com

Huntington Dies, (530) 534-1210, www.huntingtons.com

IAR Inc., (949) 443-3642, www.iar-arms.com

Idaho Knife Works, (509) 994-9394

Idaho Leather, (208) 344-2602

Interstate Arms Corp., (800) 243-3006, www.interstatearms.com

JD Western Works, (303) 663-9175

Jim Downing (The Gun Engraver), (417) 865-5953, www.thegunengraver.com

JRJ Knives, (717) 834-6265

KC Miles Leatherworks, (320) 398-2708, www.kcmilesleather.com

KIK (see Goex)

King's Gun Works, 800-282-9449, www.kingsgunworks.com

Kirkpatrick Leather, (800) 451-9394, www.kirkpatrickleather.com

Kirst Company (see River Junction Trade Co.)

Kleen-Bore, Inc., (413) 527-0300, www.kleen-bore.com

Lazy J Weapons, (817) 573-2177

Lee's Gunsmithing, (714) 921-9030, www.leesgunsmithing.com

Lee Precision, (262) 673-3075, www.leeprecision.com

Lee Shaver Gunsmithing, (417) 682-3330

Legacy Sports International, (703) 548-4837, www.legacysports.com

Legends in Leather, (928) 717-2175, www.legendsinleather.com

Liberty Arms/KBI, (717) 540-8518, www.libertyarms.com

Lone Star Rifle Company, (936) 856-3363, www.lonestarrifle.com

Luna Tech, Inc., 258-725-4224, www.pyropak.com

Lyman Products Corporation, (860) 632-2020, www.lymanproducts.com

Magma Engineering, (480) 987-9704, www.magmaengr.com

Marble's Outdoors, (906) 428-3710, www.marblesoutdoors.com

Marlin Firearms, (203) 239-5621, www.marlinfirearms.com

Meacham Tool and Hardware Co., (208) 486-7171, www.meachamrifles.com

Mechanical Accuracy, Inc., (405) 948-8613

Meister Bullets, Inc., (602) 470-1880, www.meisterbullets.com

Mernickle Custom Holsters, (604) 826-8834 www.mernickleholsters.com

MGM Targets, (208) 454-0555, www.mgmtargets.com

Midway USA, (800) 243-3220, www.midwayusa.com

Miller Enterprises, (307) 534-5871

Montana Vintage Arms Company, (406) 388-4027, www.montanavintagearms.com

Navy Arms, (201) 863-7100, www.navyarms.com

NEI Hand Tools, (503) 543-6776, www.neihandtools.com

October Country Muzzleloading, (208) 762-4903, www.octobercountry.com

Old West Reproductions, (406) 273-2615, www.oldwestreproductions.com

Old West Scroungers, (800) 877-2666, www.ows-ammunition.com

Oregon Trail Bullet Company, (541) 523-4697, www.laser-cast.com

Ox-Yoke Originals, (800) 231-8313, www.oxyoke.com

Parts Unknown, (204) 487-7185

Paul Persinger, (915) 821-7541

Peacemaker Specialists, (530) 472-3438, www.peacemakerspecialists.com

Pedersoli, 030-8915000, www.davide-pedersoli.com

Pleasant Valley Saddle Shop, (970) 669-1588, www.pvsaddleshop.com

Power Custom, Inc., (573) 372-5684, www.powercustom.com

Precision Reloading, 1-800-970-4555, www.precisionreloading.com

Rapine Bullet Moulds, (215) 679-5413

Remington, (800) 243-9700, www.remington.com

RCBS, (530) 533-5191, www.rcbs.com

R&D Gun Shop, (608) 676-5628

Red River Frontier Outfitters, (818) 352-0177

Redding Reloading Equipment, (607) 753-3331, www.redding-reloading.com

River Junction Trade Co., (319) 873-2387, www.riverjunction.com

Rocking A Brand Custom Leather, (858) 673-4021

Rod Kibler Saddlery, (706) 246-0487

San Pedro Saddlery, (520) 457-3616, www.sanpedrosaddlery.com

Scheutzen Powder Co., (800) 588-8287, www.schuetzenpowder.com

Schuetzen Gun Company, (970) 635-2409

Shiloh Rifle Manufacturing, (406) 932-4454, www.shilorifle.com

SHOOT! Magazine, (800) 342-0904 (208-368-9920 outside the US), www.shootmagazine.com

Sidekick Guncart Company, (603) 673-4270, www. sidekickguncarts.com

Silver Dollar Crafters, (928) 767-3413, www.silverdollarcrafters.com

Smith Enterprises, (480) 964-1818, www.smithenterprise.com

Snap-On Tools, (877) 762-7664, www.snapon.com

SPG, LLC, (307) 587-7621, www.blackpowderspg.com

SPEER (see RCBS/Blount)

Starline, (660) 827-6640, www.starlinebrass.com

Sturm, Ruger and Co., (928) 541-8901, www.ruger-firearms.com

Swiss (see Schuetzen Powder Co.)

Taylor's & Co., (540) 722-2017, www.taylorsfirearms.com

Ted Blocker Holsters, Inc., (800) 650-9742, www.tedblocker.com

Ten-X Ammunition, (909) 605-1617, www.ten-x.com

Texas Gunslinger, (817) 460-3840, www.texasgunslinger.com

Texas Jack's, (800) 839-5225, www.texasjacks.com

The Gun Engraver, (417) 865-5953, www.thegunengraver.com

Thompson Bullet Lube Co., (866) 476-1500, www.thompsonbulletlube.com

Thompson Center, (603) 332-2333, www.tcarms.com

Tombstone 1880, (877) 619-5672, www.tombstone1880.com

Tombstone Leather, (760) 789-6065, www.tombstonegunleather.com

Traditions Firearms, (860) 388-4656, www.traditionsfirearms.com

Trailrider Products, (303) 791-6068, www.gunfighter.com/trailrider/

Tristar Sporting Arms, Ltd., (816) 421-1400, www.tristarsportingarms.com

Uberti U.S.A., Inc., (860) 435-8068, www.uberti.com

Ultramax, (800) 345-5852, www.ultramaxammunition.com

Upper Mississippi Valley Mer., (563) 322-0896, www.umvmco.com

US Firearms Manufacturing Co., (877) 227-6901, www.usfirearms.com

U.S. Repeating Arms, (801) 876-2711, www.winchester-guns.com

Ventco/Shooter's Choice, (440) 834-8888, www.shooters-choice.com

Gunbroker.com, (404) 531-4224, www.gunbroker.com

Walter's Wads, (405) 799-0376

Wano (see Luna Tech Inc.)

Wild Rose Trading Co., (970) 259-8396, www.wrtcleather.com

Wild West Mercantile, (800) 596-0444, www.wwmerc.com

Will Ghormley, (515) 277-1898

Winchester Ammunition, (541) 464-8979, www.winchesterammo.com

Winchester Firearms, (801) 876-2711, www.winchester-guns.com

Wind River Arms & Supply Co., (307) 856-3093

Wolf Ear's Equipment, (307) 745-7135

Wolff's Custom Guns, (336) 764-5442

Wolf's Western Traders, (619) 482-1701

Didn't find a company you were looking for? Send an e-mail to info@shootmagazine.com and we'll see if we can't help you out.

Organization Directory

American Single Shot Rifle Assn., (419) 692-3866, www.assra.com

Cowboy Fast Draw Association, 800-274-1876, www.cowboyfastdraw.com

CMSA Cowboy Mounted Shooting Association, (623) 412-3036, www.cowboymountedshooting.com

International Black Powder Hunting Assn., (307) 436-9817, www.98.net/ibha/

National Muzzle Loading Rifle Association, (800) 745-1493, www.nmlra.org

National Rifle Assn., (800) 672-3888, www.nra.org

NRA Silhouette Division, (703) 267-1474, www.nra.org

North-South Skirmish Assn., (703) 478-0719

The Cast Bullet Assn., Inc., (309) 537-3662, www.castbulletassoc.org

SASS - Single Action Shooting Society, (714) 694-1800, www.sassnet.com

Didn't find a company you were looking for? Send an e-mail to info@shootmagazine.com and we'll see if we can't help you out.

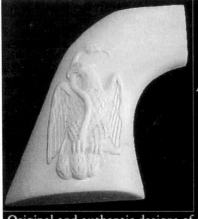
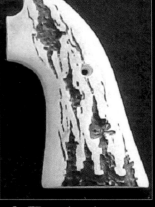

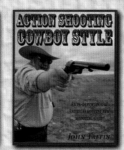

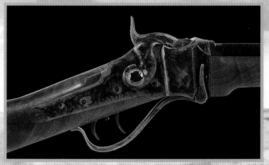

New Products 2002

MVA Model 130 - Windgauge Sporting Tang

"0" point elevation is 30 minutes lower than the Model 107/108 and is great for 22 caliber rifles. Sight has 1.3" elevation ± 14 minutes windage, and will fit all current bases. An excellent choice for those wanting a compact hunting sight.

MVA Malcolm Mounts

Patterned after the Malcolm mount, but with fewer variations. Windage adjustable to .001"; elevation adjustable to .002". Front mount adjustable for mechanical zero and when used together, rear mount can adjust for wind changes quickly and accurately. Mounts will fit all 3/4" tube scopes with the Pope-style rib. Comes with a set of dovetail mounts.

MVA Montana Magnum

MVA now offers the new Montana sized Hadley eyedisc, with a diameter of 1.95" and 15 apertures ranging in size from .021" to .115". The matte finish in conjunction with the large outside diameter virtually eliminates distracting glare, both inside the eyedisc and around the edge. The rubber O-ring on the eyedisc protects both the comb of the stock as well as the shooter's glasses. Available in different thread sizes to accommodate other manufacturers' sights. This accessory is a must for the competitive shooter!

MVA Combination Rear Sight

Patterned after the original Marble's tang sight. Spring loaded quick release staff to vertical sighting position. Graduated elevation post with locking ring. Included are a target eyedisc and the standard peep. Available for both Winchester and Marlin rifles.

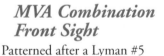

MVA Combination Front Sight

Patterned after a Lyman #5 combination front sight. Allows the shooter to select a blade or hooded pinhead. Blade is nickel silver and may be filed for exact height necessary at a specific range. Dovetail sizes to fit all production rifles and, of course, all originals.

Please call for our brochure featuring our full line of sights and shooting accessories.

Montana Vintage Arms enjoys the reputation as a manufacturer of the finest sights available.

Visit our website at: **www.montanavintagearms.com**

61 Andrea Drive • Belgrade, MT 59714 • Daytime 406-388-4027 • Evening 406-388-3405 • Fax 406-388-6503